MACMILLAN INTERNATIONAL POLITICAL ECONOMY SERIES

General Editor: Timothy M. Shaw, Professor of Political Science and International Development Studies, Dalhousie University, Nova Scotia, Canada

The global political economy is in a profound crisis at the levels of both production and policy. This series provides overviews and case studies of states and sectors, classes and companies in the new international division of labour. These embrace political economy as both focus and mode of analysis; they advance radical scholarship and scenarios.

The series treats polity-economy dialectics at global, regional and national levels and examines novel contradictions and coalitions between and within each. There is a special emphasis on national bourgeoisies and capitalisms, on newly industrial or influential countries, and on novel strategies and technologies. The concentration throughout is on uneven patterns of power and production, authority and distribution, hegemony and reaction. Attention will be paid to redefinitions of class and security, basic needs and self-reliance and the range of critical analysis will include gender, population, resources, environment, militarization, food and finance. This series constitutes a timely and distinctive response to the continuing intellectual and existential world crisis.

Recent titles:

Alfredo Behrens
REGIONAL MANAGEMENT OF ENERGY RESOURCES IN LATIN AMERICA

Robert Boardman
PESTICIDES IN WORLD AGRICULTURE

Inga Brandell (*editor*)
WORKERS IN THIRD-WORLD INDUSTRIALIZATION

Bonnie K. Campbell (*editor*)
POLITICAL DIMENSIONS OF THE INTERNATIONAL DEBT CRISIS

Bonnie K. Campbell and John Loxley (*editors*)
STRUCTURAL ADJUSTMENT IN AFRICA

Jerker Carlsson and Timothy M. Shaw (*editors*)
NEWLY INDUSTRIALIZING COUNTRIES AND THE POLITICAL ECONOMY OF SOUTH-SOUTH RELATIONS

Andrew F. Cooper
MIDDLE POWERS IN A POST-HEGEMONIC GLOBAL ECONOMY

Diane Ethier (*editor*)
DEMOCRATIC TRANSITION AND CONSOLIDATION IN SOUTHERN EUROPE, LATIN AMERICA AND SOUTHEAST ASIA

Shelley Feldman and Florence McCarthy (*editors*)
THE POLITICS OF INCORPORATION

David P. Forsythe (*editor*)
HUMAN RIGHTS AND DEVELOPMENT
THE UNITED NATIONS IN THE WORLD POLITICAL ECONOMY

David Glover and Ken Kusterer
SMALL FARMERS, BIG BUSINESS

Conflict, Peace and Development in the Caribbean

Edited by

Jorge Rodríguez Beruff
Associate Professor, University of Puerto Rico

J. Peter Figueroa
Principal Medical Officer
Ministry of Health, Jamaica

and

J. Edward Greene
Director, Institute of Social and Economic Research
University of the West Indies

MACMILLAN

First published 1991

Published by
MACMILLAN ACADEMIC AND PROFESSIONAL LTD
Houndmills, Basingstoke, Hampshire RG21 2XS
and London
Companies and representatives
throughout the world

Printed in Hong Kong   1903516382

British Library Cataloguing in Publication Data
Conflict, peace and development in the Caribbean.—
(Macmillan international political economy series).
1. Caribbean region. Economic development. Political aspects
I. Beruff, Jorge Rodríguez II. Figueroa, J. Peter III. Greene, J. Edward
330.9729
ISBN 0–333–53511–1

672853
Anc

Series Standing Order (International Political Economy)

If you would like to receive future titles in this series as they
are published, you can make use of our standing order
facility. To place a standing order please contact your
bookseller or, in case of difficulty, write to us at the address
below with your name and address and the name of the
series. Please state with which title you wish to begin your
standing order. (If you live outside the UK we may not have
the rights for your area, in which case we will forward your
order to the publisher concerned.)

Standing Order Service, Macmillan Distribution Ltd,
Houndmills, Basingstoke, Hampshire, RG21 2XS, England.

Contents

List of Tables and Figures

Tables

Figures

List of Abbreviations

AID	(US) Agency for International Development
BDP	Barbados Defense Force
CAI	Central American Initiative
CARICOM	Caribbean Community
CBERA	Caribbean Basin Economic Recovery Act (US)
CBI	Caribbean Basin Initiative
CIA	Central Intelligence Agency (US)
DEA	Drug Enforcement Agency (US)
ECLAC	Economic Commission for Latin America and the Caribbean
EEC	European Economic Community
FMLN	Farabundo Marti Liberation Front (El Salvador)
FSLN	Sandinista Front for National Liberation (Nicaragua)
IMF	International Monetary Fund
JCF	Jamaica Constabulary Force
JDF	Jamaica Defence Force
JLP	Jamaica Labour Party
MAAG	Military Assistance and Advisory Group (US)
MTT	Militia of Territorial Troops (Cuba)
OAS	Organization of American States
OAU	Organization of African Unity
OECS	Organization of Eastern Caribbean States
PNP	People's National Party (Jamaica)
PAM	People's Action Movement (St Kitts)
RSS	Regional Security System (Eastern Caribbean)
SSUs	Special Service Units
SOUTHCOM	Southern Command (US)
UK	United Kingdom
UN	United Nations
USSR	Union of Soviet Socialist Republics (Soviet Union)
US	United States of America
UWI	University of the West Indies

Notes on the Contributors

Jorge Rodríguez Beruff is Associate Professor at the Social Science Department, General Studies Faculty, University of Puerto Rico. Director of 'Peace and Development in the Caribbean' research area at the Institute of Caribbean Studies. Member of the Executive Committee of the International Peace Research Association. Author of *Los militares y el poder* (Mosca Azul, 1983), *Política militar y dominación. Puerto Rico en el contexto latinoamericano* (Huracán, 1988) and numerous research articles on related issues. Co-sponsor of the 'Peace and Development in the Caribbean Conference'.

Whitman Browne is a researcher at the Department of Labor of the US Virgin Islands. Graduate studies in Education at Lehigh and Temple universities. Author of *The Christena's Disaster in Retrospect* (St Thomas Graphics, 1985).

Neville C. Duncan is a Senior Lecturer in Political Science and Dean of the Faculty of Social Science, University of the West Indies, Cave Hill Campus. Holds PhD from Manchester University, specialises in Anglophone Caribbean political issues and has written extensively on this topic.

Isabel Jaramillo Edwards is a researcher in the North America Department of the *Centro de Estudios sobre América*, La Habana, Cuba. Specialises in Caribbean affairs and US foreign and military policy. Has published widely in Cuban and foreign journals on these topics.

J. Peter Figueroa is a medical physician specialising in epidemiology and President of the Jamaica Peace Committee. Cosponsor of the 'Peace and Development in the Caribbean' Conference.

Emilio Pantojas García is Assistant Professor of Latin American Studies at the University of Illinois at Chicago. Specialises in sociology of developing societies. In 1987, received a Fulbright scholarship to conduct field research on the impact of the export promotion programme, the Caribbean Basin Initiative (CBI), on the English-speaking countries of the Eastern Caribbean. Has published several articles on the sociology of export-led industrialisation strategies in the Caribbean. Member of the Advisory Board of the International Relations Commission of the Latin American Social Science Council (CLACSO) and of the Advisory Board of the project, 'Alternative Visions of Development in the Caribbean', of the group, Policy Alternatives for the Caribbean and Central America (PACCA).

J. Edward Greene is Director of the Institute of Social and Economic Research, University of the West Indies, Mona Campus, Jamaica. Former President of the Caribbean Studies Association. Coauthor of *Small Business in Bardados* (ISER, 1979) and many other publications on anglophone Caribbean issues. Cosponsor of the 'Peace and Development in the Caribbean Conference', and co-editor with Anthony T. Bryan and Timothy M. Shaw of *Peace, Development and Security in the Caribbean*.

E. John Inegbedion is a Nigerian PhD student in political science at Dalhousie University where he has been involved with research projects on African foreign policy and on change in Southern Africa. He is associated with the Centres for African Studies and for Foreign Policy Studies at Dalhousie University and holds a master's degree from the University of Alberta.

Raúl Benítez Manaut is a researcher at the Center for Interdisciplinary Research in the Humanities of the *Universidad Nacional Autónoma de Mexico*. Author of *La teoría militar y la guerra civil en El Salvador* (UCA, San Salvador, 1989). Coeditor of *El Salvador: guerra, política y paz (1979–1988)* (CINAS, 1988). Has done extensive research and writing on the war in El Salvador and armed conflict in Central America as well as on Cuban and Nicaraguan defense policies.

Pablo A. Maríñez is Director of Graduate Studies, Center for Latin American Studies (CELA), at the *Universidad Nacional Autónoma de México*. Editor of *El Caribe Contemporáneo*, the leading Mexican journal on Caribbean affairs. Author of *Resistencia Campesina y Reforma Agraria en República Dominicana (1899–1978)* (CEPAE, 1984) and *El Caribe bajo las redes políticas norteamericanas* (Editorial Universitaria, 1987) and numerous articles on Caribbean topics.

Humberto García Muñiz is a researcher at the Institute of Caribbean

Studies, University of Puerto Rico. Obtained Master's degree from the Institute of International Relations at Port-of-Spain, Trinidad, presently a PhD student at Columbia University. Former editor of *Caribbean Monthly Bulletin* (Institute of Caribbean Studies, UPR). Author of *Puerto Rico and the United States: United Nations Role, 1953–1975*, (Revista Jurídica, 1984), *La estratégia de Estados Unidos y la militarización del Caribe* (Instituto de estudios del Caribe, 1988) and several research articles on security issues in the Caribbean.

Dion E. Phillips is Associate Professor at the Social Science Division, University of the Virgin Islands. PhD in Political Sociology from Howard University. Coeditor of *Militarization in the Non-Hispanic Caribbean* (Boulder: Lynne Rienner, 1986). His research and writing has concentrated on Eastern Caribbean defence and security. Presently working on the military and society in Barbados.

Lloyd Searwar is Visiting Fellow at the Institute of International Relations, University of West Indies, St Augustine. He has been a senior member of the Guyana Diplomatic Service and was more recently Foreign Affairs Adviser in the Caribbean Community (CARICOM) Secretariat. He has served as a member of two Commonwealth high-level expert groups dealing respectively with North/South Negotiations and the Problems of Small States.

Timothy M. Shaw is Professor of Political Science and International Development Studies at Dalhousie University. He holds a PhD from Princeton University and has been a visiting faculty member at the universities of Ife (Nigeria), Zambia and Zimbabwe and at Carleton and Makerere (Uganda) universities. Amongst his recent co-edited books are *Africa in World Politics, Corporatism in Africa, Coping with Africa's Food Crisis, Studies in the Economic History of Southern Africa* and *Peace, Development and Security in the Caribbean.*

Alma H. Young is Professor of Urban and Regional Studies at the University of New Orleans. She co-edited (with Dion E. Phillips) *Militarization in the Non-Hispanic Caribbean* (Boulder: Lynne Rienner, 1986), and has written extensively on political developments in the Caribbean. She is a past president of the Caribbean Studies Association.

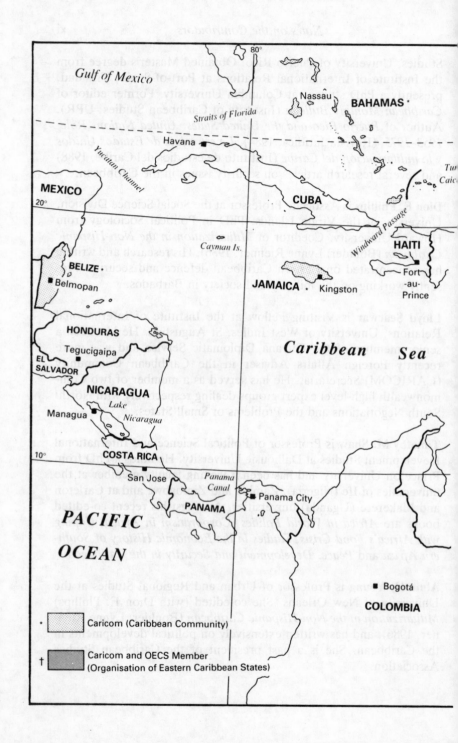

Caricom (Caribbean Community)

Caricom and OECS Member
(Organisation of Eastern Caribbean States)

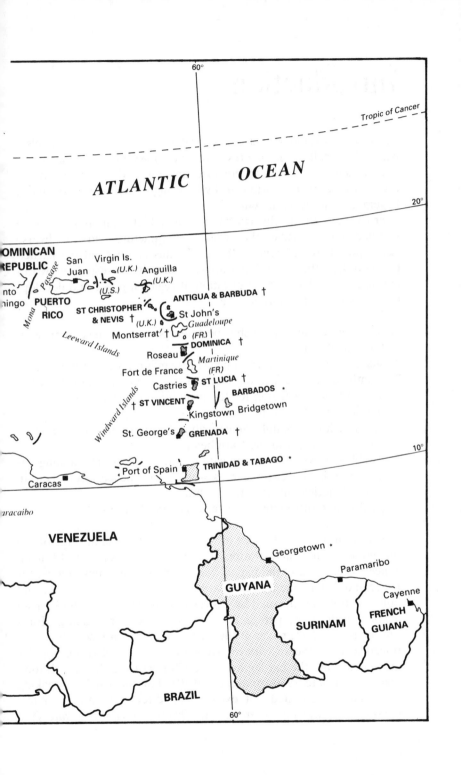

Introduction

Peace and development are inseparable in the Caribbean as elsewhere. This collection, one result of a mid-1988 international conference in Jamaica, seeks to advance analysis and discourse on the regional case of the Caribbean by focusing on security, diplomacy, hegemony and development.

From the outset, the conference aimed at examining, from a Caribbean perspective, the regional conjuncture and the diverse issues posed by the general theme. It thus emphasised the participation of Caribbean scholars who were already interested and working on topics related to the question of regional peace and development. Its stated objectives were:

1. to examine the relationship between peace and development in the Caribbean;
2. share the results of current peace research relevant to the region;
3. identify areas of concern in need of research and resources within and without the region for the promotion of peace research and the dissemination of results;
4. examine how research can contribute to efforts to promote peace and development in the Caribbean;
5. establish links of communication and collaboration among researchers in the Caribbean as well as with peace researchers in Latin America and worldwide; and
6. publish and disseminate the results of the Conference.

The conference took place in the context of the final stage of the second Reagan administration. Understandably, one of the main concerns reflected in the papers was to analyse the implications, for peace and development in the Caribbean, of the main economic and military strategies pursued by US regional policy during the Reagan years as well as the perspectives for change under a George Bush presidency. In fact, much of the current Caribbean research can be traced to the concern with interrelated processes of rising popular movements and the hardening of the US regional policy which took place in the late 1970s and early 1980s. For the English-speaking Caribbean, which had not experienced direct US military interventions, the invasion of Grenada in 1983 was obviously a watershed event. The concern with US policy, however, does not obscure the fact that the role of other international actors – USSR, Great Britain, France, Holland, Canada, Mexico and Venezuela – must also be taken into account to develop a balanced assessment of the political and economic forces at play in the region.

Furthermore, several of the essays included in this volume focus on the role of internal political forces and economic and social processes in particular countries and subregions as important factors in creating conditions or hindering the possibilities for peace and development. Despite the different degrees and forms of dependence exhibited over time by Caribbean societies, adequate attention must be given to internal political processes and to specific national characteristics to understand their interactions with external forces and diverse outcomes. Finally, all the contributions – explicitly or implicitly – reflect a sharp concern for the formulation of alternative economic and political strategies, based on Caribbean realities and interests and capable of (i) promoting peace, regional stability and development and (ii) counteracting existing tendencies towards militarisation, authoritarianism, violent conflicts and interventionism. They take into account that at the root of the crisis of the region are socio-economic problems endemic in the Third World: poverty, unemployment and the maldistribution of resources.

While much of the dynamics of the debates ensuing from the presentations and the discussion cannot be adequately captured in the pages that follow, the present contributions are revised versions. They benefited greatly from the cut and thrust of the conference, some details of which are provided below. These discussions also served to identify general areas for future research.

An important aspect of the debate had to do with the diversity of prevailing conceptions of the Caribbean and the consequent viability of a truly regional response to common challenges. This discussion served to underscore the inherent difficulties, apparent even among Caribbean scholars, in formulating a broad regional project capable of overcoming segmentary or narrow responses to the issues of peace and development. However, the cross-cultural and transnational character of the dialogue served to illuminate many common problems faced by Caribbean political economies, notwithstanding their obvious diversity, and to reaffirm the importance of regional integration and collaboration as an essential ingredient for the construction of peace.

Since the conference took place, many of the issues that concerned the participants have surfaced in so many ways in various parts of the world as well as in the Caribbean itself. On a world scale, a new process of détente between the US and the USSR has gained momentum with bold initiatives in the field of nuclear and conventional disarmament, mainly centred in Europe. Long-standing regional conflicts, such as the Iran–Iraq war, the war in Cambodia, South African interventions in Namibia and Angola, and the struggle in Afghanistan, are being confronted and resolved through multilateral negotiations. The Central American war can also be included, to a certain extent, within this general process of resolution of regional conflicts through the favourable balance of the Contadora, Esquipulas I and II, and Tela negotiations. The dismantling of the Nicaraguan *contra* army, among other recent agreements, will certainly contribute to defusing conflicts and will have important implications for the Caribbean situation as a whole.

These developments, though obviously favourable to world peace and conducive to a new global environment for regional initiatives, will not automatically transform the geopolitical realities let alone political economies of the Caribbean or the dominant matrix of international and internal conflicts. In fact, recent events have confirmed the relevance and importance, for the future development of the Caribbean, of the issues discussed at the conference. Among others, we could mention the spontaneous popular explosion in Caracas, resulting in hundreds of deaths, which was sparked by deepening of Venezuela's economic crisis and IMF-imposed austerity measures; the assassination of the primary Colombian presidential candidate by drug cartels and the subsequent internal upheaval; the intensification of the crisis in US-Panamanian relations leading to the US invasion of Panama; the persistence of authoritarian military rule in Haiti; the serious crisis at the highest levels of the Cuban leadership provoked by the corruption of key officials by drug interests; the continued deadlock in US-Cuban relations; the consolidation of the US military presence in Puerto Rico; the continued decline in the living standards of vast sectors of the population in many Caribbean societies; and the reluctance of the Bush administration to significantly depart from the prevalent military and foreign policy approach to the region. In short, interventionist inclinations of imperialist interests have not ended, they are merely being articulated and interpreted in different ways as the 1980s give way to the 1990s.

Reflective of the different levels and approaches to analysis of the Caribbean political economy, we have grouped the essays in three parts. Part I, 'Overviews and Approaches', includes three contributions which deal generally with some of the main elements of the contemporary *regional situation in global perspective*. Alma Young analyses the relationship among the notions of peace, democracy and security with special reference to the Caribbean but places them within the broader framework of modern strategies for the subordination of underdeveloped countries. She explores the implications for national sovereignity and democratic development of policies based on the concepts of 'low intensity conflict', 'anti-terrorism', and 'war on drugs' currently being applied to the region. Young also makes an important distinction between what has been called 'redemocratisation' – which implies an important political role for the military – and 'participatory democracy' which requires real political participation of popular sectors, and stresses the importance of deemphasising military security issues in regional cooperation schemes.

The chapter by Emilio Pantojas, on the other hand, shows how the restoration of US hegemony in the Caribbean Basin under the Reagan administration was not as one-tracked as is commonly believed but followed a multi-faceted military/economic strategy. Pantoja's use of the Reports of the Santa Fe Committee (1981) and the Kissinger Commission (1984) to support this view makes for a fascinating analysis. It is in this context that the Caribbean Basin and the Central American Initiatives take on new meaning. The economic restructuring of the region which was to emerge from these proposals was to constitute the basis of a long-term solution by the US to the economic crisis of the region.

Finally, Isabel Jaramillo provides a Cuban perspective regarding current perceptions in the region of that country's defence policy and its relationship to the US military stance and Cuban foreign policy aims. The more recent developments in Cuba around the 'Ochoa affair', however, dramatically pose the issues of control over the security establishment in a socialist society and of the weight of the military aspects of security in Cuba's internal and external policies.

In Part II, 'Case Studies of Small State Militarisation', we have included five in-depth analyses of *national cases*, three from the English-speaking and two from the Spanish-speaking Caribbean, that illustrate both the great diversity in specific circumstances of different countries and sub-regions and the presence of common processes of militarisation promoted by a combination of internal and external factors. Pablo Mariñez examines the changing political role of the military establishment in the Dominican Republic and the meaning of the process of 'professionalisation' with regard to the military's new articulation within the state apparatus. He stresses that while professionalisation, as practiced in that country, transforms the political role of the military, it does not imply a diminished share of state power or the elaboration of effective mechanisms of civilian control. Humberto García describes the dynamics of defence policy and planning in post-independence Jamaica (1962–88). His analysis pays careful attention to the balance of political forces in three phases of Jamaica's development as well as to the role of the former metropolitan power and the growing military influence of the US. Dion Phillips contributes a similarly solid study on the case of Barbados, a country which has played a pivotal military role in the Eastern Caribbean. The recent emergence of military structures in hitherto non-militarised Eastern Caribbean island nations, specifically St Kitts–Nevis, is described in Whitman Browne's essay. The Mexican researcher, Raúl Benítez Manaut, focusses on the defence policies of Nicaragua and Cuba in the context of current regional geopolitics. He also examines the validity of some of the ideological premises of US military policy in the Caribbean.

The third and last part of the book – 'Comparisons and Implications' – contains three important contributions which propose *alternative paths* to regional security compatible with democratic development, national sovereignity and the peaceful resolution of conflicts. Lloyd Searwar analyses fully the consequences of 'location in a sphere of influence'. This explains how, for example, the US could exercise supervisory intervention without direct military challenge by the other major power. The implication of this perspective is that once a superpower self-defines its own security interests it automatically also tends to be concerned with the 'choice of internal system and development strategy by the states located in its sphere of influence'. In this way, there is a tendency towards a convergence in the internal pattern and organisation of neighbouring states. Thus Searwar examines the root causes of the weakening of regional bodies such as CARICOM and, consequently, the constriction of the autonomy of small Caribbean states. He also delineates several viable initiatives that would promote regional peace and development, among which the strengthening of the regional integration movement is of paramount importance.

On the other hand, the examination of the issues surrounding the Grenada invasion of 1983 leads inevitably to the question as to whether small states have real choices in defining both their sovereignty and their security interests. Neville Duncan's chapter tackles this issue as well as the new forms of interventionism in the post-Grenada Caribbean. His conclusion is that peace and security can only be assured in the area when internal interference is absent and when the emphasis on Cold War politics is reduced or removed. In this respect, initiatives towards integration, such as in the Eastern Caribbean, and the Zone of Peace proposals still represent important avenues for alternative approaches to regional security. Judging from the history of Europe and Japan, Duncan's point of view deserves much attention.

Finally, Timothy Shaw and John Inegbedion analyse alternative regional security arrangements and peacekeeping initiatives in Africa and the difficulties which these have confronted due to the emerging international division of labour and internal political economies. Their contribution establishes interesting parallels with the Caribbean and suggests a useful comparative framework for approaching the different dimensions of internal, regional and global conflicts.

Taken as a whole, the essays in this volume pose important conceptual questions related to the analysis of current peace and security issues in the Caribbean. In the first place, the relationship between the concepts of peace and development, which may superficially appear evident, is in fact complex and elusive, and must be examined in the framework of a broad conception of the present regional situation, the potential for change and the conflicting projects of existing social forces. These concepts may refer us initially to the problem of how economic resources are being presently allocated between military and non-military purposes, both in market and socialist economies, and the related capacity of Caribbean societies to face external debt problems, prevent the deterioration of social services and reduce poverty. It is this dimension which Isabel Jaramillo underscores. However, as is stressed in the contributions of Alma Young, Emilio Pantojas, Neville Duncan and Lloyd Searwar, these concepts also refer us more broadly to the problems of popular political participation, of the specific class interests embodied in different 'development' models, of the implications of security policies for the viability of profound social changes and of the external autonomy of Caribbean societies.

Indeed, several of the essays illustrate the need to place the analysis of peace and development in the context of the related concepts of democracy – under which the question of civilian control

of the military could be subsumed – and social change. It is interesting to note that both concepts run through most of the regional and
national analysis. This is the case, for example, in the studies of
Humberto García, Pablo Mariñez and Dion Phillips. Likewise, the
different meanings of 'integration' currently in debate in the Caribbean also have an important bearing in the way we approach the
question of peace in the region, as Searwar and Duncan clarify. In
addition, several of the essays indicate the need to develop a more
rigorous conception of imperialism and interventionism, both because of the new forms of articulation between its economic and
politico-military aspects (Pantojas) and of the formulation of more
subtle and ideologically effective mechanisms of projecting power
such as the war on drugs (Young and Duncan). Finally, it is important to give proper consideration, in a comprehensive consideration of
the perspectives for regional peace and development, to the shifting
articulation of the Caribbean in the world economy as well as its role
in the global political arena. That is, how regional and global trends
interact, and in which way the latter represent not only important
constraints but also possibilities for constructive change. This is
precisely the theoretical approach of Shaw and Inegbedion in the
case of Africa, and a conceptual concern which appears in several
other essays.

A volume such as this clearly cannot encompass all the issues
raised by what is an important set of contemporary debates in the
Caribbean about perspectives and policies. We envisage it as a
contribution to these debates and a stimulus for further research. In
addition, the 'Peace and Development in the Caribbean' conference
served to identify other general questions that need to be tackled
with great rigour by peace researchers in the future. Among these are
the present role of peace movements in the region, the knowledge
and attitudes of the people themselves throughout the Caribbean to
questions of peace, security, external intervention and militarisation,
the content and viability of the Caribbean Zone of Peace proposal
and of other alternative security approaches, the relevance of renewed efforts at regional cooperation and integration and the necessary linkages between research, popular groups and organisations and
practical political projects which favour regional peace and development. It is to this agenda for future research and responsible political
commitment of Caribbean scholars that this book contributes.

Since the essays in this volume were written, several events have
taken place. Among these are the transformation in Europe includ-

ing Gorbachev's initiatives in the Soviet Union, a united Germany and the prospects of 'Europe 1992'; the release of Nelson Mandela; the holding of general elections in Nicaragua and calls for electoral democracy in Guyana; the annexation of Kuwait by Iraq; the attempted *coup* in Trinidad and Tobago by the Musileen. For scholars in Latin America and the Caribbean, lessons from these regional and international events require that we sustain the dialogue and foster greater commitment to peace and security in the world.

This book contains, then, a selection of edited papers presented initially at the 'Peace and Development in the Caribbean' Conference held in May 1988 at the University of the West Indies' Mona Campus in Jamaica. The conference was jointly organised and sponsored by the International Peace Research Association (IPRA), the Institute of Social and Economic Research (ISER) of the University of the West Indies, and the Jamaica Peace Committee (JPC). It brought together 36 academic researchers from the Spanish- and English-speaking Caribbean, Central America, Mexico, Brazil, the United States and Canada.

The editors wish to recognise the assistance of two former secretary generals of IPRA, Chadwick Alger and Clovis Brigagao, as well as Jean Christie of Inter Pares in obtaining the funds for the Jamaica Conference and for their support in all the stages of its organisation. Likewise, we thank the Jamaican functionaries, administrative personnel and academics of the University of the West Indies and of the Institute of Social and Economic Research, particularly Ms Joan Rawlins, who ensured that the event was carried out under the best possible conditions and in an atmosphere of Caribbean hospitality. Finally, we must mention the support provided by the Institute of Caribbean Studies of the University of Puerto Rico, Río Piedras Campus, in all the tasks related to the editing of this book.

JORGE RODRÍGUEZ BERUFF
J. PETER FIGUEROA
J. EDWARD GREENE

Acknowledgement

The editors and publishers wish to thank the following for permission to reproduce copyright material: Frank Cass, for Chapter 5, updated and revised from H. García-Muñiz, 'Defence Policy and Planning in the Caribbean: An Assessment of Jamaica on its 25th Independence Anniversary', *Journal of Commonwealth and Comparative Politics*, vol. 27, no. 1 (March 1989).

Part I
Overviews and Approaches

1 Peace, Democracy and Security in the Caribbean
Alma H. Young

INTRODUCTION

The aim of this chapter is to consider the relationship among the concepts of peace, democracy and security within the context of the Caribbean. Caribbean states, like those throughout the Third World, are insecure domestically and internationally. Insecurity stems from the relative vulnerability and lack of manoeuvre which Third World states have on economic, political and military levels.[1] Geopolitics has vastly limited their autonomy by stymieing possibilities for indigenous developments and choices. In recent years the most obvious manifestation of this encompassing insecurity is the turn towards authoritarianism and the reliance on repressive measures of social control. A discussion of this latter, more limited, sense of security (i.e. the military aspects) will form a major part of this chapter. We will suggest that a fostering of democracy, in both its political and social aspects, will bring security to the Caribbean, a security that remains elusive to the area.

According to classical liberals, the relationship between peace and democracy was simple; free institutions are inherently peaceful and furthering such institutions is the most effective way to foster peace.[2] The normal working of a free society in all its diversity serves to restrain the growth across the community of any consuming issue that leads, if frustrated, to widespread social and political violence. A free society is contrasted with an authoritarian, highly centralised one, where a loss on one issue may result in a loss on all. 'With so much at stake, violence comes easily, especially by rulers who use repression and terror without possible dissent and sources of opposition.'[3]

According to his tabulations, Rummel suggests that over the last 150 years, no wars have occurred between democracies. This contrasts with 152 wars between democracies and non-democracies and 194 wars between non-democracies.[4] Thus Rummel concludes that a world at peace can be achieved in the long run through the spread of liberal democratic institutions.

The modernisation theorists postulate that economic security (i.e., development) will create the objective conditions for social equality as well as provide the basis for a democratic political life.[5] However, during the initial stages the accumulation of capital is necessarily accompanied by impoverishment of the working classes. In time, though, social misery and despotism will be progressively overcome by capitalist expansion. Therefore, today's developed countries form images of developing countries as they will be tomorrow. The modernisation theorists assume that integration into the world economic system is basically favourable and that development proceeds at a pace which is governed by internal conditions found in each country.

The world systems theorists contend, on the other hand, that the emergence of capitalist expansion on a world scale entails an inherent inequality, which prevents the reproduction of the kind of economic development in the Third World which we see in the developed world today.[6] Social inequality and the absence of democracy are thus, in the developing world, the product of capitalist development.

Samir Amin has demonstrated that the worldwide expansion of capital is accompanied by a growing inequality in the social distribution of income in the periphery, while at the system's core it effectively creates the conditions for a lesser degree of social inequality. He views social equality as the foundation of democracy. His research shows that

1. 25 per cent of the population disposes of 10 per cent of total income in the core and 5 per cent in the periphery;
2. 50 per cent of the population disposes of 25 per cent of total income in the core and 10 per cent in the periphery;
3. 75 per cent of the population disposes of 50 per cent of total income in the core and 33 per cent in the periphery.[7]

Amin also states that his evidence suggests that income is not becoming more equal in the periphery.[8] Therefore, he argues that distortion in income distribution is a condition of capital accumulation on a world scale. 'The objective of the capitalist West is to subordinate the subsequent evolution of the Third World to the requirements of the redeployment of transnational capital.'[9]

Thus we see the growing polarisation between the needs of the core and those of the periphery. This polarisation is responsible for the appearance of socially and politically unacceptable regimes in the periphery, where democracy is the exception rather than the rule. These regimes serve to repress the demands of the working class for social and political equality, as Third World leaders pursue development through economic subordination to the core. Amin suggests that the only positive prospect for avoiding capitalist relegation to the periphery is 'delinking' on the basis of a popular national social alliance.[10] ('Delinking', according to Amin, 'is the need to submit foreign relations to the logic of an internal popular strategy of development, as opposed to the strategy of adjusting internal development to the constraints of the global expansion of capitalism'.) Amin further argues that delinking, however, is possible only if democracy is present, a democracy that incorporates both the Western bourgeois concept with its emphasis on respect for rights and legality, freedom of expression for a diversity of opinions, institutionalisation of electoral procedures and separation of powers, as well as a social dimension ('social justice') which allows for/encourages 'popular participation'. For Amin democracy can only take root if it inscribes itself within a perspective which moves beyond capitalism.

DEMOCRATIC EXPERIENCE IN THE CARIBBEAN

To the extent that there has been democracy in the periphery in the past it has been as a result of popular participation, of working class struggles. In the English-speaking Caribbean it was the labor rebellions of the 1930s that provided the genesis for self-government and political independence within a democratic framework of the Westminister model. Starting in St Kitts in 1935 and ending with Jamaica in 1938, the revolt by the working class brought demands for social and political change. However, as Ken Post has shown so well in the case of Jamaica, the rebellion was really an occasion for the exploitation of working class militancy by local elites, who went on to become 'the neo-colonial ruling class'.[11] The faith of the working class in Alexander Bustamante, who had no intention of challenging colonialism or capitalism, contributed to the failure of the 1938 uprising. While some of the labour demands of the workers were met, the leadership and the party (i.e., the Jamaica Labor Party) stymied the possibility for significant political and social change through their inability and unwillingness to let the voice of the working class be fully heard.

The early leadership of the People's National Party (PNP) did not auger well for significant change either.[12] It was difficult to think of the PNP in the early days as a nationalist party: in 1938 Norman Manley spoke only of making Jamaica 'ripe' for self-government and did not demand self-government until much later. Up to independence the leadership of the party continued to have a strong identification with the colonial authorities, in large measure because the party was dominated by a fraction of the industrial bourgeoisie. Between 1955–62 the PNP developed no mass movement towards independence.[13]

In 1972 the PNP was able to recapture the government by orienting itself towards the general discontent, especially towards the Black Power and Rastafarian movements. The general liberalisation of the government and the reforms instituted succeeded in shifting significant working-class votes to the PNP, enabling them to sweep the polls in 1976. But Manley's decision in 1977 to accept an IMF loan on harsh (even punitive) terms resulted in a massive reduction in living standards for the working class. This alienated much of the government's popular support.[14] By the next election the PNP was roundly defeated.

Of course part of the PNP's defeat came as a result of the destabilisation efforts undertaken by the United States and international organisations and by massive financial assistance to the Jamaica Labour Party by transnational capital. But as Fitzroy Ambursley argues, the main reason for the PNP's defeat was because there was no revolutionary dynamic in Jamaica.[15] The ultimate weakness of the PNP was its failure to unite and mobilise small peasants, farm workers, urban wage earners and casual labourers who comprise the social and political majority of Jamaican society. The PNP never had an organic relationship with the working class for, as Ambursley argues, its trade union was really a patronage arm of the party. Thus Ambursley concludes that

> The PNP's history reflects the low level of national consciousness in Jamaica . . . and throughout the English-speaking Caribbean, where long years of chattel slavery and colonial rule served to retard and deflect national awareness. Unlike India or Africa, nationalism does not pervade the body politic. Bustamante's election slogan in 1944, 'self-government means slavery', encapsulated this paradoxical and somewhat schizophrenic relationship between underdeveloped nationalism and its labourist surrogate.[16]

In a recent paper I have argued with Dennis Young that what we have seen in many of the movements to achieve political and economic independence is 'dependent nationalism'.[17] While the term may appear contradictory, it is really a reflection of the extent to which political developments in the periphery are constrained by economic and political factors in the core. More often than not, the leaders of these movements have looked outward for assistance in their 'struggle' with the metropole without first attempting to develop internally those resources necessary to confront the core. Political mobilisation tends to be perfunctory and disorganised; there tends to be no sustained process of educating the working class about the issues and forces that confront them. Salvation is expected to come from without rather than from within.

This has been especially true in the English-speaking Caribbean where the process of decolonisation was gradual and peaceful; instead of the power being wrested from the coloniser there was a process of accommodation between the coloniser and the colonised. Part of the reason for this is that the interests of nominally 'national' actors tend to be tied to institutions outside the nation. Thus, even during the nationalist era, when the orientation of national leaders was expected to be most radical, the nominally domestic forces were themselves profoundly conditioned by the insertion of the nation into the world system. The nationalist orientation tends to be much more a matter of rhetoric than action to bring about systemic change. The possibility for a meaningful democracy is lost.

A good example of dependent nationalism is the nationalist movement in Belize, and particularly the impact of the Anglo-Guatemala dispute on local politics (i.e., Guatemala's controversial claim to the territory of Belize).[18] The dispute has been the central issue in Belizean politics since the 1950s, when the nationalist movement began. Yet neither government nor opposition has sought to mobilise the working class on the basis of this issue. Instead, they have constantly looked outward to the core for a possible resolution, without mobilising support at home. The Guatemala issue resulted in Belize being frozen in a transitional political state (between colonial status and independence) for 20 years, and it continues to hamper the full realisation of sovereignty for the nation after several years of independence. Because of Guatemala's continued threats, Belize has found it necessary to maintain the protection of the British government. Even though Belize is an 'independent' nation, there are over 1600 British soldiers on Belizean soil.

Belize's independence continues to be compromised by Guatemala, which does not recognise its sovereignty. For example, for the past several years over 3000 Guatemalans have visited Hunting Caye, located within Belizean territorial waters. They come without benefit of visas or any other official permission of the Belize government.[19] Such incursions were not allowed during colonialism.

In the English-speaking Caribbean the prospects for participatory democracy appear limited. The leadership of the major political parties is likely to remain bourgeois, opting for reformist measures rather than systemic change and therefore seeking periodic acquiescence from the working class by means of the ballot box but discouraging popular initiatives. The mechanisms for popular participation (e.g. trade unions, mass media, political organisations, educational institutions) all remain highly centralised and under the control of the local state. Within the political arena, no more than two political parties predominate, parties that long ago reached an accommodation with the state. The possibility that third parties, especially those on the left, will emerge as major actors on the electoral scene is unlikely. Yet, the left historically has had a significant impact on the development of democracy in the Caribbean: it has been in the forefront of protests for political rights and the struggle for independence.[20]

What is the future role of the left likely to be in the Caribbean? Perry Mars and others suggest that it should assume the role of opposition, exposing the range of contradictions inherent in the socio-political system. Thus the left would create an openness in the political culture that was not allowed by the British during colonial domination and which still has not taken hold. The left's role, then, would be to push democracy further.

Pursuing that role will be difficult, however, for governments in the region have not reached an easy accommodation with the left. Mars notes, for example, that Jamaica and Guyana, with the greatest history of leftist activity, are now the most militarised.[21] The types of weapons being purchased by Caribbean governments (and others in the Third World) suggest they are meant to be used not against external invaders but against internal protest movements of all kinds.[22]

WAR ON TERRORISM

Throughout the Third World we see a decline in the demand for sophisticated arms, and a growing market for less-sophisticated weapons and support systems, and for spare parts and ammunition. One of the reasons for this shift in priorities is the growing incidence of insurgency and 'low-intensity' warfare in the Third World.[23] Low intensity conflict is often the outward manifestation of the struggle for change, generally within national boundaries, as the dispossessed seek inclusion and meet resistance. Out of concern over such low-level conflict, many Third World governments now emphasise purchases of small arms, helicopters, off-road vehicles and other such items; items to be used against their own people. Low-intensity conflict (including terrorism, insurgency, counter-insurgency and small-scale conflicts) have become in the 1980s a major strategic concern of the United States and its client regimes. As the US Under-Secretary of Defense, Fred C. Ikle, has observed: 'Today one out of every four countries around the globe is at war. These are not wars . . . where armies roll across borders, [or] where hundreds of aircraft fight for the skies. Rather they are insurgent and local conflicts in which people get killed . . . by grenades, bullets, mines [or] bombs dropped from aircraft.'[24] The US government's concern over low-intensity conflicts has been embodied in what has come to be known as a 'War on Terrorism', which seeks to mobilise public support in the US for prolonged undeclared war throughout the Third World. As Sara Miles has pointed out:

> 'Terrorism' has become a label for virtually all forms of conflict that emanate from the real processes of change in the Third World. These conflicts, whatever their true source and character, can be made to represent frightening and irrational forces. While Americans may not be moved by administration insistence that faraway revolutions represent a threat to their national security, terrorism personalizes the threat. And when counterterrorism is equated with counterinsurgency, US involvement in low-intensity conflict may come to appear as a matter of self-defense, or immediate concern to ordinary citizens.[25]

Local government's use of weapons against protest movements in the Caribbean and throughout the Third World (and in the US) is part of what James Petras terms a global network of state terror.[26] He suggests that the political purposes of state terror are to destroy challenges to capitalism, to defeat the attempt by the working classes and social movements to change the ownership of property and distribution of wealth. There is also an attempt to destroy the burgeoning institutions of popular participation so that the organised demands of the working classes cannot be articulated or heard. For Petras, the growth in global state terror has paralleled the growth in global capital expansion.[27] He argues that, as the contradictions inherent in capitalism became more apparent and the political and economic crises grew, the result has been intensified class conflict. The increasing levels of class conflict led the US and its client regimes to rely heavily on military repression. Clive Thomas gives the same rationale for the growth in authoritarian regimes in the English-speaking Caribbean, regimes dependent on repressive apparatuses.[28] Petras argues further that the long-term, large-scale nature of capital movements required systematic and sustained repressive activity. Thus a new terror network, involving systematic information collection, total warfare tactics affecting civilians and combatants, and high-tech firepower, were among the key changes introduced. Effective state terror against social movements accompanied and facilitated the principle of accessibility for capital and became one of the major factors creating investors' confidence in the regime.

The US has become the organisational center that provides the expertise, financing and technology to service client regimes and their terrorist institutions. One of the main ways that it supports state terror is through foreign police training. In 1974 the US Congress banned the government from providing training and equipment to foreign police. But Congress allowed the Reagan administration to re-institute foreign police training in Central America and the Caribbean to counter what the administration labeled Nicaraguan and Cuban 'terrorism'. As Miles has pointed out: Members of Congress who hesitated to endorse aid to military dictatorships or repel long-standing bans on US police aid, are more willing to take a stand against 'terrorism'.[29] Thus we see how well-chosen is the term 'terrorism', since it conjures up malevolence and can mean whatever one wants it to mean.

The Reagan Administration's Regional Security System (RSS) for the Eastern Caribbean included police counterterrorism training. The Central Intelligence Agency (CIA) has begun recruiting US police for temporary CIA duty to assist in its war against 'terrorism' abroad. Meanwhile the Drug Enforcement Agency continues to assist its foreign counterparts in 'narcotics control'.

Martha Huggins suggests that the quintessential example of politicised policing is the training by one country of another's police and security forces.[30] Given the unequal distribution of power between the trainer and trainee, police training by another state reduces the international and internal autonomy of the host country. What is more, such training increases the involvement of the police within their own national politics and transforms such police into global actors through relations with the donor country.

A situation that is even more disturbing, according to Huggins, is the fact that the training of civilian police is being conducted as a military function.[31] Specifically, US police trainers have usually come from the military, not civil police agencies. The techniques taught and the equipment provided are oriented towards military and not civilian social control. Finally, a central objective has been intelligence gathering for the US. Usually such intelligence gathering has been to monitor internal political threats to US economic interests or to a political regime allied with it.

The training of national police by foreign governments, especially by the US and its allies, is likely to increase. The US has demonstrated a willingness to use third countries and private citizens to carry out illegal training or to support covert operations with foreign governments, when such support could not be given through official US government channels.

The chief US ally in the exporting of terror in recent years, especially in Central America and the Caribbean, has been Israel.[32] Starting in the late-1970s, Israel's overseas activities, from the US point of view, were significant in that they circumvented the restrictions on US assistance to repressive regimes imposed because of President Jimmy Carter's human rights policy. The case of Guatemala is well known: between 1977 and 1981, Israel was Guatemala's sole arms supplier. Israeli assistance to the Duvalier dictatorship in Haiti began during the Carter administration. It was also between 1977 and 1981 that Israel began to engage in counter-insurgency assistance in Latin America and the Caribbean – in Guatemala, El Salvador and Haiti – filling the counterinsurgency gap left by the US. During the Reagan administration, Israel again fulfilled a specific role. Israel's interventions were then to circumvent US public opinion and, specifically, congressional restrictions on the implementation of executive policies. Several instances are a matter of public record: Israel helped by funding $21 million into El Salvador in 1981 when funds in the US foreign aid budget had run out and, in 1984, when the CIA requested Israel to provide financial assistance to the contras after Congress had refused to approve a covert operation budget of the White House.

We have also seen that increasingly the traditional restraints embodied in international law are explicitly rejected by the US in favour
of unilateral terrorist acts. International air piracy and the mining of
international shipping routes and national harbours accompany
public funding of mercenary terrorist forces in Central America, and
elsewhere. Such acts continue a long history of violating domestic
and international law (for instance, the overthrow of the Arbenz
government in Guatemala and the Allende government in Chile) in
order to ensure that the internal security and political climate of
those countries would be receptive to US interests.

Petras suggests that the US seeks to secure through state terror
what it has been unable to achieve in recent years through the
economic marketplace; namely, the maintenance of the capitalist
model of accumulation.[33] In order to achieve this aim, the US is
willing to sacrifice the titular heads of client regimes in order to
destroy the movements for social change and thus preserve the state
apparatus.[34] The US and its media propagate the notion that the
object of popular social movements is merely to dispose of a political
personality and not to transform the socio-political system. We are
told that the aim is to get rid of the dictator and thus gain democratic
credibility. We have witnessed recently the fall of Marcos and Duvalier from power, falls orchestrated by the US only after large seg-
ments of the populace protested against the incumbent regimes. In
order to forestall further protests and the possibility that significant
concessions will have to be made, the US intercedes and 'encourages'
the dictator to leave. As seen in Haiti, the democracy promised is
really a facade; it can best be described as a 'redemocratisation which
secures the machine guns'.[35]

The case of General Manuel Antonio Noriega, Panama's outlawed
dictator, presents the perfect example of global state terrorism in
action.[36] Noriega's association with the US began early: he allegedly
worked for the CIA while at military college in Peru, supplying
information on suspected leftists among his fellow cadets. Under
General Omar Torrijos, Noriega was given control over military
intelligence as well as criminal investigations, customs and immigration. During his 13 years on the job Noriega built his power base and
collected dossiers on anyone who might ever be an enemy. His job
made Noriega useful to the US intelligence community, which
wanted to know everything that might affect the security of the
Panama Canal and the US Southern Command headquarters nearby.

Noriega is alleged to have worked for both the CIA and the Defense Intelligence Agency.

Because of his usefulness, the US for a long time seemed willing to ignore stories about Noriega's corruption. For instance, he allowed the US to operate an electronic surveillance station in Panama; he allowed the training of contra soldiers in Panama and the setting-up of dummy corporations for use in funding them; and he gave almost free rein to the activities of the US troops along the canal. As long as Noriega allowed the US to further its foreign policy objectives, he was safe. However, as it became obvious that he was assisting Cuba and Nicaragua to evade US trade embargoes and had allowed the Soviet KGB to set up operations in Panama City, the CIA became disenchanted with their 'intelligence asset'. Increasing Panamanian cooperation with the East bloc forced the Reagan administration into action. When allegations of Noriega's involvement in political corruption and murder surfaced in Panama in mid-1987, the US decided not to oppose an indictment against him. Thus, in February 1988 federal grand juries in Miami and Tampa indicted Noriega on charges of drug trafficking, money laundering and racketeering: the first time the US had charged the leader of a major allied country with criminal acts.

Among other charges, the grand jury in Miami accused Noriega of helping members of the Medellin cartel, the violent Colombian drug ring, by providing safe airstrips for their cocaine shipments and by laundering the cartel's profits. The Panama case shows the extent to which the illicit drug industry can penetrate the borders of sovereign nations through buying off the defenders of the nation (i.e. the military and the police). In Colombia and in neighboring countries there are charges that military and police leaders are collaborating with Colombia's cocaine cartel. US prosecutors charge that Col. Jean-Claude Paul turned Haiti into a haven for drug shipments and have indicted him on narcotics-trafficking charges. Military officers in Honduras are also reported to be involved in trafficking.[37] Some have suggested that the military should not be involved in the fight against drugs, except as support to the police during drug raids. Otherwise the chance is too great for corruption of the military.

The war on drugs currently being waged in the Caribbean is orchestrated by the US and is another instance of these countries being drawn into its orbit. The tactics on how to fight against drugs and the equipment to be used are dictated from Washington. For example, in Belize the government's decision to acquiesce in the Reagan administration's demands that marijuana fields be sprayed aerially with the controversial herbicide paraquat helped to lose the governing party the election in 1984. For fear of having US aid cut off or curtailed, Caribbean leaders respond to its demands. As Neville Duncan has noted, it is the US which decides whether the individual countries are doing enough to combat the drug problem.[38]

More insidious than having policy dictated from outside is the fact that under the rubric of fighting drugs, Caribbean countries are fighting their own people. For instance, when Errol Barrow became Prime Minister of Barbados in 1986 he said he would de-emphasise the military. He ended recruitment for the security forces but kept the same size force. He assured the citizens that the force would be used against drug traffickers, not against Barbadians.[39] Surely some Barbadians are involved in drugs. More importantly, because of the fear of drugs among the middle class, in particular, there is the possibility that enemies of the government can be accused of drug trafficking, whether true or not, and repressed with impunity. The growth of the drug industry reflects the inability of the formal economies in these countries to respond to the needs of the people. Thus the stage is set for protests and the growth of social movements. But, in the name of fighting drugs, protests can be foiled and dissent weakened. Repressive actions in the US and throughout the Caribbean are on the rise.

While Caribbean leaders have been enthusiastic in their endorsements of the objectives of the US anti-narcotics efforts, they are becoming increasingly concerned and annoyed with some of the tactics employed which have impugned the reputations of a few leaders. Particularly incensed are Prime Ministers Lynden Pindling of the Bahamas and Edward Seaga of Jamaica, both mentioned in US congressional testimony by convicted drug dealers. US courts have convicted former government officials from Surinam, Belize and the Turks and Caicos for drug involvement. The leaders complain that their sovereignty is being infringed upon and their officials publicly smeared by witnesses of questionable credibility without the chance to respond. In a letter to President Reagan the leaders of CARICOM cited attempts to extend US authority 'into the neighboring countries of the region without regard for the sovereignty and independent legal systems of these countries . . . often in violation of the universal principles of natural justice.'[40] The question remains whether the leaders' concern for 'natural justice' will extend to the working classes of the Caribbean.

THE REDEMOCRATISATION PROCESS

Throughout Central America and Latin America, there is much discussion about the 'redemocratisation process', or the withdrawal of the military from positions of government and the subsequent installation of democratically elected civilians. As the military return to the barracks, the question is to what extent does the political order really become democratic?

Unfortunately the 'democracy' which has become fashionable lately is often a shallow interpretation of the real concept, and the elements chosen to characterise it serve the self-interests and specific purposes of the groups advocating it. The Reagan administration has called Latin America's efforts to create a democratic order 'the most stunning and moving political feat of recent years'. The US points with pride to the democratic transitions taking place from the Dominican Republic and Grenada to El Salvador and Guatemala. Yet this redemocratization is limited in scope, with the military still playing a controlling role in the political process.

Petras suggests that the redemocratisation process can be characterised by four features.[41] First, the military regime attempts to control the progression of 'redemocratisation' by favouring civilian partners who emphasise legal-political changes over socio-economic structural transformations. These chosen civilian partners focus on changing institutions of government and not the state. The military also encourages 'incremental change' – the process is staggered in discrete stages, thus allowing for the dispersion of the opposition. This enables the military and its favoured partners to bargain and trade off changes for continuities.

Third, Petras argues that in order to segment the opposition the military establishes 'parameters' as to who is eligible to participate and who is excluded. The purpose of this is to divide 'moderates' from 'radicals', so that the latter can be marginalised and reduced to a secondary force. Finally, the military returns to the barracks as a way of pre-empting anticipated opposition. The process of redemocratisation 'reflects the military's difficulty in ruling, its growing sense of political isolation, its realization that the process of conflict could escalate to a point where the situation could completely escape from their control and present for them totally unacceptable alternatives'.[42]

Therefore, the redemocratisation process can be seen as a pre-emptive strike by the military in the face of the deepening economic crisis and growing social movements with their increasing struggle to create political space. The military's tactical retreat allows it to choose among political groups within the opposition. Its concern is to shift the problem from the street to the negotiating table where it can be more easily handled. The decision to withdraw to the barracks 'is much more a decision to avoid the totally unattractive choices inherent in a deepening polarisation than a conversion to democratic politics'.[43]

Because of the military's carefully planned redemocratisation strategy and the kinds of commitments the civilian groups must make to gain power, the policies of the new civilian government are circumscribed significantly. Legal and political changes come rather easily, but profound social and economic initiatives are seldom taken. As a result, social and economic discontent is likely to remain just below the political surface. The threat that it might erupt into violence leads to a possible return to authoritarian rule.[44]

CONCLUSION

Except for Grenada, the security forces in the English-speaking Caribbean have not assumed power directly, nor do they play a major role in the political life of the countries. Yet democracy is far from secure in the region.

While there is much talk these days about democracy in the Caribbean, we see that such discussion goes hand-in-hand with a war on terrorism. The latter is carried out by a global network which reaches into every country in the region, affecting civilians and combatants alike. This war is insidious, with its emphasis on intelligence gathering and propaganda. Dissent of any kind becomes dangerous. In pursuit of its goals of protection of its enonomic interests and continued US hegemony, the managers of the global network have turned to acts of international crime, not the least of which is the penetration of the drug industry into more and more countries and the ensuing corruption. Borders become permeable by transnational criminals as well as transnational capital. The training of local police by this global network makes the Caribbean state even more vulnerable, as those whose job is to defend it are receiving instructions from outside. The insecurity of the state and its leaders is compounded rather than relieved. It is no wonder that instead of democracy there is 'redemocratization'. Democracy can never mean simply the removal of the military from direct power.

Democracy in the Caribbean has centered, historically, around an accommodation among competing elites. The circle of elites has widened over time, but it has not focused attention on the mobilisation of the masses. Minimal input from the masses has resulted in few changes to the status quo, certainly not the profound social changes needed to enable them to participate fully in the social and economic life of their countries. In praising Costa Rica for its heritage of liberal democracy, President Oscar Arias concluded that 'the democratic system should struggle to distribute power, economic and political, and this is a difficult struggle because power tends to become concentrated, so we need to find mechanisms to distribute it . . . We need economic democracy because liberal democracy is insufficient.'[45]

The same statement could be made throughout the Caribbean; yet the concept of social democracy enabling equal political participation seems to be an ideal that distances itself more from reality each day. The use of terrorism as a scare tactic to hide repression of dissident groups and social movements and as a mechanism for intelligence gathering and social control is having the desired chilling effect on attempts to mobilise for political and economic participation.

Yet mobilisation must continue, for a desirable democracy is one that incorporates and enfranchises the majority of its citizens. Democracy must be reflected not just in electoral results but in changes in living conditions for the majority of the people. Since the great majority of people in the Caribbean are in an underprivileged position relative to a minority, then democracy needs also to be defined 'as a system that makes it possible for the people to steadily improve themselves economically, socially and culturally'.[46]

Though definitions of democracy vary,[47] it seems that a common denominator is that mechanisms must be available that allow/ encourage effective participation by individuals in the decisions that most affect their lives. It also seems that there should be a broad interpretation of the kinds of issues that affect the lives of individuals. The model of citizen participation seems an appropriate one for fostering democracy, for it encourages the development of citizen competence and well-being, promotes public discussion and community interaction, and creates a variety of organisations that are accountable at the grass-roots level. The building of self-esteem and a sense of community means that the citizens will no longer be apathetic but will be mobilised sufficiently to make demands on the system and hold leaders accountable for their decisions. The citizen participation model could be the first step in what Amin terms 'delinking' and could bring about the kinds of change that are reflective of democracy. The maintenance of the status quo is antithetical to democracy.

Within the Caribbean there are several points at which the building of a citizen participation model might take place. One is through independent organisations like the church and the universities, where issues can be addressed in a systematic way and also where technical assistance can be offered to community groups to facilitate their development. Second, people need to be organised where they live and work – in their neighbourhoods, in schools, at their workplaces, and the first issues they attack should centre around shelter, jobs, education and food. The organising of squatter settlements in Mexico, for example, gives an indication of how successful groups can become in demand-making and how helpful outside groups, like universities, can be in facilitating that process.

Third, the Left must continue its efforts of opposing and critiquing and work to educate the citizens to raise their consciousness about their rights and offer its analysis of situations of major importance to the society. The Left must serve to mobilise the citizens on the basis of ideology – to continue to be the conscience of the government. Fourth, there must be an insistence on the fuller development and strengthening of regional organisations, from the Caribbean Community (CARICOM) to the University of the West Indies system to the Caribbean Conference of Churches and others. Less emphasis should be placed on bilateral arrangements (as in individual Caribbean countries with the US) and more effort put toward regional cooperation. Regional cooperation should be centered around quality of life issues rather than issues of security. These are some of the mechanisms that will free the Caribbean from being held hostage by the demands and requirements that come from outside the region and from leaders who act as clients for interests from outside. Only then can the needs of the Caribbean begin to be addressed, within a climate of cooperation and with a people mobilised for effective political and social action.

If we are to have democracy in the Caribbean, then the voice of the people must be heard. The practicing of formal democracy every five years is not enough. It will never create the conditions necessary for sustained socio-economic change. The working class, the peasantry and others who are in effect disenfranchised must find a way to participate fully in the affairs of the state. Instead of having policy imposed from above, the people must be given an opportunity to participate in the making of policy. In this sense, democracy is discussion. The fuller the discussion the more likely that initiatives will be taken that respond to the needs of those affected most deeply. In this sense, the people are the best assurance of keeping local state borders from being permeated by outside forces that have little interest in the welfare of the working classes. The people are the best defenders of the state. Perhaps such democracy will lead ultimately to peace.

Notes

1. Caroline Thomas (1988) *In Search of Security: International Relations in the Third World* (Boulder, Co: Lynne Rienner), p. 4, cf. 1–9.
2. See this discussion in R. J. Rummel (1984) 'On Fostering a Just Peace,' *International Journal on World Peace*, I, 1 (Autumn), pp. 4–15.
3. Rummel, p. 9.
4. Rummel, p. 12.
5. See for instance Daniel Lerner (1958) *The Passing of Traditional Society* (Glencoe, Ill.: The Free Press); and S. M. Lipset (1959) 'Some Social Requisites of Democracy', *American Political Science Review*, 52 (March), pp. 850–76.
6. See for instance Samir Amin (1974) *Accumulation on a World Scale: A Critique of the Theory of Underdevelopment.* New York: Monthly Review Press; and Immanuel Wallerstein (1979) *The Capitalist World-Economy* (Cambridge: Cambridge University Press).
7. Samir Amin (1987) 'Democracy and National Security in the Periphery,' *Third World Quarterly*, 9, 4, October, p. 1132.
8. Amin, p. 1139.
9. Amin, p. 1146.
10. Amin, p. 1148.
11. See Winston James' review of Ken Post's *Arise Ye Starvelings* in the April 1983 issue of the *New Left Review*, pp. 85–91.
12. See Fitzroy Ambursley (1981) 'Jamaica: The Demise of "Democratic Socialism"', *New Left Review*, 128, August pp. 76–87.
13. Ambursley, p. 78.
14. Ambursley, p. 82.
15. Ambursley, p. 86.

16. Ambursley, p. 86.
17. Alma H. Young and Dennis H. Young (1988) 'The Impact of the Anglo-Guatemala Dispute on the Internal Politics of Belize,' *Latin American Perspectives*, 15, 2, Spring, pp. 6–30.
18. Young and Young, pp. 12–26.
19. *Amandala* (Belize), April 28, 1988, p.c.
20. Perry Mars (1988) 'Left Wing Politics and Caribbean Democracy.' A paper presented at the 14th International Congress of the Latin Americans Studies Association, New Orleans, March.
21. Mars, p. 25.
22. Michael Klare (1987) 'The Arms Trade: Changing Patterns in the 1980s', *Third World Quarterly*, 9, 4, October, p. 1267.
23. Low intensity conflict involves both military (a la guerilla warfare) and political war (a la civic action to win the hearts and minds of the citizens) within a non-conventional theatre of operations. Civilians are very much the victims of such warfare. As Isabel Jaramillo has said, low intensity conflict is low for the United States (the major protagonist) but not for the impacted countries.
24. As cited in Klare, p. 1269.
25. As cited in Gregory Shank (1987) 'Counterterrorism and Foreign Policy', *Crime and Social Justice*, 27–28, pp. 33–65.
26. James Petras (1987a) 'Political Economy of State Terror: Chile, El Salvador and Brazil', *Crime and Social Justice*, 27–28, p. 88.
27. Petras (1987a), p. 90.
28. Clive Thomas (1984) *The Rise of the Authoritarian State in Peripheral Societies* (New York: Monthly Review Press).
29. As quoted in Shank, p. 60.
30. Martha K. Huggins (1978) 'US-Supported State Terror: A History of Police Training in Latin America', *Crime and Social Justice*, 27–28, pp. 1209–1210.
31. Huggins, p. 150.
32. Jan Nederveen Pieterse (1987) 'The Washington – Tel Aviv Connection: Global Frontier Management', *Crime and Social Justice*, 27–28, pp. 1209–10.
33. Petras (1987a), p. 91.
34. Petras (1987a), pp. 91–2.
35. Petras (1987a), p. 108.
36. This account is taken from *Newsweek*, 15 February 1988, pp. 8–13; also see *The New York Times*, 9 February 1988.
37. *The Washington Post*, April 11, 1988, p. A/7.
38. Remarks made by Neville Duncan at the Conference on Peace and Development in the Caribbean, Kingston, Jamaica, May, 1988.
39. Dion E. Phillips (1988) 'The Defense System in Barbados, 1962–88', A paper presented at the 12th International Conference of the Caribbean Studies Association, Guadeloupe, May.
40. 'Caribbean leaders bristle at drug war tactics', *Times Picayune* (New Orleans), 3 September 1988, A–16.
41. James Petras (1987b) ''The Redemocratization Process', *Contemporary Marxism*, 14, pp. 1–15.

42. Petras (1987b), p. 6.
43. Petras (1987b), p. 7.
44. Petras (1987b), pp. 10–14.
45. Quoted in Craig W. Auchter (1988) 'Democracy for Masters or Majorities? A Comparative Analysis of Political Development in Central America', A paper presented at the 14th International Congress of the Latin American Studies Association, New Orleans, March n.p.
46. Ifgenia Martinez (1988) 'Mexican Democratic Current', *World Policy*, Spring, pp. 343–44.
47. See Auchter (1988) for a discussion of the three traditions of democracy: Marxist, liberal and organic.

2 Restoring Hegemony: the Complementarity Among the Security, Economic and Political Components of US Policy in the Caribbean Basin During the 1980s
Emilio Pantojas García

INTRODUCTION

There is considerable consensus on the fact that US policy in the Caribbean Basin (i.e. in the Caribbean and Central America) under the Reagan administration was aimed at restoring American hegemony in its so-called backyard. Many US analysts seem to believe, however, that such hegemony is defined primarily by military supremacy and the ability of the North American state and capital to impose unilaterally their interests and views in the region.[1] Indeed, the high profile of the Reagan Doctrine, according to which the US government is willing to use force to contain the advance of Communism, led to this perception. But this view of hegemony is very narrow and sees force as the main means of exercising political domination.

In this chapter such a view of hegemony is rejected. Hegemony is understood here in the Gramscian sense as including both the capacity of a dominant group to lead through ideological means (i.e. persuasion) as well as the capacity to impose the dominant group's interests through force (i.e. repression) but with persuasion being the dominant means of exercising political domination. Hegemony is, therefore, domination by consent, repression being a last resort element in situations of hegemonic dominance. Hegemony implies not merely the capacity to impose the interests of the dominant group(s) against resistance, but rather the capacity of the dominant group(s) to articulate and transform (coopt) the interests of the subordinate groups. So, hegemony assumes the ability of dominant groups to incorporate in a subordinate manner the interests of the subordinate groups to their political project and thus achieve domination through consent rather than repression.[2]

According to this definition, then, the restoration of US hegemony in the Caribbean Basin entails the reorganisation of the system of political, economic and military relations with the governments of the region in order to restore the congruency of US leadership in these three spheres; or, put another way, the restoration of American hegemony implies the restructuring of US/Caribbean Basin relations in such a manner as to present US capital and the state as social forces capable of advancing not only their own interests but also the interests of the local propertied and governing sectors allied to them.[3]

As the Reagan presidency has come to an end, it becomes easier to appreciate the complementarity of the different components of that administration's policy toward the region. Although in the short term the dramatic escalation of American military presence in the Caribbean Basin gave the impression that the US was following a one track policy, the turn of events has seen a shift to a multifaceted attempt to restore American dominance in the region. This evolution in the Reagan administration's policy is perhaps best reflected in the contrasts between the two major Reaganite policy statements on the region: the reports of the Committee of Santa Fe and of the Kissinger Commission in 1980 and 1984, respectively.[4]

It could be argued that these two reports correspond to the two phases of the Reagan policy in the region. The report of the Committee of Santa Fe represents the heavily militaristic, unilateral and short-term view of the early Reagan years. The Kissinger Commission report exemplifies the longer-term and multifaceted approach that began to take shape at the end of the first term of the Reagan presidency. Although they both share the strategic goal of contention and rollback of 'communism' in the region, as well as the framework and rhetoric of East–West confrontation, they also reflect different approaches to achieving these objectives.

Here I propose to analyze each of the main components of the Caribbean Basin policy of the Reagan Administration and how these complement each other in configuring a long-term project of solution to the political crisis of the region in a manner consistent with the US goal of restoring its dominance and leadership in the region. First, I

discuss the security component. This consitutes the key to understanding the whole of the Reagan policy in the region since security
concerns have been the most invoked reason of the Administration to
justify its interventionism. In fact, the short-term response of the
Reagan Administration to the regional crisis and the crisis of American hegemony in the region was military escalation within the
framework of East/West confrontation.

Second, I analyse the two main economic proposals of the Reagan
Administration for the region: the Caribbean Basin Initiative (CBI)
and the proposals of the Kissinger Commission formulated as the
Central American Initiative (CAI). The process of economic restructuring that these proposals were trying to stimulate constituted the
basis of the Reaganite project for a long-term solution to the economic crisis in the region.

Finally, I examine American efforts to rearticulate its political
alliances in the region. Here, special attention is given to the reasons
why the US is sponsoring elections and elected regimes throughout
the region against the initial expectations that it would support
authoritarian anti-communist regimes.

THE STRATEGIC COMPONENT

North American security policy in the Caribbean during the Reagan
presidency is shaped by the thinking of the so called New Right.
According to this line of thought, World War III – the war between
the East and the West for world supremacy – has already begun and
the West is losing it. For the New Right the loss of the Vietnam war
and the consequent weakening of the power and will of the US to act
effectively as the global police of Western capitalism (i.e. the
Vietnam syndrome), led to the adoption of accommodationist policies, such as *détente* and trilateralism, in dealing with the Eastern
bloc. These 'speak soft' and 'carry no stick' policies, so to speak,
allowed significant advances during the 1970s, to 'Soviet backed'
liberation movements throughout the Third World. The triumphs of
socialist and anti-imperialist forces in Asia (Vietnam, Laos and
Cambodia), Africa (Angola, Zimbabwe and Ethiopia), and Latin
America and the Caribbean (Chile and Peru in the early 1970s and
Guyana, Jamaica, Grenada and Nicaragua in the latter part of the
decade) were clear signs for the New Right of who was ahead in
World War III. Moreover, the fact that these geopolitical 'losses'

were accompanied by the strengthening of Third World coalitions inimical to Western capitalist interests, as best illustrated by the strengthening of OPEC and the success of the Arab oil embargo in 1973, reinforced the view of the New Right and gave it some legitimacy among US public opinion.[5]

Throughout this period of decay in US power in the world, the fact remained, however, that the US was the one nation with the main responsibilities for the worldwide security of Western capitalism. If any further geopolitical losses to the West and Western capital were to be avoided, reasoned the New Right ideologues, the political shortcomings of the post-Vietnam era had to be overcome. The accommodationist policies that had permitted major Soviet gains, even in America's backyard – the Caribbean Basin – had to be reevaluated and changed. The new American policy for the 1980s had to go back to the 'get tough' attitudes of the Cold War in the 1950s and 1960s. Only now a greater emphasis should be put on the roll-back and containment of Soviet expansion in the Third World, specially in the Caribbean and Latin America. The new 'cold war' would be fought, therefore, mainly in the Third World rather than in Europe. The counter offensive of World War III would not be fought in conventional terms either but rather in an unconventional form that would come to be known among the military establishment as 'low intensity conflict'.[6]

In the scheme of the American New Right, Central America and the Caribbean would become the testing ground for this new policy. To 'draw the line in El Salvador', as Secretary of State General Alexander Haig so graphically put it, meant for the New Right the start of World War III's counter offensive. This would signal the 'comeback' of the US as the worldwide guardian of Western capitalism, the guarantor of free access for Western capital to the markets and resources of the Third World.

The framework of this comeback of the US as the undisputed power in the American hemisphere would be provided by a 'modernised' version of the Monroe Doctrine. This modernised version of the old American interventionist policy was originally advanced in the report of the Committee of Santa Fe. In brief, it called for the reassertion of US economic and military power in the region and the strengthening of US allies through the revitalisation of cold war Inter-American structures such as the Rio Treaty and the Organisation of American States.[7]

The military corollary of the 'modern' Monroe Doctrine was

advanced later in a study prepared for the US Air Force by David
Ronfeldt, of the Rand Corporation. According to it, the strategic
principles guiding the reassertion of the Monroe Doctrine required
that:

1. The Caribbean Basin be secure for US presence, power, and
   passage;
2. Hostile foreign powers be prevented from acquiring military bases
   and facilities there;
3. Foreign balance-of-power struggles be excluded and prevented
   from destabilising the region; and
4. Few US military resources be dedicated to protecting interests and
   assets there.[8]

Thus, within this logic, the thrust of American security policy in
the region should be aimed at rolling-back Soviet and Cuban gains
allowed by the weakness of the US in the recent past. The New Right
strategists perceived the Soviets as positioning themselves within a
strategic axis that mirrored the one that the US had traditionally used
to guarantee its control ('presence, power and passage') over the
Caribbean Basin. US military control of the region had traditionally
relied on a triangular axis consisting of Puerto Rico in the eastern
Caribbean, Cuba in the west and Panama in the Central American
isthmus. The Soviet axis would consist of Grenada in the east, Cuba
in the west and Nicaragua in the isthmus.

For the New Right strategists the consolidation of this 'hostile axis'
would represent a threat to US dominance in the region in various
ways. First, the possibility of building an Isthmian canal in Nicaragua
would render US control over the Panama canal virtually useless for
either economic or military purposes. Second, the Soviet presence in
Nicaragua could provide them with a Pacific base in the American
hemisphere, which would pose a new threat to growing US Pacific
interests. Finally, the consolidation of the axis could serve as the
platform from which to spread Soviet/Cuban influence throughout
the Caribbean, Central and South America through the support of
low intensity conflict.[9]

It is with this scenario in mind that the Reagan Administration
would embark upon a major escalation of its direct military presence
in Central America and the Caribbean for the purpose of rolling-back
'Soviet/Cuban gains' in these regions. The main objectives of this
display of American military might were to overthrow the revolution-

ary governments of Grenada and Nicaragua and to contain the advance of insurgent movements in El Salvador. A longer-term goal would be the neutralisation or 'Finlandisation' of Cuba.

The groundwork for the escalation of the US military presence in the Caribbean Basin had been laid by the Carter administration with the creation in 1979 of the Joint Caribbean Task Force in Key West and the stationing there of the Rapid Deployment Forces. This was followed by increased manoeuvres in the Roosevelt Roads naval base in Puerto Rico and the establishment of American military facilities in Honduras, where major exercises were also conducted. These 'muscle flexing' exercises, as the Reagan Administration called them, culminated in the 1983 invasion of Grenada. By 1983, the US military presence in the Caribbean Basin had reached a new peak since World War II. Aside from the significant increases in the number of troops stationed in the region and the establishment of new military facilities between 1980 and 1983, military aid to US allies in Central America increased by 1840 per cent from 20.7 to 401.7 million dollars. In the Caribbean, where there were no major armed insurrections, US military aid increased by 904 per cent from 8.7 to 87.4 million dollars. The US government also tried to revive the Central American Defense Council (CONDECA) and created the Regional Security System (RSS) in the Eastern Caribbean in 1982.[10]

But while in the short-term the East/West confrontation logic served to justify the increased military presence of the US in the Caribbean Basin, this very strategic logic would dictate a shift in policy. For, if the long-term objective of this policy was to restore US hegemony in the region, an extended massive direct military presence ran counter to this very objective. As defined in the earlier quotation from Ronfeldt, the principles guiding the military corollary of the 'new' Monroe Doctrine dictated not only the exclusion of the region from 'foreign balance-of-power struggles', but also the allocation of 'few US military resources' for the protection of American interests in the region. To have to divert too many military resources on a permanent basis to protect American interests in the Caribbean and Central America would actually hamper the US ability 'to act as a world power in a global balance-of-power system'.[11]

Quite apart from the logic of the global balance-of-power mentality, there were other elements acting to effect a shift in US security policy in the region. First, despite all the ominous scenarios about the fall of the region to 'the red menace' presented by the domino theories of the New Right ideologues, neither the European allies of the US nor the Democrats in the US Congress fully supported the policy of military escalation. It could be said that these groups only tolerated that policy but did not fully support it. Second, after the first three years of increasing military aid and direct US involvement in Central America, it was clear that, short of a US invasion, no military victory could be achieved over the Sandinistas in Nicaragua or over the Frente Farabundo Martí de Liberación Nacional (FMLN) in El Salvador. And despite all the bragging and chest pounding that succeeded the Grenada invasion, US strategists knew that there could be no cheap military victory in Central America. Third, although a military defeat of the Sandinistas or the FMLN was not in sight, American military escalation in the region had succeeded in halting, if not reversing, the advance of revolutionary forces. That is, containment had been achieved in Central America through military escalation and in Grenada the revolutionary process had been rolled back through an invasion. Finally, American military strategists had become convinced that the only hope to 'win' the war against insurgents in Central America was to fight it on its own terms through counter insurgency.

Thus, by the end of the first term of the Reagan presidency a consensus emerged among members of the Administration in favor of adopting a new approach to US security concerns in the Caribbean Basin. This new approach would be based on the premise that any longer-term security policy in the region should involve only a minimum of military resources. As Ronfeldt so aptly put it:

> [B]ecause the traditional strategic principles advise against applying US military power, they suggest reliance on a broad concept of security that integrates political, economic and military dimensions and seeks primarily nonmilitary solutions to security problems.[12]

The low-intensity conflict approach consists of a multifaceted counterinsurgency strategy. The recipe is not new: it was used in the 'pacification' programmes in Vietnam and the counter-insurgency programmes in Latin America during the 1960s.[13] The idea is to fight a war against 'communist insurgents' on all fronts to win the hearts and minds of the population before the insurgents do. That is, to wage a war simultaneously in the economic, social, ideological and military 'fronts', transforming society into the battlefield. The aim is to conquer people not just geographical terrain. So economic and social reforms (i.e. civic action programme) will accompany covert military operations and a well orchestrated propaganda campaign to publicise the advances of the war against 'communism'. If war is the extension of politics through force, as the Pentagon followers of Klausewitz argue, then the only way to win a war in Central America is to provide the population with an alternative to the type of society offered by the insurgents. Military power can win battles: only political and economic reforms can win the war.[14]

The appointment of the Kissinger Commission in 1983, the intensification of the 'covert' war against Nicaragua that same year (best exemplified by the Administration's intervention to unify the Nicaraguan opposition in UNO – the National Opposition Union – and the granting of the first direct Congressional allocation to the *contras*) reflect a shift towards this new approach. This was also the year in which Vice President Bush and Ambassador Jeane Kirkpatrick visited El Salvador to support the creation of a constitutional and elected form of government. The emphasis in Nicaragua would shift to the 'invisible' war and in El Salvador to the professionalisation of the army and the enhancement of its counter-insurgency capabilities through the ill-fated *Plan Nacional*.

By January 1984, when the Kissinger Report was released, the pieces of the new strategy were to come together. The efforts to develop and implement a comprehensive economic and political alternative to the socialist experiments in Grenada and Nicaragua were to be intensified. Having achieved partial containment through military escalation the Administration's attention turned to the long-term security concern of stabilising the region the American way; a new 'pax Americana' was to be sought.[15] To this I turn my attention now.

THE ECONOMIC COMPONENT

The Kissinger Report viewed military aid to US allies as a 'shield' that would allow economic and social reforms to proceed.[16] Within the new approach of the Reagan Administration, the economic programs for the region should promote types of development that were congruent with the long-term security and economic interests of the US. The question then was what would this entail? Would the economic programmes of the Reagan administration be designed to reconstruct and reinforce traditional economic arrangements in the region? Or would they be designed to promote economic reforms? If the latter was the case, what kind of reforms would be promoted by US economic policies for the region?

Traditionally, the Caribbean Basin has been a supplier of primary commodities, raw or semiprocessed, to the US. Indeed, during the 1970s the US imported from the region about one-fifth of its crude oil needs, about one-half of its petroleum products and about 90 per cent of its bauxite. The region also provided one-third of the sugar, one-fifth of the coffee and 70 per cent of the bananas imported by the US.[17] Traditionally, the Caribbean was considered also a key route for US trade.

President Reagan repeatedly pointed to these traditional functions of the region as key elements of US security interests in the region. The importance of maintaining secure sea lanes for access to basic goods and raw materials, in the event of an East/West conventional confrontation in other strategically important parts of the world, has continually been used by the US President to justify the military escalation in the region to both American and international public opinion.[18]

Yet, it would be difficult to argue that sugar, bananas, bauxite or even oil constitute the driving forces behind US economic interests in the Caribbean Basin in the 1980s. The sugar support program of the US goverment has aimed at achieving self-sufficiency in the production of sweeteners by the early 1990s. This has resulted in the reduction of sugar imports quotas for the Caribbean sugar producers by nearly 50 per cent producing a dramatic decline of the value of sugar imports between 1983 and 1986 of 205 million dollars. Imports of crude oil and petroleum products from the Caribbean Basin have also declined dramatically from 5145 million dollars in 1983 to 1448 millions in 1986, a 72 per cent drop. Bauxite imports have faced a similar fate, experiencing severe fluctuations since 1984.[19] In fact, US refineries and mining concerns, such as Exxon in Aruba, Reynolds in Jamaica and Alcoa in the Dominican Republic, have recently shut down major operations.

So, US economic policy in the Caribbean and Central America is not intended to revitalise sugar, banana or coffee plantations. Neither is it aimed at restoring mining enclaves or mineral-based processing operations. Declining commodity prices over a long period of time, the strengthening of the dollar between 1980 and 1985, higher interest rates than rates of return on investment in the region and political instability have combined to make the region unattractive to US investment in these types of economic activities.

As Table 2.1 shows, between 1980 and 1985, there has been i) a decline in US investment in those CBI eligible countries where agricultural and primary-based industrial production are the main activities and ii) an increase in those countries that are financial centres or tax havens, such as the Bahamas, the Cayman Islands and Panama.

Yet, despite the lost attractiveness of the region to capital, the fact remains that both the US state and US capital consider the Caribbean and Central America to be their backyard. Moreover, the elements that articulate policy for these sectors consider that if this backyard is to remain 'secure for US presence, power and passage' something would have to be done to restore economic growth in the region and reintegrate it dynamically into the global circuit of US capital accumulation. The aim of US economic policy in the region then is to promote economic growth by stimulating investment and trade in new areas of interest to US capital. This, it was thought, would restore dynamism to the region's economies, facilitating their reintegration to the global circuit of US capital in a dynamic manner. In turn, this would alleviate the economic crises underlying political upheaval in many of the countries of the region.

It is within this framework, that I shall call 'reintegrationist', that the Reagan Administration formulated the CBI in 1982 and the Central American Democracy, Peace and Development Initiative, also known as the Kissinger Plan, the Jackson Plan or the Central American Initiative (CAI), in 1984.

The CBI grants duty-free entry to the US market to products of 27 Caribbean Basin countries for a period of twelve years, provided that certain conditions are met. The Caribbean Basin Economic Recovery Act (CBERA), enacted in 1983 and in effect since January 1984, constitutes the legal base of the CBI. It grants duty-free status to all products from CBI beneficiary countries except apparel and textiles, petroleum products, footwear, canned tuna, flat goods (i.e. gloves, wallets, handbags) and luggage.

In order to become a CBI beneficiary country, the government of any of the 27 eligible countries listed in CBERA, must: a) request CBI beneficiary designation from the US president; b) not be communist; c) not have nationalised or confiscated property of US citizens; d) not provide special treatment and advantages to products of developed countries that compete with US products; e) provide the US fair access to its markets and resources; and f) not engage in practices that distort international trade.[20]

Table 2.1 US direct investment in the Caribbean basin, 1980–85 (million dollars)

	1980	1981	±%	1982	±%	1983	±%	1984	±%	1985	±%
Caribbean[1]	2,283	2,563	12.3	1,915	-25.3	1,855	-3.1	1,860	0.3	1,716	-7.7
Central America[2]	1,038	1,046	0.8	741	-29.2	685	-7.6	794	15.9	675	-15.0
Subtotal	3,321	3,609	8.7	2,656	-26.4	2,540	-4.4	2,654	4.5	2,391	-9.9
Panama–Bahamas											
UK Colonies[3]	6,861	7,370	7.4	8,959	21.6	10,559	17.9	10,886	3.1	11,513	5.8
Total CBI	10,182	10,979	7.8	11,615	5.8	13,099	12.8	13,540	3.4	13,904	2.7
Total World	220,177	236,081	7.2	227,841	-3.5	230,503	1.2	238,034	3.3	254,661	7.0

Notes: 1. Includes Anguilla, Antigua, Barbados, Dominica, Dominican Republic, Grenada, Guyana, Haiti, Jamaica, Netherland Antilles, St Kitts, St Lucia, St Vincent, and Trinidad and Tobago.
2. Includes Belize, Costa Rica, El Salvador, Guatemala, Honduras, and Nicaragua.
3. Includes the British Virgin Islands, Cayman Islands, and Monserrat.

Source: John Rutter, *International Direct Investment: Global Trends and the US Role,* Vol. II (Washington, DC: US Department of Commerce, n. d.).

These requirements for country eligibility are complemented by requirements on product eligibility. Aside from excluding the products listed above, the CBERA stipulates that CBI duty-free products must: a) not cause or threaten to cause serious injury to similar or directly competitive products manufactured in the US (if they do the President is authorised to cancel duty-free treatment on the recommendation of a US Department of Commerce investigation); b) have a minimum local content (i.e. CBI beneficiary country value added rate) of 35 per cent of which 15 per cent can be accounted for from US made materials reducing *de facto* the local content requirement to 20 per cent; and c) undergo a process of significant transformation, so mere packaging or transshipment operations are excluded.[21]

These stipulations would automatically exclude those eligible countries that pursue socialist or mixed-economy type policies (such as Grenada before the US invasion, Nicaragua, Guyana under Burnham or Jamaica under Manley) from the duty-free benefit of the CBI. They also ensure reciprocity for the 'one-way' duty-free concession, since 'fair access' for US interests to the markets and resources of the 'beneficiary' country is a requirement of the law.

The apparently generous and far reaching privileges of the CBI affected only 7 per cent of the region's exports at the time of its announcement in 1982. At that time, 61 per cent of the exports of the 27 CBI eligible countries already entered free of duty into the US market. The remaining 32 per cent were those goods specifically excluded from the CBI, such as sugar, petroleum products, apparel, textiles, etc.[22]

The 7 per cent of the items affected by the CBI came to about 1300 products. Of these, 900 were manufactured goods and the remainder were agroindustrial or nontraditional agricultural products. It was expected that the latter category of products would benefit the most from the CBI in the short term. Exports of fresh and frozen fruits and vegetables to the US during the winter, shellfish, rum, manufactured tobacco and the like, which had been restricted by high tariffs or non-tariff barriers in the past, were expected to grow quickly. Within the manufacturing sector, electronics, sporting goods and pharmaceuticals were expected to be the most benefited but only in the medium-term. These products were already the leading manufactured exports from the region to the US and paid duties ranging from 4 to 12 per cent.[23]

The rationale behind the CBI was to encourage US investment,

Table 2.2 Changes in the value of selected nontraditional exports to the US from CBI eligible countries, 1983–86 (million dollars)

	1983	1984	±%	1985	±%	1986	±%
Agro-industrial							
Fish and shellfish	199	230.1	15.6	256.2	11.3	320.4	25.1
Vegetables	43.4	49.4	13.9	58.7	19.3	61.8	5.4
Fruits							
(except bananas)	30.6	35.6	16.4	47.9	39.2	67.9	41.9
Live plants and							
seeds	9.5	17.3	81.6	17.5	1.2	17.6	0.6
Fruit juices	1.2	8.9	668.0	13.7	53.6	16.6	21.8
Manufactures							
Textiles and							
apparel	412.2	521.8	26.6	670.9	28.6	854.7	27.4
Electrical							
machinery	354.1	468.6	32.3	368.8	−21.3	247.9	−32.8
Chemicals	143.8	173.6	20.7	158.4	−8.8	106.1	−33.0
Pharmaceuticals	65.1	69.1	6.1	88.3	27.8	148.4	68.1
Sporting goods	41.6	43.8	5.3	49.9	13.9	53.4	7.0
Total exports	9,242	9,135	−1.2	7,115	−22.1	6,500	−8.6

Source: US Department of Commerce.

and some local investment too, in nontraditional agriculture and manufacturing for export to the US. In nontraditional agriculture, export-oriented production of fresh fruits and vegetables for the US market during the winter was the main target. In manufacturing, export-processing operations, *maquiladoras* were the the main interest. US capital would use the Caribbean Basin as an export platform in electronics, for example, to compete with cheaper Asian electronic products in US markets. The region would also become the supplier of 'exotic' tropical fruits and cheap vegetables during the winter. These activities, in turn, would reestablish the dynamic linkage of the region to US capital in new areas of international production.

Table 2.2, shows that the CBI has had some success in promoting the growth in exports to the US of nontraditional agro-industrial products, pharmaceuticals and sporting goods. What the CBI has not succeeded in doing, however, is encouraging the growth of total exports. These declined by 29 per cent from 9.2 billion dollars in 1983 to 6.5 billion in 1986.

Defenders of the CBI argue that the decline in total exports is due mainly to the decline in exports of traditional products, such as sugar, petroleum products, bauxite and the like, and that the decline in exports of electronic products (electrical machinery) is due to a recession within the industry. The CBI, it is claimed by its defenders, has not failed to promote exports, it has only promoted less than were expected or needed to achieve the goal of economic growth. These arguments are correct. However, they conceal the fact that what the CBI is doing is promoting a restructuring of the export structure of Caribbean Basin countries according to US interests rather than promoting economic growth. They also fail to note the fact that the most significant growth in manufactured exports from the region was in the textile industry, explicitly excluded from the CBI benefits.

However one looks at it, the fact is that the CBI has not done much to promote export growth or reverse the declining tendency of US investment in the Caribbean and Central America. Since the enactment of the CBI, the Caribbean Basin has become less attractive to US international capital than before. While US imports from CBI eligible countries represented 3.4 per cent of its world imports in 1983, this share declined to 1.7 per cent in 1986.[24] Likewise, US direct investment in CBI eligible countries represented 1.6 per cent of global US direct investment in 1980 but this share declined to 1.1 per cent in 1983 and 0.9 per cent in 1985.

The other major effort of the US government to reintegrate dynamically the region into the orbit of US capital is the Central American Initiative (CAI), which contains the key recommendations of the Kissinger Report. The CAI aims, in the short run, to provide the basis for a politico-economic stabilisation programme. In the long run, it aims at promoting and supporting structural adjustment programs based on export-oriented development policies congruent with the CBI.

The CAI proposed to provide 8.4 billion dollars in aid to Belize, Costa Rica, El Salvador, Guatemala, Honduras and Panama over a five and a half-year period between 1984 and 1989. The original proposal for a CAI was sent to Congress by President Reagan on February 1984, a month after the Kissinger Report was submitted. Table 2.3 summarises the aid component of the CAI as presented in the original bill submitted in the House of Representatives, HR 4874.

As can be noted, the bill proposed fairly substantial allocations for Development Assistance and Economic Support Funds. The latter,

Table 2.3 Appropriation proposals for HR 4874 'Central America Democracy, Peace and Development Initiative Act of 1984' (milion dollars)

I. Economic Aid 1984–85

Purpose	Section of Act	Proposed amount 1984	1985
Development Aid (DA)	202(a) (1)–(a) (7)	$ 75.5	$ 288.1
Economic Support Fund (ESF)	203(a) and (b)	290.5	640.6
Peace Corps	204(a) and (b)	2	18.2
US Information Agency	205(a) and (b)	7	36.4
Refugee Assistance	206(a)	—	15
Housing Guaranty Program	207	—	40
Administration of Justice	208(b)	20	20
Trade Credit Insurance	209(b)	—	300
		395.0	1358.3
Subtotal (I)		$1753.3	

II. Economic Aid 1986–89

Purpose	Section of Act	Proposed amount	
Economic Aid (all categories)	212(a)	$4800	(1200/yr)
Housing Guaranty Program	212(b)	160	(40/yr)
Trade Credit Insurance	212(c)	200	(1986)
Subtotal (II)		$5160	

III. Military Aid 1984–85

Purpose	Section of Act	Proposed amount 1984	1985
Military Assistance Program	302(a) and (b)	$259.1	$222
Military Education	303(a)	—	3.9
Military Sales Financing	304(a)	—	30
		259.1	255.9
Subtotal (III)		$515	
Total (I+II+III)		$7428.3	

however, is an ambiguous classification that provides balance of payment support funds to permit imports of goods, including military equipment. In this sense, ESFs are not purely development-oriented. Other economic aid for development purposes includes 500 million dollars for a Trade Credit Insurance Program to facilitate the financing of exports and imports between the US and Central America. This program would be administered by Eximbank, the US government agency in charge of such activities.

Other programs for which funding was proposed, such as the Peace

Corps, the US Information Agency and the Housing Guarantee Program, were intended to promote a good image for the US in the region. Expenditures in these programs were part of the means to advance the strategic aim of winning the hearts and minds of the population in the low intensity war being waged by the US in Central America. The aid to the Justice Administration Program would also play a role in advancing that strategic aims but in the more directly security related way of 'rationalising' and 'professionalising' repression.

The approximately 900,000 dollars not listed in the table, would come from programs already in place, such as the Food for Peace Program or PL 480, that were included in the CAI but did not need to be included in the funding requests of HR 4874.

The bill included also a proposal to create a Central American Development Organization (CADO). This would serve as a coordinating agency for regional development, to assure that the development policies of the CAI's beneficiary countries would be consistent with regional development objectives. CADO would be integrated by representatives of the US, CAI beneficiary countries and other donor countries that would want to channel their aid through the Organization. The head of CADO would be the US representative, whose power would stem from the capacity to withold up to 25 per cent of the CAI funds to any country that would not follow CADO's guidelines.

Although Congress did not approve the CAI aid package, it has funded most of the programmes proposed in HR 4874. The 395 million dollars requested in 1984 were fully granted and almost 1 billion dollars were provided in 1985 and 1986. Despite this, funding for the CAI up to 1987 was about 760 million dollars short of the original request of the Reagan Administration.[25]

The continued pleas of the Reagan Administration for a long-term Congressional commitment to the CAI led Congress in 1986 to request the Secretary of State, the Administrator of the Agency for International Development (AID) and the Director of the Office of Management and Budget to prepare a detailed plan for fully funding the CAI. This provided the Reagan Administration the opportunity to reshape the CAI according to the wider and now more clearly defined objectives of the new counterinsurgency strategy followed after 1983.[26] Table 2.4 summarises the second version of the CAI, as presented by the administration in the report prepared at the request of Congress.

As can be observed, this updated version of the CAI articulated

Table 2.4 Central America Initiative Financial Plan, FY 1984/85–1992

	1984/85[a]	1986[b]	1987	1984/87 Subtotal	1988	1989	1990	1991	1992	1988/92 Subtotal	Total
Economic stabilisation											
ESF	707	417	538	1,662	415	286	230	130	70	1,131	2,793
Development Assistance	21	8	8	37	0					0	37
PL 480[c]	130	95	97	321	80	50	45	30	25	230	551
Trade Credit Insurance Program	(0)	(177)	(200)	(377)							
Commodity Credit Corporation	(60)	(34)	(48)	(142)							
Subtotal	858	520	643	2,020	495	336	275	160	95	1,361	3,381
Structural change											
ESF	71	9	14	94	47	150	160	100	80	537	631
DA	116	113	91	320	93	94	84	65	50	386	706
PL 480	0	0	0	0	0	31	35	40	45	151	151
OPIC Financing	5	3	3	11	3	3	3	3	3	15	26
OPIC Guarantees	(10)	(33)	(33)	(76)							
Eximbank Guarantees	(10)	(8)	(9)	(27)							
Subtotal	192	125	108	425	143	278	282	208	178	1,039	1,514
Spreading Benefits											
ESF	25	27	51	103	25	40	40	40	40	185	288
DA	160	128	219	507	120	120	140	140	120	640	1,147
PL 480	12	15	10	37	14	9	9	5	5	42	79

Narcotics	1	0	1	2	1	1	2	2	2	6	10
Peace Corps	18	11	11	39	10	10	10	10	10	50	89
Housing Guarantee	(5)	(40)	(3)	(48)							
Subtotal	215	181	292	688	170	180	201	197	177	925	1,613
Democracy											
ESF	24	5	12	41	15	20	20	20	15	90	131
DA	3	6	13	22	17	18	23	28	29	115	137
USIA	8	20	16	43	16	16	16	16	16	80	123
Subtotal	35	31	41	106	48	54	59	64	60	285	391
TOTAL											
Appropriated	1,300	856	1,084	3,240	856	848	817	629	510	3,660	6,900
Guarantees[c, d]	85	292	292	669	301	300	280	225	225	1,331	2,000
Grand total	1,385	1,148	1,376	3,909	1,157	1,148	1,097	854	735	4,991	8,900

Notes: a. Includes FY 1984 supplemental of $370 million plus $25 million of FY 1984 PL 480 reallocations.
b. Total includes $300 million requested in FY 1987 supplemental, $100 million of which is destined for El Salvador earthquake recovery.
c. Includes Section 416 commodities for FY 1986 and FY 1987. Outyear levels for Section 416 are dependent on regional allocations and future legislative actions.
d. Outyear total estimates for guarantees are projected, based on experience to date.

Source: 'Report to the President and Congress: A Plan for Fully Funding the Recommendations of the National Bipartison Commission on Central America', *Special Report*, No. 162 (Washington, DC: US Department of State, March 1987).

more clearly the distinctions on the one hand between short-term economic stabilisation and long-term structural adjustment aid, and on the other between these and the clearly politically oriented programmes. It also excludes direct military aid from the proposal, which will be dealt with separately. Finally, the new version of the CAI proposes to extend the period of funding well beyond the Reagan presidency, until 1992, as well as increasing it by 500 million dollars to 8.9 billion. A closer look at the table also shows that the ratio of economic stabilisation to structural change aid declines steadily from 1989 until 1992, while the level of funding for political programmes remains stable.

The shift in the ratio of stabilisation to structural change aid is explained in the report as follows:

> The projected assistance levels also reflect a shift in focus beginning in FY 1989, away from stabilization and toward increased emphasis on structural transformation that leads to economic growth and a broadening of its benefits. The levels are predicated on the assumption that Central American governments will implement economic measures to promote export-led growth and essential structural reforms. We hope that the major economic objective of the CAI – recovery – will be achieved by FY 1992 and that the need for economic support assistance will be less.[27]

Clearly, as is the case with the CBI, the long-term goal of the CAI was to help reintegrate the Central American economies into the orbit of US international production and trade through export-oriented economic activities. The CAI, however, would provide greater amounts of economic aid than the CBI to the Central American economies, since the free-trade incentives of the CBI alone would have very little impact given the politically unstable environment in the region.

After three years of piecemeal application of the programmes proposed in the CAI and over two and a half-billion dollars spent on them, not much has been accomplished, however. The Reagan Administration's March 1987 report, admitted that economic recovery in Central America had been slower than expected. Moreover, the new projections of the Administration's report were that full funding of the CAI would result in economic growth rates of around 5 per cent by 1992. This is 1 per cent less and 3 years later than the original projections of the Kissinger Report. Despite claims of having succeeded in reversing negative growth rates, the report admits also that capital inflows to the Central American economies are below the levels anticipated by the Kissinger Report and that any hopes of achieving the new goals hinge on the return of local capital previously transferred to US banks, the adoption of adequate exchange rates, success in promoting nontraditional exports, and increasing private foreign capital inflows through investment and lending.[28] That is, economic recovery in Central America would be contingent not only on the massive aid proposed by the CAI, but on the restoration of faith in the viability of capitalism in Central America for North American and local capitalists. In Reaganite terms, economic recovery hinges on the faith in the magic of the free marketplace.

The owners of capital, however, do not seem to be strong believers in the ability of the CBI or the proposed CAI to turn things around in the Caribbean Basin. The picture that emerges from the previous analysis, as well as from the Administration's March 1987 report and the Congressional report on the CBI released on May 1987 (known as the Pickle Report),[29] is one of failure of US economic policy in reintegrating the Caribbean Basin economies into the global circuit of US capital accumulation. The CBI, the CAI, and all the other programs that are part of US economic policy in the region, have not managed to change the fact that the region, with the exception of the larger countries and the tax havens, remains unattractive for investment to US transnational capital. Yet the Reagan Administration, as well as the US Congress, still insist on these policies. US capital supports the Administration's policy, since it also understands that even if the region is not important to its immediate economic interests, something must be done to assure accessibility to its potential resources and markets.[30]

But whether the CBI and the CAI succeed in helping to restore some dynamism to capitalist accumulation in the Caribbean and Central America within the aegis of US capital, is not the only key issue here. These policies have fulfilled with some success a more immediate political function. The CBI and the CAI have provided US allies in the region the leverage to present an alternative politico-economic project of solution to the regional crisis to both the local populations and to international public opinion. The intense propaganda campaign orchestrated by the Reagan Administration around the CBI specially and the economic aid programmes that support it in general, has had the effect of strengthening the political position of the advocates of export-oriented development in the region, the propertied classes and the technocratic middle sectors that run government. The CBI has become the 'Trojan horse' of the Reaganomics in the Caribbean Basin. CBI propaganda presents agroindustrial production for the US market as a superior economic development alternative to the inward- and regional-oriented alternatives of the Sandinistas in Nicaragua, Cooperative Socialism in Guyana, or Democratic Socialism in Jamaica.[31]

In short, I argue that the economic crises of primary-based and export-oriented economies of the Caribbean Basin have given way to two sets of alternative politico-economic projects of solution. On the one hand, there are those projects that advocate breaking away from the orbit of US capital and the redefinition of local and international economic arrangements through the creation of socialist or mixed-economy regimes and a 'new international economic order'; which I shall call 'rupturist' alternatives.[32] On the other hand, there are those projects that propose a restructuring of capitalism through export diversification. These export promotion schemes propose to transform Caribbean Basin economies into export platforms for US capital; what some call the Puerto Ricanisation or Taiwanisation of the region. These projects, that attempt to rearticulate the links between the economies of the region and the global network of US capital, constitute what I call 'reintegrationist' alternatives.

US economic policy in the region is aimed at supporting the reintegrationist political projects of the propertied classes and their allies. It must be emphasised, however, that the reintegrationist alternatives favoured by the US promote economic restructuring rather than the restoration of traditional agriculture. This would suggest that the US government, as well as US capital, favours new economic and political sectors. That is, the promotion of reintegrationist political projects in the region would be accompanied by a rearticulation of political alliances. Now I come to the final link of US policy: the forging of new alliances with emerging sectors and the displacement of the old autocracies and landed oligarchies from politico-economic power.

THE POLITICAL COMPONENT

If the oil shocks of the 1970s and the sharp decline in the prices of primary commodities marked the decline of the economic power of the landed oligarchies and autocracies that dominated the economies of the Caribbean Basin, the political crises that ensued marked the decline of their political power. In Central America, the economic crisis was accompanied by the crisis of the ruling alliance between the military and the landed oligarchy. In other countries of the region, the economic crisis came in the midst of political transitions, such as the processes of independence of the British colonies in the Eastern Caribbean that served as the backdrop to the Grenadian revolution. The focal points of the region-wide political crises were Nicaragua, El Salvador and Grenada. These are the countries where the crises reached critical points and where counter-insurgency policies would be put to the test.

As North American strategists viewed it, the triumphs of the Grenadian and Nicaraguan revolutions and the significant advances of the Salvadorean insurgents indicated an emerging trend of 'radical' (anti- or non pro-American) solutions to the political crises of oli-garchic and autocratic rule in the region. The vacuum created by the crisis of the dictatorship in Central America had brought to power in Nicaragua, and could bring to power in other countries in this area, socialist, nationalist and anti-imperialist groups and coalitions that would favour rupturist policies. In the Caribbean, particularly the English-speaking countries, the Grenadian revolution could provide a viable rupturist model to radical nationalist groups at a time of heightened power struggles brought about by the processes of inde-pendence that took place in the late 1970s.

At the political level, the priority of the Reagan Administration was to restore the stability of pro-American regimes while actively seeking to overthrow rupturist regimes and contain the advance of rupturist movements, be these the Salvadorean insurgents or the electorally oriented People's National Party (PNP) in Jamaica. The key to achieving the goal of stabilising the region from the perspec-tive of the Reagan Administration was to support pro-American regimes of any kind at any cost. The best case for this policy was made by former US Ambassador to the United Nations, Jeane Kirkpatrick, in a notorious article that earned her a place in the Administration.[33] In that article, Kirkpatrick argued that US policy should not be morally obliged to oppose pro-American autocracies since the alternatives to those regimes could be inimical to US and Western interests. Traditional autocracies, she argued, maintain a kind of political stability that crumbles rapidly when the autocrat falls. Hence, it should have come as no surprise to the Carter foreign policy strategists that the US lost all leverage in Iran and Nicaragua after the fall of the Shah and Somoza. This line of reasoning from a conservative Democrat was perfectly in tune with the views of the New Right. Kirkpatrick's arguments quickly became part of the New Right's ideology and she and Secretary of State General Alexander Haig became the key spokespersons on foreign policy for the Administration.

As expected, the Administration did everything possible to increase support to its regional allies at any cost, from certifying progress on human rights in El Salvador to restoring military aid to the military dictatorship in Guatemala. The climax of the hard line policy of the Reagan Administration during its first term was marked by the invasion of Grenada in October 1983 and the mining of Nicaraguan ports in early 1984.

Paradoxically, during the second term of the Reagan presidency the US devoted an unexpected amount of efforts and resources to promoting elections and supporting elected regimes throughout the region. Moreover, in the two countries where US military and political presence has been most felt – El Salvador and Grenada – the US has actively promoted elections and elected governments and, contrary to all expectations, it has supported political leaders that opposed the old oligarchic and autocratic regimes. The question is why? Is it that the Reagan Administration has drifted from its policy goal of stability at any cost?

Clearly, the answer to the latter question is no. The Reagan Administration's promotion of elections throughout the Caribbean Basin represents a change in tactics rather than of strategy. Stability at any cost means precisely doing whatever is necessary and effective. Whether this is invading the country or promoting elections is a decision that depends on the levels of political conflict in the US, in the country(ies) in question, and in the international forces acting at the time; in other words, it depends on the political conjuncture. The tough talk of the Reagan Administration on its readiness to use military force to achieve its goals did not mean that it would not consider other alternatives if they were politically and economically less costly than military intervention. After all, despite all of its tough talk and desk-thumping, the Reagan Administration pulled its troops from Lebanon after the bombing of the marine compound while at the same time it invaded Grenada. Why did the Reagan Administration send troops to 'rescue' students in Grenada that were not in danger but did not do the same for the American hostages in

Lebanon? Moreover, why did it not use military force to retaliate for the Lebanon bombing and used Middle East bound troops in the invasion of Grenada?[34] Despite all the heavy rhetoric of the US Administration, pragmatism is still a major force in American foreign policy.

There are three main reasons that explain the change in US policy in the Caribbean Basin toward active promotion of elections. First, as was argued earlier, military escalation had partially achieved the goal of containment. By the end of Reagan's first term the policy of military escalation in the Caribbean Basin had managed to overthrow the Grenadian revolutionary government, contain the advance of insurgents in El Salvador, initiate a devastating war in Nicaragua, and establish a military base in Honduras.

All of this, however, was achieved in the midst of heavy criticism from the US Congress and public opinion, the European allies and the Latin American community, which formed the Contadora group to provide a diplomatic alternative to US designs in the region. Herein lies the second key reason for the shift in policy: internal and international criticism of US confrontationist and militaristic policies. These policies were not limited to the Caribbean Basin, which led to the raising of strong concerns specially among the European allies. There was so much criticism of US policy that Reagan was compelled to announce a world-wide initiative to promote democracy during his visit to London in 1982. Out of this came the creation of the National Endowment for Democracy in November 1983.[35] This criticism also paved the way for the appointment of the Kissinger Commission and the CAI proposal in 1983–84.

The third, and perhaps the most important reason, for the policy change, was the fact that the political crises in the region were precisely crises of autocratic and military regimes. Any attempt simply to restore the existing regimes could only constitute a temporary and fragile solution to the crisis. By 1984, the Administration had come to realise that change was inevitable. The dam had broken and the river was flowing so to speak, the real question facing everyone was not how to stop but how to channel the force of change. The shift in policy represented an attempt to come to grips with this reality.

If we examine more closely the electoral processes in El Salvador and Grenada, we can understand better the rationale behind the Administration's tactical shift to supporting and promoting elections in the region as a means of achieving its main political goal,

pro-American stability. In both of these countries, the Reagan Administration promoted what can be termed a military-electoral path to
political restructuring.[36]

In El Salvador, the first step towards securing the continuation of
pro-American forces in power was the dramatic increase of military
aid and training. This resulted in an increased intervention of the US
in the military apparatus of El Salvador, which gave the US the
leverage to influence the politics of the Salvadorean military. Once
the US military intervention drove the war to a stalemate – i.e.
partially accomplished the goal of containment – the US had the
leverage to influence the political process in the direction of political
restructuring through elections. This is not to argue that the Reagan
Administration had the capacity to impose unilaterally a process of
political restructuring. What we are arguing here is that the American Administration came to realise two things. First, that the restoration of the oligarchic-military alliance in power would fail to provide
a durable and reliable pro-American stability. After all, it was this
very regime that was in crisis. And second, that in order to achieve a
durable solution to the crisis, which would also be congruent with its
interests, the US would have to shed old alliances and seek new ones.
In other words, the Reagan Administration, contrary to its initial
leanings, would opt for steering a process of political restructuring
rather than simply to support old allies and restore oligarchic-military
rule. This conclusion was not reached overnight, neither was it clearly
spelled out at any point. The Administration was pushed into this
course of action as it became clear that, in the short term, a military
victory over the insurgents was impossible.

It could be argued that, at first, the Administration's promotion of
elections in El Salvador was aimed at legitimising US interventionism
by providing the appearance of democratisation and reducing internal and international criticism of American support to the highly
repressive Salvadorean regime and its 'civilian' allies, the death
squads. The US did not express any preferences among the different
parties that participated in the March 1982 election for the Constitutional Assembly. The underlying rationale for this appeared to be
that none of the parties participating in the process opposed US
policy in that country. Yet another underlying reason was that the US
expected this to be an opportunity to forge a compromise among the
different pro-American factions on a consensus solution to the political crisis. It appeared that everyone was confident that, having
excluded the revolutionary forces from the election, the process of

drafting the new constitution could provide the framework for political accommodation among pro-American forces.[37]

Early in this process, however, it became evident to US strategists that restoring oligarchic rule through elections would not bring the desired long-term outcome of pro-American stability. The outcome of the March 1982 election proved the search for political accommodation to be an elusive goal. The landed oligarchy and its allies represented in the Partido de Conciliación Nacional (PCN) and the Alianza Republicana Nacionalista (ARENA) won the majority of the seats in the Assembly and were ready to resume its old practice of excluding those groups that favored any measure of political restructuring, even the moderate forces of the Partido Demócrata Cristiano (PDC). The first move in this direction was the election of Roberto D'Aubisson, the ultra-conservative leader of the oligarchy, as president of the Assembly. The next step was to designate the provisional president. Realising that a return to the *status quo ante* would only make more difficult any attempt to win a low intensity war, the Reagan Administration decided to step in and use its leverage with the military to prevent the oligarchy from controlling the process and ruining the chances of political accommodation. This would mark a shift in alliances between the US government and the fractions integrating the Salvadorean power bloc.

The political distancing of the Reagan Administration from the Salvadorean oligarchy became public when presidential envoy Vernon Walters entered the negotiations to prevent the conservative majority in the Assembly from designating a member of ARENA as provisional president and securing a voice for the PDC in the process. As a result of Walters' visit the army warned against any decision from the Assembly that would endanger the continuation of US military aid and proceeded to issue a list of three presidential candidates acceptable to the army and the US. In the end, the PCN voted with the PDC to elect Alvaro Magaña to the presidency, a compromise candidate described as a moderate.[38] From this point on the differences between the oligarchy and the Reagan Administration became greater, and US support to the Christian Democrats grew stronger.

After the 1982 election the US seemed to have become committed to the idea of political restructuring, which was a key element of the new counterinsurgency strategy. In 1983, Ambassador Kirkpatrick and Vice President Bush visited El Salvador in support of the constitutional process. There were also major reshuffles in the diplomatic personnel dealing with El Salvador and in the Salvadorean armed forces' high command.[39] The 1984 presidential election resulted in a victory for Christian Democrat candidate José Napoleón Duarté. This time, the Reagan administration had not remained neutral. According to confirmed reports, the CIA had provided economic and other kinds of support to Duarté's campaign to the detriment of his chief rival, Roberto D'Aubisson.[40] The 1985 election for the National Assembly resulted also in a Christian Democrat victory. This time it was the oligarchy that claimed fraud and accused the army of rigging the election. Paradoxically this time the army, the former champion of the oligarchy, told their old allies publicly to 'put up or shut up'. The US had not only distanced itself from the oligarchy, it had managed to distance the Salvadorean army from it too. As Allan Narin pointed out:

> D'Aubisson's defeat marked the eclipse of the Army's power base. For years the military had done the bidding of the oligarchy, and in return officers received financial rewards. US policy now replaced this symbiotic relationship with a one-sided dependency. The oligarchs no longer set policy or paid the bills; that was Washington's role.[41]

It was not that the Reagan Administration had any particular moral reasons to distance itself from the Salvadorean oligarchy. As Kirkpatrick had argued, the US should not feel morally compelled to do anything other than to preserve its allies in power in order to maintain 'stability'. The question was one of how to achieve stability in terms that were congruent with US interests; and reestablishing an exclusionary regime controlled by the oligarchy was not it. It was this interest in achieving political stability what would drive the Reagan administration to embrace 'political reform' as a key component of its policy in El Salvador and in the rest of Central America. But one should ask, what did political reform mean in the context of US policy in El Salvador?

Some analysts have argued that the US was pushing for a renegotiation of the 'dominant pact' between fractions of the oligarchy and that, regardless of any changes in appearance, this sector would remain in charge in alliance with the US.[42] This, indeed, may have been the thinking of the Reagan strategists around the 1982 election. The needs of counterinsurgency, however, dictated otherwise. In the process, American strategists came to realise that the key to winning the war was political and that some key changes had to occur.

The need to address the plea of the landless peasants, the main base of the guerrillas, led the Reagan strategists to rediscover the agrarian reform programme initiated by the Carter administration. It is true that the oligarchy had managed to block phase II, the one that affected it the most, but still it was forced to accept an 'agrarian reform' when it opposed any form of land distribution scheme. The need to address the economic crisis led the Reagan administration to promote throughout the region economic restructuring away from traditional agriculture, a key blow also to the oligarchy and a measure of support to the emerging fractions of the bourgeoisie and the urban technocracy. The need to draw support from the organised working class led to massive funding of labour organisation programs such as the American Institute for Free Labour Development's (AIFLD) Popular Democratic Unity, which organised urban and rural workers' support for the PDC.[43] Finally, the need for effective counterinsurgency led to the 'professionalisation' of the army. That is, to the reorganisation of the army in such a way that it would not be the instrument of one class only but of the propertied classes and its allies, thus becoming the guarantor of political stability among the different pro-American and pro-capitalist forces.

Simply put, the Reagan Administration was compelled to steer a process of change after realising that it would be impossible to stop it. Moreover, the administration came to realise that supporting its old allies, the traditional military and the oligarchy, would run counter to the principles of the low intensity war strategy adopted after 1983. Despite the oligarchy's resistance, the US and its new allies, the bourgeoisie and the technocratic middle sectors, have managed to establish the framework of a limited bourgeois-like democracy or, as a Central American analyst called it, a 'facade' democracy. This is a regime with limited space for popular participation, heavily dependent on the 'goodwill' of the army – which maintains veto power over all decisions, exclusionary of radical elements and ideologically anti-communist, heavily corporatist, and with a strong executive branch.[44]

The Reagan Administration by shifting its political alliances in El Salvador managed to effect political restructuring. The state apparatus has ceased to respond only to the oligarchy. It responds now to a wider coalition of propertied classes, including US capital. The oligarchy and its traditional military allies have come to occupy a secondary place in the new power bloc. New fractions of the bourgeoisie, the technocracy and the military in alliance with the US

government and capital have come to dominate the power bloc.[45] The army has been removed from the immediate task of running the government and has become the arbiter of conflicts among fractions of the power bloc and the guarantor of the interests of the propertied classes in general, rather than of any individual fraction.

This political scheme, however, is still very fragile. The oligarchy will not accept a secondary role without resistance and the insurgents will not accept their exclusion without a fight. The Duarté government has been constantly under fire trying to maintain its balance against all its opposing forces. This juggling act has been sustained by the nearly half a billion dollars a year that the US has kept pumping since 1985, which in turn ensures the army's support to Duarté. It remains to be seen if a new durable balance can be achieved and institutionalised within this new political framework.

In the case of Grenada the path to restoring pro-American forces to power and organising an electoral process that would legitimise the new groups in power resembled in many ways the experience of the Dominican Republic. First, using the old excuse of guaranteeing the security of American citizens, the US invaded the country with token support from regional forces. Then, once the 'anti-American' forces had been defeated, US officials and their local allies organised an election under military occupation with participation from a faction of the deposed group.

Taking advantage of internal dissent and power struggles inside the Peoples' Revolutionary Government (PRG), the US stepped in and crushed the revolutionary forces in Grenada. It did this, however, amidst condemnation from friends and foes alike with the notable exception of the conservative governments of the neighboring Eastern Caribbean islands, Jamaica, Israel, Chile, Guatemala, El Salvador and Uruguay. Even the staunchest of Reagan's European allies, British Prime Minister, Margaret Thatcher disagreed publicly with this action, notwithstanding that the US had supported her government earlier in the 'reconquest' of the Malvinas (Falkland) Islands.[46] Despite all the international criticism, public reaction in the US was generally favorable to the Administration's action. Although Congress initially condemned the action, eventually it agreed with the President after further review of the situation.

Having succeeded in reversing the Grenadian revolution through military force, and portraying this as an example of American determination to contain revolutionary advances in the region, the US set out to restore pro-American stability in the island-nation. At first, it looked as if the US would stay in Grenada for a long time or would transform it into a modern 'protectorate'. Within a week of the invasion the US had a team of 50 State Department officials running the country under the symbolic leadership of the Governor General, Paul Scoon. Later an advisory council was appointed to help run internal affairs.

Contrary to initial expectations, however, the US moved with relative quickness to remove the majority of its troops from the island and to set up elections. By December 1983, US troops in Grenada numbered about 300, of which some 100 belonged to the military psychological operations unit (PSYOPS). This unit had been in charge of all propaganda operations during and after the invasion, including the transformation of Radio Free Grenada into Radio Spice Island. Preparations for elections began in January 1984, with the reopening of the Office of Elections Supervisor and the initiation of procedures for voter registration.[47]

As in the case of the Dominican Republic, elections were held in Grenada under military occupation. US troops and Commonwealth Caribbean troops were in charge of keeping order in the electoral process, while officials from the US State Department coordinated the process with the collaboration of the interim government. Contrary to the Dominican experience, though, the American backed candidate was not a lieutenant of the former autocrat and US ally.

The announcement of elections gave way to the resurgeance of traditional parties and the creation of new ones. Six parties emerged to contest the elections of December 1984. The leading contestants were the Grenada United Labor Party (GULP), lead by former prime minister and US ally, Eric Gairy, and the Grenada National Party (GNP) lead by Herbert Blaize, a conservative and pro-business politician (called a moderate by US officials) that had led the 'loyal opposition' to Gairy's autocracy for a long time. The new forces in the scene were the Grenada Democratic Movement (GDM), led by Francis Alexis, the New Democratic Movement, led by George Brizan, the Christian Democratic Labour Party (CDLP), led by Winston Whyte and the Maurice Bishop Patriotic Movement (MBPM), led by Kendrick Radix.[48]

The pre-electoral consensus was that, left to run its course, an election contested by these six groups would result in the return to power of Gairy. The GULP had defeated Blaize and the GNP in six elections between 1954 and 1976, and it seemed that the strong GULP following among the poor farmworkers in the countryside was

still strong enough to return it to power. The other parties did not
have the strength to win an election and could only take votes away
from the GNP. Everyone, including US strategists conceded that a
return to power by Gairy would only lead to a reproduction of the
conditions that led to the 1979 takeover by the New Jewel Movement. Thus the US decided to step in and steer the political process in
the direction of restructuring rather than towards the restoration of
the autocratic rule of its former ally. US officials, with aid from the
prime ministers of St Vincent, St Lucia and Barbados, who had
supported the invasion, hammered out a coalition between the GNP,
the GDM and the NDP in a new party, the New National Party
(NNP).[49]

The NNP, with the full support of the US, ran a very efficient and
highly effective campaign and, as expected, won the elections. Fourteen of the fifteen seats in parliament went to the NNP, the remaining
seat was won by the GULP. The fact that the MBPM ran was
portrayed as evidence of the free nature of the elections. In Grenada,
contrary to El Salvador, the military defeat of the revolutionary
forces and the presence of the occupying American forces made it
unnecessary to exclude the rupturist forces from the election process.
As in El Salvador, however, the Grenadian electoral process should
become the arena for the pro-American forces to devise a set of rules
which would guarantee the rights of the propertied groups and would
provide a formula of political accommodation for the different fractions of the pro-American power bloc.

As in El Salvador, also, this process of political accommodation is
still to be proved effective. In August 1987, the NNP split and a new
opposition party was formed, the National Democratic Congress, led
by George Brizan and Francis Alexis. The NDC is presently the
largest opposition group in parliament with five members; Gairy's
GULP still has one member. This split in the American sponsored
coalition has raised again concerns about a possible return to power
of Gairy in the elections scheduled for 1989. Whatever the future of
Grenadian politics may have in store, the fact of the matter is that the
principal organisations contesting the next elections will be, in all
likelihood, political entities that do not question either US leadership
in the region, nor the rights of the propertied classes to own privately
the means of production. The American concerns established on the
island after the invasion, such as Johnson and Johnson, Smith Kline
et al., have nothing to fear by the coming to power either of the
GULP or the NDC.

From the previous analysis, it is clear that the Reagan Administration turned to support elections throughout the region as a means of trying to control inevitable processes of change. Elections became part of the tactics of low intensity conflict, as it was deemed impossible to win guerrilla wars all over the region which would also be costly and would divert substantial military resources away from other areas that are crucial to the global balance-of-power struggles like the Middle East.

The wheel turns full circle, then. In the short run, military escalation is used to create the political space to restore pro-American regimes in the region. Aid programmes aimed at economic restructuring through export promotion development strategies should revitalise capitalism in the region by reintegrating the Caribbean and Central American economies into the global network of capital accumulation dominated by US capital. And the promotion of elections and elected regimes should in turn restore some legitimacy to the capitalist state as well as the leadership of the US in the region. The Reagan Administration liked the formula so much that it tried it in Haiti and the Philippines. However, as mentioned, the US cannot any longer unilaterally impose this or any other model to restore pro-American stability throughout the world. Local conflicts and interests play a major role in the success of any process of politico-economic restructuring.

CONCLUSION

In retrospect, the policy followed by the Reagan Administration after 1983 became a throwback to the days of the Alliance for Progress in many respects: support of pro-American 'reformist' political forces, support of agrarian reform, promotion of economic restructuring programmes with large amounts of aid and special training to military and paramilitary forces in counterinsurgency. To be sure, Reagan's version emphasised less government-to-government aid and more private sector based market-oriented incentives and lacked the altruistic rhetoric of the Alliance; but in many respects it mimicked the 1960s counter-insurgency policies. As a New Right analyst argues, Reagan started out breaking away from the accommodation policies of detente but ended up upholding its principles. The emphasis of the Administration shifted to containment of 'Communist' advance in the region.[50] Even in Nicaragua, where the Administration did not relinquish its goal of overthrowing the Sandinista government, pressure through the *contras* (who everyone agrees lack the political and military strength to overthrow the Sandinista government) was preferred to the initial threat of US invasion.

The shift in US policy, however, responds primarily to the realisation that the autocrats, oligarchies and military elites that ruled throughout the region were no longer useful and productive partners either economically or politically, rather than to a change in ideological perspective or to pressures from American and international public opinion. On the one hand, the corruption and thievery so prevalent under the rule of these old allies of the US was a major cause of economic disruption both internally and internationally. The squandering of international loans by corrupt rulers in the midst of foreign exchange shortages and debt crises affected not only the poor and the middle sectors but also foreign investors and banks that could conduct business in those countries. In addition, US capital understands that the economic importance of the region is not traditional primary products. Any hope for economic recuperation within the international capitalist economy must address the issue of economic restructuring within the context of the New International Division of Labor. The landed oligarchies and *comprador* bourgeoisies of the region have proved to be an obstacle to economic restructuring throughout history and it does not look as if this time around there will be an exception to this pattern.

On the other hand, the perpetuation of these corrupt allies in power facilitates the identification of a political enemy for the insurgent forces. Moreover, it advances the identification of the US and the prevailing capitalist regime as forces to be rejected by any new revolutionary order, as were the cases in Nicaragua and Grenada. Furthermore, the political crises of the region are precisely crises of authoritarian rule and corrupt regimes. The peasants and the urban poor are not the only ones willing to rebel in order to put an end to these types of regimes, as the Grenadian, Nicaraguan and Salvadorean experiences show. Hence, any attempt to restore dictatorships could only result in a solidification of the broad-based popular alliances against these types of regimes. And, according to recent experiences, these alliances tend to assume a rupturist stance in view of the US's staunch support of these authoritarian and usually corrupt regimes. It is these kinds of considerations which drove the strategists of the Reagan administration to rearticulate its political alliances and to collaborate with those forces in favor of reintegration into the US sphere of influence through politico-economic restructuring.

The question remains, however, was the US able to advance significantly its goal of restoring its hegemony over the region by following the policies discussed above? The best answer to this is that it is too early to tell. Reasserting leadership over an entire region is not a goal that can be achieved overnight. None the less, some signs can be detected that could indicate if some degree of success was achieved.

On the positive side for the US, the Reagan Administration succeeded in reasserting American military supremacy in the region. The creation of the RSS in the Eastern Caribbean and the establishment of a military complex in Honduras attest to this fact. Despite the normal conflicts and contradictions (as continuing conflicts with Panama's military strongman, General Manuel Noriega, illustrate), the US remains the most powerful military force in the Caribbean with great influence over the region's military.

Economically, despite the poor performance of the CBI and other aid packages to stimulate growth, the US succeeded in compelling the majority of the governments in the region to adopt export-diversification and market-oriented development policies. Perhaps the most dramatic example of US success in this respect was the dramatic turn around taken by the Hoyte government in Guyana.

Politically, the US managed to steer the process of 'redemocratisation' in a pro-American direction. It has created a regional support networks for its allies, such as the Caribbean Democratic Union (CDU) and the Central American Democratic Union (CADU). These groups have served to coordinate political efforts and to channel support to US allies throughout the region. It also provided regional leverage for US political intervention, as was the case when the Seaga government of Jamaica mediated in the resignation of Jean Claude Duvalier in 1986.

On the negative side for the US, however, the CBI and its accompanying aid packages failed to bring economic growth to the region. Criticism over US cuts in foreign aid were accompanied by disillusionment over the possibilities of economic growth through export-diversification schemes that depend on access to a heavily protected US market. Despite all the rhetoric about the 'magic of the market', the US Congress and bureaucracy continued to follow protectionist practices. On the economic front, the reality of failure to grow has been more powerful than the promise of the free market.

Politically, the continued divergence between Central and Latin American leaders and the US government on how to achieve peace in Central America (as indicated by the prolonged life of the Contadora group and the adoption of the Arias Peace Plan) points to the faltering of US political leadership. If military escalation succeeded in creating the space for the US to steer the process of political restructuring, the failure of the US government to take a clear leadership in the peace process – in fact its attempt to sabotage the Arias Peace Plan – has rapidly eroded the political leverage gained earlier.

But perhaps the best measure of whether American hegemony in the Caribbean Basin has been restored was the lack of success in crushing the Nicaraguan revolution or in 'Finlandising' Cuba. The erosion of US hegemony in the Caribbean Basin started in 1959 with the triumph of the Cuban revolution. The success and survival of another popular revolution in Nicaragua twenty years later is a sign that American hegemony in the region continues to decline. As long as these two revolutionary governments continue to exist and to be a factor in regional politics, US hegemony in the region will be, to say the least, challenged.

Notes

1. This narrow view of hegemony is most characteristic of the North American left. They tend to view events in the region as the result of unilateral actions of the United States without regard for local conflicts and power relations. All US policies in the region are then interpreted as accessories to the military solution of the regional crisis. See for example, Edward S. Herman and Frank Brodhead, *Demonstration Elections; US Staged Elections in the Dominican Republic, Vietnam and El Salvador* (Boston: South End Press, 1984); and Allan Narin, 'Endgame; US Military Strategy in Central America', *Nacla*, vol. 18, no. 3 (May–June 1984), pp. 19–55.

2. Cf. Antonio Gramsci, *Selections from the Prison Notebooks* (London: Lawrence and Wishart, 1976), esp. pp. 55–90, 125 ff.; and Joseph Femia, 'Hegemony and Consciousness in the Thought of Antonio Gramsci', *Political Studies*, vol. 13, no. 1 (March 1975), pp. 29–48.

3. The definition of group, class or national interests is usually problematic. Normally the researcher deducts or imputes interests on the basis of statements made by representatives of such entities as governments, parties, associations, etc. or from the analysis of patterns of actions that project a logic of behaviour of the entity under study. The analysis of

such statements and patterns of behaviour must be done in a historical context, of course.

In this essay, the definition of the North American state as a capitalist one provides the basis for deducting its strategic interests; meaning by this those interests that are central to the role of the state. In my view, the very logic of global capital accumulation is what dictates the main, long-term interests of US foreign policy. The paramount interest expressed in US foreign policy is securing access for US and other allied fractions of international capital to the markets and natural and human resources of the world for immediate or future exploitation through trade and investment. Put another way, since the logic of capitalism dictates the need for constant expansion (expanded reproduction of capital), it is the interest of the capitalist state to maintain accessibility for capital to the untapped markets and resources of the world. Hence, the role of the North American state as the global police of the capitalist world – guaranteeing *unrestrained access* to the markets and resources of the world for international capital – is the driving interest behind US foreign policy and behind the core of its military and diplomatic actions throughout the world. This, however, does not negate that in many instances other immediate economic or geopolitical interests come into play and contribute to shaping US foreign policy. Thus in analysing concrete cases, one must differentiate between the long-term or strategic interest described above and immediate interests.

4. The Committee of Santa Fe, *A New Inter-American Policy for the Eighties* (Washington, DC: Council for Inter-American Security, Inc., 1980), hereafter quoted as Committee of Santa Fe, *Report*; and *Report of the National Bipartisan Commission on Central America* (Washington, DC: n.p., 1984), hereafter quoted as *Kissinger Report*.
5. Roberto Bouzas and Luis Maira, 'Algunas claves económicas y políticas para el examen de la administración Reagan', in Luis Maira, (ed.), *La política de Reagan y la crisis centroamericana* (San José: EDUCA, 1982), pp. 53–6; also Committee of Santa Fe *Report* pp. 1–2.
6. Sara Miles, 'The Real War; Low Intensity Conflict in Central America', *Nacla*, 21, 2, April–May 1986, pp. 17–46.
7. Committee of Santa Fe, *Report*, pp. 11–13.
8. David Ronfeldt, *Geopolitics, Security and US Strategy in the Caribbean Basin*; A Project Air Force Report, Prepared for the US Air Force (Santa Monica, CA.: Rand Corporation, 1983), pp. v, 7. In the first principle we can see the application of the accessibility interest explained in note 1.
9. Ronfeldt, *Geopolitics*, pp. 36–47.
10. These figures include 'Economic Support Funds', in the calculations of military aid. The ESFs are an ambiguous category that covers security related aid. For a detailed analysis of the military developments in the Caribbean Basin during this period see Jorge Rodriguez Beruff, 'Puerto Rico and the Militarization of the Caribbean, 1979–1984', *Contemporary Marxism*, 10, (1985), pp. 68–91; and Narin, 'Endgame'.
11. Ronfeldt, *Geopolitics*, pp. v, 8. Cf. *Kissinger Report*, pp. 91 ff.
12. Ronfeldt, *Geopolitics*, p. 72.

13. See for example John Saxe-Fernández, "The Central American Defense Council and Pax Americana," in Irving Louis Horowitz, Josue de Castro and John Gerassi, (eds), *Latin American Radicalism* (New York: Vintage, 1969), pp. 75–101. In this article Saxe-Fernandez discusses the connection between the creation of CONDECA and US counterinsurgency policy in Central America during the 1960s. There is a striking similarity between what he and Sara Miles describe.
14. See Miles, 'The Real War', pp. 18–25 for a good account of the debates among US strategists on low intensity conflict.
15. The policies advocated by the Kissinger Commission are a detailed version of what Ronfeldt had proposed in his 1983 report under the label of 'collective hegemony'; that is collective regional participation in achieving US security goals. Ronfeldt, *Geopolitics*, pp. 48–71. This subtle change in the Reagan administration's policy was not perceptible at the time to many liberal American analysts that interpreted the *Kissinger Report* as a mere cover for the military solution to the regional crisis. See William M. Leo Grande, 'Through the Looking Glass: The Kissinger Report on Central America', *World Policy Journal*, 1, 1 (Winter 1984), pp. 251–84; and Stephen Kinzer, "Strategic Goals Often Loom Behind Assistance for Latin Region," *The New York Times*, 12 January 1984, p. 9.
16. *Kissinger Report*, p. 84 and passim.
17. Roger Burbach and Marc Herold, 'The US Economic Stake in Central America and the Caribbean', in Roger Burbach and Patricia Flynn, (eds), *The Politics of Intervention* (New York: Monthly Review, 1984), pp. 193–98; Rafael Hernández, "Estados Unidos y América Latina: la conexión energética," *Avances de Investigación*, no. 17 (Havana: Centro de Estudios de América, 1982), p. 122; and Jenny Pearce, *Under the Eagle* (Boston: South End Press, 1982), p. 77.
18. See Ronald Reagan, 'Central America: Defending Our Interests', message to the Joint Session of Congress, 27 April 1983; and 'US Interests in Central America', televised address, 9 May 1984, in US Department of State, *Realism, Strength, Negotiation: Key Foreign Policy Statements of the Reagan administration* (Washington, DC.: Department of State, Bureau of Public Affairs, May 1984), pp. 128–31, 134–8.
19. Calculated from tables on 'Leading Items in US Imports for Consumption from Designated CBI Countries in 1986,' US Department of Commerce, 1986.
20. US Statutes, *Public Law, 98–67*, August, 1983, title II, subtitle A, section 212.
21. *Public Law 98–67*, section 213.
22. US Department of State, Bureau of Public Affairs, 'Background on the Caribbean Basin Initiative', *Special Report*, 97, 1982, p. 4.
23. For a detailed discussion on this see Emilio Pantojas-García, 'The US Caribbean Basin Initiative and the Puerto Rican Experience; Some Parallels and Lessons,' *Latin American Perspectives*, 12, 4 (fall 1985), pp. 105–28.
24. General Agreement on Tariffs and Trade (GATT), *Second Report of the Government of the United States on the Trade-Related Provisions of the*

Caribbean Basin Economic Recovery Act of 1983 (GATT, 3 April 1987).
25. US Department of State, Agency for International Development and Office of Management and Budget, 'Report to the President and Congress: A Plan for Fully Funding the Recommendations of the National Bipartisan Commission on Central America', *Special Report*, no. 162 (Washington, DC: US Department of State, Bureau of Public Affairs, March 1987), p. 18. Hereafter quoted as *Special Report no. 162*.
26. An account of the administration's efforts to persuade Congress to provide long-term funding for the CAI is given in 'The US and Central America: Implementing the National Bipartisan Commission Report; Report to the President from the Secretary of State', *Special Report*, no. 148 (Washington, DC: US Department of State, Bureau of Public Affairs, August 1986); US Department of State, *Strengthening our Development Partnership with Central America* (Washington, DC; Bureau of Public Affairs, March 1987); and *Special Report no. 162*.
27. *Special Report no. 162*, p. 5.
28. *Special Report no. 162*, pp. 10–11, 18, 22.
29. Subcommittee on Oversight of the Committee on Ways and Means of the U.S. House of Representatives, *Report on the Committee Delegation Mission to the Caribbean Basin and Recommendations to Improve the Effectiveness of the Caribbean Basin Initiatives* (Washington, DC: Government Printing Office, May 1987).
30. Caribbean/Central America Action (C/CAA) is the organisation of US capital actively supporting the administration's policy. It was created in 1980 as a business coalition to support US economic initiatives for the Caribbean and Central America especially the CBI. A 250 thousand dollars grant from the Agency for International Development got the organisation started. In the beginning, C/CAA was mainly integrated by American TNCs with interests in the region such as Chase Manhattan Bank, Tesoro Petroleum, Bank of America, Eastern Airlines, Reynolds Metals and McGregor Sporting Goods. Now, C/CAA includes Caribbean and Central American corporations among its corporate sponsors and members of the Board of Trustees. This organisation has come to play a key role in the implementation of the CBI and in lobbying for the CAI. They have created a large network of capitalists in the region and the US and serve as liaison between governments and capitalists. C/CAA, Press Package for the 11th Miami Conference on the Caribbean, December 1987; Tom Barry, Beth Wood and Deb Preusch, *Dollars and Dictators* (Albuquerque: The Resource Center, 1982), pp. 41–2.
31. The best articulated alternative regional integration model which illustrates my point is the 'Regional Alternative' produced in 1983 by the Nicaraguan Coordinadora Regional de Investigaciones Sociales (CRIES), the Instituto de Investigaciones Económicas y Sociales (INIES) and the Institute of Social Studies (ISS) in The Hague. The proposals of the alternative are clearly antithetical to those of the CBI and would promote a very different role for the region in the international division of labor. See CRIES, INIES, ISS, *An Alternative Policy for Central America and the Caribbean*; *The Hague Declaration* (Man-

agua: CRIES, INIES, ISS, 1983); the basis and implications of this document are further discussed in George Irvin and Xabier Gorostiaga, eds. *Towards an Alternative for the Caribbean and Central America* (London: George Allen and Unwin, 1985).

32. Non-capitalist and non-aligned are terms more commonly used to describe these types of political projects. These concepts, however, have different meanings and policy implications for, say, the People's National Party of Jamaica or the National Revolutionary Movement (MNR) of El Salvador and the Communist Party of Cuba or the Sandinista Front of Nicaragua. Hence, I prefer to use the term 'rupturist' to emphasise that it is the intention to break away from the orbit of US political and economic domination what these diverse groups share in the eyes of US strategists. This is the reason why the Reagan administration lumps together labels such as 'Communists' or pro-Soviet and opposes, with equal intensity, fundamentally diverse groups of nationalists, social democrats and radical socialists.

33. Jeane Kirkpatrick, 'Dictatorships and Double Standards', *Commentary*, 8, 5 (November 1979).

34. It must be remembered that the invasion of Grenada took place two days after the Lebanon events and some part of the troops used in the invasion were on their way precisely to the Middle East. Hugh O'Shaughnessy, *Grenada: Revolution, Invasion and Aftermath* (London: Hamish Hamilton, 1984), pp. 6–7; Latin America Bureau, *Grenada: Whose Freedom?* (London: Latin American Bureau, 1984), p. 14.

35. Joel M. Woldman, 'The National Endowment for Democracy', *Issue Brief* (Washington, DC: Congressional Research Services, 1984).

36. The concept was coined by Carole Schwartz and Breny Cuenca, 'El camino militar electoral de la administración Reagan para El Salvador versus la negociación política', in Centro de Capacitación para el Desarrollo (CECADE) and Centro de Investigación y Docencia Económicas (CIDE), *Centroamérica: crisis y política internacional* (Mexico: Siglo Veintiuno, 1982), pp. 107–37.

37. These arguments were shared by both North American and Latin American analysts. See Herman and Brodhead, *Demonstration Elections*, pp. 115–19; and Breny Cuenca and Carole Schwartz, 'Reagan, las elecciones y el nuevo pacto dominante en El Salvador', in Maira, *La política de Reagan*, pp. 337–64.

38. Portraying Magaña as a moderate was misleading. He was a banker who often did financial favours for the military. See Cuenca and Schwartz, 'Reagan, las elecciones', pp. 346–47; Phillip Berryman, *Inside Central America* (New York: Pantheon, 1985), p. 50.

39. Initially, these changes in US personnel and tactics, as well as US pressures over the Salvadorean military were interpreted as an attempt by the Reagan administration to 'harden' its line. See Patricia Flynn, 'The United States at War in Central America: Unable to Win, Unwilling to Loose', in Burbach and Flynn, *The Politics of Intervention*, pp. 91–131; cf. Miles, 'The Real War', p. 27.

40. On 8 May 1984, Republican Senator, Jesse Helms denounced in Congress the CIA's support to Duarte. Helms was one of the few supporters of D'Aubisson in Congress. John Felton, 'CIA Role Casts Doubt on

Salvador Election', *Congressional Quarterly*, 12 May 1984, p. 1091.
41. Narin, 'Endgame', p. 35.
42. Cuenca and Schwartz, 'Reagan, las elecciones', pp. 350 ff.; Herman and Brodhead, *Demonstration Elections*, p. 119.
43. Chris Norton, 'Build and Destroy', *Nacla*, 19, 6 (November/December 1985), pp. 26–36. In spite of all the conflict and divisions surrounding the Popular Democratic Union, the fact is that it served the initial purpose of providing a base of support for the PDC as well as providing an institutional alternative to joining the guerrilla for many.
44. The concept of facade democracy was advanced by Mario Solórzano Martínez, 'Centroamérica: Democracias de Fachada,'' *Polémica*, no. 12 (November/December 1983), pp. 40–55.
45. To say that the new dominant coalition within the Salvadorean power bloc is integrated by the bourgeoisie, the technocracy and the military is, of course, too vague. A detailed analysis of just what forces integrate the new power bloc is beyond the scope of this chapter. It is my contention that the emerging forces in the new power bloc are the middle class technocrats, such as Duarte himself, who want to advance a reintegrationist economic project along the lines discussed in the previous section. Yet another group that stands to gain from a reordering of power relations is the local industrialists linked to export processing industries or *maquiladoras*. The sectors involved in finance have a great stake in maintaining the flow of US dollars to the country and are likely to go along with US designs this may be one of the reasons why Magaña was portrayed by the Reagan administration as a moderate. Finally, the members of the army that do not have strong links to the oligarchy stand to gain more at this juncture by supporting the process of political restructuring than by opposing it. These are untested propositions that can be reasonably inferred from the arguments of this chapter and personal observations. Much research, however, would be needed to substantiate them.
46. Latin American Bureau, *Grenada*, pp. 94–6.
47. Anthony Payne, Paul Sutton and Tony Thorndike, *Grenada: Revolution and Invasion* (New York: St Martin's Press, 1984), pp. 187–9; Latin American Bureau, *Grenada*, p. 100; Patrick Emmanuel, Farley Brathwaite and Eudine Barriteau, *Political Change and Public Opinion in Grenada: 1979–1984* (Cave Hill, Barbados: Institute of Social and Economic Research, 1986), pp. 55, 63.
48. Emmanuel *et al.*, *Political Change*, ch. VII.
49. Fred Halliday, 'An Ambiguous Turning Point: Grenada and its Aftermath', *Nacla* 18, 6 (November–December 1984), pp. 29–30; George Black, 'The Americans' Man; A Talk with Eric Gairy', *Nacla*, 19, 2 (March–April), 1985, pp. 8–9; Emmanuel *et al. Political Change*, pp. 79–88.
50. Norman Podhoretz, 'The Reagan Road to Detente', *Foreign Affairs*, 63 (Spring 1985), pp. 447–64. It is interesting to note that for this New Right editor of *Commentary*, the change in the Reagan Administration's policies by the end of its first term were clearer than for the liberal analysts mentioned in note 15 above.

3 Cuba and the Caribbean: Perceptions and Realities
Isabel Jaramillo Edwards

> Let us bid farewell to arms and, in a civilized way, consecrate ourselves to the most pressing problems of our time. That is the responsibility and the most sacred duty of all the world's statesmen. That is, in addition, the indispensable premise for human survival. (Fidel Castro. 34th Period of Sessions of the General Assembly of the United Nations, New York, 12 October 1979.)

INTRODUCTION

Emphasis on the military sphere in the Caribbean countries is, in most cases, conditioned by external factors which are fundamentally related to the US geopolitical approach to the region. This emphasis is stressed even more in the case of Cuba, since this geopolitical approach, related to the perception – or theory – of the surrogate role Cuba supposedly plays as the USSR's proxy in the region, gives rise to an outdated view of the 'threats' confronting the area, diverting attention to external factors.

The consequent diversion of resources to the military and defence spheres in underdeveloped countries in general has a direct, detrimental effect, and restricts development capacity of these countries. The real threat to regional stability[1] is related to the current situation of economic decline characterised by the rise in fuel prices, the foreign debt, the drop in prices of exports in the world market, protectionism and the transfer of the problems and oscillations of the US economy (to which the Caribbean is strongly tied by bonds of dependence), as well as to the crisis in productivity, and the unequal distribution of income closely linked to problems of a structural nature.

THE CARIBBEAN

Historically, the US has considered the Caribbean subregion as its 'third border', where it principally focuses on geopolitical and security considerations. The Caribbean is 'a vital strategic and commercial artery for the United States. Nearly half of US trade, two-thirds of our imported fuel and more than half of our imported strategic minerals pass through the Panama Canal or the Gulf of Mexico. Let no one be deceived: the well-being and security of our neighbours in this region favour our own vital interests.'[2]

US hegemony in the region has gone through various stages and adjustments in keeping with global realignments and the strategic and foreign policy perceptions prevailing at different historical moments in the US. The so-called 'low intensity conflict' is articulated within the most general framework of the policy of containment. It is a concept in the realm of strategy which includes political, economic, social and military means and pressures. The objective is to 'win the hearts and minds' of the people and 'avoid certain results', obviously referred to revolutionary processes and even modernisation and/or reformism, in Third World countries which the United States deems to be contrary to its interests. It includes the use of military force as a 'deterrent' and, in an extreme phase, it contemplates the direct participation of US troops, when the country or region in question has not been able to solve the problem through internal means, implemented with US aid and advice at every level in order to achieve so-called 'nation building'.

Even after Grenada, the Caribbean – from the official US point of view – represents a 'potential threat'. The invasion of the island was a show of military strength and the circumstance of an easy victory overshadowed the disaster of the Marines in Lebanon. It also implied a warning for Nicaragua and for similar sociopolitical processes in the area. The operation was also a barometer for gauging the reaction of the USSR and Cuba, and was essentially aimed at restoring US hegemony, both in perceptions and realities.[3] In this respect, it is important to consider the theory of the Army War College, according to which the micro-states are pawns in the strategic global balance.

In Atlantic jargon, the Caribbean is a 'grey zone',[4] which rules out coordinated NATO interventions. So it falls to the United States to take part in activities defined as 'internal defense abroad'[5] in which the means applied are consistent with a preventive phase in the area, within the framework of 'low intensity conflict'.

In economic terms, the formula is basically composed of the Caribbean Basin Initiative (CBI),[6] which, as part of the Reagan administration's geopolitical project, aimed 'to assure that the nations of the Caribbean Basin continue to compete favourably compared with Cuba' and 'to guarantee a secure and stable Caribbean flank' particularly during an East–West crisis in Europe.[7] In general terms, it was aimed at orientating the region towards a single model of development based on free enterprise and private investment, preferential trade tariffs and marked bilateralism in aid programmes. The conditions imposed by the IMF, however, 'without the shadow of a doubt augur an economic disaster, a political disaster and a social disaster, and they are going to engender an unprecedented crisis of unforseeable consequences'.[8] Thus social explosions are anticipated which can only be controlled by political intervention, with the resulting restriction of political space.

The CBI increased intra-Caribbean contradictions, at a time when these countries 'need integration, need international cooperation; their development cannot be undertaken exclusively on the basis of their own resources and should not become a transnational business, but rather their cardinal objective must be well-being of their people and the consolidation of their independence and national identity'.[9]

From the Caribbean point of view the main criticism towards the CBI is that it is inadequate and internally inconsistent; that is shows no understanding of the problems of the Caribbean and that it lacks a series of ingredients, such as incentives for investors and a consideration of the service sector – particularly tourism. In addition, it does not see the infrastructure as the main obstacle to any kind of development, a constant feature in the Caribbean.[10] This explains, in part, why foreign investment has not begun to flow into the region.

As some US officials recognise, the problem with CBI is that it has created unrealistic expectations. It must be taken into account that what the US wants is 'a long-term policy . . . the kind of development that will make these countries economically self-sufficient and give them a standard of living in which there is no fertile ground for subversion as there is at present'.[11] Therefore, the recommendation of the promoters of the CBI is patience, although the needs of these countries are pressing.

As regards economic integration, this represents, for the underdeveloped countries, 'something more than a historical tendency; it is a very necessary mechanism for defending themselves against the disadvantageous conditions imposed by the industrialised countries on their economic relations and for taking advantage of the region's potential with a view to promoting economic development'. Today there are few who doubt that economic integration is, for the countries in the Third World, an alternative in the face of the crisis, a tool for survival.[12]

US policy towards the subregion – reduction of the sugar quota, protectionist practices in general and foreign debt service payments[13] – seriously affects the subregion's integrationist imperative.

Caribbean integration has also been seriously affected by issues such as the invasion of Grenada with regard to the coordination of foreign policy, and the possibility of the Caribbean states projecting joint positions with respect to regional problems, which would strengthen their bargaining power. A common, integrated Caribbean front on matters of mutual interest, as well as ideological pluralism in the regional context, seems to have crumbled.[14]

Further, the US commitment to the CBI has weakened due to strong political pressures by sectors which feel affected by it. There are contradictions among US investors and governments in the region, with the latter believing that a total economic opening to foreign investment would be a kind of political suicide. In addition to this, strong US protectionism and the reductions in sugar quotas, suggest that Washington's concern for the area only emerges at moments of crisis, when all the mechanisms created to control them are brought into play. Once the crisis is over, or at least mitigated, 'normality' returns and the focus of attention shifts to another area, where US interests are at greater risk.

In addition, the militarisation of the subregion responds to geopolitical perceptions of the United States, rather than to real needs. After the invasion of Grenada, US interest in the creation and articulation of a regional security system grew. Such a system would function on two levels: deterrent and contingent, with a system installed in the subregion also providing for an operational advance guard point.

On the other hand, subregional actors such as Saint Vincent (1984) and Barbados (1986), through their respective Prime Ministers, expressed their dissatisfaction with the growing emphasis on military components in the area when its real needs were jobs, technology, and the development and welfare of the people in general.[15]

The idea of a regional security force for the Caribbean did not materialise, given different views of the interests in question. The United States favored a large security apparatus within the context of an East–West perception, linked to its own national security and to the problems of the 'international threat'. From the Caribbean perspective, more balanced approaches seemed to centre on the idea of a normal internal security apparatus, small and proportional to the needs and realities of each country. The differences of opinion had to do with the range of operations which a regional security force would have, and also with whether or not the members of the Organisation of Eastern Caribbean States or CARICOM as a whole would participate.

What does seem to be a fact is the intention to form a fairly loose regional security system as a consequence of the lack of a unified position in the Caribbean which would allow for the formalisation of an institutional framework through which the US could establish a relation of assistance in the realm of security with the regional institution created. This would develop a new kind of linkage different from the hitherto prevalent (the bilateral one), without eliminating it. The increase in resources earmarked for the military and security spheres, linked to US interests in the subregion, reaffirms the economic-military dependence of the United States, while creating conditions – on the domestic level – for authoritarianism.[16]

US priorities in the Caribbean – mainly the English-speaking Caribbean and particularly its small countries – are based on the concept of its own security and not on these nations' economic and social development needs. The CBI, essentially, did not resolve the problems of the subregion, nor did it meet the expectations it created at the outset, while US insistence on creating political and military counter-insurgency mechanisms of dimensions previously unheard of by the people of these countries has created evident discontent.

CUBA

Although different perceptions coexist in the Caribbean[17] on security matters, the one that constitutes a primary consideration, imposed and manipulated until it becomes an argument, is that of the US.

In the context of the 'Caribbean Basin', the nature of the US perception of Cuba[18] plays a decisive role, to which we must add the belief that 'the Caribbean will face a problem of a different sort: how to arrest decay in established democratic and parliamentary infrastructures created during the recent colonial experience'.[19] Thus, the region has been relocated on a scale of strategic priorities in Washington, which in turn implements a combination of military, political and economic pressures as preventive means in an area seriously affected by the crisis.

The US view, which makes Cuba the focal point of its foreign policy towards the 'Basin', is based – apart from the trauma represented by the triumph of the Cuban Revolution – on the perceptions: 1) of the role of Cuba as a Soviet surrogate with power designs on the region; 2) on the possibility that it will obstruct sea lanes of communications (SLOCs) fundamental to the US economy and block supplies for NATO; 3) on the danger that all the countries of the region, including Mexico, will gradually 'fall', and that the US will be politically and militarily isolated. The dissemination of these perceptions through the mass media and international press agencies, precludes an alternative Caribbean perspective and prevents Cuba from being seen as a Caribbean actor with a socialist model of alternative development which has to confront an unfavorable context of constant pressures and ongoing acts of aggression. The invasion of Grenada – in a flank manoeuvre – met the objective expressed by Haig in the sense of 'going to the source'.[20]

Cuba's insertion in global security problems by the US is linked to Cuba's relations with the USSR and with its internationalist foreign policy in the Third World.

The diplomatic isolation imposed on Cuba by the US in the 1960s gradually lost ground in the 1970s[21] and, by the 1980s, Cuba had a broad range of inter-state relations with the countries of Latin America and the Caribbean, and the Third World in general, as well as globally.

Cuban foreign policy is fundamentally characterised by a combination of principles: internationalism, peaceful coexistence and the development of plural relations with the countries of Latin America and the Caribbean, and non-alignment.[22]

Non-alignment joins Cuba to the largest and most important group of Third World countries, which tries to face, in a unified manner, the main global problems affecting developing countries, while forming a movement of relative convergence and with international leverage.

Peaceful coexistence is a token of development and socialism. The struggle for peace is an essential element of the strategic objectives of Cuba's international policy.[23] While peace is necessary for development, development itself is a condition for peace.

From the point of view of US perceptions, both non-alignment and internationalism are the critical aspects. Cuba, on the other hand, understands that it is a global historical necessity that normal relations exist among all the countries of the world, based on mutual respect, recognition of the sovereign right of each one and non-intervention. Cuba believes that the normalization of its relations with the United States would be favourable for the political climate of Latin America and the Caribbean, and contribute to world detente. Cuba, therefore, is not opposed to resolving its historic differences with the United States, but no one should pretend that Cuba changes its position or compromises its principles. Cuba is, and will continue to be, socialist. Cuba is, and will continue to be, a friend of the Soviet Union and of all the socialist states. Cuba is, and will continue to be, an internationalist country.[24]

It would seem that the US perception which most clearly reveals the drive for hegemony and frustration, is that most common among foreign policy makers, namely, that Cuba 'is a grade C country which should not have a grade A foreign policy'.[25] Furthermore, 'the US is a grade A, and therefore its programme of military aid is seen as natural, while that of Cuba is not'. Cuba, 'a poor country, should not give itself the luxury of charity', so its internationalist efforts are seen as subversion.

Following this same logic, we could ask ourselves how it could be possible for a 'grade A' country like the United States to have a 'grade C' foreign policy, one that is so erratic and inconsistent, and which gathers strength and semblance of coherence only in moments of crisis, at least as far as Latin America and the Caribbean are concerned.[26]

It is clear that Cuba cannot export revolution,[27] but at the same time the US cannot stop the historic development and legitimate aspirations for change in the underdeveloped world. Nor can the US export democracy: that which it perceives and accepts as such, and which is extraordinarily similar to the US system.[28]

Internationalism is solidly based on two guiding documents of Cuba's State and Party policy: the Constitution of the Republic and the Program of the Cuban Communist Party. Internationalism, as an implicit and explicit aspect of the socialist system, 'is also a matter of conscience and . . . if there is, indeed, no conscience in the world about international collaboration, the future of the world is going to be a great disaster'.[29]

Cuba's internationalist solidarity manifests itself in many ways ranging from assistance in health, education, agriculture, construction, and various types of technical aid – which are of fundamental importance – to military assistance. Internationalist aid is offered in response to requests from the recipient countries.[30]

As for Cuban military aid, it is clear that it is limited to the needs of the country making the request, and that

> our forces will not stay anywhere one minute longer than necessary for the country and the country requesting it; our people will not delay a moment in beginning to return from the time the country where they are carrying out their missions notifies us. That is why our troops will never be a problem for any country where they are sent, nor a threat to any other country. They have gone to carry out support missions in certain countries. And, I repeat, they will not be there even one minute past the time that the country in question ask that they return. We are not defending strategic positions, nor national interests; so that there is nothing easier for us to resolve, and this principle will always be respected, along with the principle of absolute respect, of the most absolute respect for the domestic and foreign policy of the countries that have asked us for this aid.[31]

Cuba's military aid is not a norm, as it is for the US. It is an exception. It has occurred in the case of countries subjected to foreign aggressions,[32] and after other means for arriving at a solution to certain conflicts have been exhausted.

Cuba, consistent with the principles of internationalism, non-alignment and peaceful co-existence as regards regional conflicts, has called for the creation of conditions for negotiated solutions, as in the case of Central America[33] and the Southern Cone of Africa,[34] among others.

The US, as regards negotiated solutions, has in some cases promoted them from positions of force; in others shown itself to be clearly ambiguous; and finally, in others, has blocked them. In a broader context, such an attitude is precisely the opposite of what is needed for peace, disarmament, cooperation – which is not contrary to internationalism – and a New International Economic Order, specially in the Third World. The current US approach to the Third World, linked to perceptions of national security, indicates that the arena it has chosen for breaking strategic parity is none other than the underdeveloped world.[35]

Given US foreign policy's stress on national security matters,[36] various aspects of Cuba's approach to 'national security' merit consideration:

1. There are differences of opinion as to what the US and Cuba deem to be national security, derived – in the case of Cuba – from the fact that the latter has been the object of ongoing economic, political, military and psychological threats by US governments throughout its history.
2. It must be made clear that Cuba's concept of national security has nothing to do with the doctrine created by the US, and tragically transplanted in some Latin American countries.[37]
3. The concept of national security, among countries in general and in underdeveloped ones in particular, is increasingly linked to development interdependence and the need for indivisibility and equality to be included in this concept, which means that any country aspiring to security must join it to that of others and that all nations have the same right to security.[38]
4. The United States' overwhelming conventional, naval and air power superiority is totally disproportionate to the nature of the threat attributed to Cuba.
5. The most probable scenario in which it is calculated that Cuba could really be a threat[39] – according to some experts – would be in the case of a conflagration in Europe, which is highly unlikely, specially in a context tending toward global *détente* such as the current one, in which the US and the Soviet Union have signed the INF Agreements.

Since 1959, with the triumph of the Revolution, the US National Security Council began studies and set in motion all kinds of aggression against Cuba.[40] During the following years – up to the present – the US has not changed its hostile posture towards the revolution nor stopped its efforts to destroy it.[41]

Given persistent US aggressiveness, it is clear that, in the case of Cuba, defence cannot to be neglected. It is a reality imposed by the island's geographic location and by the differences in political, economic and social system between Cuba and its more powerful neighbour, the US.[42]

Although the last stage of the Carter government marked a shift in policy, US aggressiveness towards Cuba increased[43] with the coming to power of neo-conservative groups in the US in 1980. The US implemented an offensive foreign policy and consequently defence spending rose. The aim was to recover hegemony by force.

The possible forms of aggression against Cuba range from counter-revolution and harassment, military blockade, systematic attrition, and limited strike, to invasion with previous development, and surprise invasion. The most likely scenario would be a surprise attack, in the form of massive air strikes and an invasion of ground troops accompanied by systematic attrition to do away with the country's economic and political structure.

As a result of the increase in US aggressiveness, Cuba perceived that it must be prepared for two types of war: one conventional and another of the people, in order to deter an attack. Consequently, President Fidel Castro announced, on May Day, 1980, the creation of the Territorial Troops Militia (MTT),[44] and the 'War of All the People' (GTP) concept was launched.

The essence of the latter concept is the participation of the entire society, including the Revolutionary Armed Forces (FAR), whose capacity has been increased consistent with the needs of the moment,[45] for the implementation of both irregular and regular protected warfare, at all levels.[46] The entire society is organised along those lines.

The strengthening of Cuba's defence expresses 'a determination to defend ourselves, to struggle, very strongly and heroically, of which I am sure imperialism has no doubts'.[47] The measure, clearly *defensive*, implies that 'we are increasing the possibilities of peace, there is nothing we want less that war. In today's world, no person conscious of the situation and of the dangers could support a military solution of any kind.' What is involved is raising the cost of an act of aggression so much that the US will not launch an attack on Cuba.[48]

Ongoing US aggressiveness in the case of Cuba and also Nicaragua necessarily implies an increased defensive capability, which in turn affects development, given the fact that resources must be diverted to and concentrated on defence.[49] Even so, between 1979 and 1988 Cuba's average spending for the latter was about 10 per cent of the national budget, while the average outlay for education and health in the same period (1979 to 1988) was 21 per cent (see Figure 3.1).

It is absurd to think that a small country, with 10 million people, could be a threat to the security of the US, although the strength and capability of its Armed Forces are well-known. The 'Cuban problem' for the US is rather one of the perceptions of those who shape its foreign policy regarding Cuba's international activity.[50] Similarly, in

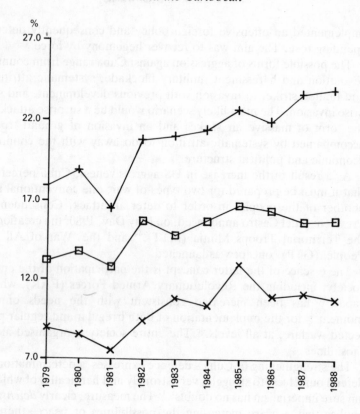

Key:

— + — Education/public health

— ☐ — Other activities–socio-cultural/scientific

— ✕ — Defence and domestic order

Figure 3.1 Proportion of the most important components of Cuba's national budget in percentages, 1979–88

Sources: 1979 Gaceta oficial 30/12/78 Law No. 20; 1980 Gaceta oficial 29/12/79 Law No. 26; 1981 Gaceta oficial 30/12/80 Law No. 32; 1982 Gaceta oficial 31/12/81 Law No. 35; 1983 Gaceta oficial 04/01/83 Law No. 40; 1984 Gaceta oficial 27/12/83 Law No. 45; 1985 Gaceta oficial 28/12/84 Law No. 47; 1986 Gaceta oficial 30/12/85 Law No. 53; 1987 Gaceta oficial 26/12/86 Law No. 58; 1988 Gaceta oficial 30/12/86 Law No. 64.

a scenario of world conflagration, Cuba would probably disappear. And it is totally ridiculous to think that Cuba could start a war against the US. The real threat for the US is not military nor has it to do with security; rather it is the perception that Cuba is a possible alternative model of development despite all the difficulties it has faced.

In a context of cooperation and integration, Cuba can play a positive role in the international scene, in consolidating links with the countries of the hemisphere in the framework of a necessary Latin American and Caribbean unity with an emphasis on the North–South perspective. At the same time, to achieve real and effective peace and development, a constructive position must be taken by the US and the industrialised world, since 'conceiving of development without peace and disarmament is impossible, thinking of peace without development would not be realistic'.[51]

It is a recognised fact that the US must again achieve a balance between its economic and security interests. The disproportionate growth of military spending and the stress on security matters has also reflected negatively on the Third World, where a maximum of resources for development is needed.

The tendency towards global defence – and the possible setting aside of bi-polar confrontation and the bi-polar approach – marks a favourable shift towards a necessary focus on the most pressing problems of development and on international cooperation, and towards the necessary search for a broad consensus regarding the creative exploration of development strategies.

It is within this framework, favoured by the tendency towards detente and by the juncture of the US elections, that proposals[52] are being made for a reversal of tendencies towards unilateralism, and studies are suggesting the demilitarisation of the Third World.[53]

Realism, objectivity, reasonableness and political determination will advance the creation of favourable conditions for the under-developed world to enter the next century with more security regarding its prospects for development.

Notes

1. Regarding different aspects of the Caribbean problem see: H. Michael Erisman, (ed.), *The Caribbean Challenge* (Westview Press, Boulder,

Colorado, 1984); Alma H. Young and Dion E. Phillips, (eds), *Militarization in the Non-Hispanic Caribbean* (Lynne Rienner Publishers, Boulder, Colorado, 1986).

2. Ronald Reagan, 'Speech before the OAS'; February 1982.
3. Cfr. Isabel Jaramillo, 'La estrategia intervencionista estadounidense hacia el Medio Oriente y en la "Cuenca del Caribe"', *Avances de Investigación* (CEA) No. 18, CEA, 1983.
4. US Secretary of State, George Schultz, has repeatedly and indiscriminately used the terms 'grey zone', and 'ambiguous challenges'. Recently, Vernon Walters, US Ambassador to the UN, during his tour of the Caribbean and Latin America, referred to 'constructive ambiguity'. All of this terminology is related to 'low intensity conflict' doctrines.
5. Manual FM-100-2o. Fort Gullick, 1982.
6. See *Fact Sheet CBI*, February 1982; T. Barry, *et al.*, *The Other Side of Paradise*, Grove Press, 1984; A. Singham and S. Hune, 'The CBI, the US Response to Non-Alignment', in *Trans-Africa Forum*, 1, 2, 1982. Also see the documents on the CBI published by *Cuadernos de Nuestra América*, 1, 4, (January–June, 1984).
7. W. Mc Donald, quoted in *NACLA*, 19, 4, (July–August, 1985); also the article by Mc Donald himself 'Atlantic Security, the Cuban Factor', in *Jane's Defense Weekly*, 22 November 1984.
8. Fidel Castro, *La Deuda Externa: selección temática*, Council of State, La Habana, 1985, p. 66.
9. Fidel Castro, *Nada podrá detener la marcha de la Historia* (Interview granted to Jeoffrey Elliot and Mervyn Dymally), Editora Política, La Habana, 1985, p. 195.
10. C. Skeete, *The English Speaking Caribbean: Current Conditions and Implications for US Policy*, Report prepared by Congressional Research Service, Library of Congress, for the Subcommittee on Western Hemisphere Affairs, US House of Representatives, US Government Printing Office, 13 September 1985.
11. Ronald Reagan, 'Statement', 26/7/83.
12. Gerardo González Nuñez, 'Notas sobre los obstáculos de la Integración en el Caribe', Manuscript, Centro de Estudios de América, La Habana, 1988.
13. Gerardo González Nuñez, 'Particularidades de la Deuda Externa en los países del Caribe angloparlante', Paper delivered at the Seminar on International Relations, Sponsored by LASA/CEA, La Habana, Cuba, July 1987.
14. L. Searwar, 'The Security of a Small State', in *CARICOM Bulletin*, 6, 1985, p. 7; A. Payne, P. Sutton and T. Thorndike, *Grenada: Revolution, and Invasion*, New York, 1984. The coordination of a foreign policy with a view to establishing an independent regional voice – one of the goals of CARICOM in 1973 – centred on two main objectives, according to Searwar. 'To assure the security of the individual member States through a limited coordinated approach towards the international community and to seek stronger support from the international system for the norms and forms of organisation that promote security and development in small countries'.

15. T. Thorndike, 'The Militarization of the Commonwealth Caribbean', paper presented at the Annual Conference of the British International Studies Association, UCW, Aberystwyth, 16–18 December 1987.
16. See Isabel Jaramillo, 'Conflicto de Baja Intensidad en el Caribe: la Fase Preventiva', in Andrés Serbín, Comp., *Venezuela y las Relaciones Internacionales en la Cuenca del Caribe* (Venezuela and International Relations in the Caribbean Basin), ILDIS/AVECA, Caracas, 1987, p. 41–60.
17. The perceptions suffer from an interpretative danger because they correspond to an intentional interpretation of reality affected by elements of propaganda, disinformation and based on real information which may conceal a part of reality itself.
18. On Cuba, see Carlos Díaz and Isabel Jaramillo, 'Cuba y el Caribe', paper presented at CALACS, Canada, October 1982. A. Payne, P. Sutton and T. Thorndike: *Grenada: Revolution and Invasion*, New York, 1984; 'The Communist Threat', in *Foreign Policy* No. 52, 1983; T. H. Moorer and G. A. Fauriel, op. cit.; Rafael Hernandez, 'La política de los EEUU hacia Cuba y la cuestión de la migración' in *Cuadernos de Nuestra América*, No. 3, pp. 83–5; 'Informe de Santa Fe' (Santa Fe Report), in *Cuadernos Semestrales* (CIDE), No. 9.
19. T. H. Moorer and G. A. Fauriol, *Caribbean Basin Security*, The Center for Strategic and International Studies, Georgetown University, Washington, DC, 1984, p. 41.
20. Cf. Néstor Sánchez, op. cit., and Moorer and Fauriol, op. cit.
21. Cuba established diplomatic relations collectively, in 1973, with Guyana, Trinidad and Tobago, Jamaica and Barbados.
22. See: L. Suárez, 'La Política de la Revolución Cubana hacia América Latina y el Caribe: Notas para una Periodización', *Cuadernos de Nuestra América*, No. 6, (July–December, 1986) pp. 137–180; and C. Alzugarary (ISRI), 'Realidades y Perspectivas de la Seguridad Nacional Cubana'. Preliminary version, 'Cuba-US Relations in the '90s' Workshop, American Studies Center, La Habana, April 88.
23. C. Rafael Rodríguez, 'Fundamentos Estratégicos de la Política Exterior de Cuba', *Cuba Socialista*, No. 1, Dec. 1981.
24. Fidel Castro, 'Report to the 3rd Congress of Cuban Communist Party', La Habana, 1980.
25. See Lars Shoultz, *National Security and US Policy Towards Latin America*, Princeton University Press, 1987, p. 265.
26. The US focuses its attention on problems when these get to the stage of open crisis; it solves those aspects in its immediate interest, and once stability is recovered, it again relegates them to oblivion. The US intervenes, but it does not take responsibility for the results of the intervention, nor for the development of the country which was 'snatched from the jaws of communism', or diverted from a course of progressive development which the US deemed harmful to its interests.
27. See Fidel Castro, 'Speech', Santiago de Cuba, 1-1-84.
28. See Howard J. Wiarda, 'Can Democracy be Exported: The Quest for Democracy in US-Latin American Policy', p. 344, in Kevin Middlebrook and Carlos Rico (eds), *The US and Latin America in the 1980s*, University of Pittsburgh Press, Pittsburgh, 1986, p. 325–51.

29. Fidel Castro, 'Speech', 4 April 1984.
30. For diverse interpretations see W. Raymond Duncan, 'Cuba in the Caribbean and Central America: Limits to Influence', in H. Michael Erisman and John D. Martz, (eds), *Colossus Challenged The Struggle for Caribbean Influence* (Westview Press, Boulder, Colorado, 1982), pp. 83–119; Juan del Aguila, 'The Politics of Confrontation: US Policy Toward Cuba', in *The Caribbean Challenge*, H. Michael Erisman (ed.) (Westview Press, Boulder, Colorado, 1984), pp. 95–116; Fidel Castro, 'Speech, 26th Anniversary of the Landing of the Granma and the Establishment of the Revolutionary Armed Forces', La Habana, 11–12–82; Barry B. Levine (ed.), *The New Cuban Presence in the Caribbean* (Westview Press, Boulder, Colo., 1983); Anthony T. Bryan, 'Cuba's Impact in the Caribbean', *International Journal*, 15, (Spring, 1985), pp. 331–47; C. Díaz, Isabel Jaramillo, 'Cuba y el Caribe', paper presented at CALACS, Canada, 1982; C. Alzugaray, op. cit.
31. Fidel Castro, 'Speech at the Military Ceremony on the Occasion of the 26th Anniversary of the Landing of the Granma and of the Establishment of the Revolutionary Army Forces', La Habana, 11–12–82.
32. In the case of South Africa's acts of aggression against Angola and Somalia's against Ethiopia.
33. See Fidel Castro, 'Interview with NBC journalist María Shriver', *Juventud Rebelde*, 28 February 1988.
34. 'Risquet Responde: Fábulas y Realidades', *Bohemia* No. 7, (8–1–88), pp. 74–8. In this interview with Jorge Risquet, member of the Political Bureau of the Cuban Communist Party, it is made clear that since 1984 Angola, by common agreement with Cuba, 'has presented a platform for a negotiated solution that would guarantee the independence of Namibia, the security of Angola and peace and stability in South West Africa. More recently Angola has made the requirements of this platform more flexible in order to arrive at an honourable arrangement, and re-initiated talks with the US with this objective. But the constructive position of one of the interested parties (which includes Angola, Cuba and the SWAPO) is not enough; also decisive is the position of the other party (that is, South Africa and the US)'. See also '¿Cuál sería la esencia de una solución negociada a los problemas de Angola y Namibia?' *Granma*, 4–2–88; 'Communique of the Ministry of the Revolutionary Armed Forces', *Granma*, 18–3–88; and 'Joint Communique of the Four-Party Meeting', *Granma*, 5–5–88.
35. *Discriminate Deferrence*, Report of the Special Commissions headed by Fred Ikle and Albert Wohlstetter, USA, February 1988.
36. See: C. Alzugaray, op. cit. For different perceptions of national security see: A. Wolfers, 'National Security as an Ambiguous Symbol', *Political Science Quarterly*, LXVII, 4, December 1952, pp. 481–502; and *Estudio sobre los Conceptos de Seguridad: Informe al Secretario General*, UN, A/40/553, New York, 1985, both cited by C. Alzugaray, op. cit.
37. C. Alzugaray, op. cit.
38. M. Gorbachev, *La Perestroika y La Nueva Mentalidad para Nuestro País y para el Mundo Entero* (Editora Política: La Habana, 1988) pp. 179–80.
39. Michael C. Desch, 'Turning the Caribbean Flank: Sea-lane vulnerability

during a European War', *Survival*, Vol. XXIX, No. 6, (Nov.–Dec., 87), pp. 448–551.

40. Tad Szulc, *Fidel: A Critical Portrait*, Morrow & Co., New York, 1986, pp. 480–1. See Fidel Castro, 'Speech on the 2nd Anniversary of the Triumph of the Revolution in Civic Square', 2 January 1961, in *El Pensamiento de Fidel Castro. Selección Temática*, Tome I, Vol. 2, January 1959–April 1961, Editora Política, La Habana, 1983, pp. 631–2. At that moment, when the attack on Cuba was imminent, Fidel Castro said he was thinking not only of Cuba, which would be selfish, we think also, with sadness, of the sacrifices that an attack on our country would imply for other nations, the dangers it could imply for humanity because above men, above individuals are nations, and above nations is humanity.

41. The US has maintained the economic blockade since 1960 and has tried to impose a diplomatic blockade, which has failed completely.

42. See Fidel Castro, 'Closing Address at the 6th Congress of the Federation of Secondary School Students', La Habana, 8–12–84.

43. See 'Informe de Santa Fe' (Santa Fe Report), *Cuadernos Semestrales* (CIDE), No. 9 (First Semester, 1981), Mexico; Isabel Jaramillo, 'La estrategia intervencionista estadounidense hacia el Medio Oriente y en la Cuenca del Caribe', *Avances de Investigación*, (CEA), 18, (February 1983); 'J. Risquet responde . . .' (J. Risquet responds . . .) *Bohemia*, op. cit.

44. See Fidel Castro, 'Speech at the 1st of May Commemoration Ceremony', La Habana, 1980, *EDS/OR* (April–June, 1980–81).

45. See 'Acerca del Trabajo Político-Ideológico para la Defensa del País', Document approved by the 10th Plenary of the Cuban Communist Party Central Committee, 24–26 December 1984, *Granma* 4–2–85.

46. In this sense, the Vietnamese experience has been a basic element to consider. It must also be stressed that in 1981 President Fidel Castro referred to the need for Cuba to learn to defend itself and the need to rely on the collective effort of the people themselves to face a US act of aggression.

47. Fidel Castro, 'Speech at the Closing Ceremony of the 4th Congress of the UJC (Young Communist Union)', La Habana, 4–4–82. *EDS OR* (April–June, 1982). On the economy see Fidel Castro, 'Conclusiones en el VII Período Ordinario de Sesiones de la Asamblea Nacional del Poder Popular', *Bohemia*, January 1985.

48. C. Alzugaray, op. cit.

49. 'Risquet responde . . .', op. cit.

50. See Lars Schoultz, op. cit., pp. 260–7.

51. Fidel Castro, 'Encuentro Internacional de Intercambio de Ideas sobre los Problemas del Mundo Contemporáneo', *Granma*, 6–11–87.

52. In the Annual Report of *Diálogo Interamericano* (Interamerican Dialogue) the governments of the hemisphere are urged to reverse the tendency towards unilateralism which threatens peace and economic development and it calls on the industrialised countries to renew their support for the economic growth of the Latin American and Caribbean region.

53. In a recent study carried out jointly by Soviet and US experts, including

G. Arbatov, member of the Soviet Communist Party Central Committee and Director of the United States and Canada Institute of the Soviet Union's Academy of Sciences, and William Colby, ex-director of the CIA, among others, the proposal is made to demilitarise the Third World, limit programmes of military assistance to 'what is necessary for legitimate self-defence, and to deal with regional disputes mainly through international bodies, which would strengthen the role of the UN'.

Part II
Case Studies of Small State Militarisation

Part II

4 The Armed Forces in the Dominican Republic: Professionalisation and Politicisation*

Pablo A. Maríñez

INTRODUCTION

The Armed Forces have had a supreme influence on the political life of the Dominican Republic ever since the country achieved independence in the middle of the last century. But it is only this century, over a period of 56 years, that the military has, directly or indirectly, exercised political power. So, the related policy of professionalisation of the Armed Forces of the Dominican Republic is one of the themes on the military question which has aroused major interest on the part of national public opinion during the past few years.

Does such professionalisation imply the apoliticisation and institutionalisation of the Armed Forces? Were not the Chilean, Uruguayan and Argentinian Armed Forces, (to mention only three), the main examples of professionalisation in all of Latin America, and was it not precisely these which have demonstrated the greatest politicisation of the continent?

With respect to the Dominican Republic, the following questions occur to me: What type of professionalisation can be aspired to in a country where the military, in order to achieve the grade of professional, have to be instructed and trained in foreign schools or in their own country by foreign experts? What degree of professionalisation can be achieved in a country which depends on one single foreign supplier of arms, and which has not had the opportunity of elaborating or selecting its own security doctrine, which doctrine is imposed from abroad? And finally, what possibilities exist for the institutionalisation of the Armed Forces in a country where even the

* Translated from the Spanish by Elma Shelley.

State has not achieved this level in its political system, particularly with its civil servants in the State administration.

There are several degrees of professionalisation with different contents according to the particularities of development of the Armed Forces and the national and international historical context in which they are produced. From this perspective, I consider that the degree of professionalisation of the Armed Forces of the Dominican Republic does not include depoliticisation nor institutionalisation. On the contrary, professionalisation, given the historical context in which it occurs, implies greater politicisation of the military institutions. It is for this reason that the mentors of this policy have been very careful not to make reference to the North American influence in the very core of the national army, nor to outline the character of the national security doctrine, for to do so would be to manifest the degree of politicisation which professionalisation has implied. Also, the project of civic action of the Armed Forces has been presented to national public opinion as a humanitarian activity, totally divorced from politics, when in reality it constitutes a substantial part of the internal security doctrine, which is closely related to the degree of military professionalisation.

TRAINING, SUPPLY OF ARMS AND IDEOLOGY

After the military intervention of 1965 the US Government focused its attention on at least two basic aspects of the Dominican Republic Armed Forces: military training and the question of ideology. This task was under the Military Aid and Advisory Group (MAAG) whose numbers were increased substantially for these objectives while a significant number of Dominican Republic officers were selected to attend training courses in military schools situated mainly in the US and the Canal Zone.

In the years immediately following the military occupation, the control of the Dominican Republic Army was effectively exercised through members of the MAAG. David Fairchild, an official of USAID who lived in Santo Domingo from 1966 to 1967, would afterwards declare that 'if one wanted to know something about the Dominican Republic Armed Forces one would have to go first to the MAAG. If one called the military they would not know what to say. They would immediately put the question on hold and call Adviser of the MAAG' (Cuello, 1973, p. 96). In this vein, Alexander Firfer,

Director of USAID in the country during May 1965 (in September 1968 he was appointed AID Regional Director in Vietnam), indicates the following:

> On the other hand is the fact that the military is obviously sitting around waiting for the MAAG to tell them what to do. It is also obvious that the President has less power over the military than the MAAG. The Mission of 65 MAAG members live, eat, sleep with these fellows. The San Isidoro Military Base rarely has less than 10 North Americans about the place. And the amount of military aid totals some three and a half million dollars, which for such a small country means a lot of money. (Cuello, 1973, p. 99)

The total number of Dominican Republic soldiers who attended courses in US schools up to the mid-1980s and particularly in the period 1977–86, is not available, but the information that I have managed to obtain throws some light on the matter. From 1950–83 the Dominican Republic sent 4714 students to training schools in the US. From 1950–63 only 955 soldiers attended, whereas from 1964–79, 3262 students attended and from 1980–83, 496 participated. This represents an average of 73, 217 and 128 students per year, in each one of the three periods cited. From 1975–79, 268 Dominican Republic soldiers attended the Military School of the Americas, located at Fort Gulick in the Panama Canal Zone, of which at least 90 were instructed in counter-insurgency and 21 in military intelligence, including 6 in interrogation (Klare and Stein, 1978, pp. 168–9).

In 1973 a group of 10 US instructors operated in the Dominican Republic, the largest number registered for any Latin American country; these instructors taught courses in tactical operations for a period of 18 weeks. From 1969 to 1973 at least four Dominican Republic soldiers took courses in anti-terrorist training in the US Bombardment School in Los Fresnos, Texas. These were to be in charge of the operations of the para-police group that operated in the Dominican Republic precisely during those years, under the same name of the Democratic Anti-Communist and Anti-Terrorist Front, but which the people called 'The Gang', for in fact they operated like paid thugs. During 1969–73 alone, the para-police groups that operated in the country assassinated at least 329 persons (Gomez, 1984).

This intensification of the training of the Dominican Republic military, however, does not correspond with the supply of arms that the US provided. During the entire period after the US intervention the country's armament was not upgraded. I understand that this phenomenon is explained in the light of the new security doctrine encouraged by the US Government, according to which the national army was assigned the task of defending the ideological frontiers; in other words, the internal frontiers. The figures registered in the US Military Sales Programme for the Dominican Republic are extremely low; it seems that the major part of the armaments were acquired through financial arrangements and have consisted of weapons for internal repression and the provision of modern rifles. From 1970 to 1979, the country invested under $1.5 million in the importation of light arms (Cordero, n.d.).

While the training operation was being carried out, within the Dominican Republic Armed Forces an intense effort of anti-communist indoctrination was being developed, and the sector of the military Constitutionalists disarticulated, despite the fact that according to the Act of Reconciliation signed in 1965, they had to be reintegrated. Those who were not sent abroad to Diplomatic posts were retired or dismissed; many had to go into exile; others were assassinated. While the Constitutionalist officers were exposed to this situation, those who were outstanding for their servile attitude to the US troops in 1965–66 achieved the most important positions of command. Of the 43 generals of Balaguer's Government in 1978, at least 11 of them had demonstrated their subservience to the US Government during the period of the military occupation (Mariñez, 1986). That sector of the officer corps constituted the strongest support of Joaquin Balaguer during his 11 years in government, while at the same time serving as the conduit of communication between the Pentagon and the Dominican Republic Armed Forces.

Following the unfavorable results of the May 1978 presidential elections, this sector attempted a Coup d'Etat in favor of Balaguer. US intervention was not hesitant so immediately 'General Dennis McAuliffe, Chief of the Austral Command in Panama, telephoned General Beauchamp to advise him of the consequences the Coup would have' (Szulc, 1978, p. 7). The generals behind the Coup were forced to withdraw their orders and to negotiate with the successful candidate of the PRD. Later, President Antonio Guzmán took advantage of the presence of a US delegation of high-ranking officials to retire several of the generals involved in the failed coup. During the course of his 4 years government Guzmán sent into retirement a number of generals he found in active service, but promoted others to that rank.

However, at the end of the decade of the 1970s, US control of the Armed Forces had been consolidated to such an extent, at least ideologically, that the Pentagon was in a position to allow the sacrifice of some of the Dominican officers who had collaborated in the restructuring of the institutions of the Armed Forces. Their exit at that time represented no danger whatsoever to the political-military stability of the country, nor did the reincorporation of some Constitutionalist officers, as in fact did later occur. Thirteen years of intensive work of the part of the Pentagon in the Dominican Republic had been sufficient to evolve a new stage of the Armed Forces under the banners of professionalisation, depoliticisation and institutionalisation, in accordance with the process of democratisation that was inaugurated in 1978. New officers with a higher degree of professionalism in terms of capability and theoretical knowledge of counter-insurgency, assumed high-ranking military commands as would happen in the period 1978–86.

The flow of Dominican Republic officers and cadets attending training courses in US military schools was steady. At the same time, there was no lessening of exchange of awards, social functions, receptions, lunches, etc., offered for the officer members of the MAAG,[1] or the visits to the country made by US military personnel.[2] All of this can be interpreted as a simple expression of the good relations existing between two states. However, certain statements or behaviours of some of the Dominican Republic and visiting US officers would lead anyone to suspect that this was an example of a colonised army that had degraded itself by losing its true identity and coming to consider itself subject to the decisions of a foreign power. Many facts serve to illustrate this point: I will refer to some of them.

In March 1982, based on the news that the US planned to establish a military base on Haitian territory, the Secretary of State of the Dominican Republic Armed Forces, Lieutenant General Mario Imbert McGregor, declared the following in the national press: 'We have a base close by which is Cuba, a Soviet base; therefore I welcome the fact that the North Americans should approach closer, because the only thing that ensures democracy here and defends the system are the Americans' (*El Nuevo Diario*, 13 March 1982). A few months before, in October 1981, based on the demotion (from Admiral to the rank of Lieutenant Colonel of the Dominican Republic Navy) of retired officer Lajara Burgos, this Lieutenant General denounced the case to President Ronald Reagan in correspondence sent through the US Embassy in the country (*El Caribe*, 31 October

1981). This fact in itself is extraordinary, but assumes even greater dimensions when the petitioner was not sanctioned in any way for petitioning a foreign government to solve internal problems which are the sole province of the Dominican Republic's sovereignty.

On the other hand, we have the high number of US officers, Admirals and Generals, who visit the country frequently, and take the liberty of making statements on internal and external policy, as if they were in one of their colonies, without any Dominican Republic authority raising even the most elemental note of protest.[3]

THE RISE AND CONSEQUENCES OF ANTI-COMMUNISM

The death of Trujillo coincided with the reformulation of the US hemispheric security doctrine in which the counter-insurgency type of struggle displaced conventional warfare. During the period 1961–65, the advance of the counter-insurgent character within the institutions of the Armed Forces was not significant because, among other reasons, the military had been dragged into the partisan political struggle by the leaders of the Right. In the barracks these found an excellent breeding ground due to the anti-communist ideology existing in them which was reinforced by the new reformulation of the security doctrine.[4] In this context, after a military coup in September 1963, at the end of the same year the Armed Forces were obliged to confront a resurgence of guerilla activity in the country. In effect, during the last days of November 1963 six guerrilla fronts made up of 160 men appeared in various locations. In actual fact very few of them managed to organise themselves as such and to remain in the mountains for a significant period of time. If the Armed Forces had little counter-insurgency training, the guerrillas seemed to be even less prepared. According to a later statement by one of the fighters who managed to survive, '90 per cent of the comrades who went up to the mountains, had not handled a weapon, much less knew how to use it' (Raful, 1983, p. 711). This evaluation may be a little exaggerated but when at the end of 1963 the guerrillas decided to give themselves up to the troops, they were shot. However, the guerrilla uprising caused certain contradictions or at least created disaffection amongst politicians and some military personnel. An Air Force pilot refused to bomb the guerrillas and deserted with his plane to Puerto Rico; and a member of the Triumvirate that governed the country resigned his post in protest against the shooting of the young fighters.

In this way the new national security doctrine whose aim was the defense of internal frontiers had passed its first test. A preliminary evaluation would indicate that in the new context the military would involve itself more in political activity in the country.

In 1964 and during early 1965 corruption had reached its height in the Armed Forces on par with the continued influence in the barracks of political leaders. The military challenge in the barracks was expressed in the formation of rival groups. The San Cristobal group, led by Colonel Neit Nivar Seijas, made up of officers of the province whose name they adopted, was the one which had strongest ties, including family relationships, with the Trujillo family; the San Isidro Group, situated in the main Air Base in the country, was the group in which anti-communist ideology had penetrated most profoundly, at least at the level of the person who emerged as their leader, Colonel Elias Wessin y Wessin; and finally, a group of honest and national-istic military personnel was formed which opposed corruption and proposed the return to the constitutional regime of Juan Bosch. This group was led by Colonel Rafael Fernández Domínguez. The struggle between the first two groups heightened to the extend that in June 1964 the explosives of the 27 February Military Camp, con-trolled by the San Cristobal Group, were detonated with the aim of weakening it in terms of weaponry (*Ahora* No. 64, 20–6–64). It is within this military struggle that the insurrectional movement of 24 April 1965 arose, in which the Armed Forces institutions were not able to cope with the new strategy of popular struggle with which they were faced, and had to resort to US military troops. Only in this way was defeat avoided.[5]

One of the justifications given by Washington for intervening was that within the insurrection movement there was a group of 52 communists. The statement was laughable as some of the names of the list were duplicated, others were of persons who were outside of the country as well as of people who were already dead. However, this justification constituted the element that gave ideological force to the intervention and framed it within the US doctrine of hemispheric security: to avoid the expansion of communism in the world. The problem lay in that the main leaders of the constitutionalist move-ment, Colonel Caamaño Deñó and ex-President Juan Bosch, could not be suspected of being communists. Caamaño had studied in US military schools and led the main counter-subversive corps created by the US in the Dominican Republic; also his father had been an outstanding pro-Trujillo soldier who enrolled in the army during the military occupation of 1916–24 (Hermann, 1980). Bosch, for his part, had dedicated his life to the defence of representative democracy.

However, the same course of events modified the ideological concept of both leaders. Caamaño went to Cuba and from there prepared an armed expedition with which he intended to open a guerilla front in the country (Hermann, 1980); Bosch began to make harsh criticisms of imperialism and declared himself Marxist.[6] In this way, the April insurrection which had been classified as communist from its inception, in light of US interests, found its best empirical proof of the fact that communists, with a great talent for deception, had effectively infiltrated the country and constituted a real danger to democracy and particularly to the existence of the Armed Forces. For this reason, from 1966 the US military advisers and the different courses taken by the Dominican Republic troops and officers emphasised the ideological aspect of anti-communism. This position was to be reinforced within the Nixon national security doctrine which placed the causes of revolution in the sphere of subversion.

Over the past twenty years anti-communist propaganda has played an outstanding ideological role in the Armed Forces institutions, including the army barracks. During that time the existence of posters in the barracks with messages such as – 'Soldier: All those who do not believe in God are enemies of mankind, and Communists do not believe in God'; 'Soldier: Communism means backwardness, death, hunger and malnutrition' – became the norm (*El Sol*, 13–5–81).

There was no doubt that the Armed Forces, as in the best times of the Cold War, had declared war on communism,[7] which had to be fought on all fronts. For this reason Commissions composed of high-ranking officials were organised to tour the military installations in the country and to read out an anti-communist manifesto.[8] According to the officer corps of the Dominican Republic, in this war undertaken against communism the enemy had reached the barracks hence the need to detect them and to take steps to prevent their continued infiltration. With this objective in mind, special measures were taken to screen the aspiring recruits to the Armed Forces. These officers managed to prove that indeed some of the applicants were 'labeled as communist activists' (*Listin Diario*, 12–9–81) and so it was decided that 'in-depth screening would be carried out constantly within the ranks of the armed forces institutions', giving rise to 'dishonorable discharge of several agents of that institution who were linked with marxist doctrine' (*Ultima Hora*, 12–9–81).

ADVANCE OF COUNTER-INSURGENCY PLANS

After the US military intervention at least three events occurred from which it is possible to visualise the character of the counter-insurgency plans that the Dominican Republic Armed Forces were able to put in practice at any given time.

The first occurred in 1972 when an offensive was launched against a young, armed group, members of the so-called Resistance Commandos who, as was later known, intended to prepare an urban guerrilla front in conjunction with the one that Caamaño would later establish in the mountains of the Dominican Republic. Two aspects of the confrontation of January 1972 were evident. One of them was the strategy of the Dominican Republic Armed Forces of launching a massive attack right from the start in order to annihilate the enemy immediately. The army and the police mobilised hundreds of soldiers[9] armed with high powered rifles, mortars, 105 millimeter cannons, tanks, assault vehicles, helicopters and reconnaissance planes against a group of six guerrillas. It was also rumored that they were aided by the US military from Puerto Rican bases. The other aspect was the dubious preparation of government troops, if one considers their superiority in terms of weapons, and numbers, and the factor of surprise. They had approached and surprised the guerrilla group when the latter were still in the stage of preparation and in a place not of their choosing for the battle. In spite of these favourable elements, the Armed Forces had to fight for several hours and even suffered a high number of casualties.

The second event took place in February 1973 when a group of six combatants under the leadership of Caamaño Deñó disembarked in the country in order to open a guerrilla front. With regard to the weaponry used by the armed forces – which of course included the most modern in existence in the country – and by the participating counter-insurgency battalions, perhaps the most important aspect to be considered was that of the immediate measures undertaken on the national level, above all in the urban centers. The country was virtually militarised, the National University closed, the main roads and places with access to the capital city were under the control of counter-insurgency troops; simultaneous to these operations, the homes of the main political, union, student and general opposition leaders were raided and they were taken prisoner. Communication links were under strict security measures, etc. In this way potential sympathisers were prevented from giving any sort of support to the struggle and, in fact, groupings of the Left did not have time to react to the events. When they realised what had happened they went on the defensive, that is to say, they sought a safe refuge in order to avoid being captured.

Under these conditions and in spite of having aroused sympathy among the peasant population of the area, according to the testimony of one of the survivors, the guerrilla uprising did not manage to get past the initial stage and, after a few battles, was defeated in a matter of weeks. Only two members of the armed invasion managed to remain alive (Hermann, 1980).

The third event occurred on two separate dates – April 1984 and January–February 1985. On the first, a mass demonstration took place to protest the high cost of living, caused in part by the conditions imposed by the IMF. The outcome of three days of popular uprising was more than one hundred dead and hundreds wounded. Because the demonstration was spontaneous and unexpected, the security forces were not able to act with the speed that the occasion demanded. On the first day the national police went out on the streets, and although they were a militarised police force with counter-insurgency battalions, they were unable to contain the demonstration. On the second day the army brought out their special counter-insurgency battalions and only in this way was the situation controlled (Mariñez, 1986a).

In January 1985, before the announcement of the signing of a Stand-by Agreement between the government and the IMF, the Armed Forces elaborated a National Counter-Insurgency Plan to be put into practice as soon as the above-mentioned Agreement was signed. The plan included, *inter alia*, the following:

1. Drawing maps of the different rapid access routes to marginalised neighbourhoods and other areas considered dangerous to the military.
2. Aerial photographs of marginalised neighbourhoods, cane fields, wooded areas, etc. in order to study carefully those places and their location. And
3. A study of the penetration of mobile units of the army corps in zones where access was difficult.

Given these security measures, the demonstrations did not take place, at least not on the date announced. In fact the people turned to a new method of struggle, for which the counter-insurgency plans were inoperable. Between 28 January and 10 February more than 100 partial strikes, organised by the Popular Struggle Committees (CLP), took place throughout the whole country. The first of these was staged in the marginalised neighbourhoods of the capital, but immediately spread to other provinces, and on 11 February the National Coordinating Committee of Popular Organisations, made up of more than 50 entities, 32 of which were CLP, called a 24 hour general strike and was able to paralyse 90 per cent of the country's activities. The elite counter-insurgency battalions – outstanding among which were the 'Green Berets', the 'Red Berets', the 'Mountain Hunters' and the 'Macheteros', as well as the plans which had been drawn up and the weaponry that was mobilised – were unable to abort the general strike.

Faced with such an organised demonstration, the President of the Republic was obliged to announce the revision of some economic measures, basically those related to the price increases which had been decreed for certain food items, and to promise new social service measures.

The military high command took advantage of this evident loss of popular support for government to play a greater role in the political life of the country, as well as to gain some benefits for their institution which were translated basically into the acquisition of new armaments such as combat planes, patrol launches, etc.

THE PROGRAMME OF CIVIC ACTION

The civic action activities of the Armed Forces began in 1961 but it was only after the US intervention in the mid-1960s that they expanded and acquired a true national aspect. This programme is registered within the security doctrine that the US articulated and exported to other countries to form part of the counter-insurgency strategy.

According to Joseph Comblin, civic action is:

a defence against subversion; it is preventive action and it is also a response. The military is called upon to undertake public works for the welfare of the population (roads, public buildings), health services, social services, etc. In summary, civic action consists of undertaking governmental tasks. Thanks to the conceptualization of this civic action, the military is convinced that only they are capable of organizing the development of the country. (Comblin, 1978, p. 169)

Comblin points out that apart from the social assistance given by the Armed Forces to 'people seduced by revolution, the civic-military action would show them that the government was more efficient than the revolution in addressing their needs' (p. 58).

The majority of the news articles that appear in the Dominican Republic on the subject of the civic action undertaken by the military, generally present it as a simple humanitarian act on the part of the armed services for the good of the civilian population. However, in at least one article in the Armed Forces magazine, the true counter-insurgency character of the project is set out. This article points out that the increase in civic action work by the Armed Forces in the country of the past few years 'has tended to improve living standards of many sectors of our population and is one of the main means of preventing subversion contributing, at the same time, to the strengthening of relations between the civilian and military populations'.[10] What the author of the article does not point out is that this strengthening of relations has a military intelligence objective, in that the civic action allows the army not only to obtain the approval of the population, but also to uncover existing problems and therefore to be able to take preventive measures.

The civic action project in the country is made up of two basic sections; that is, public welfare activities that are carried out by 'specialist personnel (engineers, communications technicians, etc.)' and various activities in areas such as education, health and sports. (EOPR, 1972, pp. 105–7). As will be observed, the execution of this project implies a close relationship between civic action and the professionalisation of the Armed Forces. The former is subject to the latter. If the Armed Forces rely on a low level of technicians and members of various professions (educators, doctors, engineers, etc.) the civic action would remain at the level of donations, delivery and distribution of foodstuff, clothing and other articles of use to the civilian population. The Dominican Republic has at least seven officers who have attended civic action courses at the *Escuela de las Américas* in the Panama Canal Zone, during the period 1970–75 (Klare and Stein, 1978, pp. 168–9).

If the civic action project is not a simple humanitarian activity but forms part of the security doctrine, its execution on a national level corresponds to the needs of the country's counter-insurgency strategy, and will therefore not be a casual matter. In this sense, apart from the incomplete information available to me, I perceive clearly at least two aspects. The first is that the major percentage of the civic action programme has been concentrated in the rural areas, while the minor part corresponding to urban areas has been directed at marginal neighbourhoods. The second aspect is that the rural population of the south, followed by the north-central area, is notoriously privileged; the eastern area has been less fortunate. If we reflect on this, we find that the privileged areas, in terms of the civic action, are those which were the scene of armed struggle during the last four decades, or which at least have been chosen as a disembarcation point by fighting groups of exiles.[11] On the other hand, the eastern region has experienced no armed movements, nor has it been a disembarcation point, since the first US military occupation (1916–24), when the rebels called 'Gavilleros' operated there. In addition to this, one would have to ascertain the importance of the peasant movements in the regions and specific localities in which the greatest concentration of civic action has occurred.

Finally, the civic action project carried out in the country has relegated to second place the 'works of public welfare' and has focused fundamentally on the so-called 'various activities'. In these, great importance has been placed on the tasks of donations (food, clothing, shoes, etc.); on services such as soup kitchens (in 1979 the latter was distributing 'a monthly average of 1 million food rations among underprivileged persons');[12] on literacy training (in 1981 a total of 21,310 persons were made literate); on vocational training (in 1982 21,947 young people graduated with various skills);[13] and finally, on health related activities such as immunisation, dental services, donations of medicines, etc.

OTHER ASPECTS OF THE SECURITY DOCTRINE

There are two other aspects which I wish to touch on briefly – the defence of national borders and natural disasters. I have attempted to find the elements which make up the security doctrine on national borders, outside of the available documentation, but this has not been possible. Nor has it been possible with respect to Haiti, a country which I suppose should occupy an outstanding position for the Dominican Republic Armed Forces,[14] given its historical background and being the only country with which the Dominican Republic has borders.

With the type of weapons existing in the country and the training that the Dominican Republic military receives, tending towards counter-insurgency, it is very difficult for them to have a defence strategy in case of an external attack.

Do the Dominican Republic Armed Forces rely on US military defence in case of an external attack? If we subscribe to the actual security doctrine supported by the US and to the strategic location occupied by the country, we would be inclined to think that, in effect, such reliance exists. With respect to natural disasters, if we take into account the role played by the Armed Forces during the disasters of Hurricane David and the storm Frederick in 1979, when thousands of people died and losses were estimated at hundreds of millions of dollars, I also would have to conclude that the Armed Forces lack a real defence plan for cases such as these.[15] The substantial part of the rescue operation, distribution of food and evaluation of the disaster, was carried out by 275 US pilots (including 60 members of the Puerto Rican National Guard), who worked intensively in the country and who utilised Hercules C-130 and UH-1 rescue helicopters, as well as other transport and rescue vehicles (*El Sol*, 13–9–79). On that occasion the Dominican Republic government, under pressure from the US Embassy, refused the help offered by Cuba.

THE ARMED FORCES UNDER BALAGUER

Up until the beginning of this century, the Dominican Republic Armed Forces did not display even the most elemental principles of a professional army. Neither had they achieved a national character. Its members not only lacked adequate uniforms and arms, but also received their salaries with irregularity, which obliged some of its members to dedicate themselves to other activities outside of the army in order to ensure their livelihood. In turn, the political strife between regional factions in a society in which the State had not yet managed to consolidate itself and to acquire a true national character, was expressed in the Armed Forces, which could not be an exception within the society. They also were broken up into regional factions and participated in the political disputes over the control of power.

However, during the dictatorship of Trujillo, above all in the last 15 years, the Armed Forces achieved considerable development. Trujillo founded the infrastructural bases on which the present Dominican Republic Armed Forces institutions would rest. However, professionalisation of the Armed Forces, in the modern sense of the term, was far from being achieved. The dictatorial regime itself obstructed this possibility. With the aim of ensuring greater loyalty to his person, Trujillo gave preference to the recruitment of the peasantry and illiterates in general to the Armed Forces. At the beginning of the 1959s, the Dictator even prohibited soldiers from studying at the University (Alvarez, 1978, p. 2). His objective was to keep the Armed Forces as far away as possible from the civilian population; and above all to prevent them from having access to specific studies in order to avoid the possibility of soldiers being influenced by political ideas opposed to the regime. Under these conditions, understandably, soldiers could only acquire a certain degree of education within the military academies and the training offered in them was very limited; only two years of study was required to become a cadet, later increased to four years.

The Armed Forces constituted, in fact, the principal instrument of domination at the service of Trujillo, but the latter was very expert with regard to espionage, control and repression, including torture of political prisoners. In the 1950s the much feared Military Intelligence Service (SIM) was created, which, as well as controlling the same Armed Forces institutions 'attempted to link and compromise the total Armed Forces in criminal acts through political repression' (Valera Benítez, 1984, p. 22), for which its members were made to spend a period of training in the torture chambers of the dictatorship, with the aim of hardening them and making them feel committed to the regime of Trujillo (Valera Benítez, 1984, p. 25). Outside of this political task of a police nature, one could not say that the Armed Forces achieved any training that would permit the army to assume political power. Quoting Bartlow Martin, following the fall of Trujillo in 1961, 'the military did not want to govern. They understood nothing of this. They only knew that they hated and feared communists' (p. 114). The very fact that the Armed Forces were an instrument of political domination at the service of a leader, prevented them from having a real institutional character. Trujillo had his relatives and friends appointed to high military posts (Ganlindez, 1956, p. 313).[16]

Understandably, the degree of professionalisation within the Armed Forces until 1961 was extremely precarious, and was practically reduced to the permanency of its members in the occupation of bearing arms, discipline and specialised knowledge of the use and management of the instrument with which they exercised legitimate violence.

During the period of transition between 1961 and 1965 – one of the periods of greatest political instability in the country and which in turn would have the deepest repercussions within the Armed Forces is when the first steps were taken towards a true process of modernisation, which was to be consolidated after 1966, fundamentally in terms of training and the formation of a military doctrine of war. But this process of modernisation would have the particularity of being assumed, in terms of implementation and evaluation, by foreign forces, which would imply a denationalisation of the Armed Forces on the ideological level. During this period, institutionalisation achieved no advances, in that, on the political level, the anti-communist indoctrination was heightened,[17] and the military barracks were flooded with the propaganda and intrigue of the political parties. It is within this framework of professionalisation that the Armed Forces were obliged to hand over the government to a triumvirate of civilians after the Coup d'Etat of 1963. At that time the Armed Forces did not have military personnel trained for the army to take over, for example, the office of Secretary of State, the leadership and management of State agencies and enterprises, as in later years they were able to do.

After 1966, the professionalisation process would be deepened and consolidated during subsequent years. This would take place within the context of a demoralised army, as, if it were not for US intervention, it would have admitted defeat in the armed confrontation. For this reason, the US army would acquire greater authority in the development of its restructuring plan, assessment and training aimed at professionalisation.[18] However, the training offered, in accordance with the needs of the new model of the US doctrine, was not limited to the strictly military aspect, but encompassed political and administrative training in such a way that the Armed Forces relied on teams of professionals prepared to take on the tasks which, up to that time, had been reserved for civilians.

The internal conditions of the country were to make possible the development of this project. On the political level, the conservative Reform Party, under the leadership of Joaquin Balaguer, achieved hegemony among the different sectors of the oligarchy and the local bourgeoisie, thus displacing the other right-wing parties that proliferated in the country up to that time. Within the barracks also the influence of other political organisations was displaced, leaving the government party with a virtual monopoly within the Armed Forces. In addition, of the three military groups that had been in conflict over the control of the Armed Forces, the Constitutionalists were effectively excluded. For this reason only the San Cristobal and San Isidro Groups remained within the barracks and became known as the Neit Nivar Seijas Group and the Pérez y Pérez Group respectively, an allusion to their respective leaders, and whose conflicts would be instrumental in permitting President Balaguer to achieve equilibrium within the Armed Forces and in this way avoid any coup attempt. For greater security, those officers who through their political ambitions, represented a potential danger to military stability, that is to say, to the political stability of the government (as would be the case of the controversial General Elias Wessin y Wessin), were retired.

In this way, perhaps for the first time in the history of the Dominican Republic, the barracks became an extension of the government party; where high-ranking officers made political speeches in support of the President, above all during electoral campaigns; propaganda of the Reform Party was pasted up in army camps, and soldiers patrolled the streets carrying that Party's flag. This was one of the most visible manifestations of the politicisation of the Armed Forces, and generated the greatest protest on the part of the population as well as criticism from the other political parties.

However, a more significant form of politicisation, though less noticeable, was occurring: the participation of the military in political decision-making of the state administration. It was during Balaguer's government that the military for the first time and in a systematic and constant manner, were able to participate directly in the state apparatus, in ways that traditionally had been reserved for civilians. Some secretariats of the state, such as the Foreign Affairs Secretariat of the Presidency, and certain state agencies such as the Agrarian Reform Institute, were occupied by active or retired generals; also, high-ranking officers became managers of some state enterprises. This is perhaps the most novel and important aspect that the professionalisation and politicisation process of the Armed Forces presented during the twelve years of Balaguer's government. The state positions occupied by military personnel, as well as the technical and intellectual training they required, in the main were fundamentally of a political character. In this manner, the Armed Forces entered a new phase through which were created the conditions for them to cease being used politically by the governing party. The military found themselves able to participate in the political life of the nation, at the service of a party, or if necessary, as an independent institution.

This process of professionalisation of the Armed Forces cannot be separated from the new model of capitalist accumulation that had begun to develop during the government of Joaquin Balaguer. After 1966, North American capital investments in the country increased considerably; various sectors of the national economy, among them mining, finance and to a large extent industry, came under the control of transnational capital. For this reason, within the framework of foreign capital the need arose to form military cadres not only with counter-insurgency training, but also with the ability to maintain the functioning of the political and economic life of the country, at least at the most vital levels, if this should become necessary. It is a fact also that for the first time the military was given the opportunity of participating in a significant way in the process of capitalist accumulation. Consequently, its integration and commitment to the Balaguer government was not only politically and ideologically motivated, but economically as well. As a result of the corruption and various mechanisms of political influence, dozens of high-ranking officers became powerful millionaires, with the added novelty that they did not limit themselves to investing in the agricultural sector as had traditionally occurred, but began to invest in some industrial areas, in commercial and financial activities.

While the process of professionalisation of the Armed Forces advanced, the level of politicisation was not limited to the previously indicated aspects of active participation with the government party and traditional anti-communist indoctrination, but included terrorism. In effect, motivated by a McCarthy-type anti-communism, the Armed Forces, particularly the national police force, became a machinery of planned criminality, to the point where the major part of a whole generation of Marxist leaders and activists were eliminated.

Contrary to what occurred during the Trujillo dictatorship, when he made military personnel participate in torture and criminal activities in order to commit them to his policy, in this new phase the Armed Forces acted *motu propio*, that is to say, within a general plan, under US supervision. These repressive tasks, which formed part of the counter-insurgency and of the preventive war strategies, seem to have played an outstanding role in the system of promotion and upward mobility within the military. The numbers of military persons who were promoted after having been identified as guilty of some political crimes are not few.[19] None has been charged or brought to justice, and when the Government was obliged to do so because of public pressure, they were soon set free and, what is more, given greater privileges. This situation, together with the other elements of public order already pointed out, seems to constitute the greatest obstacle to compliance with the established system of promotions, as well as the organic law of the Armed Forces.

In certain aspects, Balaguer managed this institution by the same method applied by Trujillo, that of rotating military commands, promotion or retirement, for reasons of a partisan political nature, with the intention of maintaining power or of creating favourable conditions that would facilitate his presidential re-election. For this reason, high-ranking officers who demonstrated political loyalty were not only promoted rapidly but had high commands rotated between them; some of them even occupied the same command more than once. On the other hand, other officers who were not outstanding in the area of planned criminality or who did not 'manifest absolute loyalty to his policy, spent more than ten years in the same rank, even though they attained sufficient merits for promotion, that is if the organic law had been complied with.[20] This situation of privilege and political affiliation of high-ranking officers with Balaguer continued after 1978, when he was electorally defeated, with the incorporation of some officers, in a retired capacity, into the Reform Party, where they carried out militant political activities; others preferred to establish their own political parties, although always allied with Balaguer.

PROFILE OF PROFESSIONALISATION IN THE GOVERNMENT OF THE PRD

The advances achieved by the *Partido Revolucionario Dominicano* (PRD) in the period 1978–86 in its policy to develop true professionalisation of the Armed Forces, is a far cry from that which the Government has announced. However, some achievements have been made, although very few of these tend to modify substantially the profile of professionalisation.

To the existence of modern hospitals, a radio station, recreational clubs and residential neighbourhoods for military personnel, has been lately added inauguration of an army museum and a social security institution. These contribute, without a doubt to giving the Armed Forces greater independence from civilian institutions, which constitutes one of the aims of professionalisation. But perhaps more important are the advances achieved in academic military training. The study plans have undergone modification, to include such subjects as Constitutional Law and Human Rights, among others. The number of military personnel that has to go abroad to study will possibly decrease in the coming years due to the inauguration of new academies, among them one for the Air Force and another high level one from which officers of the rank of Major will graduate. However, we understand that professionalisation of the Armed Forces, in spite of the advances pointed out, will experience great difficulties in achieving major advances if the existing pattern of recruitment is not modified.[21] This consists of a traditional system of recommendation in which credits for studies seem to be of little importance. The emphasis placed on high level academies, of maintaining existing conditions, could give rise to stratification within the Armed Forces, where soldiers have little access to officer rank, which would be reserved only for those who join up through the cadet academies. Only the police force seems to have introduced some important requirements for those who aspire to join it.

With regard to military hardware, for many decades and until mid-1984, no important renovation had been carried out. However, the government acquired some Coast Guard launches in 1974 which allowed greater control of the coastal areas of the Dominican Republic.[22] Some Dragonfly and A-37 aircraft have also been acquired which are destined to substitute the obsolete air defence that consisted of 9 P-51 planes dating from World War II. During the past 25 years only twelve T 34B planes, used for training students, were acquired, according to the military authorities. The P-51s were sold to a US company as museum pieces.

On the political level, with the government of the PRD the Armed Forces abandoned the role they had developed as a machinery of planned criminality to which I have referred; also political activism, which was exercised in the barracks in favour of the government party, has been modified. However, statements of an evidently partisan political nature, generally used as a means of achieving certain political and economic privileges from the executive power, continue to be made by high-ranking officers. They have not abandoned the practice of a high-ranking officer of the Armed Forces accompanying the President of the Republic when he goes on tour or makes a public statement, as was done during the Balaguer regime.

In his frequent visits to military camps the same President habitually praises the professionalisation of the Armed Forces, but in fact what he does is take advantage of such opportunities to engage in political propaganda in favour of the government party of his own self.[23]

The inclusion of military cadres in state positions has continued at a constant pace.[24] In 1980 there were at least 19 high-ranking officers carrying out administrative functions in various State institutions and four officers (two of them retired with diplomatic posts at Ambassadorial level) (Rivas, 1980). But more significant than these isolated cases is the role of planning and coordination that the Armed Forces have begun to play in some areas of the national economy; or the demonstrated ability that they have to replace the service of certain professional or non-professional civilian sectors of the country. At the end of 1982 the Dominican Republic cement factory was militarised and all its workers laid off. The reason given was that it was operating at a loss for want of planning. In a very short time the factory began to function within a capitalist framework. In May 1985, when the Dominican Republic Medical Association went on strike demanding salary increases and improved working conditions, the government made military hospitals available to the general public and so neutralised the strike's effect.

As will be observed, the so-called depoliticization of the Armed Forces that the PRD proclaims has managed to circumscribe the elimination of planned criminality and, fundamentally, to tone down the blatant forms of military support for the government party. The other elements of a political nature, including the anti-communist campaigns in the barracks, have not been modified in any way.[25] That is to say, what the PRD has achieved, at least in part, has been to reduce substantially the partisan activism in the barracks, but not the politicisation of the same.

In 1976, during the regime of Joaquin Balaguer, a Brigadier General stated in a speech that 'the apoliticism that certain sectors wish to inculcate in us is an outdated concept, it is as out of place as the spear or the arrow on the battle field'. This same General, who was outstanding for his political speeches in praise of the Presidents, among other things, was later to be appointed to the post of Secretary of State for the Armed Forces by Salvador Jorge Blanco, and after his retirement at the end of the PRD's term of office, indicated his intention to work in the political arena with ex-President Salvador Jorge Blanco. He would follow the same path taken by other high-ranking officers with ex-President Joaquin Balaguer.

With regard to the institutional aspect of the Armed Forces, in spite of everything that has been said to be achieved, no real achievements whatever seem to have been attained. It is true that the frequent transfers no longer take place neither does a high-ranking elite exist that used to capture all the high commands. Yet the promotion and retirement of military personnel continues to be a preserve of the President of the Republic and is hardly ever carried out in accordance with the organic law of the Armed Forces. Promotions and retirements take place at any time during the year, on an individual or group basis, on many occasions by Presidential Decree. At the end of 1985 Jorge Blanco justified the mass retirement of more than 90 officers on the grounds that there had been a bottleneck in the military hierarchy that prevented the promotion of new officers. If his reasons were correct one would have to arrive at the conclusion that the promotion system is inoperative, in that it does not permit upward mobility based on length of service, training, etc.

The President of the Republic continues to manage the Armed Forces using the same criteria with which he operates the civil state sector, where the merit system does not exist. Professional merit is preceded by political affiliation. It is for this reason that changes of government produce massive lay-offs of employees. With respect to the Armed Forces, each new government reinstates the officers of its political preference who the previous administration had retired. This explains the large number of officers who have been promoted and retired in the past twenty years. Only the government of the Revolutionary Dominican Party (PRD) retired close to one hundred generals[26] and at the same time promoted a comparable number to that rank over an eight year period.

Notes

1. See *Revista de las Fuerzas Armadas*, publication of the State Secretariat of the Armed Forces of the Dominican Republic from 1975 to 1983.
2. See *Revista de las Fuerzas Armadas* from 1967 to 1983.
3. Ex-President Juan Bosch referred to the visit to the country made in February 1980 by General Robert Schweitzer, Director of Strategy,

Plans and Policy of the US Army and said the following: 'If a general of another nationality were to arrive in Washington and behaved in the way General Schweitzer behaved in Santo Domingo, President Carter would not have received him.' (*El Sol*, 5–2–80). In March of 1985 Admiral Wesley McDonald, Chief of the Atlantic Fleet and US Naval Commander, visited the Dominican Republic and was asked by a journalist if the US would be prepared to intervene again in the country. He stated that intervention could not be discounted 'depending on the scenario present at a given time, especially if the elected government of the day requested assistance. There are many variables that make it impossible to answer the question. There are many points in the questions that I as a military officer could not answer at this time . . .' (*El Nacional*, 21–3–85).

4. The best collection of documents, articles and communiqués that reveals the anti-communist position of the Dominican Republic Armed Forces during the period 1961–62, was compiled by that institution.

5. An ample bibliography has been compiled on the US military intervention of 1965, the following may be cited: (Gleijeses, 1985; Kurszman, 1966; Lowenthal, 1977; Moreno, 1973; Ricardi, 1974; Selser, 1966; Slater, 1976; Szulc, n.d.). For a wider bibliographic reference see (Maríñez, 1985).

6. In 1977, Bosch, responding to a question on how US propaganda contributed to his becoming a marxist, stated that 'All this induced me to read Marx and Engels, because if they accused me of being a marxist without my knowing what marxism was, I should study it to know on what the accusations were based, and on reading Marx and Engels I realised that Marxism was historic truth, true philosophy, true theory and finally the universal truth. I must confess that I have to thank also the dirty propaganda of the North Americans for calling my attention to Marxism; and I am grateful because knowledge of marxism has made me a new man; new in terms of ideas, in my concept of life and the world, as well as physiologically because the renewal of the thinking mechanism in one's head reflects a renewal of the whole body' (Grimaldi, 1985, p. 60).

7. In April 1981 the Chief of Staff of the national army stated that the communists are 'the leaders and messiahs of those who proclaim that they must destroy the Armed Forces' (*El Sol*, 29–4–81). Three months before, in January of that year, the Secretary of State of the Armed Forces stated 'it is not true that the military was going to put attacks on communists on hold . . . as the Armed Forces we have to defend ourselves, it is the communist leaders who affirm that in order to win they must first destroy the Armed Forces and if they proceed in this manner they are not our friends'.

8. During his visit to the country in 1981, Vice-President Bush launched an attack on communism and especially on Fidel Castro. Forty-eight hours after his departure an Armed Forces Commission of high-ranking officers initiated a tour of the barracks carrying with them the same anti-communist line (*Ultima Hora*, 15–10–81).

9. According to the then Chief of Police, General Neit Nivar Seijas, 250 men were used in the operation of which only 30 men saw action, 'but what the journalists who were on the scene saw of the events appeared to

them to deal with thousands of soldiers and police. Uniformed police and secret service, as well as Special Operations, members of the San Cristobal battalion and the First Brigade together with forces of San Isidro participated'. (*Ahora*, No. 427, 17–1–72).

10. 'Breve Bosquejo de la Acción Cívica de las Fuerzas Armadas'. *Magazine of the Armed Forces*, No. 188, June 1972. The article appears signed with the initials EOPR, p. 106.

11. The anti-Trujillo expedition of 1949 took place in Luperon, Puerto Plata province on the north coast of the country (Arvelo, 1982); the 1959 expedition took place in three different places, Constanza in the Central Cordillera and on the north coast province of Puerto Plata, Maimon and Estero Hondo (Hermann, 1980; Delancer, 1979; Vargas, 1981); the guerrilla action of 1963 took place in the Cordillera Central, although seven political-guerrilla zones existed which covered practically the entire country (Despradel, 1983); Caamaño's guerrilla landing took place on the south coast in Playa Caracoles, Ocoa Bay (Hermann, 1980); a second guerrilla landing made up of some of the survivors of the first, also took place on the south coast (*Ahora*, No. 605, 16–6–75).

12. In March 1985, based on a series of student protests demanding the re-establishment of university dining-room service, the Armed Forces offered to supply 'technical personnel and all the machinery necessary to make functional the dining-room of the Autonomous University of Santo Domingo'. The collaboration was offered through the administrator of the Armed Forces Dining Rooms, (*Hoy*, 2–3–86).

13. The Vocational Schools were founded in 1966 under an agreement between the government of the Dominican Republic and the International Agency for Progress. Originally the Vocational Schools were aimed at offering a career to military personnel close to retirement, so that they could enter civilian society with greater ease. Later the Vocational Schools opened their doors to the civilian population, a large percentage of which entered. There are twelve Vocational School Centers from which more than two thousand graduate annually, in more than 20 different areas, amongst which are: arts and crafts, weaving, bricklaying, plumbing, industrial soldering, industrial sewing, nursing, painting and decorating, cosmetology, etc.

14. It is true that the frontier region is considerably militarised with barracks and forts; also the third and fourth army brigades are located fairly close to the frontier.

15. According to the ex-Secretary of the Armed Forces, Lieutenant General Manuel Antonio Cuervo Gomez, the Armed Forces 'have elaborated contingency plans in the case of a natural disaster. These plans are revised periodically, up-dated and put in force, according to the magnitude of the event that produces the disaster' (*Magazine of the Armed Forces*, No. 284, April–June, 1985, p. 11). Although the contingency plans have been put in place they have not been outstanding in their effectiveness.

16. In spite of this, during the dictatorship some military conspiracies took place which were discovered by Trujillo's espionage service. In a July 1946 report from the US Embassy in the Dominican Republic to the US

Secretary of State, it was reported that the army troop plans to bring down the government 'were frustrated by the arrest of the officers and civilians involved . . . The plan was to take the General Andrews airport and the Fort Ozam arsenal. It was hoped that by controlling the munitions in the fort, the Dominican Republic army would be rapidly dominated and that large sections of the army would assist the troops that had revolted . . . It is understood that each one of the officers involved selected two soldiers to help them in the uprising and that each soldier in turn selected three others and that this chain was maintained to induce a considerable number of soldiers to assist in the uprising . . . It is said that thirty soldiers were executed shortly after the 'trial' and that the Artillery company was disbanded and its troops divided among various army units across the country' (Vega, 1982, p. 309). It is very difficult to obtain information on this type of activity as the media at that time did not gather it and the conspirators in the main lost their lives. However, subsequently the names of other military personnel who also participated in some plots were discovered.

17. The arrival of Batista to the Dominican Republic after his overthrow in Cuba in January 1959, considerably influenced the anti-communist propaganda in the Dominican Republic barracks. Batista and his companions gave several accounts of executions of Cuban military personnel by the revolutionary forces led by Fidel Castro.

18. 'The National Army of the Dominican Republic is made up of Brigades, Battalions, Companies, Platoons and Squadrons. The Brigades consist of two or four Battalions and are made up of approximately 600 members. The Battalions consist of two or four Companies made up of approximately 144 members. The Companies in turn comprise two to four Platoons, the latter comprising three or four Squadrons of approximately 9 men: 8 men led by a Corporal. This number of men can vary according to tactical organization' (Brea Franco, 1983, p. 424). The army is made up of 4 Brigades, a general office of military training, a presidential guard and specialised battalions; the Navy with two naval bases is made up of the Office of Chief of Staff as well as three major sections: general command; the air force is structured like the army and has two air bases (Brea Franco, 1983, pp. 424–6).

19. This procedure seems to have been going on for a long time in the country, Bosch states that 'After Trujillo assumed power it was easy to get to the point where one day during a pro-Trujillo demonstration, for example, an enemy was killed. In his last days Trujillo used to ask an officer, out of the blue, 'How many have you killed?' He did this when he invited officers to lunch or dine with him' (Bosch, 1964, p. 192). In 1970, Balaguer, trying to justify a series of political crimes committed in the country, stated the following: 'It is not a secret to anyone that the Police force was infiltrated during a certain period by a large number of common delinquents who were incorporated into the force under the false assumption that it was easier to ensure public order with the cooperation of these delinquents rather than with their submission to the law by means of physical force and coercive constraints. Many of the criminal acts which have caused great consternation among the citizens,

were perpetrated by these delinquents in uniform, who, for the commission of these crimes, acted under the protection of the impunity that their ties with the police force afforded them' (Balaguer, 1979, p. 107).

20. 'Military rank will be granted by means of a rigorous hierarchical scale, for years of service and exceptionally for merit, under conditions indicated in the present law and in the relevant regulations' (Article 72); In peace time the minimum period of effective service in the rank considered appropriate for promotion is the following: Cadet and Marine Guard, 4 years; Second Lieutenant and Frigate Ensing, 3 years; First Lieutenant, 4 years; Major and Captain, 3 years; Lieutenant Colonel and Frigate Captain, 3 years; Colonel and Navy Captain, 4 years; Brigadier General and Admiral, 3 years; Mayor General and Vice-Admiral, 4 years. (Organic Law of the Armed Forces, No. 873, 1978, *Official Gazette* No. 9487).

21. 'Entry to the Armed Forces shall be voluntary in peace time and compulsory in time of war or civil disorder at which time total or partial mobilisation will be decreed' (Article 30); 'Entry by enlistment will be made under contract between the Dominican Republic represented by the respective Chief of Staff and the enlistee, who will be obliged to serve for a period of four (4) years. All members of the Armed Forces who have completed the period of enlistment and who wish to re-enlist must do so through the same unit to which they were attached. In no instance will members who have completed their period of enlistment in another branch of the armed forces or who have been discharged for any reason be admitted to the ranks of the armed forces' (Article 32); 'Entry to the Armed Forces as Officer, Cadet or Marine Guard will be by appointment issued by the Executive Powers, in accordance with the requirements set out in this law' (Article 37). (Organic Law of the Armed Forces, No. 873, 1978, *Official Gazette*, No. 9487).

22. The stagnation and decline of the navy led Montes Arache to point out in August, 1986 that 'Before we had a real navy, but it has deteriorated (. . .) Now what we have is an institution of minor units. Naturally the navy is made up of ships. Today we do not have the same ships as before, but we have the same staff. We do not have what we had before, a real navy' (*El Nacional*, 15–8–86).

23. In December 1985 'Yesterday President Salvador Jorge Blanco distributed thousands of pesos among the members of the Armed Forces and the Police, during a visit to two military camps and a police station' in the city of Santiago; 'Jorge Blanco distributed 50 pesos to officers and 25 to enlisted men, as an additional gift over and above the double Christmas salary' (*El Caribe*, 18–12–85).

24. Paradoxically, however, the Armed Forces have not been able to do without civilians in carrying out specialised task; for this reason the category of *co-opted* exists within the Dominican Republic Armed Forces, which refers to professionals who join the armed forces to offer their services. This fact is a clear reflection of the limitations of professionalisation of the Armed Forces since these have to resort to the civilian population to cover their needs. For the functioning of the Escuela de Estado Mayor contracts had to be signed with several Universities in the country in order to establish the teaching staff of the military center.

Article 40 of the Organic Law speaks to the incorporation of co-opted persons as follows: 'The Major General of the Armed Forces will recommend to the Executive General of the Armed Forces will recommend to the Executive Powers, through the Secretary of State of the Armed Forces, when technical needs arise, that the Chief of Staff be authorized to contract the services of officers, professionals or foreign missions to act as advisers, professors or technicians . . .'

25. In March 1985, the Secretary of State of the Armed Forces stated the following during a speech whose content and form resembled that of an ultra-conservative priest of the 19th century: 'Gentlemen, it would be monstrous to think as many do now, that religion, faith in Jesus Christ, devotion to the Mother of God, are questions of a different era.' 'There is nothing more absurd than believing in the diabolical voices that speak through the press, through radio and television. Many times in deliberate and premeditated interviews we see the venom of Satan spewing from the mouths of pseudo-sociologists, pseudo-economists and pseudo-scientists who feed on atheism and pervert children and young people, corrupting the innocent and taking advantage of ignorance and misery' (*El Nacional*, 20–3–85).

26. In 1986 when Balaguer became President of the Republic, there was a total of six generals on active service, at the end of his term of office in 1978, he left 45; of these President Antonio Guzmán (1978–82) retired 36, but with the promotion of others he left 35 generals on active service; Salvador Jorge Blanco (1982–86) promoted several officers to the rank of general by January 1986, but in total he retired 57.

References

Alvarez, Virginia, 'La otra cara de Pérez y Pérez' (entrevista, *Ahora*, No. 777, 2–10–78, pp. 11–16.

Arciniegas Valentín, Nelson Antonio, *Historia de la marina de guerra*, Editora Nivar, Santo Domingo, 1984.

Arvelo, Tulio H., *Cayo Confite y Luperón, Memorias de un expedicionario*, VASD, Santo Domingo, 1982.

Balaguer, Joaquín, *Memorias presidenciales*, Imp. M. Pareja, Santo Domingo, 1979.

Bosch, Juan, *Crisis de la democracia de América en la República Dominicana*, Centro de Estudios y Documentación Sociales, A. C. México, 1964.

Brea Franco, Julio, *El sistema constitucional dominicano*, Vol. II, Universidad Nacional Pedro Henríquez Ureña, Santo Domingo, 1983.

CEFA (Centro de Enseñanza de las Fuerzas Armadas), *Libro Blanco de las Fuerzas Armadas y de la Policía Nacional de la República Dominicana: Estudio y pruebas documentales de las causas del movimiento reivindicador del 25 de septiembre de 1983*, Ed. del Caribe, 1964.

Comblin, Joseph, *El poder militar en América Latina*, Ediciones Sígueme, Salamanca, 1978.

Constitución de la República Dominicana, Junta Central Electoral, Santo Domingo, 1985.

Cordero, Fernando, *Importaciones de armas livians en: Argentina, Brasil, Colombia, Costa Rica, Chile, República Dominicana, Perú, México y Venezuela (1970–79)*, Instituto de Estudios Latinoamericanos, Stockholm, n.d.

Cuello, José Israel, *Siete años de reformismo* (Taller, Santo Domingo, 1973).

Deláncer, Juan, *Primavera 1959, Constanza, Maimón y Estero Hondo*, Imprenta Amigo del Hogar, Santo Domingo, 1979.

Despradel, Fidelio, *Manolo Tavarez en su justa dimensión dimensión historica. Las Manaclas, diario de la guerrilla*, Alfa y Omega, Santo Domingo, 1983.

EOPR, 'Breve bosquejo de la Accion Cívica de las Fuerzas Armadas', *Revista de las Fuerzas Armadas*, No. 188 (June, 1982).

Fernández, Arlette, *Coronel Fernández Domínguez, fundador del movimiento militar constitucionalista*, Editora Cosmos, Santo Domingo, 1981.

Gaceta Oficial, No. 9487, 'Ley orgánica de las fuerzas armadas', No. 873, Santo Domingo, 1978.

Ganlíndez, Jesús de, *La era de Trujillo*, del Pacífico, Santiago de Chile, 1956.

Gleijeses, Piero, *La crisis dominicana*, FCE, México, 1985.

Gómez, Luis, *Los derechos humanos en la República Dominicana, (1492–1984)*, Universitaria, Santo Domingo, 1984.

Grimaldi, Víctor, *Los Estados Unidos en el derrocamiento de Trujillo*, Imp. Amigo del Hogar, Santo Domingo, 1985.

Hermann, Hamlet, . . . *De héroes, de pueblos* . . ., Alfa y Omega, Santo Domingo, 1980.

Klare, Michael T. and Stein, Nancy, *Armas y poder en América Latina*, Era, México, 1978.

Kurzman, Dan, *Santo Domingo, la revuelta de los condenados*, Martínez Roca, Barcelona, 1966.

Lowenthal, Abraham F., *El desatino americano*, de Santo Domingo, Santo Domingo, 1977.

Mañón, Melvin, '¿Los militares al poder?', *Ahora*, No. 550–54 and 561–563, May–August, 1974.

Maríñez, Pablo, *Resistencia campesina, imperialismo y reforma agraria en República Dominicana (1899–1978)*, Ediciones CEPAE, Santo Domingo, 1984.

Maríñez, Pablo, *Injerencias, agresiones e intervenciones norteamericanas en la República Dominicana. Bibliografía básica para su estudio* (Universitaria, Santo Domingo, 1985).

Maríñez, Pablo, 'República Dominicana: entre las imposiciones del FMI y la respuesta popular (1983–1984)', *El Caribe Contemporáneo*, (UNAM, México), No. 10, 1986.

Maríñez, Pablo, 'República Dominicana: veinte años después de la intervención norteamericana de 1965', *El Caribe Contemporáneo*, (UNAM, Mexico), No. 11, 1986.

Martín, John Bartlow, *La crisis dominicana desde la caída de Trujillo hasta la guerra civil*, Ed. de Santo Domingo, Santo Domingo, 1975.

Moreno, José A., *El pueblo en armas. Revolución en Santo Domingo*, Tecnos, Madrid, 1973.

Oficina Nacional del Presupuesto, *Presupuesto Nacional Ejecutado, 1966 a 1983*, Santo Domingo.

Osorio Lizarazo, J. A., *Al bacilo de Marx*, La Nación, Ciudad Trujillo, 1959.

Peláez Ruiz, Eugenio José, *Código de justicia de las fuerzas armadas*, Ed. Corripio, Santo Domingo, 1984.

Piñeyro, José Luis, *Ejército y sociedad en México: pasado y presente*, Universidad Autónoma de Puebla y Universidad Autónoma Metropolitana-Azcapotzalco, México, 1985.

Piñeyro, José Luis, 'Seguridad nacional en América Latina. Propuesta metometodológicas', *Nueva Sociedad*, No. 81, 1986.

Raful, Tony, *Movimiento 14 de junio. Historia y documentos*, Alfa y Omega, Santo Domingo, 1983.

Ricardi, Antonio y otros, *La revolución dominicana de abril vista por Cuba*, UASD, Santo Domingo, 1974.

Rivas, Ubi, 'La reorientación de las fuerzas armadas en el gobierno del PRD', *El Sol*, 17–1–80.

Rivera Cuesta, Marcos, *Las fuerzas armadas y la política dominicana*, Imp. Talleres de Artes Gráficas de Luly, Santo Domingo, 1986.

Selser, Gregorio, *¡Aquí Santo Domingo! La tercera guerra sucia*, Palestra, Buenos Aires, Argentina, 1966.

Slater, Jerome, *La intervención americana*, Santo Domingo, 1976.

Szulc, Tad, *Revolución en Santo Domingo*, Santo Domingo, n.d.

Szulc, Tad, 'La crisis dominicana', *Vanguardia del Pueblo*, No. 146, 2–8–78.

Trujillo, Rafael L., *Discursos, mensajes y proclamas*, (Vol. 5 and 10), El Diario, Santiago, 1946 and 1951.

The Military Balance, 1975 to 1985 (Institute for Strategic Studies, London).

Vallejo, Rubén Darío, 'Trayectoria de las fuerzas armadas de la República', *Revista de las Fuerzas Armadas*, No. 261, 1981.

Valera Benítez, Rafael, *Complot Develado*, Taller, Santo Domingo, 1984.

Vargas, Mayobanex, *Testimonio histórico, junio 1959*, Cosmos, Santo Domingo, 1981.

Vega, Bernardo, *Los Estados Unidos y Trujillo. Colección de documentos del Departamento de Estado y de las fuerzas armadas norteamericanas*, (Vols I and II), Fundación Cultural Dominicana, Santo Domingo, 1982.

Vega y Pagán, Ernesto, *Síntesis histórica de la guardia nacional dominicana (génesis del actual ejército nacional)*, Atenas, Ciudad Trujillo, 1953.

5 Defence Policy and Planning in the Caribbean: the Case of Jamaica, 1962–88*

Humberto García Muñiz

> By supporting the efforts of others to strengthen their defense, we frequently do as much for our own defense budget. Security assistance to others is a security bargain for us.
> President Ronald Reagan's Message to Congress, 14 March 1986.[1]

INTRODUCTION

The aim of this chapter is to examine defence policy and planning in Jamaica during the years 1962 to 1988. This study will be broken down into three phases, which are roughly consonant with the periods in power of the two main political parties, the Jamaica Labour Party (JLP) and the People's National Party (PNP). The first phase lasts from 1962 to 1972, the second goes from 1973 to 1980, and the third starts in 1981 up to October 1988.

In this study the term 'defence policy' refers to the broad military objectives of a country and the identification of perceived threats, while 'defence planning' deals with the organisation of military forces needed to deter those threats or face them if they are carried out.[2] For each phase a succinct socio-economic and political background is provided, with a short reference to the foreign policy objectives/initiatives, military politics and to the international environment, emphasising developments that influenced defence policy and planning.

The next step is an analysis of the defence planning process during each period using four categories. These are: employment policy

---

* 'Defence policy and planning in the Caribbean: An Assessment of Jamaica on its Twenty-fifth Independence Anniversary', *Journal of Commonwealth and Comparative Politics*, 27, no. 1 (March 1989), 74–102.

(plans of manpower and material used to deal with a perceived threat and/or actual conflict), acquisition policy (kinds of military equipment procured and its sources), deployment policy (positioning of men and material in times of peace and conflict) and declaratory policy (public statements of defence plans and policies). Finally, a short analytical summary for each period is presented. The work ends with a comparison of the three phases of Jamaica's defence policy and planning.

1 INTERNAL SECURITY AND THE QUEST FOR STABILITY, 1962–72

After more than 300 years of colonialism, independence finally came to Jamaica on 6 August 1962, following a bitter referendum which practically divided Jamaicans in half over whether the island should remain in the Federation of the West Indies or go it alone. The JLP, led by Alexander Bustamante, received the most votes and to him fell the honour of leading the first British colony in the Caribbean to political sovereignty. It was also the first compelled by Britain to establish a defence force in order to achieve independence, followed in the same month by Trinidad and Tobago and four years later by Guyana.[3]

Prior to independence, Jamaica's declaratory stand on defence, together with most British colonies in the region, had already been voiced when it rejected in 1960 a position of neutrality between East and West and accepted 'a West Indian partnership role in Western Hemisphere defence'.[4] Also before independence, in February 1961, an agreement was signed between the United States and Great Britain (on behalf of the Federation of the West Indies), by which the US returned all the lands it leased in Jamaica during the Second World War, except the rights to a 100-acre plot for a long range navigation system which reverted to Jamaica in 1964.[5]

A few eyebrows (mainly of the opposition PNP, which was not consulted) rose when, but one week after independence, Prime Minister Bustamante, in a case of external balancing, invited the US to establish a military base whenever it desired to do so. This position corresponded to Jamaica's policy of industrialisation by invitation which targeted the establishment of import-substitution and export-oriented manufacturing enterprises. On this issue both political parties were in agreement. In the 1950s, during the period of internal self-government, the PNP, led by Norman W. Manley, promoted massive inflows of North American capital for the development of the bauxite industry, branch plant manufacturing and the expansion of the tourist industry.

Simultaneous to the growth of US direct foreign investment came an increasing pattern of trade dependence on the US market for exports and hard currency earnings. A significant element of US-Jamaica relations during the 1960s was 'the guns/ganja/organised crime nexus', with its resulting arms smuggling into Jamaica in payment for ganja (marijuana).[6]

From 1950 to 1968 Jamaica experienced an average real economic growth of 4 per cent, but in societal terms the results were social and economic inequalities. Income distribution data revealed that in 1958 the highest 5 per cent of earners consumed some 20 per cent of national income, while 60 per cent of the population accounted for only 18 per cent of the income.[7] Unemployment increased, particularly after the closing of Britain as a migration outlet in 1962. Rapid urbanisation and the growth of shantytowns resulted partly from the mechanisation/introduction of labour saving techniques in agriculture and better communication with the urban centres. In 1960 the national average of unemployment was 13 per cent, while in Kingston it rose to 19 per cent.[8]

Moreover, the correlation between race and social class was high at this time. One could speak of the black lower classes, the brown middle classes and the white or light-skinned upper classes. The capitalist class was (and still is) easily identifiable, particularly when most were of Jewish and Arab ethnic origin dating back to mercantile families of the late 19th and early twentieth century.[9]

In 1962, according to Michael Handel's criteria of power, Jamaica was within the category of a micro or mini state.[10] Its population was 1.6 million people, with an area of 4411 square miles, a GDP of J$756.9 million (in 1968), a small domestic market, high dependency on foreign markets for imports and exports (bauxite and raw sugar) as well as for capital, a very vulnerable open economy, and no R & D.[11] In military matters, it had extremely limited capabilities to defend itself from external aggression and was totally dependent upon foreign countries for weapons acquisition (no indigenous arms production). With respect to the international system, its interests were limited; it had no influence in the balance of power and could be easily penetrated. Furthermore, Jamaica is located at the northern tier of the Caribbean, falling under those states 'toward whose

domestic behaviour the United States has always been particularly
sensitive' for its 'negative effects on its own security'.[12]

The international environment Jamaica was born into was a bipolar one. The Cold War was in one of its most intense stages. Cuba's
alignment with the Soviet bloc appeared to shatter US historical
inviolability in the region.[13] For Bustamante it provided opportunities to continue being vociferously anti-communist. Now he
became anti-Cuban as well, banning the importation of communist
literature, withdrawing passports to whoever visited Cuba and
breaking trade and diplomatic relations with the island.

However, consular relations were maintained because of the large
number of emigrants that had gone earlier in the century to work
mainly in the Cuban sugar industry or in the US base in
Guantanamo.[14] Yet, during the 1960s, the influence of Cuba in the
internal politics of Jamaica was negligible.[15] In terms of Cuba and
most other foreign issues, Jamaica's foreign policy synchronised US
positions, in accordance with the acquiescent adaptation model.[16]

In 1962 the defence establishment was composed of two main
security forces: the Jamaica Defence Force (JDF) and the Jamaica
Constabulary Force (JCF), as the police is officially called. The
former became operational in July of that year. Its stated roles were
to defend the country from external attack, and to aid the civil power
in emergency situations and maintain essential services.

On the dissolution of the Federation of the West Indies, the 1st and
3rd battalions of the Federal West India Regiment (FWIR), which
previously had been the Jamaican Regiment (JR), became the main
component of the JDF.[17] The JDF was organised into regular and
part-time (national reserve) elements, both tri-service in composi-
tion. The regular element comprised the force headquarters, 1st JR
battalion at Up Park Camp (with ranger companies deployed in
Kingston, Montego Bay, Mandeville and May Pen), the air wing, the
coast guard, the depot at Newcastle and several logistic units providing administrative backing, for a total approximate strength of 1000
men.

The JDF was the only operational element in the ministry of
defence, a portfolio kept by the prime minister, who also retained the
ministry of external affairs. As a result, the defence portfolio and
foreign affairs were closely linked under the prime minister. Here it is
worth noting that even though Jamaica has a parliamentary system of
government, the party leadership generated by its political culture
was (and continues to be) authoritarian: 'The party leader is invested

with an ultimate authority and becomes a sort of transcendental, larger-than-life figure who must not be criticised nor questioned.'[18] Thus, it follows that all important defence decisions were made by the prime minister, who is also the party leader, in consultation with a very small group of advisors.[19]

The other main security force, the JCF, was administered from the ministry of home affairs, together with the electoral office, bankruptcy, criminal justice and administration of law, among others. As the 1960s wore on the JCF proved unreliable and inefficient. A pattern therefore developed whereby the JDF was frequently called to back the JCF in emergencies as well as in routine checks.[20]

The immediate precedent for this pattern took place before independence when in June 1960 a combined 1000-men security sweep (the police, the Royal Hampshires and the FWIR) quelled the so-called 'Henry rebellion'.[21] The combined operations of the security forces in the face of domestic instability was the employment policy that Jamaica inherited and continued to enforce. Just after its formation, the JDF, together with the national reserve, carried out joint exercises with the JCF in order to practice the use of military communications networks.

In April 1963 the drills became deeds. A JDF convoy of nine vehicles, including two armoured ones, went to Coral Gardens to assist the JCF in the capture of six Rastafarians who had attacked a Shell petrol station. The initial action of a tactical pattern of joint operations of the security forces having begun, successive JLP prime ministers mobilised the JDF in similar situations. In so doing they always decried the damage suffered by the image of Jamaica as an attractive place for foreign investment and as a tourist haven.

Though the British garrison left in 1962, the remaining seconded British officers in JDF top positions must surely have had no qualms in the application of their legacy. A British joint services training team remained until 1971. The military intelligence officer was British up to the early 1970s. Most JDF officer-cadets went to British military schools, particularly Sandhurst. In 1965 most of the British seconded officers left. The new JDF Chief of Staff, Brig David Smith, and his second in command, were naturalised citizens born in the Bahamas and Barbados, respectively.[22]

Jamaica had only been independent for a year when a Military Assistance Agreement was signed in June 1963 with the US without prior notification to parliament. The purpose of the US was only 'to improve the capability of the Jamaica Defence Force to maintain surveillance of the island's north coast, 90 miles from Cuba'.[23] Prime Minister Bustamante failed in his goal of signing a defence treaty with the United States. Conscious that Jamaica would gravitate towards its orbit, the US was only interested in integrating Jamaica to its well-controlled inter-American system, even though it is not until 1969 that Jamaica was admitted in the Organisation of American States:

> The UK is gradually withdrawing from the Caribbean. Its influence . . . will remain a factor in post-independent Jamaica for some time to come . . . [i]ts unwillingness to assume substantial economic or military commitments in the area will soon become apparent to Jamaica which we expect will look increasingly to the United States. The Premier of Jamaica has already asked for a Defense Agreement with the US. We have replied that the island's security could be preserved best by membership in the OAS and that as an OAS member Jamaica could participate in the activities of the Inter-American Defense Board.[24]

The acquisition policy of the JDF was congruent with an internal security-oriented defence planning.[25] Most of the air wing and coast guard equipment came from the US but the light weapons of the JDF were British. Lacey concluded: 'The JDF was modelled and run on a British blueprint. Such military aid as given by the US and Canada fitted in in that context.'[26]

Canada's role was secondary compared to either Britain or the US. A bilateral Military Training Agreement signed in September 1964 was a Jamaican attempt to broaden its training opportunities since vacancies in British military schools were very scarce. Contrary to Britain, Canada assumed most of the training costs. In the 1960s a special relationship grew between Canada and the air wing. Light aircraft training was given in Canada and a Canadian private company set up shop at Up Park Camp, flying Bells similar to the ones of the JDF.

During the 1960s both Canada and Britain established training exchanges with Jamaica.[27] The US military top brass in the Caribbean visited Jamaica and the JDF homologues reciprocated.[28] The JCF received training (including seconded officers), specialised equipment, and technical and financial assistance, in accordance with the counter-insurgency doctrine the US favoured in the mid-1960s. Due to the size of Jamaica, this assistance 'resulted in a certain degree of "Americanisation" in the police force, particularly as a result of exposure to US police techniques, procedures and style'.[29] US assistance to the security forces can only signify its approval of the inward oriented defence planning of Jamaica.

Unprecedented political violence, complicated by a wave of strikes, erupted from February 1966 to March 1967, lasting over a month after the general elections. Political warfare between party groups and gangs rose to such levels that a state of emergency was declared in October 1967 to apply to West Kingston. Joint JDF-JCF forces carried out house-to-house searches. The involvement of the political parties came into the open by the finding of instruments of violence in their local headquarters.

The roots of party violence lie in a system of two competitive, trade union-linked parties (with a mass, cross-class membership), seeking to allocate scarce resources. By way of political patronage the loyal supporters of the ruling party receive the scarce benefits available. This clientelistic relationship generates an inter-party antagonism which is directed at 'the same class of impoverished and socially disadvantaged [which] have the misfortune of supporting the wrong party'.[30] Clientelism serves as an escape valve for the social anger of the poor, reducing the energy they can direct against the propertied classes.

Political violence was not new to Jamaica, but for the first time firearms were widely used. Before the general elections (which were won by the JLP), the national reserve was also mobilised. The JDF assisted the police in controlling political disturbances. Both forces together patrolled West Kingston. However, even though the violence was politically inspired, the JDF acted impartially and not against the opposition PNP.[31]

The event that really frightened the government was the October 1968 riots that followed the exclusion of Dr Walter Rodney. Dr Rodney, a Guyanese historian teaching at the Mona campus of the University of the West Indies (UWI), was banned for alleged 'black power' subversive activities. It has been noted that the violence was aimed at property (not persons), with very little political motivation and organisation. The students' protest marches sparked an explosion of discontent by Kingston's urban poor and lumpenproletariat.

During the first decade of independence it was clear that the main function of the JDF was to intervene to sustain the socio-economic and political *status quo*:

In Jamaica, the military appears well socialised through a long history, training with overseas military forces and the receipt of foreign military assistance, into the function of defending the ruling segment of society and the substantial foreign investments against the threats of the impoverished majority.[32]

In sum, the JDF was created as the result of British pressure, although there was in Jamaica a military tradition and social conflicts and tensions that provided rationale. It remained under British influence and tutelage during the 1960s. The JDF was mobilised to assist the police, even unnecessarily at times; its role then being to search for lawless elements, to patrol the streets, and see to the maintenance of essential services, along with the destruction of ganja cultivation. In his study of this decade Terry Lacey concluded that:

> the main role of the Jamaican army was that of an internal security force, even though its training and operations were clearly geared to giving aid to the civil power and latterly to a potential counter-insurgency role.[33]

Thus the JDF arms inventory was designed for internal security purposes. Most of it, except light weapons, came from a bilateral agreement with the US. The United States was the sole supplier for the coast guard and the principal supplier for the army and air wing.[34] The latter could only deal with search and destroy operations, transport of a few men and aerial reconnaissance; the former with coastal surveillance and search and rescue operations.

The JDF was under the direct command of the prime minister. Its mobilisation was his sole decision. The JDF–JCF joint defence planning shows that the maintenance of domestic stability took precedence in its deployment policy. JDF forces were deployed near Kingston at the Up Park Camp headquarters. Also Montego Bay was well protected because of its importance as a tourist mecca, vital for the island's image.

The declaratory defence policy of the Jamaican government comprised two elements. One was alignment with the US and a constant attack against Cuban communism. The other was its offensive from the Rodney riots onwards against alleged black power subversives. The type of equipment and training given by the US to security forces, was the result of the counterinsurgency policy pursued in response to the Cuban Revolution. There was consensus between the

JLP and the PNP on their diagnosis of the main security threats as internal and on the manner in which to face them. Consequently, there was a congruity among the British legacy (personified in the JDF officialdom), the US as principal donor and Jamaica as recipient, that internal security was the main aim of the latter's defence policy and planning.

2 COPING WITH DESTABILISATION, 1973–80

In the first decade of independence, Jamaica's GDP grew at an annual rate of 6.5 per cent in real terms.[35] Yet, the unemployment rate doubled to 24 per cent; illiteracy and malnutrition were endemic.[36] Due mainly to 'popular discontent,' the PNP, headed by Michael Manley, won the 1972 general elections.[37] In contrast to previous and future campaigns, the political violence decreased, though both parties 'actively campaigned with their armed escorts during the 1972 electoral struggle'.[38]

Much has been written on Manley's first administration, but for the purposes of this article I will emphasise three elements which had a direct effect on defence planning. Here two decisions were of significance, one dealing with foreign policy (close relations with Cuba) and the other with the domestic political arena (the commitment to 'democratic socialism'). Both had great internal and external impact.

Two years before assuming power, Manley proposed in his article 'Overcoming Insularity in Jamaica' an active, non-aligned, pro-Third World foreign policy within a regionalist framework.[39] A logical, yet unmentioned, sequel was a rapprochement with Cuba. It took place in 1973, when in unison with the other independent Commonwealth Caribbean states, diplomatic relations were established with Cuba.

Relations with Cuba included Manley's travel with Fidel Castro to the non-aligned summit in Algiers in 1973, a state visit by Manley to Cuba in 1975 and a return visit by Castro in October 1977, and agreements in technical assistance for school, health, housing, mini-dam construction and fishing. According to Manley, US-Jamaican relations began to deteriorate after his support of Cuba's action in Angola. He points at this episode as the start of a US campaign to destabilise his regime.[40]

The second element was the PNP's declaration of commitment to 'democratic socialism' in 1974. This was a return to its roots as the PNP declared itself socialist (of the British Labour Party type, influenced by Fabianism) in 1940, but then assigned its ideology a low profile. Instead, in 1952, the small, hard working and influential Marxist wing, known as the '4-Hs', was expelled.

Closer relations with Cuba and the commitment to 'democratic socialism' had an immediate internal effect: it led to the withdrawal of support by and from the capitalist class. Manley's radical rhetoric and initiatives in foreign policy became confused and confounded with his reformist internal policies.

The third element that affected defence planning was the economic situation. At the start of the 1970s the economy was characterised by its dependency on the foreign-owned and controlled bauxite/alumina, tourist and export-agriculture industries. These industries were not expanding; the economy was stagnant. The Manley government confronted a balance-of-payments crisis in its first year in power. The situation worsened with the economic crisis that hit the world capitalist countries following the rise in the oil prices: the island's oil import bill increased from J$65 million in 1973 to J$177 million in 1974.[41] The inherited economic situation, the world crisis, and its own economic policies ended in a dismal economic performance for the PNP administration, with a very important role played by the International Monetary Fund (IMF). Extended analyses of this period have already been made, so for my purposes it must be noted that throughout this period Jamaica suffered an acute dearth of foreign exchange, which hindered its ability to acquire equiopment for the security forces.[42]

During the general elections of 1976 and 1980 violence rocked Jamaica. In the first electoral contest there were more than 500 fatalities and in the second 889 persons died. Manley belatedly accused the US of organising a destabilisation process.[43] He claimed that the JDF and police heads also viewed the threat as external and implied that the JLP played an active role too.[44] A new method of protest, national in scope, involving the blocking of roads was organised in 1979 by the JLP. It paralysed the economy for three days.[45]

The Manley regime countered by strengthening the security forces and creating the Home Guard (HG). The HG, a system of recruiting voluntary help for the police, was an important modification to its employment policy. It added a new force with 'the potential to shift power into the hands of the people in the neighborhood . . . to be the eyes and ears of the communities'.[46] The HG received basic training in small firearms and patrol duties. Its members were given arms when on duty, which always was under the direction of the JCF. In

May 1976 its membership was 1574, in December of the same year 1984 members and by 1980 over 9000 members.[47]

The JLP bitterly opposed its creation and refused to join the organisation. Instead, it pledged its support to the security forces because, in its view, the HG was modelled on the 'people's militia' of the communist countries and the PNP intention was to replace them with the HG.[48] The JLP called for more government support for the security forces. In particular it noted the lack of adequate equipment and cars. Not only was bipartisan consensus shattered in economic and ideological matters, but also in security issues as well. The HG never fulfilled its original mission and became a living proof of government's inability to mobilise the country and control the violence.

Operational defence planning was still done jointly by the JDF and the JCF. In 1974 an important change confirmed the internal security role of the JDF. A ministry of national security and justice was created where the JDF and JCF, as well as the legal and penal systems, were administered jointly.[49] In late 1973 Lt Col Rudolph Green was appointed Chief of Staff.[50] During his tenure Manley always appointed a trusted person (Eli Matalon, Keble Munn and Dudley Thompson) as minister, though he retained the post of minister of defence.[51] As the creation of the HG shows, the political directorate was still at this time the most important participant in the defence planning process. However, its control over the security forces, particularly over the JDF, was weakening.

The strain caused by the economic crisis, political polarisation and political violence took its toll on the JCF and the JDF.[52] As previously noted, since independence the security forces played an important role in the maintenance of the government in power by their repeated interventions in favour of domestic stability. In reality the issue was not whether the JDF would intervene in politics, but to what extent and by what means.[53]

In his pioneering work, Malcolm McFarlane mentioned several factors that might have checked a broader involvement by the JDF.[54] First, the British values of professional conduct and personal behaviour inculcated in the Sandhurst-trained officers. It is important to note that the average length of military service of the JDF top military officers was at least 25 years and that there was an 'old boy' service network, which even included ex-servicemen of the British armed forces.[55] Second, although their social origins were more and more from lower-middle and working classes, their education geared them towards the values and aspirations of the dominant classes.[56] A third factor was the small size of the force.

During the Manley administration the crisis of confidence was such that even with these possibly inhibiting factors some undercurrents in the JDF surfaced canvassing a wider role in the society. In 1977 a JDF major wrote in *Alert* that the force *'can serve as a catalyst'* in the development of Jamaica and

> must be used to inculcate discipline and productivity in the minds of the citizenry. If this were not done the JDF will be *defaulting in its responsibility as the prime guardians of the state and moderniser.*[57]

In a menacing tone, at least as it appears to me, he wrote:

> Governments of Jamaica must, *if they are to avoid increasing the risk of military intervention*, recognise that the military despite its better education, good conditions of service and generally high levels of welfare, is not [an] exclusive, closed society. It is sprung from the womb of society and therefore feels empathy with the sympathy for the privations for the rest of the nation. *Jamaican Governments must direct their military into the development of the country, making use of the structure, organisation, skill and discipline which is inherent in military bodies.*[58]

By the end of the Manley years a sector within the security forces sided with the opposition JLP.[59] On 22 June 1980 there was even a coup attempt by 33 JDF members, together with a minuscule rightist party, which the JDF Chief of Staff Maj Gen Robert Neish crushed before it unfolded.[60] The Manley administration had lost control of the security forces.[61]

Manley's views on these events deserve to be quoted *in extenso* because he argues that the class extraction of the officers and their British training influenced their stance:

> To begin with, the officer group of the Jamaica Defence Force is traditionally drawn from upper and middle class families, and class bias persists, despite training. As the establishment increased its campaign amongst the middle classes and as the latter, angered by shortages and frightened by anti-communist propaganda, became increasingly hostile to our government, the officer group reflected

this mood. Even the lower ranks began to succumb . . . Then too, the entire traditional system of military training is designed around the concept of an enemy. Most of our officers had been to Sandhurst. They had been exposed to a world configuration in which the enemy is seen through the eyes of the MI5. For people of this class background, early cultural experience and training, it is extremely difficult to accept a foreign communist – and perhaps even a local socialist – is not an enemy.[62]

At this critical juncture Manley called for general elections. In October 1980 the PNP was defeated and power transferred to the JLP. The resilience of Jamaican formal democracy passed a difficult test. The election was the ninth under universal suffrage granted in 1944. The JLP and PNP have alternately won two consecutive elections and lost in the third attempt. The antagonism of these clientelistic, multi-class parties was well grasped by Manley when he wrote: 'In the end, supporters of the two parties tended *to become more like members of opposing armies* than citizens with different views about their country'.[63] Yet the presence of an alternate two-party system was the most important inhibitory factor for a coup.

A clear expression of the security forces' anti-PNP position can be seen in their voting behaviour during the 1980 general elections. While their voting turnout was lower than the national average (65 per cent compared to 87 per cent), the turnout for the JLP was a little above the national average (56 per cent to 51 per cent). But the outstanding result was that its turnout for the PNP amounted to 9.3 per cent as opposed to the 35 per cent national average! The security forces bias towards the JLP is more obvious in the examination of the military/police voting box that was located in Up Park Camp, which accounted for 14.3 per cent of the security forces voters list. Here the JLP received 76 per cent of the votes and the PNP 5.6 per cent. Mark Figueroa judges that 'there is sufficient evidence, with respect to sections of the security forces, for one to be concerned about their even handedness'.[64]

A surprising development, completely different from Manley's developmental priorities, was the increase in military expenditures during his first term. The violence forced the government to spend more on the security forces. The government's estimates of expenditure for major military equipment in the year 1974–75 was J$924, 159, but it was obliged to spend J$2,469,100, a 167 per cent increase.[65] The major increase in purchases from the US was in the

Foreign Military Sales (FMS) programme.[66] The most significant of the military hardware procured were two Beech transports and three Bell helicopters.

Based on the Jamaican dollar value of its arms import trade in the period 1973–80, the US was the principal supplier (76 per cent of its procurement for the years for which data have been found).[67] Britain was in second place (12 per cent). In third place, as supplier from 1968–71, was Canada, which appears only as a minor source of re-exports.[68]

In the second term of the PNP, paradoxically, there was a reduction of military expenditures, although the violence was more endemic. The main reason for the decrease was the economic crisis that engulfed Jamaica in the late 1970s. The foreign exchange reserves were simply not sufficient to permit the purchase of the necessary material.

Procurement of military hardware from the US military establishment dried up from 1977 to 1980.[69] The only remaining connection with the US arms market were commercial sales. In 1979 and 1980 they also decreased substantially. Ten V-150 Commando APC and the six 81mm mortars were bought from private suppliers.[70] Jamaica did not accuse the US of applying a restricted transfer policy, but this was the military side of the destabilisation process. Manley himself was conscious as early as 1976 that Jamaica lacked the funds to purchase the necessary wherewithal:

> We had put money into the police, upgrading their equipment, salaries and numbers. But it was obvious that no amount of money that we could afford would create a police force that could really control the situation.[71]

Meanwhile the JLP, courting the JDF and the JCF, accused the government of weakening the security forces by not providing the weaponry and the equipment necessary to protect the society. Its campaign stressed the PNP's alleged plan to replace the security forces with the HG and some 1500 Cuban-trained *Brigadistas*.[72]

During this period there was neither a direct British presence in the JDF nor British soldiers training in Jamaica's tropical terrain. However, the security connection with British military tradition not only continued but expanded as JDF men went to India for training.[73] In 1975 a Canadian team provided assistance from an aircrew and technical standpoint on the operation and maintenance of the recently acquired Bell helicopters.[74] The following year, 179 members of the security forces trained in Britain and 17 in Canada.[75] In 1977 22 policemen went to Britain and Canada for some courses.[76] The only official security connection with the US took place in mid-1974 when the JDF and the JCF joined the US Drug Enforcement Agency (DEA) in anti-drug operations.[77]

A novel development in security issues was the training by Cuba of eight security personnel in charge of VIP protection.[78] Equally new was the re-export in 1979 to Cuba of seven items worth J$30,000 under the 'Tanks and other armoured fighting vehicles' category of the island's trade statistics.[79] Another significant initiative was the assistance programme to Grenada which saw deputy superintendent, K. S. Morgan, and a sergeant offering a three-week training course in 1979 and then staying on at the police training school, which was inaugurated in July 1980.[80]

The deployment policy was the same as in the previous period; the forces were located near Kingston and important urban centers. In at least eight of the 15 constituencies of Kingston and St Andrew, political gangs were moving freely. Stone concludes:

> These constituencies have the heaviest concentrations of urban poor and many of their communities provide the hard core militants willing to risk life and limb in defence of the party and willing to carry out daring physical attacks on the party's real or imagined enemies.[81]

The tactical pattern of joint operations by the security forces remained the same. The only change was in the weaponry of the gangs, which was obtained either from the ganja trade or from political party officials. Up to 1976 the 365 Magnum was the most common weapon in use. In 1980 many M-16 and some A.K.47 assault rifles and sub-machine guns were in use by '"garrison communities" . . . [which] . . . control clearly defined boundaries and territories where political protection insulates them from the reach of the security forces'.[82]

In brief, the formulation of defence policy and planning in the Manley regime was in the hands of the political leadership. It differed from the first phase in that its operationalisation was affected in the late 1970s by the open identification of a sector of the security forces with the opposition JLP.

Defence policy and planning was directed at combatting domestic instability which it perceived as caused by the US in collusion with the JLP. The declaratory policy just hinted at this view. Its employment policy, particularly the creation of a ministry of national security and justice and of the HG, was focused to face an internal war. Its procurement was directed to obtain military hardware to fight domestic violence. Thus the acquisition patterns did not change much when compared with the first phase.

Notwithstanding this, and contrary to the previous period, Manley's foreign policy took Jamaica out of US military programmes, forcing it to buy in the private supplier market. This was the military effect of the destabilisation process. The training of the security forces continued to follow British traditions. Relations with the US military establishment became for all purposes non-existent.

The economic situation led to a foreign exchange shortage which limited Jamaica's ability to purchase weapons from any source and to combat the political violence successfully. The Cuban connection was circumscribed to specialised security training and to the re-export of some weapons, but significantly none was related to the JDF or the JCF. The sending of JCF personnel to Grenada for training purposes was a new initiative which did not last long because the PNP lost the general elections soon after. These links denoted a willingness to assist Caribbean governments with similar foreign policy positions and also facing US hostility and growing regional isolation.

3 US PENETRATION AND THE SUB-REGIONAL DIMENSION, 1981–88

On 1 November 1980 Edward Seaga was sworn in as prime minister. In less than a year diplomatic relations were broken with Cuba and relations with the US reverted to an all-time high. Seaga was the first foreign leader to visit Reagan's White House. Jamaica was second to Israel in 1981 and 1982 as per capita recipient of US assistance. Seaga continued playing on the two themes that had gained him the favour of US conservative circles: anti-communism and free enterprise. In short, Jamaica was presented by the US to the international community as a model for democracy and the free market in the Third World.[83]

The economic crisis and the political violence had left Jamaica in shambles. Unemployment in 1972 was 184,000; in 1980 it was 270,000.[84] Standards of living fell by 25 per cent. Net foreign exchange reserves were at -J$900 million in 1980, a fall of 1014 per cent.[85] Between 1972 and 1979 the GDP fell from J$2244 million to J1933 million, a fall of some 14 per cent.[86] The security forces too were devastated, as if they had just been through a war. In June 1981, when announcing an increase in military expenditures, Seaga described the security forces as 'run down, in the case of the JDF, to 25 per cent of their capabilities; in the case of the [JCF] . . . half of their fleet was immobile'.[87] A year later Seaga declared his intention to develop 'well equipped security forces to deal with disorder'.[88] The military share of GNP under Seaga climbed for the first time over the 1 per cent bracket and remained there for three consecutive years.[89]

Under the JLP administration, the employment policy underwent a change. From guarding the main urban areas, the JDF range was expanded island-wide. A secondary school constructed by Cuba in Montpelier became a military camp, giving the JDF access to western, central and eastern Jamaica.[90] In 1985 the JDF camp in Moneague was upgraded.[91] The elimination of the HG in 1981 left the JDF and the JCF to combat, jointly, any domestic menace. The scrapping of the HG was Seaga's decision, with the acquiescence of at least the JCF, which was never happy about its creation.

Important modifications in acquisition policy also came after Seaga's election. The trend towards US dominance in Jamaica's arms imports culminated in the years 1981 to 1984, with its percentage increasing to 96 per cent.[92] Britain's share became minuscule, most likely limited to the small weapons of the JDF which are 'almost exclusively of British origin'.[93]

However, the radical change was in US military assistance. Over 95 per cent of military assistance for Jamaica since independence falls within the years 1981 to 1986.[94] This acquisition style follows a replacement surge pattern.[95] On the one side, the thrust of the financial assistance is funnelled through Military Assistance Programme (MAP) Merger Funds, which meets obligations for payment of FMS purchases.[96] The FMS programme for Jamaica is for the purchase of armoured cars, trucks, vehicles, helicopters, patrol boats, radio communication equipment, spare parts and maintenance of aircraft.[97]

Together with Haiti, the Dominican Republic, Belize, Antigua/Barbuda, Grenada and St. Kitts/Nevis, Jamaica became a beneficiary of the Strategic Defense Acquisition Fund (SDAF).[98] In terms of the JDF budget, assistance from other states, such as the US, are separate and apart from the provision by the Jamaica Government but in instances where the assistance is of a Capital nature it is regarded as part of the Capital Budget.[99]

On the other side, the US International Military Education and Training (IMET) programme is directed to expand the JDF managerial, technical, tactical and training skills base.[100] Training has been both in and outside of Jamaica. By 1986 approximately 30 per cent of JDF members had received training under IMET.

The US military establishment sees IMET as a vital programme for its ideological content, military-to-military contacts, and in the establishing and maintaining of long-term security relationships with nations important for US security:

This program has great potential for influencing foreign governments, whose representatives are trained by US personnel and exposed to the United States, its people, culture, and policies. *Frequently, students later assume senior leadership and management roles in their governments.*[101]

In this light, a new element in US military assistance in the Caribbean in the 1980s is the use of the US national guard. In January 1983 an agreement was signed between Jamaica and the US, by which the national guards of Puerto Rico and the US Virgin Islands and the JDF could exchange personnel.[102] In early June 1987 JDF and Barbados Defence Force men, together with soldiers from the Dominican Republic, were training with US national guard of Puerto Rico in Camp Santiago, Puerto Rico, in an annual exercise which started to be held after the coup by the New Jewel Movement in Grenada.[103]

From 1981 to 1983 US official objectives were to strengthen the 'western orientation and professionalism of the JDF', improve its capability to meet possible threats from externally supported subversion and to cooperate with Jamaican authorities, mainly in drug enforcement matters.[104] These aims are all related to an internal projection capability of the JDF, which is the main goal:

An adequately equipped and trained security force can play a key role in Jamaica's recovery by helping preserve Jamaica's democratic tradition against internal threats. For years the Jamaica

Defense Force has served as a reliable, apolitical and constitutional military force.[105]

As stated above, one task envisioned by the United States for the JDF includes the eradication and interdiction of drugs. The US DEA estimated in 1987 the value of the ganja crop for the economy at US$82 million annually.[106] Since September 1986, Jamaica has launched the most concerted anti-ganja campaign in its history. The drive is in the hands of the JDF, with the assistance of US DEA agents.[107]

Recent US legislation ties progress in drug eradication and interdiction to the disbursement of economic and military aid.[108] In 1987 Jamaica received US$1.5 million, in 1988 US$3.4 million, and US$1 million was asked from Congress for 1989.[109] Noting that 'if there were no buyers, there would be no sellers', Prime Minister Seaga, not satisfied with US efforts, questioned the 'Star Wars' defence system when the United States 'could not stop commuter planes carrying ganja'.[110]

The JCF appears to have been sidestepped in the campaign for drug eradication. There are reports that senior JCF officials are implicated in the drug trade. However, a recent Americas Watch's report on human rights in Jamaica revealed that under an Anti-Terrorism Assistance (ATA) programme, the JCF received US assistance and added that it was 'unaware of a problem of terrorism. . . of the sort that the ATA is intended to combat'.[111]

In October 1983 the well known events of Grenada took place and Jamaica played an unexpected, important role. First, it was one of the leading Caribbean countries (the other was Barbados) that tried to legitimise US military intervention by means of a formal request of the Organisation of Eastern Caribbean States (OECS) to the United States, even though it was not a member of that organisation. Second, JDF men were in the initial contingent of the Caribbean Security Force (CSF) (renamed later the Caribbean Peacekeeping Force) and Col. K. Barnes was its head and Maj. A. Douglas operations officer.[112] Third, over 300 JDF soldiers remained in Grenada for more than two years to perform security roles: 'The experience gained from our 21 Years of Internal Security Operations in Jamaica was used effectively and efficiently in Grenada.'[113] In 1985 an officer from the JDF coast guard went to assist in the training of the Grenada coast guard.[114]

Elsewhere I have argued that the OECS petition served as a smokescreen for the acceleration of a US offensive in military training in the Commonwealth Caribbean that had started as a consequence of the March 1979 coup by the New Jewel Movement in Grenada and of which the establishment of the Regional Security System (RSS) in 1982 is the prime example.[115] The RSS is the brainchild of the US military establishment, with perhaps some minor input of its Eastern Caribbean allies. In this case, the idea of regional integration, long present in the political consciousness of the Caribbean, was warped to promote US security interests, oddly enough in its traditional bilateral manner.

Suffice it here to emphasise that though there was a convergence of interests between some governments of the Eastern Caribbean islands and the US for the establishment of some sort of security scheme, Barbados Prime Minister Tom Adams' stillborn initiative of a regional defence force indicates disagreement over the mechanism to be created. Adams' initiative was buried with him in March 1985. The required funds for its operationalisation were not forthcoming from the US. As usually happens, he who pays the piper calls the tune. Not only has the US with Britain as a minor partner and Canada in a still lesser role, equipped the defence forces of Jamaica, Barbados and Antigua and the special service units of the rest of the islands, but it has also trained and exercised with them for sub-regional internal security purposes.

It is within the context of the RSS that Jamaica has broken its tradition of non-cooperation with other Commonwealth Caribbean forces.[116] It seems that Jamaica is being groomed to serve as a US proxy in the Commonwealth Caribbean. Such a role is implied in US Department of State security assistance documents, as in its latest request to Congress:

> Our military assistance will also foster a continued close relationship between the JDF and the US military, and will promote the JDF ability and willingness to participate in joint operations with friendly forces to further regional security and support US foreign policy objectives.[117]

Extremely important in this respect has been its participation in four military exercises with US forces and the RSS, of which Jamaica is not a member.[118] The aim of the exercises is the same: 'to integrate

Troops from the Caribbean region and US Troops' in a scenario where 'insurgents . . . engaged in subversive activities' were destroyed.[119]

The latest exercise took place in mid-September 1987 at the JDF's camp in Moneague, St Ann. Total participation for the manoeuvre, code-named 'Exercise Trade Winds', was 300 troops of all ranks, including 120 JDF members , 120 from the RSS and 60 from the US army.[120] Yet, JDF relations with US military forces not only include exercises in Puerto Rico and manoeuvres with the RSS, but also contacts in the US naval base in Guantánamo, Cuba. In August, 1988 twenty-five JDF soldiers went to that base to participate in a drill and shooting competition.[121].

The US military assistance programme for 1989 aims at the JDF acquisition of MAP-provided vehicles, boats and aircraft, the training of maintenance personnel, and the continuation of the education of JDF officers.[122] It should be noted that Hurricane Gilbert, which hit the island hard in mid-September 1988, damaged and destroyed JDF equipment.[123] It is obvious that US military assistance will continue for some time, though it may start to decline soon due to the limited absorptive capability of the JDF. To a lesser extent, it will also be affected by Jamaica's ability to pay FMS loans. For example, as of 30 June 1985, Jamaica had due and unpaid US$134,000 and rescheduled a debt of US$277,000.[124]

This military activism of Jamaica in the Caribbean takes place at a time when a reorganisation of US military structure in the Caribbean and Central America is due. At present the Caribbean falls within the maritime-oriented, US Navy-controlled Atlantic Command (LANT-COM), the one in charge of the Grenada invasion. There has been a lingering debate on whether the Caribbean remains in LANTCOM; passes into land-oriented, US Army-dominated Southern Command (SOUTHCOM); or a new unified command is created covering the Caribbean basin, giving military form to this geostrategic concept.[125]

Under the new law reorganising the Department of Defence approved in 1986, the US President is required to review periodically (at least every two years) the allocation of missions, responsibilities and forces of the combatant commands. Specifically the law says that within a year a first review must be done considering a 'revision of the geographic area for which [SOUTHCOM] has responsibility so as to include the ocean areas adjacent to Central America [and] elimination of the command designated as United Forces, Caribbean'.[126] These provisions seem like a Congressional command for the transfer of the Caribbean to SOUTHCOM.[127] The modification of US military command structure undoubtedly is an important development whose consequences for the implementation of US military policy in the Caribbean and Central America need to be studied.

Jamaica's involvement in the Caribbean also extended into its foreign policy.[128] In April 1987 staff members of the Kingston-based Caribbean Democrat Union (CDU) were in St Lucia to help the United Workers Party in its re-election campaign.[129] Also important were Seaga's failed attempts to change CARICOM by bringing in pro-US states, such as the Dominican Republic and Duvalier's and post-Duvalier's Haiti, as well as the cordial relationship with Puerto Rico. Under Seaga, Jamaica's foreign policy in the Caribbean was actively pro-US and free enterprise, conservative, and security conscious of the internal situation of other Caribbean islands.

Within this picture of the US as the principal supplier and trainer to the JDF and the new surrogate status of Jamaica in the Commonwealth Caribbean, it is noteworthy that in 1985 the JDF reached out to Britain and Canada.[130] In May the exchange programme with Britain was renewed.[131] With Canada the 1964 training agreement was replaced in July 1985 by a new one.[132] In October 1987 eighty JDF soldiers completed a course in mechanised training in Canada as part of a reciprocal exchange with the Canadian army. Canadian forces were based at Moneague and participated in 'jungle' exercises.[133]

In addition to the historical links between the JDF and British military tradition, it may be speculated that the reason for this move was to counteract US influence. The situation arises that the most senior JDF officers were trained within British army values of professional conduct and personal behaviour, yet Britain's interests, and consequently its influence, in Jamaica and the wider Caribbean has diminished considerably. However, the training of young officers and many enlisted men imbibing US values may be worrisome when it is crystal clear that one of IMET's objectives is to penetrate the military establishment that it trains: 'provides a valuable channel of communication and influence with foreign militaries worldwide'.[134] In the JDF, the military intelligence unit is said to have been trained and in the 'closest basis with the United States'.[135]

Nonetheless, US penetration of the JDF is compatible with Seaga's policies in areas of Jamaican life other than security:

In a real sense, the World Bank, the IMF, and Washington have been more important in shaping the direction of economic and social policies in the country since 1980 than any domestic interest, pressure group, or source of policy influence.[136]

However, even with massive US financial assistance since Seaga took office – more than US$775 million –, the support of the international financial institutions, and the commercial banks, Jamaica has been unable to achieve sustained economic growth.[137]

In spite of the strained economic situation there has not been the level of protest or violence that marked the Manley period. In 1985 the PNP organised a roadblocking action similar to the one instigated by the JLP in 1979. It lasted two days and seven civilians were killed. Carl Stone, the leading Jamaican political sociologist, tells of a case where the governing JLP 'intimidated groups with interest in protest action with a strong presence of heavily armed political mercenaries.'[138] These actions, together with government's priority upgrading of the security forces, put fear in people's minds that a repressive response would be the answer to protests and manifestations – popular or political – of discontent.

To further complicate matters, in mid-October 1987 a retired JDF colonel wrote in the *Gleaner* that the new generation of officers born after Independence now replacing 'the traditional leaders . . . will not be as predictable as the old stager who brought in Independence.'[139] Col. MacMillan added that whatever the differences between the security forces, they shared one important position: 'the majority have lost faith in the politicians'.[140] Referring to the lack of national consensus to face the crime wave hitting the island, he said

it is quite possible that in the not too distant future some young army officers may decide that they would make better leaders by virtue of their discipline, training and mistaken administrative ability, with or without the initial co-operation of their brothers-in-arms.[141]

The *Gleaner* found that the young officers had some corporate grievances, such as 'declining professional military standards, a rapidly declining standard of living and a gross inability to address the mounting welfare problems that confront the men they had been trained to lead and serve'.[142] It added that 'far from plotting and scheming the young officers' were leaving the JDF 'in epidemic proportions'.[143] Without referring to the new surrogate role of the JDF, Chief of Staff Neish replied that the retirement numbers were the same as in the past and repeated the traditional line on the JDF internal role: 'we will continue to work alongside the JCF to prevent unlawful acts, apprehend criminals, eradicate ganja and destroy the drug trade'.[144]

For most of the years of this period the political panorama was unstable. The Grenada events provided Seaga with an opportunity to call a snap general election in December 1983 in order to ride the short-lived pro-JLP popularity wave that Jamaican involvement occasioned. The PNP boycotted the polls, charging that the JLP breached a pledge that elections would not be held until several electoral reforms were effected. As a result the JLP won all 60 seats in parliament.[145] In 1986 the PNP bounced back by winning convincingly (57 per cent to 43 per cent) the local government elections, with Manley returning to power for a second government in mid-1989.

Even though the economy improved in some sectors in 1987, the situation changed radically with the devastation of the country by Hurricane Gilbert. To assist in the restoration efforts, contingents of 30 BDF men, 53 TTDF men and around 40 GDF men arrived in late September to stay for at least two weeks.[146] Gilbert's immediate political effect was a pro-Seaga surge in the polls (PNP 51 per cent to JLP 49 per cent). Elections had to be postponed at least until the restoration of electricity. Carl Stone commented that 'the longer the election is delayed, the more this will favour a revival of the earlier large PNP majority'.[147]

Elections were held in mid-April 1989. It is important to note that the PNP has been tight-lipped all throughout this period on the ongoing penetration of the JDF by the US military establishment, or for that matter, on practically all issues dealing with the security forces.[148] This is so because the PNP has been careful not to antagonise the US. Its rhetoric and programme moved to the centre in order to gain some support from the Jamaican middle and capitalist classes as well as to allay US anxiety over the return to power of Michael Manley.

In the third phase, then, Jamaica's defence policy and planning underwent fundamental transformations. Defence policy and planning were directed only at internal security issues up to 1983. However, the Grenada events indicated that Jamaica was willing to serve as US proxy in the sub-region, if not for intervention at least for security roles. The deployment of a JDF contingent for a lengthy stay in Grenada attests to the addition of this new element in Jamaican defence policy and planning. Jamaica's participation in the joint

US/RSS military manoeuvres and the military exercises with the BDF, soldiers from the Dominican Republic and the US national guard of Puerto Rico staged in Puerto Rico confirms this fact. Its acquisition policy shows that the US dominates the supply of the necessary material and training to the JDF.

Apart from US military assistance, military expenditures show an increasing trend. The reality is that at present the JDF is in the process of being penetrated by the US military, a radical shift that may push out the British tradition predominant in the force since its inception and which might lead under certain circumstances to a wider presence of the JDF in the civil and political arena. The equipment acquired is consistent with the internal security orientation of the JDF, though not opposed to the new sub-regional projection as there is no more professional and better equipped force in the Commonwealth Caribbean. This sub-regional projection could range from security roles (as in Grenada after the invasion) to intervention under the RSS scheme, in all probability with the United States providing the necessary transportation.

CONCLUSIONS

In sum, the defence policy and planning in the three phases was oriented to internal security concerns. The employment, deployment and acquisition policies of the security forces – the JDF and the police – were designed to meet domestic instability and violence. The political directorate, particularly the Prime Minister, was the guiding force behind the formulation of defence planning, while the operational aspects fell in the hands of the security forces.

Both political parties expressed consensus on the internal security threat, but differed on its source. The JLP saw black power and Cuba as the main source, while the PNP accused the US of acting in collusion with the JLP to occasion its destabilisation. In the second period the economic and political crisis brought changes in employment policy (the creation of the HG) and in procurement policy (the closing of the US military arms market and its reliance on private suppliers).

More important was that the crisis affected the traditional loyalty to formal democracy of a sector of the security forces and led it to act against the government. In this period the first attempt of supplanting the government by a sector from the JDF took place. Voices within the military were heard calling for a leading role for the JDF in the development of Jamaica. The polarised partisanship that cuts Jamaican society was felt within the security forces.

Under Seaga the most important modification to Jamaica's defence policy and planning is the new role of the JDF as a US surrogate in the sub-region. The US is now the pre-eminent power in the supply and training of the JDF. The supposedly main custodians of Jamaican sovereignty – the JDF – are in the process of assimilating the doctrine, tactics and world view which define the political action of its main supplier, the US.

The internal political consequences of these new developments are still too early to ascertain, but the United States is buying security at a bargain in the Commonwealth Caribbean, even though new economic and politico-military developments might in the short- or medium-term affect US security assistance and even its military structure in the Caribbean region. US plans for stability in this sub-region seems to centre around the RSS and Jamaica, instead of a large-scale direct military presence. In short, the US has expanded its military involvement in the security of the sub-region and in doing so has increased its penetration of the security forces in the area. In the third phase again voices extolling the virtues of military leadership in the society have reappeared. Though it seems that this JDF faction is not the dominant one, it is noteworthy that it feels secure enough to express its views openly in the political debate.

Notes

1. US Department of State, 'Freedom, Regional Security and Global Peace', *Special Report No. 143*, Washington, DC, 1986.
2. See S. G. Neuman, 'Defense Planning in Less Industrialized States: An Organizing Framework', in S. G. Neuman (ed.), *Defense Planning in Less Industrialized States* (Lexington, 1984), pp. 1–27.
3. Barbados was the only one not forced to establish a defence force. For a detailed analysis of the formation of these defence forces see M. R. M. McFarlane, 'The Military in the Commonwealth Caribbean: A Study in Comparative Institutionalisation', PhD thesis, The University of Western Ontario, 1974, pp. 147–67.
4. Sir J. Mordecai, *The West Indies: The Federal Negotiations* (Evanston, 1968), 270.
5. In 1940 Great Britain, in exchange for some 50-odd over-aged destroyers, granted the United States the rights to lease areas in eight of

its Caribbean colonies, including Jamaica. For the text of the 1961 agreement see R. Preiswerk (ed.), *Documents on International Relations in the Caribbean* (Río Piedras; St Augustine, 1970), p. 630.

6. T. Lacey, *Violence and Politics in Jamaica 1960–1970* (London, 1970), 159.
7. N. Ahiram, 'Income Distribution in Jamaica', *Social and Economic Studies* (Jamaica), 13, 3, (1965), p. 343.
8. Lacey, *Violence*, 17.
9. See C. Stone, *Class, State and Democracy in Jamaica* (New York, 1986), pp. 38–40.
10. M. Handel, *Weak States in the International System* (London, 1981), pp. 47–53.
11. Central Planning Unit, *Economic Survey 1969*, 3.
12. V. A. Lewis, 'The Caribbean State Systems and Contemporary World Order', in C. Stone and P. Henry (eds), *The Newer Caribbean* (Philadelphia, 1983), p. 135.
13. See D. Ronfeldt, *Geopolitics, Security and U.S. Strategy in the Caribbean Basin* (Santa Monica, 1983), pp. 22–5.
14. Bustamante himself migrated to Cuba in 1905 where he worked with a tramway company which operated in Cuba and Panamá. After two or three years he was transferred to Panamá, but he returned to Cuba in the 1920s, where he stayed working as a member of the special police force before moving to New York, shortly before the fall of the dictator Gerardo Machado in the early 1930s. See G. E. Eaton, *Alexander Bustamante and Modern Jamaica* (Kingston, 1975), pp. 14–15.
15. See Lacey, *Violence*, pp. 146–7.
16. For an analysis of the model in this case see V. A. Lewis, 'Issues and Trends in Jamaican Foreign Policy 1972–1977', in C. Stone and A. Brown (eds), *Perspectives on Jamaica on the Seventies* (Kingston, 1981), pp. 42–8.
17. For a short historical overview of the JDF see *Tenth Anniversary 3rd Battalion The Jamaica Regiment 1962–1972* (Kingston, 1972) and 2 Lt T. Reid, 'Military in Jamaica', *Alert* (organ of the JDF) 10 (1982), pp. 14–15, 21.
18. Stone, *Class*, 53.
19. Only for a short period of time, when Donald Sangster was prime minister, the two positions did not coincide. See E. H. Stephens and J. D. Stephens, *Democratic Socialism in Jamaica* (Princeton, 1986), pp. 42–6.
20. It is important to note that the JCF is a paramilitary force (armed, under one central direction and with some military training). For an analysis of the JCF relationship with the government see Lacey, *Violence*, pp. 102–6, 115–43.
21. The rebellion was planned by a Rastafarian group led by Rev Claudius Henry and an armed militant black group from New York, the First Africa Corps. See H. Campbell, *Rasta and Resistance. From Garvey to Walter Rodney* (New York, 1987), pp. 103–4.
22. Brig Smith fought in the Second World War, joined the JR in the 1950s and went to the Imperial Defence College, London, in 1964. See O. L.

Levy and H. P. Jacobs (eds), *Personalities Caribbean 1971–1972* (Kingston, 1971), p. 598.

23. *Declassified Document Quarterly Catalogue* 9, (1983), 001018, US Department of State report, 'Briefing Paper for the President. Subject: Meeting with Jamaican Prime Minister, Sir Alexander Bustamante', n.d., 4.

24. Ibid., 001019, US Department of State memo, 'Jamaica Scope Paper', 22 June 1961, p. 2.

25. For a detailed inventory and acquisitions of the JDF military equipment see *The Military Balance* (London, various years) and the *SIPRI Yearbook* (London, various years).

26. Lacey, *Violence*, p. 152.

27. Bermudan soldiers were also involved in 1968 in the British army jungle warfare exercises. See Ibid., 151 and Capt B. Blake (1JR), 'First Jamaica Defence Contingent on Training in Canada from 21 May–19 June, 1971', *Alert* 4, October, 1971, 33–4.

28. Throughout the years the JDF has assisted government departments with work of a technical nature and in one of these the JDF, the geological survey department, the UNDP-FAO water resources project, and the US National Aeronautics and Space Administration (NASA) collaborated in an airborne remote sensing survey over the island. See Maj J. B. Williams, 'The Defence Force and NASA', *Alert* 4 (October 1971), pp. 13–16.

29. Lacey, *Violence*, p. 155.

30. Stone, *Class*, p. 56.

31. See Lacey, *Violence*, pp. 87–94, 114–15 and McFarlane, 'The Military', pp. 224–8.

32. McFarlane, *Ibid.*, p. 358.

33. Lacey, *Violence*, p. 115.

34. A sole supplier is a single donor which supplies all of a particular type of weapons system to a recipient. A principal supplier is a single donor that has supplied 60 per cent or more of a particular system to a recipient, but other suppliers have also made other systems available. In the Jamaican case the percentages might not be so clear cut, but my intention is to note that British arms supplies and the training of the security forces in Great Britain mean that ties with the former colonial power remained. See A. Leiss, *et al.*, *Arms Transfers to Less Developed Countries* (Cambridge, 1970), p. 84.

35. M. Manley, *Jamaica: The Struggle in the Periphery* (London, 1982), p. 37.

36. A. Payne, 'Jamaica: The Democratic Socialist Experiment of Michael Manley', in A. Payne and P. Sutton (eds), *Dependency under Challenge. The Political Economy of the Commonwealth Caribbean* (Manchester, 1984), p. 19.

37. M. Manley, *The Politics of Change. A Jamaican Testament* (London, 1974), p. 222. Michael was elected head of the PNP when his father Norman retired in 1969.

38. H. Campbell, 'Crime and Violence in Jamaica Politics', *Caribbean Issues* (Trinidad and Tobago), 2, 1976, p. 29.

39. M. Manley, 'Overcoming Insularity in Jamaica', *Foreign Affairs* 49, (1970), pp. 100–10.
40. Manley narrates a lunch in Jamaica where Kissinger said 'he would appreciate it if Jamaica would at least remain neutral on the subject of the Cuban army presence in Angola'. He adds that the US Secretary of State sent 'a message' by mentioning a Jamaican proposal for a US$100 million trade credit. After the announcement of support to Cuba nothing else was heard on the trade credit. Manley, *Jamaica*, pp. 116–17.
41. A. Payne, 'Jamaica', 27.
42. See N. Girvan, R. Bernal and W. Hughes, 'The IMF and the Third World: The Case of Jamaica, 1974–1980', *Development Dialogue* 2, (1980), pp. 113–55 and C. Edie, 'Domestic Politics and External Relations in Jamaica Under Michael Manley', *Studies in Comparative International Development* 21, 1, 1986, pp. 71–94.
43. Destabilisation, he writes, 'describes a situation where some source either inside or outside a country – or perhaps two sources working in concert, one outside and one inside – set out to create a situation of instability and panic *by design*'. Manley, *Jamaica*, p. 138 (emphasis in the original).
44. After Edward Seaga took over the leadership in 1974, the JLP moved close to conservative circles in the US. It can be said that the JLP penetrated the US political system. See V. A. Lewis, 'The Small State Alone: Jamaican Foreign Policy, 1977–1980', *Journal of Interamerican Studies and World Affairs* 25, 2, (1983), pp. 150–5. In another work I discussed the role of the JLP as a 'disloyal opposition', a concept drawn from J. J. Linz, 'Crisis, Breakdown, and Reequilibration', in J. J. Linz and A. Stepan (eds), *The Breakdown of Democratic Regimes* (Baltimore, 1978), pp. 15, 30–2, 40–5. See. H. García Muñiz, *La Estrategia de Estados Unidos y la Militarización del Caribe* (Río Piedras, 1988), pp. 108–10.
45. See Stone, *Class*, p. 194.
46. M. Kaufman, *Jamaica Under Manley* (Westport, 1985), p. 116.
47. Ibid. and Stephens and Stephens, *Democratic Socialism*, 133.
48. See Manley, *Jamaica*, p. 85.
49. The new administrative arrangement, coupled with the violence, affected the management of the security expenditures: 'From the mid-1970s, the degree of aggregation for both police expenditures and the Jamaica Defence Force is very great. The breakdowns into operating and capital costs cannot be considered very reliable for those years.' N. Ball, 'Jamaica', *Third World Security Expenditures: A Statistical Compendium* (Stockholm, 1984), p. 50. See also I. Kaplan *et al.*, *Area Handbook for Jamaica* (Washington, DC, 1976), 284.
50. Lt Col. Green took over from Brig Dunstan Robinson, who was appointed in May of the same year. Lt Col. Green joined the JR in 1946 and attended the Army Staff College, UK, on 1964. See O. L. Levy and H. P. Jacobs (eds), *Personalities Caribbean 1972–1973* (Kingston, 1973), pp. 471–2 and C. Neita (ed.), *Who's Who in Jamaica 1969* (Kingston, 1973), p. 182.

51. The three had military service in the Second World War: Matalon in the Royal Canadian Air Force, Munn in the Canadian Army, and Thompson in the Royal Air Force. See C. Neita (ed.), *Who's Who in Jamaica 1963* (Kingston, 1963), pp. 264, 283, 383.

52. The only instance of JDF-JCF conflict in the 1970s I have found is told by JLP Deputy Leader Pearnel Charles, then a political detainee and presently public utilities and transport minister. He writes that some policemen were shot and injured in retaliation by the killing of a JDF soldier by the police. For a time the island-wide joint patrols were suspended. Charles was detained after tapes of police and military radio transmissions were found in his possession. See P. Charles, *Detained, 283 Days in Jamaica's Detention Camp Struggling for Freedom, Justice and Human Rights* (Kingston, 1977), pp. 123–6.

53. Early in the 1970s a Canadian security specialist warned: 'But where external threats are minimal, internal security becomes the primary reason for the existence of military forces. If called out too often, such forces cease to be a deterrent and do work that should more properly be done by the police. In such circumstances it is often difficult to maintain military efficiency; *but these military forces may become a threat to the civil power.*' R. A. Preston, 'Caribbean Defense and Security: A Study of the Implications of Canada's "Special Relationship" with the Commonwealth West Indies', *The South Atlantic Quarterly* 70 (Summer, 1971), p. 320 (my emphasis).

54. See McFarlane, 'The Military', pp. 325–28.

55. There are organisations of ex-servicemen, such as the Jamaica Legion. In the mid-1960s there were also organisations linked to the British forces, such as the Royal Air Forces Association. See ibid., 326 and Jamaica Information Service, *The Handbook of Jamaica for 1966* (Kingston, 1966), pp. 888–9.

56. It should be noted that in 1976 a JDF Women's Unit was formed. See 2 Lt S. M. Taylor, 'Women in the JDF', *Alert* 10 (1982), pp. 45, 49.

57. Maj. A. Douglas, 'The Role of the Jamaica Defence Force in Developing Jamaica', *Alert*, (1977), p. 33 (my emphasis). In 1980 Maj Douglas advocated conscription: 'The society must be organised, motivated and disciplined. We in the Jamaica Defence Force have a responsibility to endure that the appropriate vehicle, National Service (conscription), is enacted in the not too distant future'. Maj. A. Douglas, 'A Case for National Service in Jamaica', *Alert* 8, 1980, p. 17.

58. Ibid., pp. 31–2. (My emphasis) In a recent study on the Guyanese military, the definition of militarisation utilised fits neatly the approach advocated by Maj. Douglas. Militarisation is defined as 'a condition in which increasingly large portions of the population and resources of a society become progressively involved and dominated by, or inducted in one way or another into military and para-military institutions. It is a condition in which military type institutions become viewed by a ruling elite as an organisational panacea for the "ills" of external defence indiscipline, social instability, and problems of mobilisation, control, and development within a society. It is a social condition in which regimentation is seen as a way of life.' G. K. Danns, 'The Role of the

Military in National Security in Guyana', *Bulletin of Eastern Caribbean Affairs* (Barbados) 11, 6, 1987, p. 23.

59. See Stephens and Stephens, *Democratic Socialism*, 238–41. In addition to the political motivations behind the coup attempt, general dissatisfaction, demoralisation, and a breakdown in the middle management due to a leadership crisis within the JDF were major factors. Interview with anonymous JDF officer, Kingston, May 1988.

60. See Kaufman, *Jamaica*, 188–9. Maj Gen Neish was appointed chief of staff in 1979. The pro-JLP sector in the JDF favoured Neish's appointment because he was seen as easy to manipulate and politically neutral, in contrast to Trinidad-born Col. K. Barnes, who was regarded as very professional and difficult to control. (Interview with anonymous JDF officer, Kingston, May 1988) Maj Gen Neish joined the FWIR in 1958; attended the Royal Military Academy, Sandhurst, UK; the School of Infantry, UK; Army Aviation Instruction Course, Canada; and Army Staff College, UK. See A. L. Levy and H. P. Jacobs (eds), *Personalities Caribbean 1982–83* (Kingston, 1983), p. 470.

61. A leftist UWI lecturer, Mark Figueroa, noted in early June that the independent actions of the security forces directed against government personnel and supporters were 'ominous signs, particularly in the context of open calls and other incitements from the reactionary for the overthrow or "under-throw" of the Government'. M. Figueroa, 'Ominous Signs', *The Jamaican Daily News*, 9 June 1980, 6. See also I. Villar, H. Dilla and I. Jaramillo, *Crisis, Proceso Político y Alternativas en la Sociedad Jamaicana Contemporánea* (La Habana, 1983), pp. 113–17.

62. Manley, *Jamaica*, 201. It is interesting to note that Maj Gen Neish, together with Seaga and other major public figures have been described as 'socially white from the propertied elite'. G. Beckford and M. Witter, *Small Garden . . . Bitter Weed. The Political Economy of Struggle and Change in Jamaica* (London, 1980; 2nd expanded edn 1982), p. 130.

63. Ibid., 51 (my emphasis). Campbell claims that because 'the ruling petty bourgeoisie cannot guarantee the total allegiance of the police or the army it is necessary for the party to maintain a constant supply of thugs'. Campbell, 'Crime and Violence', p. 31.

64. M. Figueroa, 'An Assessment of Overvoting in Jamaica,' *Social and Economic Studies*, 34, 3, 1985, pp. 90–91. He suggests that the rank-and-file soldiers that supported the PNP were most of the abstentions 'because they perceived their officers and the majority of their colleagues to be leaning in the direction of the JLP and were intimidated' (p. 88).

65. See *Estimates of Expenditure for the Year Ending 31 March 1975, passed by the HR on 30 May 1974*, 382 and *Estimates of Expenditure for the Year Ending 31 March 1976 passed by the HR on 30 May 1975*, 401.

66. See US Department of Defense (DOD), *Fiscal Year Series as of September 1982* (Washington, DC., 1982), pp. 356–57.

67. These imports probably fall under the Commercial Sales of the United States, which usually is police-type equipment. Percentage estimates from Department of Statistics, *External Trade 1973, 1975, 1977–80*.

68. Ibid., *External Trade 1969–71*. The small re-exports trade is mainly with the United States, Britain and some Caribbean countries.
69. See US DOD, *Fiscal Year Series*, pp. 356–7.
70. The armoured vehicles were bought in the US and the mortars in Britain.
71. Manley, *Jamaica*, p. 84.
72. See Stephens and Stephens, *Democratic Socialism*, 229–30.
73. A former military officer trained in India said: 'Its culture is Commonwealth.' Interview with a former JDF officer, who asked not to be cited by name, Kingston, May, 1988.
74. Maj. L. Harbord, 'Canadian Military Assistance', *Alert* 4, July, 1975, p. 10.
75. Stephens and Stephens, *Democratic Socialism*, p. 135.
76. See *Caribbean Monthly Bulletin* (Puerto Rico), 11, 12, 1979, p. 6.
77. See Capt. C. L. Kirkcaldy and Lt C. Taylor, 'Diary of events', *Altimeter* (organ of the JDF air wing) 4, July, 1975, p. 5. Reportedly the senior military attache in the US Embassy in Kingston was meeting prior to the coup attempt with JDF officers. These meetings sometimes were in the Up Park Camp. See E. Ray and B. Schaap, 'Massive Destabilization in Jamaica, 1976 with a New Twist', *Covert Action Information Bulletin*, 10, 1980, pp. 7–17.
78. See Manley, *Jamaica*, p. 231. A US Foreign Service officer says that under the construction agreement with Cuba of the 1200 men that went to Cuba for training several hundred received 'special military training', J. D. Forbes, *Jamaica: Managing Political and Economic Change* (Washington, DC, 1985), p. 23.
79. See Department of Statistics, *External Trade 1979*. The only previous arms trade with a communist state was in 1968 when it imported from Czechoslovakia one unit under the category 'Revolvers and Pistols' worth J-35. See Department of Statistics, *External Trade 1968*, p. 130.
80. The two officers went at Grenada's request. See 'Police Being Upgraded', *The Free West Indian* (Grenada), 17 November 1979, 15 and Grenada, Ministry of Information, Government Information Service News Release 981/80, 4 November 1980.
81. Stone, *Class*, p. 57.
82. Ibid.
83. The Report of the Atlantic Council's Working Group on the Caribbean Basin says: 'Jamaica, the largest and the most influential nation of the subregion, should be identified as a model of democratic mixed-enterprise development for other countries to emulate.' R. Kennedy and G. Marcella, 'U.S. Security on the Southern Flank: Interests, Challenges and Responses', in J. R. Greene, B. Scowcroft, *et al.*, (eds), *Western Interests and U.S. Policy Options in the Caribbean Basin* (Boston, 1984), p. 231.
84. '1981–82 Budget Debate Presentation by the PM, Hon Edward Seaga', Agency for Public Information, 16 June 1981, p. 6.
85. F. Ambursley, 'Jamaica: From Michael Manley to Edward Seaga', in F. Ambursley and R. Cohen (eds), *Crisis in the Caribbean*, New York, 1983, p. 85.

86. News Release No. 555/81, Agency of Public Information, 10 March 1981, p. 4.
87. '1981–82 Budget Debate', p. 55.
88. Quoted in L. Edmondson, 'Jamaica', in J. W. Hopkins (ed.), *Latin America and the Caribbean: A Contemporary Record* (New York, 1983), p. 592. See also Villar, Dilla and Jaramillo, *Crisis*, pp. 158–72.
89. See US Arms Control and Disarmament Agency, *World Military Expenditures and Arms Transfers, 1985* (Washington, DC, 1985), p. 68.
90. See *Latin America Regional Reports: Caribbean Report*, 20 August 1982, p. 3.
91. Ibid., 27 September 1985, p. 3.
92. Percentage estimate from Department of Statistics, *External Trade 1981, 1983 and 1984*, pp. 387–8, 389–90, 384–5.
93. Included here are the SLR rifles, the Sterling sub-machine gun, the GMPG general purpose machine gun and the 81mm mortar. A. J. English, 'Jamaica', *Armed Forces of Latin America* (London, 1984), p. 295.
94. Percentage estimate from US DOD, *Fiscal Year Series*, 356–57 and US DOD, *Foreign Military Sales, Foreign Military Construction Sales and Military Assistance Facts as of 30 September 1986* (Washington, DC, 1986), pp. 6–7, 48–9.
95. The surge pattern is a 'special case of accretion in which a very large increase occurs over a very brief time-span'. Leiss, *Arms Transfers*, p. 62.
96. MAP Merger Funds are non-repayable and cannot be used to finance procurements from US commercial suppliers. See US DOD, *Foreign Military Sales*, p. iv.
97. This information is from the US Department of State (DOS), *Congressional Presentation, Security Assistance Programmes* for the fiscal years 1981 to 1988. US assistance also included the loan of a power barge from the US navy that would provide 25mgw of back-up capacity. See 'A Report to Parliament on the Administration's Second Year in Office: Statement by the PM Edward Seaga, to the HR, 2 November 1982', Jamaica Information Service, 11 November 1982, p. 31.
98. The SDAF is a revolving fund established in 1982 to finance the acquisition of defence items and services 'which enhances the US Government's ability to meet urgent foreign needs for military equipment. . . [and to] . . . promote cooperative forward planning by allied and friendly governments.' US DOS, *Congressional Presentation . . . FY1988*, 352.
99. Letter of Maj. J. A. Prescod, HQ, JDF, Up Park Camp, Jamaica, to Humberto García Muñiz, New York City, 18 July 1987.
100. See US DOS, *Congressional Presentation . . . FY1988*, 352.
101. The Organization of the Joint Chiefs of Staff (OJCS), *United States Military Posture FY1985*, 82 (my emphasis). According to a 1980 survey by the US DOD, 25 presidents/heads of state, 160 cabinet ministers/legislators/ambassadors, 258 chiefs of staff and 1834 general/flag rank had attended US senior military schools as foreign students. See The OJCS, *United States Military Posture for FY1984*, 53.

02. See 'Exchange Program Between Puerto Rico, J'can Army Men', Jamaica Information Service News Release 104/83, 19 January 1983.

03. See 'Guardsmen, Caribbean soldiers train', *The San Juan Star* (Puerto Rico), 6 June 1988, p. 13. For a fuller discussion on this topic and the wider Jamaica-Puerto Rico relations see J. E. Rey Otero, 'Cooperación intergubernamental en el Caribe: Puerto Rico y Jamaica', in A. Medina Villalba (ed.), *La Transnacionalización de Puerto Rico en la Década de los 80* (Río Piedras, 1984), pp. 73–87.

04. US DOS, *Congressional Presentation . . . FY1982*, p. 437.

05. US DOS, *Congressional Presentation . . . FY1986*, p. 405.

06. Unofficial estimates run much higher to almost US$1 billion. See 'Marijuana Production Worth US$1 billion', *Caribbean Contact* (Barbados), March, 1987, p. 2.

07. In Puerto Rico a JDF soldier was sentenced in 1988 to two years in prison for drug possession. He was arrested at customs with two pounds of ganja when he arrived in a JDF aircraft to take part in military exercises staged by the US National Guard of Puerto Rico. See 'Pot pleading', *The Daily News* (US Virgin Islands), 30 April 1988, p. 5.

08. See 'Jamaica: Fear of US Aid Cutoff Sparks Tougher Anti-Drug Drive', *Inter Press Service*, 10 December 1986 and 'United States: 20 Countries Cooperating with Anti-Drug Campaign', *Inter Press Service*, 2 March 1987.

09. See *The Jamaican Weekly Gleaner*, 21 November 1988, p. 28, and US DOS, *Congressional Presentation . . . FY1989*, p. 203.

10. 'Seaga Raps US Drug Enforcement Efforts', *The Jamaican Weekly Gleaner*, 25 July 1988, p. 11.

11. Americas Watch, *Human Rights in Jamaica* (New York, 1986), p. 4.

12. Jamaica contributed the most men to the CSF, followed by Barbados. Their role was proxy-like in the sense that the United States could perform the security tasks, but decided against it because 'for political reasons . . . it is best that some other state do the job for it'. S. R. David, 'The Use of Proxy Forces by Major Powers in the Third World', in S. G. Neuman and R. Harkavy (eds), *The Lessons of Recent Wars in the Third World: Comparative Dimensions*, vol. 2, (Lexington, 1987), p. 200.

13. Capt V. H. Anderson (HQ, JDF), 'Operation "Urgent Fury"', *Alert*, 11, July, 1984, p. 21.

14. See HQ, US Forces Caribbean, 'Caribbean Regional Coast Guard Program', *DISAM Newsletter*, Fall, 1985, p. 55.

15. See H. García Muñiz, *Boots, Boots, Boots: Intervention, Regional Security and Militarization in the Caribbean 1979–1986* (Río Piedras, 1986); D. E. Phillips, 'Barbados and the Militarization of the Eastern Caribbean', *Bulletin of Eastern Caribbean Affairs* 11, 6, January/February, 1986, pp. 8–18; and A. Walker, 'Security of the Eastern Caribbean', *Jane's Defence Weekly*, 17 January 1987, p. 61.

16. The only previous exceptions, to my knowledge, were at least two meetings of the chiefs of staff of the JDF, the Trinidad and Tobago Defence Force (TTDF) and the Guyana Defence Force (GDF) in 1969 to discuss coordinating activities for internal security purposes and a

short visit of the JDF chief of staff to Trinidad and Tobago during the 1970 mutiny. See McFarlane, 'The Military', 206 and Preston, 'Caribbean Defense', 330. Personal links among the officers of these forces should exist, particularly those formed in training. For example, Maj Gen. Neish and TTDF army chief of staff Col. J. L. Theodore served in the JR and attended Sandhurst at the same time. See 'West Indians in Pass-out at Sandhurst', *The Jamaican Daily Gleaner*, 3 August 1961.
117. US DOS, *Congressional Presentation . . . FY1989*, 200.
118. In one of the exercises British troops participated and in another St Vincent and Barbados abstained from sending men.
119. Lt D. G. Pryce, 'Exercise "Ocean Venture"', *Alert*, 12, August, 1986 p. 9.
120. See '"Exercise Trade Winds" in Action' and 'Regional Security Teams on Exercise', *The Jamaican Weekly Gleaner*, 21 September 1987 pp. 25, 27.
121. See *The Jamaican Daily Gleaner*, 18 August 1988.
122. See US DOS, *Congressional Presentation . . . FY1989*, pp. 201–2.
123. See 'PM Says JDF to Do Home Surveys', *The Jamaican Weekly Gleaner*, 5 December 1988, p. 8.
124. See US General Accounting Office, *US Security and Military Assistance: Programs and Related Activities – An Update*, GAO/NSIAD–85–158, 30 September 1985, pp. 15–18.
125. For a discussion on the US military command structure see García Muñiz, *Estrategia*, pp. 219–32, 270–2.
126. US *Statutes at Large*, vol. 100 (1986), 'Goldwater-Nichols Department of Defense Reorganization Act of 1986', Sec. 212.
127. For further information on SOUTHCOM see Raúl Leis, *Comando Sur Poder Hostil* (Panamá, 1985) and Gen Paul Gorman (US Army, Ret) 'C³I: USCINCSO's Perspective, 1983–1985', *Defense Analysis* 4, 3 1988, pp. 307–20.
128. For a valuable discussion of Jamaica's integration record see A. Payne *Politics in Jamaica* (London, 1988), pp. 149–77.
129. The CDU groups the right-wing parties of the Commonwealth Caribbean and its president is Seaga. The organisation is linked to the International Democrat Union, the conservative opposite to the Socialist International, of which the PNP is a member. See 'St. Lucia Outside Interference in Elections Charged', *Inter Press Service*, 2 April 1987.
130. The Bermuda Regiment resumed its training exercises in Jamaica in February 1987, after stopping them in the mid-70s. See F. McKnight 'Bermudan Soldiers Here on Training Exercise', *The Jamaican Weekly Gleaner*, 16 March 1987, p. 24.
131. See *Caribbean Insight*, July, 1985, p. 8.
132. Ibid., August, 1985, p. 8.
133. 'Soldiers Attend Course', *The Jamaican Weekly Gleaner*, 9 November 1987, p. 2.
134. US DOS, *Congressional Presentation . . . FY1988*, p. 55.
135. Interview with anonymous JDF officer, Kingston, May, 1988.
136. Stone, *Class*, p. 179.

137. From 1981 to 1988 Jamaica received over US$390 million in Economic Support Funds which are earmarked 'to achieve the US foreign policy objective of alleviating economic and political disruption that threaten the security of key countries, by fostering economic development and reform in those countries.' US DOS, *Congressional Presentation . . . FY1988*, p. 56.
138. Stone, *Class*, p. 178. In this vein, early in 1987 the Supreme Court ordered the government to pay a sum to a member of the small Marxist-Leninist Workers Party of Jamaica who was tortured by the police in May 1983. JCF brutality has been under discussion since the 1960s. The Americas Watch report quoted above highlighted the issue, but it was also heavily criticised. One critic, Carl Stone, noted: 'Some of the bad eggs in the Police Force operate outside of the disciplinary reach of the Police High Command because they are mercenaries in the pay of powerful politicians which make them untouchables.' C. Stone, 'The Police and our Rights', *The Jamaican Daily Gleaner*, 1 October 1986.
139. 'No JDF Plot to Overthrow the Govt.,' *The Jamaican Weekly Gleaner*, 19 October 1987, p. 2.
140. Ibid.
141. Ibid. (my emphasis).
142. Ibid. A military informant stated that soldiers were 'leaving camp at night to sleep in their houses due to the bad conditions of the barracks'. Interview with JDF officer, who asked not to be cited by name, Kingston, May, 1988.
143. Ibid. McFarlane had noted: 'dissatisfied officers of the JDF prefer to resign, rather than to precipitate a crisis as in Trinidad and Tobago, is an indication of their newly-found values'. McFarlane, 'The Military', p. 327.
144. 'Neish: JDF Firmly Behind Fight Against Crime', Ibid., p. 3.
145. Due to the events in Grenada the JLP intensified its anti-communist campaign by accusing the Soviet embassy in Kingston of espionage. For details see A. Payne, P. Sutton and T. Thorndike, *Grenada: Revolution and Invasion* (New York, 1984), 210–13.
146. See 'Carib Troops Come to Help', *The Jamaica Weekly Gleaner*, 3 October 1988, p. 11.
147. C. Stone, '"Gilbert" Swings Public Opinion Towards Seaga', *The Jamaican Weekly Gleaner*, 17 October 1988, p. 9.
148. The PNP shadow minister for national security, K. D. Knight, is a well known criminal lawyer 'with some knowledge of the police, but not of the JDF'. Interview with a former anonymous JDF officer, Kingston, May, 1988.

6 The Development of the Military in Post-Independent Barbados
Dion E. Phillips

INTRODUCTION

There are a limited number of studies on the post-independent military in the Anglophone Caribbean in general and Barbados in particular. Two principle reasons account for this. It is only within the last two decades or so that the new nation states of the subregion have had thrust upon them the responsibility for external affairs and defence, including the creation of defence forces. Previously, defence was the prerogative of the British government. In other words, the phenomena of 'a local army' did not exist.

However, when the defence force entered the arena with the advent of independence, unlike Jamaica, Trinidad and Tobago, Guyana and Belize, who started defence forces, respectively, to coincide with the event of independence, the formation of a defence force in Barbados, officially named the Barbados Defence Force (BDF), came in 1979, 13 years after its actual attainment of political independence. Since its creation, there has been but a single study dealing exclusively and comprehensively with the origin, organisation and behaviour of the post-independent military in Barbados.[1] This chapter is an updated version of that very work. Specifically, the period covered is 1966 to 1987, although I do provide a brief overview of the existence of the military during the colonial years.

Then, too, the *lacuna* in regard to substantive research on the military in the Caribbean is partly a consequence of the fact that social scientists have tended to shun the detailed, micro-study of elites, not to mention the military. Apart from the recency of its existence, the difficulties encountered in the process of studying the military revolve around having to investigate a topic as esoteric as defence which, by virtue of its importance is isolated from public scrutiny. And so, because defence forces operate in an environment of secrecy, security and confidentiality, this reality makes data gathering difficult and is a militating circumstance in its selection as a legitimate area of study. The defence force is a politically sensitive area of research. As a result, any one trying to obtain relevant information concerning it is viewed with suspicion which, in turn, inhibits the research process.

Notwithstanding the aforementioned existing conditions, in recent years the existence of the military in the newly independent Caribbean nation-states has aroused interest and concern among politicians, policy makers, academics and other observers. There are five major defence forces in the Anglophone Caribbean, namely, in the countries of Jamaica, Trinidad and Tobago, Guyana, Barbados and Belize. Antigua and Barbuda is the only member of the seven-country Organization of Eastern Caribbean States (OECS) grouping with a defense force. Currently, there are no full-fledged defense forces in the remaining OECS countries of Grenada, Dominica, St Kitts and Nevis, St Vincent and the Grenadines, St Lucia and Montserrat. However, Grenada did have a Peoples Revolutionary Army when Maurice Bishop and the Peoples Revolutionary Government were in power. The defence force of Barbados is of particular interest because of its manifest military importance. The US Agency for International Development (USAID) in 1982 stated: 'Barbados is a vital cog in the regional security posture. The country has important physical assets whose use by a hostile power would be detrimental to US interest.'

Such significance is exemplified by the fact that a detachment of the BDF rendered support to the 28th Airborne Division and other elements of the US military establishment when the United States elected to invade the tiny island of Grenada in October 1983. Also, the BDF serves as the nucleus of the Regional Security System (RSS). The RSS is the first and only genuine military alliance in the Caribbean. Its member states are the OECS countries and Barbados; the latter's BDF chief of staff serves as the RSS coordinator.

PRE-INDEPENDENCE YEARS: 1627–1966

The colonial history of Barbados and the other British colonies is one in which the military featured prominently. Britain played a vital role in its attempts to keep Barbados and the other colonies in line with its national interests. Part of this strategy involved the use of various forces, namely, the militia, West India regiments, the police after emancipation, and, in subsequent years, the Volunteer Force, the Barbados Battalion and, finally, the Barbados Regiment, with the latter serving as the precursor to the BDF.

In general, the militia units in Barbados, were maintained primarily to pacify the large slave population.[2] The first units were raised in 1640 'for the protection of the island'. When slave revolts were uncovered in 1649, 1675 and 1692, militia units were rapidly deployed 'to defend the colony from the blacks from within'.[3] The Barbados militia was often sent to other Caribbean islands to quell unrest. The most significant of these was the opposition to Oliver Cromwell in 1649. The historian Ligon refers to Barbados in 1688 as 'a potent colony and able to arm ten thousand men'.[4]

In addition to the existence of militia units in Barbados, the British government decided to defend its West Indian possessions with regiments of slaves – initially manned by creoles but subsequently and predominantly by blacks born in Africa.[5] Few whites seemed able to survive military service in the tropical climate. In 1795, two regiments of blacks were started; within three years there were twelve, many of which were shortlived. When the Bussa rebellion, broke out in April 1816, the insurgents were suppressed by several local militia units in conjunction with the first (Bourbon) West India regiment.[6]

The militia forces in Barbados were succeeded in the post-emancipation period by the police force.[7] In 1834, one year after emancipation, the legislature passed an Act establishing a single force for the whole island.[8] Six years later in 1840, a unit of detectives was formed. In 1882, a new Police Act provided that the term 'Police Force' should mean and include the land police, the Harbour police and the Corps of writservers. The year 1945 was a watershed for the police force. Superintendent W. A. Calver of the Metropolitan Police, London, (later Commissioner of Police in Jamaica) made the following report:

> Change is constant. In Barbados as in other progressive countries, the change in business, political and social lives and the development of all institutions, have reflected themselves upon the force. The police are, therefore, required to be completely modern, individually efficient, and generally confident and contented, to ensure that it is foremost among the essential services.[9]

Consequent to such recommendations, important changes have taken place in the police force since 1945.

The Barbados Volunteer Force was established in 1902 under the provisions of the Volunteer Act 1901–21. It was formed to provide the internal security requirements of the island when the locally stationed Imperial troops left to take up other duties in St Lucia. As a body, it was called upon on two occasions to go overseas to protect the interest of the Imperial Government. The first occasion was in 1907 when a detachment of volunteers and police were sent to St Lucia to suppress strikes and rioting by coal carriers which were potentially harmful to the British Navy and Merchant Marine in the Caribbean which needed coal for fuel. The second was in 1942 when a crisis threatened the peace and stability of the British colony of Dominica which developed owing to the presence of 5000 Martiniquians exacerbating food shortages and causing social strife. Also, soldiers from the Volunteer Force of Barbados were involved, at low levels, in World War II.

On the home front, the Volunteer Force was called out on 27 July 1937 to assist the police in their response to civil disturbances which had started the day before.[10] These disturbances were allegedly instigated by Clement Payne, a Trinidadian, who had agitated for better conditions and preached trade unionism. The unrest resulted in 14 persons being killed and 47 wounded. In terms of the role of the Volunteer Force in restoring order, it expended twelve rounds of ammunition and a single arrest was made by Major Walcott.

In 1941, the Volunteer Force was taken over by the Imperial Government (British War Office). Its name, structure and role were changed and it was replaced by a body of full-time soldiers called the Barbados Battalion, South Caribbean Force. One West Indian detachment, which included a Barbadian unit, was trained. During the Second World War, approximately 60 Barbadians reached as far as Italy during the war of Lorence. However, the battalion did not go to the front of the war because they were regarded by General Alexander of the British Eighth Army as unfit. Upon their return to Barbados, the 'island battalion', as it was called, continued its training program until the end of the war and was eventually disbanded in March 1947.

In July 1947, the Barbados Battalion was replaced by a part-time volunteer body called the Barbados Regiment. The bill to change the title 'Barbados Volunteer Force' to 'Barbados Regiment' was passed in the House of Assembly in December 1948. This came in the wake of the re-constitution of the Volunteer Force after the demobilisation of the troops and the disbanding of the Barbados Battalion of the South Caribbean Force. The Barbados Regiment essentially continued the work that the Volunteer Force had begun.

During the period of its existence from 1948 to 1979, the only real challenge the Barbados Regiment faced was the devastation caused by Hurricane Janet in September 1955. Under the command of Colonel O. F. C. Walcott, the regiment was involved in road clearing as well as administrative and security tasks.

The black soldiers of the militia and West India regiments bore arms and were part of a military elite though few, if any, rose to a rank beyond that of a senior noncommissioned office. Also, while Barbadians and other West Indians did participate in both World Wars on the side of the British, their recruitment and organisation tended to follow the customary ethnic groupings. Moreover, even though they served beyond the shores of the Caribbean, West Indian units were regarded as support, rather than genuine combat elements. In fact, after World War I and II, respectively, these West Indian forces were demobilised. Hence, during the colonial years, a strong martial tradition was not cultivated and sustained by the British. And so, with the coming of the BDF in 1979, Barbados had no solid experience with a standing army.

INDEPENDENCE WITHOUT AN ARMY: THE FORMATIVE YEARS, 1966–79

Supposedly, one of the conditions for formal independence of the new Commonwealth states as imposed by the United Kingdom was the establishment of a defence force. Before the demise of the West Indies Federation, there was a proposed plan to establish a Federal Defence Force to service its ten member countries. It was scheduled to be headquartered in Trinidad. After the Federation collapsed and Jamaica proceeded to independence in 1962, the latter formed a defence force, many of whose members were Jamaica nationals previously enlisted with the Federal West India Regiment (see previous chapter).

The creation of a defence force as a condition to independence was again exemplified by the actions of Trinidad and Tobago as they too embraced independence in 1962, months after Jamaica. Moreover, the apparent universality of this criteria was echoed by Eric Williams, a leading Caribbean historian, scholar, and Prime Minister of Trinidad and Tobago, and one known at the time for his anti-colonialist posture. He stated that:

> The fact of the matter is that a new independent country is expected, even required by the ex-colonial power, to have some sort of defense force. The British Government made this quite clear when it set out eight criteria of independence at Jamaica's request at the time of the break-up of the Federation. The former British Prime Minister, Sir Alexander Douglas Home, reiterated this fairly recently when in replying to a question on the prime considerations for the grant of independence, he stated: It is essential that a country concerned has an efficient army – no matter how small – loyal to the legally elected government, and an efficient police force.[11]

When Guyana moved to independence in 1965, it too followed suit and made arrangements for the creation of the Guyana Defense Force.[12] With Barbados, the pattern would change.

Under the leadership of Errol Barrow, a World War II air force veteran, and the Democratic Labour Party, Barbados became independent on 30 November 1966. However, unlike Jamaica, Trinidad and Tobago, and Guyana, there were seemingly no formal plans at the time for the creation of a defence force and neither was the omission of this alleged independence requirement a matter of urgency. Rather, during the first 13 years of its existence, the police force was the factotum and security mainstay of the nation-state. Moreover, unlike Eric Williams who asked the United States to surrender the base of Chaguaramas, Barrow permitted the US naval facility in St Lucy, with its sixty US marines and where eighty locals were employed, to remain in post-colonial Barbados for the entire duration of his twenty consecutive years in power.

Although Barrow and the Democratic Labour Party relied on the police as their sole source of internal security for many years, eventually they were instrumental in starting a Coast Guard Service. This maritime body was an arm of the Barbados Regiment and its base at the time was located, not at the Wharf, Bridgetown, the present headquarters of the Coast Guard, but at Scarborough, near Oistin in Christ Church. The Barbados Regiment, the only other military body in existence during the first stint in government of Barrow and the Democratic Labour Party was a 'militia territorial force which consisted of one battalion equipped with light arms' and which was essentially engaged in ceremonial activities, drills, and sporting activities.[13] It is, however, noteworthy that when the Democratic Labour Party left office in 1976, it left proposals for the creation of a defence force of about fifty to eighty persons.

Two years after the Barbados Labour Party (BLP) was in power, the US hinted to the Barbados government that it was considering pulling out of the naval base it had maintained since 1956 at St Lucy because it was considered to be technically obsolete. The base, which was used for sophisticated undersea communications and information gathering, was closed eventually on 31 March 1979.[14] The BLP when it came to power in 1976 had rejected the idea of a standing army. However, because of hostile actions against the Tom Adams BLP government, the Cubana airline crash and the Sidney Burnett-Alleyne invasion scare in particular, coupled with other developments in the region and the world at large, and with little or nothing to do with the US naval base's departure, the BDF was started on 9 August 1979.[15]

THE ORGANISATIONAL STRUCTURE OF THE BARBADOS DEFENCE FORCE

The BDF is headquartered at St Ann's Fort, the Garrison, St Michael. St Ann's Fort is a pre-existing military facility left by the departing British garrison which has remained somewhat dormant, although put to limited used over the years by the Barbados regiment and sundry elements. Because of the 'new needs' of the newly constituted BDF, the latter has been able to convert existing resources in accordance with infrastructural expansion. Among the features that are found at St Ann's Fort are a ration room, gymnasium, officers' mess rooms, kitchen and dining hall, Hodson hall which serves as a conference room, guard room, parade grounds, medical facility, and other fixtures.

Apart from the headquarters, the BDF has two stationary camps. The St Lucy camp is located at Harrison in St Lucy, Barbados' northernmost parish. This facility was formally occupied by the US Naval Facility. Another camp is located at Paragon, Christ Church, adjacent to the Grantley Adams international airport. This property was formerly the premises of the High Altitude Research Project

(HARP) and the Space Research Corporation (SRC), run by Cana-
dians.

The organisation of the BDF is shaped in accordance with the
British model; however, because of local needs, this military establishment has undergone major alterations in its short existence. The
present BDF, incorporates five squadrons, namely, a regular administrative element, a regular infantry arm, the Barbados regiment, a
pioneer squadron and the Coast Guard service. Additionally, there is
also the Cadet corps and other ancillary units.

The administrative squadron or first squadron is the command and
control headquarters of the BDF. This unit includes the central
procurement and accounting offices as well as the central pay and
record office. This squadron also provides communication, clerical,
stores food, transportation, engineer and material support to all
other BDF squadrons. The second regular squadron is the infantry
arm of the force which is, in fact, the principle fighting or combat
unit. It is comprised of rifle men or snippers who are regarded as a
'strategic military reserve'.[16] Another squadron of the BDF is its
reserve infantry, until 1979 better known as the Barbados Regiment.
The Barbados Regiment which predates the formation of the BDF
was, upon the creation of the latter, integrated into the BDF. The
operational control of this body of part-time soldiers comes under the
immediate rubic of its own commander. A fourth squadron of the
BDF is the Pioneer section which was instituted in April 1984. It
supplies the BDF with such personnel as carpenters, masons,
plumbers, electricians, and welders.

The BDF has the responsibility for the Cadet Force which is
comprised of students most of whom are enrolled in government-
aided secondary schools. The Cadet Corps scheme was originally
formed in January 1909 and was, at that time, attached to the
Barbados Volunteer Force. Once limited to four, the number of
cadet companies has risen to 18, and now encompasses most of the
secondary schools in Barbados; one independent company also
exists. Additionally, the BDF has a role in assisting the National
Youth Service Scheme, formed in 1979, and whose camp is located at
Harrison's Plantation in St Lucy.

Also, the BDF has a Woman's Army Corps formed in November
1984.[17] As of May 1987, this female section of the reserve had not
received the status of a company. A corps of drummers was started in
December 1985.[18] One outstanding feature of the BDF is the medical

reception station located at the BDF headquarters. This unit has the capability of housing 12 in-patients, performing minor surgery, and providing outpatient medical and dental care. In the event of mass casualty disaster, the medical service unit can be extended to accommodate as many as 70 in-patients for a few days.[19]

Until Errol Barrow and the DLP were returned to power in May 1986, the BDF had established a growing small air wing which widely depended on the retention of the air services of the government-owned Aero Services with a fleet of six planes. The air wing of the BDF, which is shrouded in secrecy, seems to have regularly engaged the services of two planes, namely, a 402 Cessna and a Skyvan.

The Cessna 402 was purchased at Fort Lauderdale, Florida.[20] It has a passenger capacity of six persons plus two pilots and a cruising speed of about 190 knots. Also, it has a flight duration of about six hours and a range from Puerto Rico to Trinidad. Though in its normal configuration it was a corporate plane it is modified for aerial surveillance as well as search and rescue.

As for the 19-seater Skyvan, it was acquired in December 1984 from Short Brothers in Northern Ireland for approximately $3 million BDS and was the largest of the fleet. This twin-engine aircraft which served as the backbone of the air wing has a takeoff weight of 13,700 pounds and a cruising speed of 150 knots. It was designed to take off and land on unprepared airstrips no more than 1000 feet in length. During Prime Minister Bernard St John's, tenure in office, (he was Tom Adams' successor) in his capacity as Minister of Civil Aviation, he proposed a site for the construction of a separate hangar at Grantley Adams airport, Barbados' sole airport, to accommodate the then envisaged expansion of the air wing of the BDF.[21] However, thereafter, he and the Barbados Labour Party were voted out of office.

With the return of Barrow and the Democratic Labour Party (DLP) to power, the BDF airwing was downgraded to the point of selling the BDF Skyvan to the government of Guyana in July 1982.[22] In keeping with this unprecedented tilt toward the privatisation of some government-run concerns, Errol Barrow even threatened to dissolve Aero Services, many of whose civilian pilots serviced the BDF's air wing because of a paucity of military personnel trained in aviation and aeronautical engineering. In fact, Caribbean Airways, a commercial airline that was headquartered in Barbados, was part-owned by the Barbados government, and which carried the country's national flag was closed. Even though the much heralded promise by the DLP to drastically reduce the BDF, if and when returned to power, was not fulfilled, its decision to sell the Skyvan, an aircraft that was used exclusively by the BDF, did not only cripple the air wing but effectively reduced its capacity for rapid deployment.

The Barbados Coast Guard squadron, although somewhat autonomous, is an integral part of the BDF and is considered as its maritime arm. The Coast Guard headquarters are located at HMBS Willoughby Fort on the Pierhead, Bridgetown, in the parish of St Michael. This new facility, having formerly been located at Scarborough Christ Church, was completed and commissioned in February 1982. The compound is comprised of, among other components, a woodwork shop, a main shop, a power distribution room, a guard room, the amenity block, junior ratings quarters, a control operations room, and the commander's office.[23]

The Barbados Coast Guard has a naval fleet of seven vessels as well as a number of rubber dinghies. The seven vessels of varying size, power and utility are the HMBS Trident, the HMBS Enterprise, the HMBS Excellence, the HMBS George Ferguson, the HMBS J. T. C. Ramsey, the Commander Marshall and the T. T. Lewis. The Trident is the coast guard flagship and the most formidable of the vessels. Costing some $20 million BDS ($10 million US), it was purchased from Brooke Marine of Lowestoft, England which designed and built it. It is a 37.5 metre ship with two 3000 Pasmore Valenta diesel engines and is capable of cruising 2500 to 3000 miles at a speed of 12 to 14 knots. Its top speed is 30 knots which makes it the fastest vessel in the fleet. Also, it is fitted with communications and navigational (radar and radio) equipment and has a life-saving capacity designed to provide rescue facilities for 200 personnel. Most importantly, the Trident carries two anti-aircraft guns, one mounted up front which has a caliber of 40 millimetres and one mounted in the stern which is 20 millimetres.

The Excellence is a 22 metre vessel designed to carry an eleven member crew. Unlike the Trident, it travels at the much slower speed of 9.6 knots but is capable of 6000-mile endurance stints. The Excellence as well as the now defunct Enterprise were both shrimp trawlers that were converted to serve as coast guard vessels at Swan Hunters in Trinidad.

Other ships in the seven-vessel Coast Guard squadron are the J. T. C. Ramsey (P05), the Commander Marshall and T. T. Lewis, each of which are 12 metres in length. These small-size boats fitted to carry a crew of four were all designed and built by Halmatic-Aquarias of

Havant, England, and are each capable of reaching speeds of up to 24 knots. Purchased in November 1974, some four years before the Coast Guard became a part of the BDF, the J. T. C. Ramsey is the oldest of the fleet.

In September 1986, the original HMBS George Ferguson (P04), a 20-metre boat and once the fourth largest member of the fleet became non-operational. This craft was wrecked in the Tobago Cays, a cluster of uninhabited islands off St Vincent, when it was being taken to Grenada for repairs. The BDF Commander, Rudyard Lewis, promised a full inquiry into its wreckage. However, in August 1987, the Coast Guard, with US assistance, acquired two new launches to replace the damaged HMBS George Ferguson as well as the HMBS Enterprise.[24] These two 22-foot vessels cost $104,000 US and are equipped with 155 horse power outboard engines.

CRITERIA FOR THE ENLISTMENT AND TRAINING OF BDF REGULARS AND OFFICERS

The selection of individuals into the ranks of the BDF is voluntary and without regard to sex, race, colour, religion or class. An individual can be recruited if he or she is between the age of eighteen and twenty-five at enrollment. However, the age limit is extended to accommodate persons with 'special skills'. The prospective soldier or sailor is not required to have any designated level of formal education. However, the applicant is required to complete an application form obtainable from the headquarters of the BDF at St Ann's Fort or the Government Sales Booth in Independence Square, Bridgetown, the capital, or from HMBS Willoughby Fort, the Wharf, also in Bridgetown, in the case of the Coast Guard. Applicants for all branches of the BDF must produce, prior to selection, a police certificate of character and proof of educational background as a prelude to an interview.[25]

If the candidate is accepted, he or she is enlisted as a recruit only if there are vacancies. Upon enlistment, all recruits, regardless of which branch of the BDF they may wish to join, must complete a sixteen-week basic infantry training course. At any time during the course, a recruit may opt out if he or she so chooses.

Having completed basic training, one is then eligible to join the BDF as a regular soldier or sailor.

In order to commence a term of office with the BDF, however, one is required to sign a contract to serve in the regular army or coast guard for three years and, if leaving after that period, to complete a further three-year period in the reserve class II. This class of reserve has no military obligations to fulfill but can be called out in times of national emergency. However, if the enlistee wishes to continue in the BDF, he or she can apply to renew his or her engagement for a further three-year period.

Similar to the regulars, officer selection in the BDF is made without regard to sex, race, colour, and religion. However, dissimilar to the selection of regulars, it appears to be based primarily on educational achievement and leadership skills. The prospective officer cadet must be in possession of at least six or more Caribbean Examination Council 'O' level passes or have credentials of an equivalent standing or standard. Two of the six passes must be in English and Mathematics.[26] Applicants must be in the age bracket of 17½ to 25 years and be physically fit in accordance with specified medical standards. Unlike regulars, who apply to the staff officer attached to the administrative unit of the BDF at headquarters, the initial application of the officer cadet must be sent directly to the BDF Chief of Staff who is also an *ex-officio* member of the Barbados Defense Board. Applicants must be recommended by a headteacher, minister of religion, a Justice of Peace, or some other similarly prominent citizen of the community. Also, the officer-cadet applicant is required to appear before an interview panel, whereupon, if he or she meets the approval of said panel, one is again further evaluated for consideration by an Officer's Selection Board. In the event of being chosen, he or she is then eligible for officer training.

In regard to occupational mobility, the specific criteria that are used in the BDF as a guide for promotion are not specified. There is no Promotions Advisory Board or its equivalent. A publication written by the BDF Public Relations Division entitled 'A Career in the Defense Force' states that 'there are sample opportunities for promotion with resulting salary increases'.[27] Of course, it is to be presumed that promotion is determined by length of service, success at promotion examinations, and recommendations by commanding officers.

BRIEF HISTORY OF THE STRENGTH AND BUDGETING SUPPORT OF THE BDF

Until 1979, when the Barbados Defense Force Act authorised the formation of a bona fide defence force, or army, the police comprised the only genuine security force in Barbados. In fact, unlike Jamaica, Trinidad and Tobago, Guyana, Grenada under Bishop and even Belize, none of the Commonwealth Caribbean countries, except Barbados, ever had and still do not have full-fledged armies. In the absence of a defence force, the police, in the tradition of a constabulary, was charged with the combined functions associated with a police and defence force.

When Errol Barrow and the Democratic Labour Party took Barbados into formal independence in 1966 and during their uninterrupted twenty years' stay in power, a defence force never came to fruition. Rather, the Democratic Labour Party created a coast guard and retained the Barbados Regiment, a body used largely for ceremonial occasions, which existed in the pre-independence period. However, in 1976, they left behind proposals for the creation of a defence force of about fifty to eighty persons.

In the initial years of the Adams regime, the idea of a defence force was downplayed. The position of Adams and the Barbados Labour Party in the September 1976 general election read: 'Internally, the defence forces will be limited to such as are adequate to maintain law and order.'[28] However, by 1979, Adams and the Barbados Labour Party made an about-turn and created a full-fledged defence force, which incorporated the pre-existing Barbados Regiment.

Given 'the winds of change' in the Caribbean at the time, as early as November 1980 the Carter Administration officials made manifest the 'special military role' that it envisioned for Barbados. Although a year earlier ineligible for foreign military sales credit, William G. Bowdler, assistant secretary of state for inter-American affairs, in his testimony before Congress proposed $5 million to help Barbados buy communications and navigational equipment to 'strengthen the security of the entire Eastern Caribbean'.[29] As a consequence of assistance that was received, the BDF did experience modest growth but still remained a structurally undifferentiated military establishment and essentially a token defence force. By 1984, its strength had crept up to a reasonable size. According to statistics that were provided by Chief of Staff Rudyard Lewis to US Secretary of State George Shultz on the occasion of Shultz's visit to Barbados in 1983, the BDF was 610 strong. It was comprised of 250 regulars, 270 reserves, and 90 coast guardsmen.[30]

However, in the latter phase of the Adams administration, the size of the BDF spiralled to approximately 1800 persons. This figure came to light when Errol Barrow, upon being returned to office in an

Table 6.1   Estimated organisational strength of the security forces in
Barbados, 1984 and 1986

| Security forces | Estimated organisational strength | |
	1984	*1986*
Police[a]	1,156	1,500
Defense Force[b]	610	1,800

Notes: a. Police force figures include members in the police band
    b. Defense force figures are inclusive of the Coast Guard
Source: Figures on the Police Force were obtained from the 1984, 1986 Joint
    Estimates on the Government of Barbados; whereas, figures on the
    Defense Force were supplied by newspaper accounts.

election race against the Bernard St John-headed Barbados Labour
Party (Tom Adams having died in office) was in his capacity as Prime
Minister, Minister of Defense and Security and as such was Chairman
of the Barbados Defense Board, automatically privy to such a stat-
istic.

Previous knowledge of the actual size of the BDF was highly
esoteric and withheld from the Barbadian public. So much so, that
while serving as leader of the Opposition and shadow minister for
Defense and Security matters, Barrow was known to have remarked:
'The size of the defense force is the biggest secret in Barbados. I had
to ask a foreign government what the size of the Defense Force
was.'[31]

The expanded size of the BDF, which serves as the nucleus of the
Regional Security System (RSS), found justification in the unsettling
events which transpired in Dominica in 1979, Barbados in 1980, and
particularly Grenada in 1983. In the post-Grenada period, prior to
Barrow's return to power, the increase in the size of the BDF was
dictated in large measure, by future Barbados Labour Party considerations which envisaged the 'rise again' of the Caribbean left and
similar forebodings, a sentiment which found a 'community of
interest' with the Reagan administration's hegemonic policy toward
the Caribbean and Central America.

Table 6.1 provides the estimated strength of the armed forces in
Barbados. The strength of the Barbados military in 1984 was 610.
Between 1984 and 1986, the military has increased by 1190 personnel, and by so doing has tripled in strength to a size of 1800. It is
noteworthy that, because of this astronomical growth during the said
two-year period, the BDF has come to outstrip that of the police by

Table 6.2   Local expenditure on Barbados' military institution, (Barbados Defense Force), 1978–86* (in 000 BD$)

1978	1979	1980	1981	1982	1983	1984	1985	1986
1,764	2,405	3,475	8,380	10,485	13,303	15,757	19,920	16,900

Note: Budgetary allocations for the Barbados Coast Guard are subsumed under the BDF.

Source: Accountant General.

over 200 personnel. The trajectory was presided over by PM Tom Adams who concurrently served as 'the architect behind the military build-up in the Caribbean subregion in the 1980s'.[32] During Bernard St John's brief stint as Prime Minister, he adopted the same military mind-set as his predecessor. However, after Errol Barrow and the Democratic Labour Party were reinstated, there was not a reduction in the BDF's size as was promised but rather a curtailment of recruitment. Barrow assured the members of the BDF that their jobs are safe as 'it is not the intention of the government to exacerbate the high level of unemployment which already exists by wholesale re-trenchment in the Force itself'.[33]

Expenditure on the military parallels the increase in its size over the years. Table 6.2 provides figures on expenditures on the military between 1978 and 1986. In 1978, the year before the BDF was formed, the government expended a total of BDS $1.7 million on the military. It is noteworthy that since 1979 and commensurate with the growth in size, there has been a corresponding steady growth in the amount of government funds devoted to defence requirements. This pattern is borne out by the fact that in 1985, as much as BDS $19.9 million was spent on the military.

Moreover, despite pronouncements by the Barrow administration while in opposition and even after being returned to government that the size of the BDF was too large, there has been no cut in the size of government expenditure for the defence force, given the fact that the BDF received in the estimates of 1987/8, the full $16 million which it had asked for. In fact, it was the only department to have received every penny that was requested.

Needless to say, much more is expended on the BDF than is reflected in the annual budget releases of the government. This is so since the budget allocations for the military exclude expenditures for arms and ammunition which are purchased externally.

INDIVIDUAL AND GROUP TRAINING OF THE BDF

The training of a defence force, along with its structure, size and expenditure, provide an indication of the uses to which it has been put or for which it is being prepared. In this regard, the BDF is no exception.

Relative to the BDF, there are two types of major training. First, there is training that involves individual specialisation and formal course attendance. And second, there are group training programs that are undertaken along two lines. One brand is based on training exclusively among the units of the BDF. The other takes the form of joint exercises which are conducted on the basis of an exchange programme with military forces of one kind or another.

As a matter of course, all the members of the BDF undergo initial training along British Army lines. As reflected in its sixteen-week Basic Infantry Course which is a requirement for all recruits, the BDF has inherited British military training and tradition, including civil-military relations which has served as the basis for the formation of the BDF.

After enlistment as an officer or into the ranks, both the members of the regular forces as well as the reservists, whether in the defence force proper or the Coast Guard, are required to fulfill the statutory yearly training requirements; these are (1) one three-hour evening training per week; (2) one weekend every month; and (3) one fortnight every year.

INDIVIDUAL TRAINING

The BDF was not only set up, organised and trained initially in accordance with the British Army model but the vast majority of its senior officers, if not all, are British trained including Rudyard Lewis, its Chief of Staff and Commanding Officer.[34] While a member of the West Indies Regiment in Jamaica, Lewis was one of the three Barbadians to be trained at the Royal Military Academy, Sandhurst, and remained in Jamaica in soldiering when the West Indies Federation collapsed in 1962. Lewis returned to Barbados in 1980 to assist in the establishment and professionalisation of the BDF and was appointed its Brigadier when Colonel Leonard Banfield retired.[35] Lewis is not alone and could be part of an incipient 'BDF Sandhurst Connection'.

Subsequent to the formation of the BDF in 1979, at least two young commissioned-officers have received training to be professional soldiers. These are Captain Sean Reece who attended Sandhurst from September 1981 until April 1982 and Mark Ince who was a student there in the 1983–84 years. Based on his performance in said course, Ince gained himself the 'stick of the Honour', an award presented to the Best Overseas Cadet. Even before undergoing overseas military training, officer-cadets have a high level of education. Evidently, only the best qualified academically are selected for officer training.

Attendance at Sandhurst for both these highly credentialed officer cadets was for a period of six months of intensive training. The main emphasis of the course was on military exercises which are held in various parts of the United Kingdom and often times on the European continent. More specifically, as an integral part of the Sandhurst course, priority is typically given to tactics and the use of weapons in defence and attack. All cadets are given an opportunity to act as platoon or section commanders in field manoeuvres. Mark Ince remarked that 'there were really tough occasions, designed to find out whether the cadets could use the military skills they had learned in conditions of great discomfort, sometimes freezing weather and with sleep often denied them'.[36] One of the highlights of the officer-Cadet training is exposure to a full scale mock battles with armour.

Also, in regards to the training of recruits in the BDF, it is noteworthy that in 1984 some 22 Barbadian officers in the British Army who had completed compensionable service returned home to assist in the development and expansion of the BDF. At such time, one British army major was on loan to the BDF. However, by April 1987, this number had increased to four. In addition, in 1987, there were a further five British Loan Service personnel attached to the headquarters of the Regional Security System (RSS) to assist with defense planning and operations.[37]

Officers of the BDF, along with police and soldiers from St Vincent, Antigua and Barbuda, have received two week courses in hygiene, water duties and pest control. Such courses were conducted by the Royal Army Medical corps of the British Army and financed by the British government. Officers of lesser rank have received intensive training throughout their careers; for example, drill courses at such places like the School of Infantry in England and the Queens Division in Cambridge. A few Barbadian military personnel have attended the two-and-a-half month junior non-commission officer courses as well as the combat engineering course, both in Jamaica. Officers have also benefited from stints with the Trinidad and Tobago Defense Force and the Venezuela military.

In regard to the coast guard, the bulk of their training has been undertaken by the British, the US and, to a lesser extent, Canada. Above and beyond assistance in the constructing and equipping of the Barbados Coast Guard base at Fort Willoughby, British military aid comes, more so, in the form of personnel rather than hardware. Under the Loan Service scheme, British Navy and Royal Marine personnel are loaned to the BDF to share their expertise and assist in training. In 1987, there were four such personnel on loan to the coast guard, some twenty Barbadians including three officers, namely, Charles Belle, Kingsley Jones and Wilbert Kirton, who spent six weeks training in seamanship, navigation, firefighting, boarding and armament in British waters.

The US government has acquired 16 new island class patrol boats for law enforcement and eradication of drugs in the insular Caribbean. Since 1964, the US Coast Guard has conducted sessions with coast guard units in Barbados and other Eastern Caribbean countries.[38] In regard to Canada, 58 persons from various coast guards in the region, including persons in Barbados, were trained in 1984 at the Canada Coast Guard College in Sydney, Nova Scotia. Also, a two week training course in Marine Search and Rescue techniques was sponsored by the annual Caribbean Maritime Training Assistance Program.

Official data showing the proportion of officers to enlisted persons and the rank and file within the regular BDF as well as the official size of the reserve are not available. This inadequate data base is a barrier to rigorous analysis, but it can be supplemented by conjecture based on other materials and on personal observation. Unlike the Coast Guard, the naval arm of the BDF, where many of the officers and even the Coast Guard Commander are non-nationals, most of the BDF commissioned officers are Barbadian nationals.[39]

As a result of the preponderance of British training of most of the BDF officers who serve as role models for many of the junior officers and other ranks, the BDF seem to have imbided the British Army code of personal and professional conduct. However, the BDF has not confined training to Commonwealth countries alone. While training in Britain and Canada has not been discontinued, BDF military personnel have also been sent to the United States for training, whereas, prior to 1979, few Barbadian military personnel

Table 6.3   Military personnel of Barbados and select Eastern Caribbean countries trained under the International Military Education and Training Program, 1950–85

	1950–78	1979	1980	1981	1982	1983	1984	1985	1950–85
Antigua	—	—	—	—	—	9	9	11	29
Barbados	—	1	13	12	10	22	22	18	98
Dominica	—	—	—	7	1	6	16	8	38
Grenada	—	—	—	—	—	—	—	18	18
Montserrat	—	—	—	—	—	—	—	—	—
St Kitts/Nevis	—	—	—	—	—	—	10	7	17
St Lucia	—	—	—	2	3	6	15	12	38
St Vincent/ Grenadines	—	—	—	1	—	8	12	14	35

Source: US Department of Defense, *Foreign Military Construction Sales and Military Assistance Facts*, 30 September 1985, Washington, DC, Data Management Division, Comptroller, DSAA, 1985, pp. 302–81.

had received such training. However, the picture has since changed dramatically.

Current evidence suggests a new stage in the security policy of Barbados relative to its inclusion in the International Military, Education and Training Program. Official US Government data indicate that the BDF has received increasing support from the US. According to Table 6.3, between 1966, the year of independence, and 1978, the US did not provide a single official from that country with military training and just one in fiscal year (FY) 1979; however, in FY 1980 alone, the year after the formation of the BDF, the US trained as many as 13 military personnel from Barbados, a number that has since ebbed and flowed at about this level; by FY 1983, the total trained by the US in one year ran as high as 22 Barbadians.

The prime purpose behind extending such military aid is to establish relationships between the US military establishment and the BDF. In fact, in the post-Grenada invasion period, the US has come to replace Britain as the principal guarantor of Barbados' security. This view was corroborated by PM Tom Adams in an address to the Royal Commonwealth Society in London in December 1983, some weeks after the Grenada action, when he stated that that had been the 'watershed year in which the influence of the United States, willy-nilly, came observably to replace that of Great Britain'.[40] In a very definite way, the Carter Administration, particularly during the Tom Adams years, recognised Barbados as a major ally in the subregion and moved to form a 'special military relationship'. Washington's concern regarding unsettling developments in the Lesser Antilles resulting from the Grenada's socialist-oriented revolution explains Barbados' unprecedented prominence. Indeed Karen Young noted that:

> There have been reports that the United States hopes to turn the island of Barbados perhaps the closest US ally in that region, into a sort of 'Iran of the Caribbean.' Barbados maintains the only army-like defense force in the area and many within the Pentagon and Carter Administration would like to see it as the center of a regional defense force. But Barbados so far has balked.[41]

In fact, this 'special relationship' between the United States and Barbados was laid earlier with the appointment, unlike previous years, of senior career diplomats as ambassadors to Barbados and the Eastern Caribbean.[42] Moreover, the increasing security importance of Barbados was indicated in the visits of top-ranking military officers.[43]

GROUP TRAINING – LOCAL

In regard to local field training camps that are carried out among the units of the BDF within and/or around Barbados, the location and frequency of such exercises vary in order to make the BDF personnel familiar with the Barbadian terrain. In similar regard, these local training camps are carried out in various parts of Barbados including the rugged Scotland District in St Andrews as well as in the 'country areas' of St Philip, St Joseph and so on. As a consequence, 'inhabitants. . . are now getting quite used to see groups of soldiers in full fighting order walking fast up hills and doubling on the flat and down hills early in the morning'.[44]

The exercises carried out locally by the BDF not only allow officers in charge of squadrons and companies to supervise closely and assess the performance of officers and other ranks under their command, but also have a psychological impact on the Barbadian public. These exercises help to instill a feeling of security among the population at large.

One such operation code-named 'Away All Vessels' took place in March 1986 in which, for the first time, all the Coast Guard vessels and crew took part in an all day naval exercise off the south coast of Barbados. This exercise involved 105 men from the Coast Guard and 45 from the commando squadron of the BDF.[45]

Such manoeuvres have the likely effect of demonstrating to the Barbadian public that the BDF will resist the enemy and has no intention of capitulating. They are also a display of the coercive apparatus at the disposal of the government and are therefore meant to serve as a deterrent to would-be 'enemies of the state'.

GROUP TRAINING – OVERSEAS

Group training with overseas troops is a fairly regular feature of the operations of the BDF. From its very inception in 1979, the BDF has been involved, in varying degrees, in joint exercises with foreign troops.

The first such military exchange program took place between the BDF and the US Virgin Islands National Guard in 1980. A similar programme was undertaken by the Puerto Rico National Guard in 1980 and again in 1982, 1985 and 1987.[46] The objective behind these agreements on military cooperation is echoed in the ideology of the Army War College which states:

> *Exchange of small units.* The exchange of ideas and goodwill achieved by exchange programs of small units can produce great compensations. For example, the work carried out by the Puerto Rican National Guard in helping the Dominican Army solve a problem of munitions storage was praised by the Dominican leaders. Similar results were obtained in Barbados. The exchange of small units can even improve the capability of the foreign units and *the climate for coalition cooperation*. Confidence and respect for the United States Navy can be gained at low cost with specialized teams . . . the task of small unit exchange is two-fold – to improve both the image of the United States and the military capabilities of the countries in the region.[47]

The National Guard has therefore been assigned the task of assisting with the training of the BDF in keeping with the objective of 'coalition cooperation'.[48]

Also, the Barbados Coast Guard have engaged in bipartisan joint manoeuvres with the St Vincent and the Grenadines Coast Guard in the Grenadines. And so, initially, the training programmes of the BDF with overseas personnel were modest and rudimentary. However, in the post-Grenada invasion period, this pattern changed dramatically and took the form of programmes of a counter-insurgency nature.

According to Diederich:

> The smell of cordite hardly had time to dissipate in Grenada when special forces training teams from Fort Bragg, North Carolina, began landing in neighboring islands with new weaponry.[49]

Beginning in November 1983, these US teams were involved in the training of select members of the police force in five of the seven OECS countries and soldiers in the BDF and the Antigua and Barbuda Defense Force. They were trained in US Special Weapons and Training Methods and other elements of the US National Guard programme. Also, such items as jeeps, armoured cars, trucks, high-powered weapons like M-60s, M-16s and communication equipment were delivered.

These special teams are called Special Service Units (SSUs) and are being coordinated under the rubric of the RSS. Given the size of the BDF, relative to other security forces in the Eastern Caribbean, and the fact that its Chief of Staff is also coordinator of the RSS which is headquartered in Barbados, the BDF forms the nucleus of the RSS.

Figure 6.1 not only diagrams the relationship between the seven RSS member countries as one level of cooperation but points to a second and more profound level of coordination which exists between RSS and the extra subregional military establishments of the US, Britain and Canada. This second coordination is facilitated by the existence of manoeuvres carried out in RSS member countries and in Caribbean waters. These joint manoeuvres, involving the SSUs, serve to reinforce and solidify the training that was begun in 1983.

Between 1985 and 1987, there have been a series of four major multinational manoeuvres involving the BDF, other Caribbean forces and the US.[50] The first such major manoeuvre took place in St Lucia and was code-named 'Exotic Palm'. It took place in September 1985 and involved sea and air action utilising US and British forces

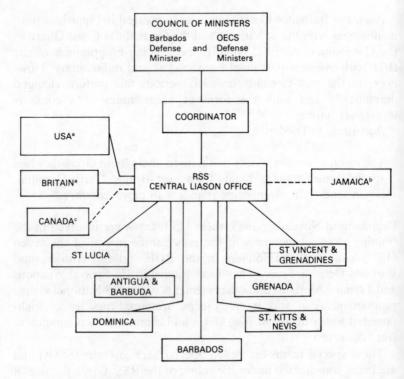

Figure 6.1   RSS and US, British and Canadian Military Establishments: an organisational chart

Notes: a. The boxes labeled US, Britain, and Canada are meant by their size here to reflect the relative extent of the involvement of these countries in the RSS.

b. Though a participant in RSS activity, Jamaica, as indicated by the --- line is not a formal member of this body. Neither are other Anglophone Caribbean countries, namely, the Bahamas, Belize, Guyana, nor Trinidad and Tobago.

c. Unlike the US and Britain, as of April 1987, Canada does not, as reflected by --- line, directly supply training, personnel, intelligence, equipment or finances to the RSS.

and all the SSUs with the exclusion of St Vincent and Grenadines. The scenario was that of a small island, 'Linus', whose government had been toppled by 50 insurgents supported by 'Carumba' and 'Niggaro' and which had requested RSS assistance.[51] The second major manoeuvre which involved OECS forces was 'Ocean Venture' carried out in April and May 1986. Although the bulk of the exercise was conducted around Puerto Rico and North Carolina, the Eastern Caribbean segment concentrated upon Grenada and involved over 1000 soldiers and police from the US, Jamaica, Antigua and Barbuda, Dominica, Grenada, St Kitts and Nevis, and St Lucia, directed by the RSS staff in Barbados. However, as the St John administration in Barbados faced the electorate, they did not partake in this manoeuvre. The third major manoeuvre and one in which both Barbados and St Vincent sent troops was 'Exercise Camille' held in Dominica in May 1987. This manoeuvre involved 700 personnel from the US, Britain, the JDF, the BDF and forces from OECS. 'Camille' was the first exercise to include units from all seven RSS member nations, including Barbados and St Vincent which had stayed away from previous manoeuvres.

The fourth and final major manoeuvre, in 1987, the second to include all units and thus pointing to a consensus, was staged in Jamaica and termed 'Exercise Trade Winds'. Total participation for the manoeuvre was 300 troops of all ranks, including 120 from the RSS and 60 from the US Army. The exercise, which was carried out in the parishes of St Ann, St Mary and St Catherine, concentrated on protective and defensive training.

Much of the overseas group training is concentrated on two major programmes. These are internal security and civic military action. To advance and implement these above-mentioned training programmes, equipment has been provided to the BDF and Barbados' military bureaucracy has been expanded and reorganised.[52]

CONCLUSION

Unlike the fellow Anglophone Caribbean countries of Jamaica, Trinidad and Tobago, and Guyana, Barbados did not enter into independence with a defence force. The BDF was started in 1979, thirteen years after independence, as an institutional response to a threatening security environment as perceived by Tom Adams and the BLP.[53] Its force structure and enlistment patterns are according to the British model. Also, beginning with the Carter years and continuing under Reagan, the BDF has experienced an unprediented growth in size as well as a steady increase in expenditures. Initially, overseas training for the BDF was provided more so by the British. However, beginning in 1983, training provided by the US and, to a lesser extent, Canada, has not replaced but is in addition to existing

British military assistance.[54] Much of this training and the acquisition of military hardware that has been provided by the US is not merely to fight drug trafficking but to better bolster internal security in Barbados and the Eastern Caribbean in the aftermath of the Grenada crisis.

Acknowledgement

For helpful comments on an earlier draft, the author is grateful to Humberto García Muñiz of Columbia University. I also wish to thank Mary Dickinson who typed the paper for publication. I bear responsibility for the contents of this article with the full knowledge that this inquiry represents a preliminary survey of the BDF. In pursuing this area of study, I am made aware that points of research interests are often closed to academic investigators for what are deemed to be security reasons.

Notes

1. Dion E. Phillips, 'The Creation, Structure and Training of the Barbados Defense Force', *Caribbean Studies*, 21, 1 & 2, 1988, pp. 124–57.
2. Jerome S. Handler, 'Freedmen and Slaves in the Barbados Militia', *The Journal of Caribbean History*, 19.1, May 1984, pp. 1–25; Peter F. Campbell, 'The Barbados Militia 1627–1815', JBMS, XXXV, 1976.
3. Hilary Beckles, *Black Rebellion in Barbados* (Bridgetown, Barbados: Antilles Publications, 1984).
4. Richard Ligon, *A True and Exact History of the Island of Barbados . . .*, (London, 1657), p. 53.
5. Roger Norman Buckley, *Slaves in Red Coats: The British West India Regiments, 1795–1815* (New Haven: Yale University Press, 1979).
6. A. B. Ellis, *The History of the First West India Regiment* (London: Chapman and Hall, 1885), pp. 166–9; Michael Craton, 'Bussa's Rebellion: Barbados, 1816', in *Testing the Chains: Resistance to Slavery in the British West Indies* (Ithaca and London: Cornell University Press, 1982), pp. 254–66.
7. Though not a bona fide police force, as early as 1705, an Act was passed to appoint 8 'Watches' in the towns of the island. Also, in 1813, to meet the increase in crime, the St Michael vestry established its own watch. Two years later, a watch for Bridgetown alone was created.
8. On 19 July 1834, parliament passed legislation establishing the Bridgetown Police with Francis Mallalieu of the Metropolitan police of London as Inspector General. In that very year, parliament passed another Act for the establishment of a Rural Police Force. The next year in 1835, a

consolidated Police Act was passed authorising the establishment of a single police force.

9. *Royal Barbados Police 150th Anniversary, 1985–1985*, p. 17.
10. *Barbados: Report of the Commission appointed to enquire into the Disturbances which took place in Barbados on the 27th July 1937 and Subsequent Days*, p. 3.
11. Eric Williams, 'The Regiment', *Journal of the Trinidad and Tobago Regiment*, I, 5, December, 1964, p. 11.
12. Other reasons which influenced the necessity for the newly independent Guyana to form a defense force was its experience of violent disorder in 1962, 1963 and 1964 when British troops had to be deployed in order to maintain internal security. Also Guyana had to cope with the territorial claims of her neighbors, Venezuela and Surinam. George K. Danns, *Domination and Power in Guyana*, New Brunswick: Transaction Books, 1982.
13. Col. Trevor N. Dupuy, US Army Ret., *The Almanac of World Military Power* (1st edn), p. 21.
14. 'US Navy to quit Barbados', *Washington Post*, 13 December 1978, p. A29.
15. Dion E. Phillips, 'The Increasing Emphasis on Security and Defense in the Eastern Caribbean', in Alma H. Young and Dion E. Phillips (eds), *Militarization in the Non-Hispanic Caribbean*, (Boulder: Lynne Rienner Publishers, 1986), pp. 42–64.
16. Los Angeles Times, 24 May 1984.
17. BDF Women Will March Separately, *The Nation*, 22 November 1984, p. 11.
18. 'Defense Force Shows What's in Reserve', *Barbados Advocate*, 10 December 1985.
19. 'PM Tours Medical Station', *Advocate News*.
20. 'Defense Force Plane Arrives', *Barbados Advocate*.
21. During the heyday of the BDF, there were discussions regarding 'the take over of the Garrison fully by the military and the removal of the Barbados Turf Club's racing to Coverly Plantation in Christ Church, "Secret Savannah Trip"', *Daily Nation*, 19 September 1985, p. 24; 'Full Locating for Pilots Soon', *Daily Nation*, 3 December 1985, p. 5.
22. 'Guyana takes over Skyvan', *Daily Nation*, 1 July 1987, p. 1.
23. Trevor Adams, 'Protecting the Water Around Us', *Sunday Sun*, 28 February 1982, p. 11.
24. 'Two new vessels for coast guard', *Daily Nation*, 26 August 1987, p. 1.
25. The Pioneer Battalion in the BDF seems to be comprised of persons who did not quite qualify academically to enter the force.
26. Basic statistical data on the social origins and pre-professional education of the officer corps of the BDF is not available. BDF commissioned officers are an exclusive group. Like their counterparts, the politicians, many officers are drawn from the prestigious government-aided secondary schools and have often served in the cadet corps of those very schools. The educational background of this 'new elite' points to the political significance of the BDF.

27. BDF Public Relations Division, 'A Career in the Defense Force', *The Young Citizen*, Volume 1, 1984–85, pp. 56, 57.
28. *Barbados Labour Party Manifesto*, 1976, p. 15.
29. John M. Goshko, 'Caribbean Ally Confront Reagan With Early Test on Military Aid', *The Washington Post*, 26 November 1980, p. A7.
30. US House of Representatives, Committee on Armed Services (1984). Report of the Delegation to the Eastern Caribbean and South American Countries, 98th Congress, 2nd session, February, pp. 1–44.
31. 'Barrow is wary of regional army', *Daily Nation*, 3 June 1986, p. 4.
32. Dion E. Phillips, 'Tom Adams: Architect Behind Eastern Caribbean Military Build-up', (memo): 'The Question of Militarization', editorial, *Barbados Advocate*, 26 January 1987.
33. *Latin American Regional Reports Caribbean*, 1988.
34. Rudyard Eggleton Carrington Lewis attended Harrison College, Barbados' leading secondary school, where he was a member of the school's cadet corps. Upon graduation, he joined the Barbados Regiment, reaching the rank of corporal before enlisting with the West Indies Regiment, the military arm of the West Indies Federation; 'Profile of a Military Leader: Brigadier Rudyard Lewis', *Nation*, 25 October 1983, p. 15.
35. The first commanders of the defense forces of Jamaica, Trinidad and Tobago, and Guyana were, in their formative years, Brigadier David Smith, Lt Colonel Peter Pearce Gould and Colonel Ronald Hope, respectively, all British-born, whereas the commander of the BDF was, from its very inception, a Barbadian national.
36. Irene Sandiford, 'Well Done, Mark', *Sunday Sun*, 6 May 1984, p. 29.
37. Mark D. Alleyne, 'Government policy is opposed to Caribbean Militarization', *Sunday Advocate*, 26 April 1987.
38. 'Three US Vessels to visit Barbados', *Barbados Advocate*, 18 September 1986, p. 2.
39. After twenty months with the coast guard, Commander James Oliver handed over his duties on April 1983 to his British compatriot Roger Porteous.
40. Speech at Royal Commonwealth Society, London, 9 December 1983.
41. Yussif Haniff, 'Barbados Warming Up For Elections', *Caribbean Contact*, August 1980, p. 16.
42. The appointment of Sally Shelton and Frank Ortiz as consecutive ambassadors to Barbados and the Eastern Caribbean under the Carter administration not only denotes the willingness to assign diplomats whose 'qualifications are not limited to connections or the size of their contributions' to political campaigns but, in part, demonstrates the new importance of Barbados and the Eastern Caribbean in US foreign policy. During such time, the following high ranking US officials paid visits: Secretary of State Cyrus Vance (1977), State department specialist Phillip Habib, President Carter's wife, Rosalyn Carter, and US ambassador to the UN, Andrew Young (1979). Although the Reagan administration seems to have reverted to the practise of politically-appointed US ambassadors in the persons of Milan Bish and Tom Anderson, as a prelude to the US invasion of Grenada, veteran career diplomat Francis

Mac Niel paid a secret visit to the area 'to sound out the view of regional leaders'. Even before the Bishop regime was toppled, Reagan visited Barbados in 1982 on a 'working holiday' at which time he confered with Caribbean heads of state. Moreover, in the aftermath of the US invasion of Grenada, though a clear set back to the left, the Reagan administration deemed it necessary to open a separate US embassy in Grenada in the Southeastern Caribbean. It must be born in mind that the move in October 1987 to close the US embassy in Antigua, reportedly the initiative of 'certain congressional elements', was opposed by the Reagan administration and underscores the importance, though diminished in the post-US invasion period, of the Eastern Caribbean to US foreign policy and planning. Tony Best, 'The Choosing of US Ambassadors', *Daily Nation*, 27 May 1987, p. 5; 'Antigua embassy may face closure', *Daily Nation*, 22 October 1987, p. 10.

43. Among those military officials who visited Barbados are Fred Ikle, undersecretary for policy in the US Department of Defense, in 1984 and Frank Butler, also of the defense department, as well as Commander-in-chief Admiral Lee Baggett, Jr. of the US Navy, both in 1986.

44. 'Full Strength BDF Improves Soldiers Skills', *Sunday Advocate*, 20 November 1986, p. 16.

45. Omowale Elson, 'A Ship-Shape Coast Guard', *Sunday Sun*, 16 March 1986.

46. In 1980, 50 soldiers of the BDF went to summer camp in Puerto Rico. In 1982, security forces from Barbados and Dominica received training from the Puerto Rico National Guard and the Jamaica Defence Force attends training sessions in Puerto Rico.

47. Strategic Studies Institute, United States Navy War College, *The Role of the US Military: Caribbean Basin.* (ACN 80049), Final Report, 26 October 1981, ch. 4.

48. Jorge Rodríguez Beruff, 'Puerto Rico and the Militarization of the Caribbean, 1979–1984', *Contemporary Marxism*, 10 (1985), p. 79.

49. Bernard Diederich, 'The End of West Indian Innocence: Arming the Police', *Caribbean Review*, 13, 2, p. 11; Barbados lost its innocence and was inducted into cold war politics in 1975 when Washington's 'displeasure' with the refuelling in Barbados of Cuban planes bound for Angola in 1975 brought this practice to a halt. For the Commonwealth Caribbean as a whole, such 'loss of innocence' was marked by US–UK tactics in Guyana to unseat the government of Cheddi Jagan when the Kennedy administration feared that a communist take over in Guyana would threaten US strategic interests. It was felt that a Guyana under Forbes Burnham 'would cause many few problems than an independent Guyana under Jagan, an avowed Marxist'.

50. Apart from these four major multinational military exercises, the region has witnessed smaller scale exercises like 'Upward Key – 85' in Barbuda involving Antigua–Barbuda, St Kitts–Nevis (for the first time) and US forces. RSS coordinator Rudyard Lewis revealed in St Lucia in 1985 that there were some exercises on other islands which "have not been publicized for one reason or another." 'Military Exercises, September 11 to 15', *Barbados Advocate*, 27 August 1985, p. 5.

51. 'Clash over Barbados Defense Force', *Caribbean Contact*, October 1983, p. 8.
52. 'Caution on Army Use', *Daily Nation*, 21 January 1985, p. 1.
53. Toms Adams, 'Signs of Progress are around us', address by Prime Minister at the 46th conference of the BLP, 20 January 1985.
54. 'Planned Schedule is under control', *Daily Nation*, 4 April 1985, p. 17; Patrick Ward, 'The End of Mark Young's Stormy Run', *Daily Nation*, 6 May 1987, p. 13.

7 Overt Militarism and Covert Politics in St Kitts–Nevis

Whitman Browne

St Kitts, Nevis and Anguilla have played an important role in the history of militarism and politics in the Eastern Caribbean. However, this has often been overlooked as part of the Caribbean story for one reason or another. Even Phillips and Young (1986), in their preliminary work on the military in the non-Hispanic Caribbean failed to mention the role played by these islands.

Sir Thomas Warner made the first British settlement in the Caribbean on St Kitts in 1624. The French, under the leadership of Belain D. Esnambac, made theirs on the same island about one year later (Innis, 1979, pp. 2–3).

In time, either acting separately, together, or against each other, those Europeans dominated the military actions on these islands. Their force destroyed the Caribs and humiliated the enslaved Africans. Early militarism here was largely in the name of nationalism – European nationalism.

On St Kitts there are names such as 'Bloody Point', where the British are alleged to have made Carib blood run like a river and, 'Brimstone Hill' – the Gibraltar of the West Indies; there the British established themselves as the dominant force in the Caribbean for years. When the French invaded Nevis in 1702, the White Militia, reputedly notorious for its cowardice, hid itself. Only 70 of 430 men challenged the invaders. It was the slaves who gave the French a real fight (Innis, 1983, p. 13). The famous English admiral, Lord Nelson, also has a legendary military and nuptial association with Nevis.

Two French invasions of Anguilla 1745 and 1796 were beaten back (Westlake, 1972, pp. 11–12). Then there was a rebellion on Anguilla against the government in St Kitts, May 1967, which forced a new, Caribbean-oriented militarism, as against the prior militarism which was an expression of European nationalism in the Caribbean area. Less than a month after the rebellion, Anguillians also participated in an invasion of St Kitts (Hodge and Petty, 1987, pp. 62–88).

Robert Bradshaw was leader of St Kitts, Nevis, and Anguilla when the rebellion and invasion occurred. Neither Caribbean governments, nor the British took him seriously when he suggested a new militarism was emerging in the Caribbean. And, except for Forbes Burnham of Guyana, Bradshaw could not get a sympathetic ear on the matter of invading Anguilla to force the island back to constitutional government. But, as he grappled with his ordeal, Bradshaw commented: 'When St Kitts sneezes, the Caribbean catches a cold.' He was reflecting on the fact that many events which shaped the entire Caribbean originated on St Kitts.

After the Anguillian revolt, it was a matter of time. Antigua, Trinidad and Tobago, Barbados, and Jamaica did experience their troubles too. That series of military-related episodes in recent Caribbean history climaxed with a disastrous invasion of Grenada in October 1983.

Today, the question of a military deterrent in the Eastern Caribbean first addressed by Bradshaw back in 1967 is no longer a laughing matter. Even Kennedy Simmonds who opposed Bradshaw's view then, has changed his mind; he now argues the relevance of Eastern Caribbean and allied militarism. But in 1967, Simmonds was an opposition politician; anti-government militarism was an option to power. Now he is leader of the government, that option has lost its attraction. Constitutional government is preferred to radical alternatives. St Kitts–Nevis, like all other independent Caribbean governments now boasts some form of overt or covert military force, allegedly to preserve political stability. In Bradshaw's terms, the entire Caribbean has caught military fever since St Kitts sneezed in 1967.

Anguilla was part of the colony St Kitts, Nevis, Anguilla. Robert Bradshaw was the premier of a political union that went back as far as 1825. It took Bradshaw about 25 years of hard political gaming to achieve Associated Statehood with Britain by 1967. More authority for internal government went to Bradshaw's Labor Government centralised on St Kitts. Britain retained the right to external security.

Statehood in Association with Britain was a political half-way house to full independence. Bradshaw himself referred to statehood as 'the emasculated device of Associated Statehood.' Like 'Federation' in 1958–62, this was new wine being poured into old bottles. It was temporary politics with permanent repercussions in the Eastern Caribbean. Neither Nevisians nor Anguillians were excited over the prospect of having more governmental authority passed to Bradshaw.

The Anguillians put action into their thoughts and revolted in May. They rose up en masse to challenge the authority of the St Kitts government. A contingent of 30 policemen was disarmed and forced to leave their island (Petty, 1983, p. 22).

Such an event was a direct challenge to Bradshaw's authority. It was unconstitutional and against his belief in a United Caribbean but, in the absence of such precedence in the Eastern Caribbean, Bradshaw must have expected the revolt to lose support and fizzle out in a short time. Such thinking was a mistake.

That initial action taken by the Anguillians was carefully planned on Anguilla and on St Thomas, USVI. It was intended to be quick, dramatic and decisive. Either all or some of that planning was done in the presence of, or with assistance from, high level opposition politicians from St Kitts (Hodge and Petty, 1987, p. 62).

Shortly before the rebellion on Anguilla, a leader of the People's Action Movement (PAM) political party on St Kitts, then the leading political force that opposed Bradshaw, made some interesting remarks about the latter and his Government in an address given at Emile Griffith Park, St Thomas. Bradshaw was criticised as offering inferior leadership to that which the opposition politician could offer. Further, threats were made that Bradshaw could not remain in power for much longer. Donald Westlake, no supporter of Bradshaw, wrote of the Anguilla affair 'P.A.M's role in all this is just slightly murky'.

Bradshaw was informed about that address. Weapons were also being purchased openly on St Thomas to 'overthrow Bradshaw'. The Premier was told to expect trouble. A supporter of his government, St Clair Tobias who lives on St Thomas, became aware of the military action being planned. Even Tobias was approached about a donation to the cause of Anguilla. Once again, St Thomas, notorious for the planning of historic revolts, found itself in that position. Three American citizens were hired as mercenaries. They were Phil Clarke, a Korean war veteran who owned land on Anguilla, and Roy Rosene and Dean Densman who lived on St Thomas. It was reported their fee could have been in the region of $100,000 (St Thomas, *Daily News*, 16 June 1967).

The military attack on St Kitts from Anguilla, with the knowledge and sanction of PAM supporters in St Kitts occurred one morning in June 1967 (Hodge and Petty, 1987, pp. 68–73). According to Hodge and Petty, 'The notion of attacking St Kitts was the brainchild of Ronald Webster and a prominent Kittitian' (Hodge and Petty, p. 62). The same authors further stated:

On Saturday, 10 June 1967, a party of armed men from Anguilla landed on St Kitts. They had two principal objectives which were interrelated. Firstly, their objective was the defence of the Anguilla Revolution. Secondly, they planned the overthrow of the Government of Premier Robert Bradshaw and the installation of a Government sympathetic to the Angullian cause. The Angullian revolutionary leaders were fearful of an invasion from St Kitts and reasoned that the best way of preventing it was to attack St Kitts and overthrow its government. Their philosophy was, 'the best form of defence was attack.' According to one of the men who was part of that historic landing: 'St Kitts was trying to get into Anguilla by fair means or by foul. We were out in the night and so forth, and we were seeing boats coming in and we figured that Bradshaw might attack us at any time, so we attacked him first' (*Ibid* p. 62).

Philosophical and credible as the foregoing might read, it does not tell the whole story. The Angullians wanted to be rid of Bradshaw and his government, but so too did the PAM politicians. That attack on St Kitts was carefully planned between Kittitians and Anguillians to overthrow the Labor Government. The Anguillian rebellion became a useful tool in the hands of desperate politicians on St Kitts willing to trade treason for political power. Despite all the other claims, the crucial factor about that invasion of St Kitts in June 1967 was to place the PAM political party in charge of the St Kitts, Nevis and Anguilla government.

No sane Anguillians would have travelled to St Kitts and attacked Bradshaw's Government without a promise of future reprieve. The Anguillans knew Bradshaw quite well. He was a law and order man, and he believed intensely in Caribbean unity. Everyone involved in the revolt and invasion must have known that both acts were treasonous. Even if the Angullians did give thought to a government independent of St Kitts–Nevis, it must have been an afterthought to a more imminent goal – an alternate government on St Kitts. The invaders were assured that once that operation began there would be a general uprising on the island.

Targets on St Kitts for the military operation included the defence force camp, Radio Station ZIZ, the electricity plant, the police headquarters, and the bulk depot for gasoline at Ponds Pasture in Basseterre. It was well-planned overt militarism with covert political intentions. However, even though some Kittitians hated the Labor

Government, and there was sympathy for the Anguillians, Kittitians had neither the guts not the military experience to participate in the successful military overthrow then. Consequently, the invasion became a fiasco.

In response to the invasion, Bradshaw heightened the state of emergency already existing in the State. The defence force was embodied and given special powers. Meanwhile, he again approached Caribbean governments and Britain to assist him militarily. Bradshaw intended to take military action and force Anguilla back into the union.

Since they were close friends, Burnham always seemed willing to aid Bradshaw. At that time too, because of continuous border disputes with some of its South American neighbours, Guyana had one of the best trained military forces in the English-speaking Caribbean. Other than Burnham, the other leaders listened to Bradshaw with his rebellion and invasion story sceptically. None was committed to repressing what they considered the rights and sovereignty of the Anguillians. Meanwhile, the PAM party undertook an aggressive program of anti-Bradshaw propaganda. It emphasised the historic negative relations between Anguilla and the St Kitts Government. And, it dared to suggest there was no invasion of St Kitts. The whole scenario, it argued, was staged by the Labor Government to gain sympathy.

Every avenue was used to make the government appear fanatical and facist. 'It declared an unnecessary state of emergency.' 'The invasion did not occur.' 'It was a ploy to arrest opposition politicians and their supporters.' Such ideas were propagated in the Caribbean and beyond through the PAM organ, *The Democrat*, through PAM's political meetings and through well-connected English and American sympathisers who hated Bradshaw for one reason or another.

Even today there are Kittitians and Nevisians who refuse to accept there was an attempted coup on St Kitts. People from other Caribbean islands greeted Bradshaw's cry of 'foul play' as if it came from an insane man who could not be taken seriously. Few believed Anguillians would stage a military attack on St Kitts. But then few people in the Caribbean understood the Anguillians' desperation for changed relations with St Kitts, or the rising politicians on St Kitts desperation for power. Even Britain refused to get involved militarily until it landed some forces on Anguilla in 1969.

The St Kitts' government was not militarily equipped to handle the crises at hand. Weapons and training for such eventualities were severely limited. Some of the top men in the police and defense forces were also suspect as to their allegiance to the government; that included Colonel John Irving Howell, Commander of the Defence Force. Little wonder, then, that those men advised the government to call off at least one planned invasion of Anguilla with a volunteer force. But they offered the government no alternative solution to the problem at hand. The leaders suggested the Anguillians were well armed and Kittitians would die in Anguilla.

Generally, just as later occurred in the Grenada affair, the leading Caribbean governments – Trinidad and Tobago, Barbados, and Jamaica – passed the issue of military action on to a foreign nation, that time Britain. They advised Bradshaw that such a matter was beyond them and should be dealt with by the British. The fact that St Kitts, Nevis and Anguilla was a colony of Britain, set up legal barriers which prevented other independent Caribbean nations from intervening. Britain, on the other hand, avoided the matter by labelling it an internal affair. Its responsibility to St Kitts, Nevis and Anguilla, an Associated State, was for external affairs only.

But Britain had another problem when contemplating an invasion of Anguilla. Two years before it refused to invade Rhodesia when it revolted, and set up a 'pigmentocracy'. Harold Wilson's Kith and Kin Statement would still have been fresh on Caribbean people's minds. Under different circumstances, even Bradshaw would have called an invasion of Anguilla by Britain racist and revolting.

Bradshaw never forgot, nor forgave those Caribbean Governments and Britain. They humiliated him and forced him to renege on two of his fundamental political principles – constitutional government, and a united Caribbean. Probably Bradshaw considered that failure to regain authority over Anguilla to be his most crushing personal and political failure. The circumstances he faced forced him to share the blame.

Since it failed to achieve its military option, the government on St Kitts opted for the next best thing – diplomacy. Bradshaw was stubborn; but so too were the Anguillians. Neither side was willing to give much. Further, in a referendum in Anguilla to decide whether Anguilla should remain a part of St Kitts, Nevis, Anguilla or go on its own, five persons voted for the return to St Kitts; 1813 voted against. (Petty, 1983, p. 26). With such a mandate, the leaders of Anguilla had no other option but to drive a hard bargain with Bradshaw.

A Caribbean conference was convened on Barbados in July 1967 to seek a solution to the Anguillian problem. Barbados, Guyana, Ja-

maica, Trinidad and Tobago, Britain, Anguilla, and St Kitts were
represented. At one point it appeared that an agreement was in the
making. Some of the Anguillians and the other participants at the
conference signed, but Ronald Webster and W. C. Richardson did
not. Later, when the Anguillian population learned of the signing,
they agreed with the hold out by Webster and Richardson. To them,
the signing was a sell out of their 'revolution'.

Among the areas of apparent agreement at that Barbados Conference were:

(11) *Amnesty.* No criminal proceedings will be taken against any
person in connection with political action against the State Government or British Government during the period from May 30th until
today, but this amnesty will not extend to criminal offenses committed outside Anguilla.

(13) *Police.* Provided there is an orderly return to lawful government, the strength of the detachment of the state police force
stationed in Anguilla during the initial steps of the return to
constitutional rule will not be greater than the detachment maintained in Anguilla in recent years.

(14) *Peace-Keeping Team.* A team consisting of police officers
provided by the Commonwealth Caribbean Governments will be
stationed in Anguilla during the initial stages of the re-
establishment of constitutional Government. This team will be
under the command of a senior police officer selected by the
Commonwealth Caribbean Governments. Its members will have
the power of police officers under the law of the state, and the state
government will take steps to secure the enactment of legislation
for this purpose. The force will not discharge the routine duties of
the state police, but will carry out a peace keeping team, the
logistic arrangements for its transport and supply and the duration
of its stay will be agreed between the governments concerned.

(16) *State of Emergency.* The present state of emergency will be
terminated as soon as possible so far as it relates to Anguilla.

(18) *Surrender of Arms.* The arms and ammunition seized from the
St Kitts detachment at the end of May will return to the State
Authorities. The people of Anguilla will co-operate in the surrender of all arms and ammunition held without licence or permission
of the Chief or Police.

The British government also agreed to a special grant of £50,000 to be spent on development projects in Nevis and Anguilla by March 1968 (Petty, 1983, pp. 27–9).

It is noteworthy that many the procedures and tentative agreements adopted at that Barbados Conference set the guidelines for future intervention of Caribbean governments in such matters in the region. The crisis in Grenada, 1983, revived many of the ideas discussed at Barbados, 1967.

Despite its failure in achieving a settlement between Anguilla and the St Kitts Government, the Barbados Conference was still useful. Some precedence was set for dealing with crises related to the new militarism emerging in the area.

When the Anguillians rejected the Barbados Agreement, first Jamaica and then Barbados withdrew from the peace keeping force. There were further meetings in August to achieve a settlement in Barbados and Jamaica, but no agreement was reached on how to deal with the peace keeping force issue.

Meanwhile, the Anguillians had moved towards setting up a new form of government. They were also making certain that the circumstances surrounding their disagreement with Bradshaw's government were presented to the world. Dr Roger Fisher, a Harvard Professor, was engaged as a consultant, and overtures were made to the UN.

Fisher wrote a Constitution for the Anguillians. It consisted of 11 sections. In mid-October Ronald Webster, Wallace Rey, Hugo Rey, Collins Hodge, and John Hodge were elected unopposed to form a new Council in Anguilla (Petty, 1983, pp. 32). Dr Fisher then wrote to the UN. That letter was a follow up to a previous attempt with Jeremiah Gumbs to put Anguilla's case to the UN Special Committee on Colonialism. The British, however, objected to two US citizens making such a presentation to the UN on behalf of Anguilla, a British Commonwealth territory. In March 1968, the Special Committee on colonialism agreed to send a mission to Anguilla to do some investigation. However, the British government did not give permission for that visit.

The Anguillian people en masse remained in dogged support of their revolutionary action. Through it, they intended to search for and find a new politics. Nothing that was happening in the Caribbean nor the rest of the world could make them think differently.

At that point, Bradshaw had few choices but to continue the negotiations on the crucial issues. There was no Caribbean or international sentiment to force Anguilla back to a union its citizens did not want. There was no force to carry out Bradshaw's wishes.

This saga with Anguilla taught Bradshaw some lessons about the realities of leading a Caribbean government. Politics in the Commonwealth Caribbean had taken on an ugly new dimension. Militarism had become a real option to those in search of political change.

Bradshaw had no alternative but to prepare to protect his integrity and the trust thousands of people had in his government. He could no longer depend on a defence force that was largely a ceremonial body or a special club to those militarily inclined.

In January 1968 Bradshaw instituted a standing military force on St Kitts–Nevis. This was not an invasion force against Anguilla. It was to maintain political stability and the integrity of the St Kitts–Nevis government.

Captain Erroll Maynard, a member of the Volunteer Defense Force, and one of the 17–22 men previously selected for special training in July 1967, was given command. That group had been trained by Geoffrey Ellis, a former captain in the British Army from August to November 1967. Ellis emphasized, invasion tactics, security work, special skills, and arms. Similar training was offered the police force. However, John Lynch Wade, then Chief of Police, and a Sergeant Fernando Marshall, argued against the further militarisation of the police. They insisted that police did not want to shoot anyone.

Citizens of St Kitts–Nevis did not grasp the need for a standing military force with the same urgency as the government. Consequently, a number of questions were raised in the community about its relevance. Not surprisingly, those accused of involvement with the Anguillian invasion were some of the governments' severest critics. There have been enduring questions, too, about the legality of such a force. In certain circles, Section 41, Chapter 181 of the Revised Laws of Federation 1961 has been used to criticise Bradshaw's militarisation through a body separate from the police force. The same rule is used to justify the present militarisation of the police. It states that the police can be used to avert external aggression.

One important feature of militarisation in St Kitts–Nevis is its proneness to political labels. Sometimes it is imagined; at other times it is real. The truth is that in Bradshaw's times with talk of a real invasion, and today, when such an invasion seems more remote, the general population does not understand the need for any military force. Such a force is maintained and justified largely at the whim and fancy of the political party that forms the government. The citizens enjoy looking at the military formations and the marches.

But uniformed men carrying weapons, and moving around the community in military vehicles is perceived as unnecessary and ever a threat to individual and political freedoms.

After a standing force separate from the police was put in place, mistrust between government and police intensified. But this movement away from harmony appears to have come from a growing feeling among the men in government that certain top police officers were disloyal and could not be trusted. Further, during both the revolt in Anguilla and the attempted invasion of St Kitts, the police seemed quite incapable of dealing with such crises. The police did not respond more favourably when it was known that selected citizens who favored the government of the day were being armed. So, the new military creation consisted of both an overt and a covert force.

The regular military had three parts: (1) a regular corps (2) a reserved corps and (3) a cadet corps. About 100 men from both St Kitts and Nevis formed the standing force. Students made up the cadet corps – between 65–75 men – and were taught leadership skills and disaster preparedness.

Much of the training for Bradshaw's new military force was done locally. At first the 17–22 men trained by Captain Ellis became a core for the few training. Later, overseas training was provided in Guyana, Trinidad and Tobago, Jamaica and England.

Between 1973 and 1979 the reserve corps attended a number of regional camps in the area. The trainees were labelled the Associated States and Montserrat Combined Corps. Each of the camps lasted ten days.

Special training teams from Britain also came to St Kitts to help train military forces there for about two months at a time. To boost standards of professionalism further, British defence advisers stationed on Jamaica visited St Kitts on a regular basis.

Guidelines as to how the military on St Kitts should conduct itself, were laid down by a Captain Oscar Pollards of Guyana. They were: (1) it should maintain internal stability, (2) except as a result of elections, it should preserve the government in office no matter what, and (3) if the military has to choose a side, let it be the side of the people.

Soldiers were admonished to be loyal to country first then to the legitimate government of the day. As far as their soldiering was concerned, the interest of society was always to be placed above the interest of a political party or group.

Bradshaw's phase of recent militarism on St Kitts–Nevis lasted

1967–81. In 1968 the military budget was about $90,000 (EC dollars); by 1972 it was about $172,000; and when that force was disbanded in 1981 its budget had reached $425,000. Most of those amounts were spent for salaries and equipment. The equipment came largely from the British government and from private sources in the US. At the time the equipment included automatic weapons and at least two armored vehicles.

During 1968–81 there was no further military attack between St Kitts and Anguilla. Their quarrel remained verbal rather than physical. Anguilla was given ambiguous political support by Britain. It managed to persist with its secession until it was legalised in 1980.

Despite the decline in a real physical threat from Anguilla, the government in St Kitts continued to maintain its military force. Threats of political instability through the physical overthrow of governments continued on St Kitts and Nevis. Nevisians were becoming more aggressive in their drive for secession. That was what forced Bradshaw to threaten, if Nevis took the route of Anguilla, that, 'There will be blood on the streets.' On St Kitts, the men accused of assisting the Anguillians with the 1967 invasion had been freed. After this release their patterns of politics continuously tended towards threatening the governments' stability. Further, repeated rejection at the polls could have heightened their frustration with a constitutional approach to politics. By the early 1970s much of St Kitts governments's military interests were focused in Nevis. The nearest point between St Kitts and Nevis is two miles whereas Anguilla is 70 miles away from St Kitts. Bradshaw was determined to make good his threat to Nevisians or, by keeping part of his military force on Nevis, to discourage the growing political protest there.

A rumour that Nevisians were planning to take over the ferry between the islands by force moved the tension in another direction. The government made certain that armed guards were placed aboard on each trip from one island to the other. Meanwhile, the military which was stationed close to Government House at Charlestown made regular patrols and camping expeditions throughout Nevis. Rumours abounded that the soldiers harassed Nevisians, including the politicians. But these rumours were denied and no legal charges were ever made.

At one time, during the heat of the secession drive on Nevis, a machine gun was taken to Nevis pier and allowed to stand there. Nevisians saw that act as particularly threatening to their person. It served only to intensify animosities between the two islands.

In retrospect, the Labor Government made an unprecedented move when it militarised St Kitts–Nevis. A standing army on St Kitts–Nevis, armoured vehicles and sophisticated weaponry suddenly bacame part of the daily scene. Even policeman on normal duties were sometimes armed. That military posture remained from 1967 until the change from a Labor Government in 1980. But circumstances forced Bradshaw in that direction. He took action he deemed necessary to protect his state from external or internal adversaries. He was committed to a strong government with internal stability. Now that many of the then-unknown factors are in, the move towards militarism at that time does not appear to be as absurd.

Those actions might well have preserved stability and a measure of unity in the state. However, that blatant move to militarism did set the stage for the present militarism in the Eastern Caribbean. Then, as now, it is only acceptable to military persons and those who hold political power. It was little wonder that the calypso "Boots' by the Mighty Gabby, a critic of growing militarism in the Caribbean, became popular with citizens but hated by the governments.

No actual fighting occurred during the fourteen years of Bradshaw's militarism of St Kitts. However, three soldiers died in accidents. In 1969 one soldier was shot while two of them played with their weapons. Another died in a vehicle accident in 1972 and the third died in a drowning mishap at Bassterre pier in February 1980. Ironically, the soldiers were returning to St Kitts after being asked to evacuate Nevis by the new government.

The military had been labelled a 'Labor Army'. But, as it had been advised by Captain Pollard during training that after a legitimate election it would allow the legally elected government to assume power, the military did not intervene in what was a smooth transfer of power from one political party to another. Captain Maynard, head of the military, and Joseph Francis, head of the police force, went to Premier Simmonds and pledged loyalty after the new government was installed. However, both men were Labor Government loyalists. Few people, including themselves, expected they could survive in those positions for long. In St Kitts, the die is cast. Any leadership in the police or military demands loyalty to the political party, not competence or loyalty to the country.

Under the new government a coalition between the PAM and Nevis Reformation Party (NRP), the military, instituted in 1968, lost favour. That was the very organisation that had frustrated the political aspirations of politicians in both parties.

But, the force could not be disbanded without proper preparation and adjustment in society. The new government needed time to decide what it should do to the body now destined for a changed role in society. The premier did suggest the soldiers become more involved in community work. However, that was never followed with specifics. And, since Captain Maynard's men were trained as a fighting force, he did not initiate any community service either.

Soon after the government changed the military, dominance on St Kitts–Nevis shifted from the army to the police. The new government did not trust the military; neither did it trust the leadership of the police. Eventually, a former policeman, a known supporter of PAM's politics, was brought home from New York to head the police and all new military organisations. That created by Bradshaw was officially disbanded September 1981.

By this time the force had been relegated to a very low profile in society. It was only highlighted at ceremonial parades such as Remembrance Day and the Queen's Birthday. Whether or not the people supported the military presence on their islands the parades were great spectacles. Everyone loved the drama and the antics of presentations such as 'beating the retreat'.

Whatever Premier Simmonds felt about Bradshaw and the move to militarism in the late 1960s he had revised his thinking in 1980. The need for some form of military force to protect Caribbean islands was not imaginary, it was real. Since Bradshaw's action in 1967–68 a number of events in the Caribbean had testified to his sanity. Even Premier Simmonds was prepared enough to understand that reality: the islands need some defence capacity more versatile than the police.

The 1970s saw a new nationalism, interpreted as a new radicalism, in the Caribbean. It was unprecedented in modern times. The newly independent natives were carving a path towards their future. And they were attempting to break some of the traditional dominance of foreign nations. New sympathies had emerged towards Cuba, especially in Jamaica and Grenada. Several times in 1979 *NewsWeek* alleged that the whole Caribbean area including St Lucia and St Kitts was turning to communism, and was on the verge of political explosion.

Almost 20 years before, when Castro caused a similar eruption in the Caribbean, the US invoked its right to intervene on the strength of the Monroe Doctrine. Now Carter's Administration sent Philip Habib, a veteran diplomat, on a trouble shooting mission to the area.

His recommendations were: (i) the US set up an embassy in Antigua; (ii) increased economic aid to the area; and (iii) increased military aid to governments sympathetic to democracy.

Meanwhile, the US established a military-oriented task force in Florida. It was to monitor military and political trends in the Caribbean. At the same time, it was expected to maintain a high state of readiness in preparation for rapid deployment.

When President Reagan came to office in 1981 the forces and strategies that would manipulate and control Caribbean governments were already in place. All the ultra-conservative Republican government had to do was state its agenda of back to the *status quo* for the Caribbean. Then Reagan had to let Caribbean governments know they could not support an agenda different from that proposed by the US. As benefits for supporting this agenda, they were promised economic aid, on the one hand, and military aid on the other. The 'communists' were supposedly everywhere in the Caribbean and they had to be uprooted.

Caribbean governments knew quite well that the real fear in the area focused around economics. The communism scare was more fiction than fact. All the islands, even Cuba and Grenada, then declared communist islands, were struggling to cope with high birth rates and unemployment, a better educated populace, and inefficient political systems. These factors threatened the power brokers. They had to design new strategies for the 1980s. A cornerstone to this new design was militarism.

History absolved Bradshaw. Militarism for political control in the Caribbean was no longer a haphazard matter. It had become both Caribbean and international policy by the early 1980s.

When Premier Simmonds came to the leadership of St Kitts–Nevis in 1980, he too was forced to accept the option of militarism for political control. His perceived reality, and the reality of the Caribbean accepted by the US, left no other option than some form of militarism for new governments. In a House of Assembly of 9 members, the Simmonds Government held 5, the opposition 4. At the same time, there were threats that the Labor Government would soon return to power, probably by clandestine means. Grenada was then considered a dangerous spectacle in the Caribbean. Simmonds' naivete, too, in terms of history and politics, also left him pliable to the force being exerted by international politics.

The new government's approach to the military was different from Bradshaw's. A Special Service Unit (SSU) was created within the police force to perform activities different from those of the regular police. They conduct drug raids in the mountains; they do special security work; and they will be expected to lead the defence, if ever there is a rebellion, or invasion against the current government.

Other differences between the force that defended Bradshaw's government involve the issues of covertness and independence. Bradshaw's force was trained by British troops but it performed independent operations. The present force performs many operations in co-operation with US and other Caribbean troops. Through a memorandum of understanding signed in 1983, St Kitts–Nevis SSU has also been aligned to others throughout the Caribbean; i.e. Barbados, St Vincent, St Lucia, Dominica and Antigua.

At present the SSU on St Kitts–Nevis stands at over 60 men. The government's sources for military equipment and military aid are Britain, the US, and Canada. Since the Grenada invasion the US has easily become the chief supplier of military equipment to the Eastern Caribbean. The government on St Kitts–Nevis continues to receive equipment, training and other forms of technical military aid.

As a back-up to the SSU the volunteer defence force has been reinstated to the position it held before Bradshaw's militarisation. But that too is equipped with better weaponry, although it does not receive the same training as the SSU. However, the defence force does continue to meet regularly. Its command, like that of the SSU, is highly politicised.

Since the 1980s Caribbean politics has increasingly moved to the right. At the same time, most of the politicians have become fascinated by the prestige of power and would do anything legal or illegal to keep it. Because of illegal practices, not even the election process is considered free of tampering anymore. Thus the growing trend towards militarism in the area is seen in some circles as a force that can undermine traditional democratic processes. Further, as Caribbean governments continue their move to the right, they have become part of the East vs. West international conflict. Eugenia Charles of Dominica, James Mitchell of St Vincent and the Grenadines, and Kennedy Simmonds of St Kitts–Nevis have on occasion made public statements on international matters to which their islands have no immediate connection. On those occasions, it was obvious these leaders were deliberately taking the US position.

Britain remains a force in the Caribbean through its long colonial domination of the area. But its own economic problems, and probably Prime Minister Thatcher's world view, limit its present day involvement in and aid to the area. Canadian aid appears altruistic, but in the real world of politics there is 'no free lunch'. The USSR makes few open moves in the Caribbean, other than in Cuba; perhaps the crisis of her ships being turned in the opposite direction during the early 1960s is not forgotten. Meanwhile, the US is in the business of aid to the Caribbean in the form of the CBI, USAID, etc.

At the same time, the US government makes no excuses over the fact that its aid is linked to political goals, votes in the UN, and other aspects of ideological dependency. During Maurice Bishop's era in Grenada, the US made elaborate efforts to prevent aid reaching it. Teachers from that island, for example, could not be invited to workshops paid by USAID funds.

The militarism Bradshaw employed back in the 1960s was a necessary evil. It was a desperate response to a real political threat. Few citizens understood or accepted the politics behind that need for militarism, but it was overt while the politics largely covert. Militarism in St Kitts–Nevis now may be more covert than overt, but the related politics remain covert.

When the militarism is overt, the citizens know the military is there; it is uniformed and obvious. Maybe the downside to the existence of such a force is the overt physical and psychological damage it can do to a society naive about militarism.

The upside to the militarism sponsored by PM Simmonds, is its lack of overt psychological and physical threats to citizens' well-being. There are many factors in its downside. The lack of openness limits honest information about it. For instance, citizens of St Kitts–Nevis were told that 'Tradewinds 88', a joint military operation between the US and the Eastern Caribbean staged on St Kitts, in May 1988, was to prepare them for hurricanes. Yet no civilians were involved in the exercise.

Foreign forces play too large a role in the activities in which the SSU engages. Sometimes even local drug operations are supervised by US troops. Further, no details have been given to citizens about the scope, roles of intentions of the alliances that have been formed. It was a surprise to both the police and other citizens when members of the unit were assigned to Grenada in 1983.

The politics and economics of this form of militarism exact too much in terms of political and financial costs from the islands. A government cannot afford to continue colonial relations in an independent country as its sovereignty and its security will be both undermined. And, since St Kitts–Nevis has been struggling to avoid economic bankruptcy, financial priorities for the country must be carefully chosen. Now many questions remain about whether at this time, the military is one. Even though the SSU is a small body, the financial cost of maintaining it is growing. It now stands at about EC$6.5 million.

Probably the worst aspect of the new militarism in St Kitts–Nevis is the politics it is supposed to defend. Caribbean society today is a product of ideological pluralism. Even the present government on St Kitts–Nevis was once a strong proponent of such pluralism. However, now in the Caribbean, including St Kitts, there is a growing movement to limit political debate. Indoctrination is being proposed over reason. Ideological pluralism is being criticised as a foreign destabilising force in the region. Leaders such as Eugenia Charles of Dominica and Kennedy Simmonds of St Kitts lament constantly about 'foreign ideology', but foreign ideologies have always shaped the region.

To counter ideological pluralism, a number of Caribbean leaders have chosen to become linked to a conservative oriented movement – the Caribbean Democratic Union (CDU) – which is linked with other such movements in the US. It has also been sighted as having received funds from the Iran *contra* caper supervised by former US security director Oliver North. There is growing belief in the Caribbean that the CDU, the SSU and the present drive towards unity may all be part of such a foreign conservative political strategy. Thus, the present militarism on St Kitts can be seen as very much a part of a political mission. That mission has an agenda hidden from the citizenry.

To date, the military on St Kitts has had its best success against the Rastafarians. Its next phase might well be against those others who openly support ideological pluralism. However, if the military resorts to brutality and to ignoring citizens' rights, it will further limit itself in the society. No recent move to militarism on St Kitts–Nevis has been acceptable to all. Consequently, the politicians resort to duplicity. Even though Bradshaw argued his turning to militarism was legitimate he met concerted opposition from the citizenry.

As politics goes, even on St Kitts–Nevis, the ability of government to satisfy the social economic and emotional goals of its people increases its longevity. Meanwhile, too much military presence, no matter how subtle, can disrupt the whole social and political process. That was the case in Grenada.

However, cost of military equipment, the growing sophistication of military technology, and limited manpower availability prevent the military on St Kitts–Nevis from becoming an effective deterrent to serious invasions from outside. Cuban troops, or a small well trained mercenary force, can still overrun St Kitts–Nevis and overthrow the government in a short time. Probably, this is one reality which makes alliances secret or otherwise a necessary feature of the present government's move to militarism.

In the real world of Caribbean politics the St Kitts–Nevis government hardly expects an attack from Castro's Cuba, and an internal revolt is dependent on how sensitive the said government's policies are to the needs of the people. These two factors, plus that variable of subtle politics, compels the rationalisation of the existing militarism on St Kitts–Nevis. But other factors have to be examined critically. Is militarism in St Kitts–Nevis today intended to be defensive, or coercive? Can it ensure the nation's sovereignty and the right of the people?

Sadly, the militarism on St Kitts–Nevis gives government a false sense of security. Since the US plays a dominant role in its sustenance, that very militarism leaves the nation's sovereignty and security inherently underminded. This is so because the training style, the exercises, etc., are determined by the US. Thus local military operations now or later remain dependent. And if ever there is a popular disagreement between citizens and government any issue of the people's rights may put the military in an unenviable position. Such a situation might bring some interesting things to light in terms of the military's true allegiance.

The current militarism in the Caribbean islands may also be part of an attack on their institutions. It is a subtle attack. Even governments sworn to protect the rights of their people can be aiding its success. Contrary to what Caribbean governments are told by foreign politicians and evangelists, the attack on Caribbean institutions is not from communism. Neither is it from a conventional military force. The attack is from foreign cultural and economic forces that are overwhelming the area in the 1980s and 1990s. Now, just as ideological pluralism has become an endangered species in the Caribbean, one can begin to envision a similar fate for cultural pluralism in the near future. And the culture that is being eliminated is Afro-Caribbean – the politics, the food, the economics and the music.

Maybe the present trend to militarism on St Kitts–Nevis brings more problems than it solves. The government should examine its level of productivity and the structure of its education. It should also examine the nature of its dependency, and the myths it continues to accept. Then it may begin to understand the fragility of its assumed security.

When these realities are seen in their true light, government may decide to build a progressive not a restrictive military. Such a military would be prepared for proper, independent intelligence gathering. It would promote a programme of education for independence. And it will be prepared to promote creative productivity.

St Kitts–Nevis needs this new military. By re-arming its forces, selecting relevant goals, and listening to the people, government can become better equipped to take an independent, positive approach to its real battles – those of economics. These are the critical battles that confront Caribbean governments today.

If there is no rethinking on militarism in St Kitts–Nevis, the present trend will magnify, not minimise, the country's problems. For, the government will remain fixated on illusions, while being oblivious and insensitive to realities that concern the people. But then, according to Karnow (1983) 'waging a war is simple, running a country difficult'. The militarism in question is a cop-out: it can only anticipate problems that are unreal, and it offers no long-term social, political or economic solutions to real immediate problems at hand.

Bibliography

Barry, T., Beth, W. and Prousch, D. *The Other Side of Paradise* (New York: Grove Press, 1984).
Browne, W. T. *The Christena Disaster in Retrospect* (Charlotte Amalie, VI: St Thomas Graphics, 1985)
The Daily News, St Thomas, V. I. 16 June 1987.
Hodge, N. and Petty, C. L. *Anguilla's Battle for Freedom 1967* (Anguilla: Petrat Publishing, 1987).
Innis, P. *Historic Basseterre* (Offset Commercial Printers, Basseterre, St Kitts, 1979).
Innis, P. *Whither Bound St Kitts–Nevis* (Antigua Printing and Publishing, Antigua, 1983).
Karnow, S. *Vietnam* (New York: Viking Press, 1983).
NewsWeek, US Edition, 26 March, 28 May, 27 August 1979.
Petty, C. L. *Anguilla*, Express Lithographics (Surrey, England, 1983).
Westlake, D. E. *Under an English Heaven* (New York: Simon and Schuster, 1972).
Young, A. H. and Phillips, D. E. *Militarization in the Non-Hispanic Caribbean* (Boulder: Lynne Rienner, 1986).

8 Nicaragua, Cuba and the Geopolitical Challenges in the Caribbean on the Threshold of the 1990s*
Raúl Benítez Manaut

In this chapter, I analyse the geopolitical situation of the Caribbean Basin in the 1980s and the specific roles of Cuba and Nicaragua in the region. The redefinition of US priorities due to the consolidation of the Nicaraguan revolution and the failure of the 'roll-back' policy based on the support of counter-revolutionary groups is an important change in the regional situation. Another important aspect is the Cuban presence, both in the internal aspects of the revolution of its defence doctrine, which has developed the concept of 'war of all the people' (territorial militia), and in the regional dimension. The development of the Salvadorean revolutionary movement and the serious internal political situation in Panama are also relevant elements in the present conjuncture.

In the Caribbean, US hegemony is being redefined in order to avoid the consolidation of certain processes of social change that have the tendency to be non-aligned. That was the obvious meaning of the intervention in Grenada in 1983. That action was undertaken with the purpose of reversing the tendency towards the erosion of US power, which had weakened significantly since the revolutionary victory in Nicaragua in 1979. I should also take into account the change in attitude of the larger countries of the Basin which showed very active positions of influence in the early 1980s, as expressed mainly through the activities of the Contadora Group (1983–86).

Another important factor has been the transformation of the international environment towards the solution of important regional conflicts such as Afghanistan, Angola and the Iran–Iraq war. This must be given due regard in view of the dependence of the Nicaraguan counter-revolutionaries on US assistance, the key role of Cuba

* Translated by Jorge Rodríguez Beruff and Dale Matthews.

in the Angola negotiations and the close relationship between Cuba and Nicaragua. Furthermore, the progress made in global negotiations between the US and the USSR concerning nuclear disarmament has had the effect of revaluating conventional war, which implies that a greater geostrategic importance is attached to the Caribbean Basin.

The change of government in the US in 1989 does not represent a substantial change in the policy towards the Caribbean formulated by Reagan. The aim of isolating Nicaragua and the reliance on force – both dissuasive and demonstrative – will continue under the Presidency of George Bush. He has stated that he will consolidate the conservative offensive begun by Reagan, a philosophy which has been clearly stated with regard to Latin America since 1980.[1]

GEOPOLITICAL CHANGES IN THE CARIBBEAN IN THE 1980s

The geopolitics of the Caribbean underwent a series of profound transformations in the post-war period. The Caribbean changed from a natural zone of influence of the US and Britain (closely following the design of Alfred Mahan, one of the founders of geopolitics[2]), further consolidated during the Second World War,[3] to a situation of hegemonic decline after the Cuban revolution. In the 1970s, non-aligned and centrifugal tendencies became stronger. In this respect, the struggle of the Omar Torrijo's government in Panama to modify the Canal treaties stands out. This was achieved in 1977 with the signature of the Carter–Torrijos Treaties and their subsequent ratification in 1978 by the US Senate. Likewise, Mexico and Venezuela sought to enlarge their respective spheres of action: Mexico vigorously supported Panama and reactivated its relations with Cuba, and Venezuela sought new markets for its petroleum exports. At the same time, the People's National Party, led by Michael Manley, of social democratic orientation, obtained an electoral victory in Jamaica and governed from 1973 to 1980.[4] Manley reestablished relations with Cuba while Jamaica became one of the most active non-aligned governments in the world scene. This erosion of US hegemony was brought into sharp relief by the overthrow of Somoza in Nicaragua in July 1979.

During this period, the US carried out, due to its military defeat in Vietnam, an important revision of the main postulates of its foreign policy. The Vietnam experience forced US strategic thinking to revise its approach to the Third World. It was in this context that the Carter–Torrijos Treaties – which provide for Panamanian control over the Canal and for a gradual dismantling of the military complex of the US Southern Command until 1999 – were signed. However, a foreign policy debate began to take place within the Carter administration. This placed great emphasis on the concern that the continuation of the original course of the administration could further compromise US hegemony and consequently threaten national security. Thus, in June 1979, the US attempted to send a multilateral military force to Nicaragua to prevent the total disbandment of the National Guard and the *sandinista* victory. This was prevented by the Organization of American States (OAS), due to a Mexican initiative which upheld the principle of non-intervention.[5]

As a result of the revision of the US strategic postulates, a *Rapid Deployment Force* was established to prevent military stalemates. Its creation was announced by President Carter in October 1979 in the immediate context of the crisis in Iran and the revolution in Nicaragua.[6] Developments in Iran provoked concern in the US due to the larger dimension of the Middle East conflict and the perceived threat to maritime lines of communication. Likewise, the Caribbean Basin was considered of great strategic importance, particularly the Panama Canal and the oil supplies from Mexico and Venezuela. Thus, when the Reagan administration took over, a new 'geography of conflict' had emerged related to the possibility of a prolonged war with the USSR. According to the new perspective, it was vital to exercise naval superiority in the Caribbean Basin and to 'diminish vulnerabilities'. The latter meant that a non-aligned country or island in the region was considered a potential threat to US national security.[7]

The first concrete step was to reconsider and upgrade the military importance of the Southern Command (SOUTHCOM), which had been almost dismantled in the second half of the 1970s.[8] SOUTH-COM, under General Paul Gorman, was assigned tasks such as 'the containment of Cuban and Soviet expansionism in Central America', and new functions related to threats to US security including the control of the drug traffic.[9] Among the functions of SOUTHCOM, I would mention the training of troops from the Caribbean Basin, the control of US troops in Honduras, and the organisation of manoeuvres and military exercises. These have been held in a large naval scale since Ocean Venture 81 while major land exercises have been held since Big Pine I (Honduras, February 1983). SOUTH-

COM also performs the function of directing the operations of the Salvadorean Army against the FMLN. This task is carried out by the US Military Group stationed at the US embassy which, since its establishment in 1980, directs the counter-insurgency war.[10] These military activities are explicitly undertaken to confront and contain the alleged expansionism of Cuba and Nicaragua. In the case of Nicaragua, containment is effected through the application of the 'low intensity war' doctrine in its modality that calls for the creation of counter-revolutionary forces.

These two countries are accused of promoting instability in the region. Consequently, they are ranked as the main threat to be faced by US defence policy in the Caribbean Basin. For this reason, I consider it essential to ascertain the real role played by Cuba and Nicaragua in the existing regional geopolitical and military correlation of forces.

THE BALANCE OF MILITARY FORCES IN THE CARIBBEAN BASIN

In order to analyse the balance of military power in the Caribbean Basin with objectivity, we must, first, consider military effectiveness in each country; second, take into account the armaments available to these forces, particularly those considered of an offensive character; and, finally, consider those countries and major powers which, without being geographically in the Basin, possess a military presence.

We have divided the Basin into several subgroups of states: 1) the *Insular Caribbean*, subdivided in the Larger and Lesser Antilles; 2) the *Continental Caribbean* made up of Belize, Guyana, French Guiana and Surinam, which for historical reasons has national-state characteristics similar to those recently decolonised countries of the Insular Caribbean; 3) *Central America*, composed of Guatemala, El Salvador, Nicaragua, Honduras, Costa Rica and Panama and 4) *the larger countries of the Continental Caribbean*: Mexico, Venezuela and Colombia.

Among the major powers which have an active presence in the Caribbean region, the US is dominant, having exercised regional hegemony since the late nineteenth century. The US has permanent military contingents in Panama, Puerto Rico (for our purposes, Puerto Rico belongs to the US), Guantánamo (Cuba), Bermudas, Honduras and El Salvador. To a smaller degree, England, France,

Table 8.1   Total military forces in the Caribbean basin, 1987–88

Larger Antilles	206 715
Lesser Antilles	7,630
Continental Caribbean	483,065
US military forces	20,850
USSR, UK, France and Holland	4,100
Irregular forces	42,000–43,000
Estimated total	765,000

Sources: IISS, *The Military Balance 1987–88*, IISS, London, 1987; US House of Representatives, *Report of the Delegation to Eastern Caribbean and South American Countries*, Washington, DC, GPO, 1984, p. 12; Dion Philips, 'The Increasing Emphasis on Security and Defense in the Eastern Caribbean' in Alma Young and Dion Phillips, *Militarization in the Non-Hispanic Caribbean*, Lynne Rienner, Boulder, Co., 186, p. 59.

Holland and the USSR also have a military presence. The latter sporadically carries out military exercises in the region and maintains a close military relationship with Cuba. The political and military relationships established through diverse training and assistance programmes and the extreme dependence of some countries on tourism and foreign financial centres should also be taken into account.

The military and police forces of all the countries in the Caribbean Basin, including the military forces of other powers and the existing irregular forces, amount to some 765,000.

To establish which are the existing real or potential threats, we must distinguish those forces which have an offensive capability from those destined to the defence of the countries or to internal police or military functions (e.g. to combat insurgent armies or the drug traffic). It is also important to consider possible war scenarios and potential tendencies towards military alliances.

The largest, best-trained and best-equipped forces are the Cuban, followed by the Colombian, Mexican, Venezuelan, Nicaraguan, Salvadorean, Honduran and Panamanian. In general terms, given the peculiar history of conflict between Cuba and US over the last thirty years, the militarisation of that island has a largely defensive character. Just as important is the case of Nicaragua since the victory of the *Sandinista* revolution, a conflict that has important geopolitical and military implications since 1981, when the first funds to support the creation of the *contra* forces were approved by the US National Security Council.[11]

The case of the Mexican Army is peculiar since, like Costa Rica, Mexico is one of the least militarised countries of the region, taking into account its geographical, economic and demographic dimensions. The Mexican Armed Forces have a defensive doctrine and do not possess modern weapons (they just have 11 F-5 supersonic planes). Within the Armed Forces, the infantry is given priority. Even in the case of serious border conflicts, such as the one Mexico had with Guatemala between 1980 and 1984, Mexico has solved them through diplomatic negotiations.

Colombia, El Salvador and Guatemala are experiencing acute military conflicts, where insurgent forces play an important role. These three countries use their well-equipped and well-trained Armed Forces in internal counter-insurgency. For this reason, it is difficult for their armies to participate in conflicts outside their borders and this situation will probably not change in the short term. However, these three countries have faced border tensions with neighbouring states that at times have been conflictual and have affected the region's geopolitics. Colombia has an ongoing dispute with Venezuela over the Gulf of Maracaibo; Guatemala has made claims on the territory of Belize, and El Salvador went to war with Honduras in 1969. These conflicts have generally been resolved by means of international negotiation.

The cases of Honduras and Panama have common elements. They represent situations of military colonisation by the US, which make them important enclaves for that country's strategy in the region. However, SOUTHCOM, which is based in Panama, will have to be dismantled by 31 December 1999, when the Canal and its adjacent areas will also revert to Panamanian control. Its Armed Forces support this nationalisation process. The Carter–Torrijos Treaties also contain a clause which provides for the future neutrality of the Canal and of the Defense Forces of Panama.[12] Honduras, on the other hand, is undergoing a process of consolidation in the US military presence under Protocol III of the 1954 bi-lateral military treaty, with the foreseeable consequence of making permanent the presence of US military forces, bases and communications installations.[13] This rehabilitation of Honduras is quite important to the US because of the redefinition of the role of conventional war in its military strategy and to permit the dismantling of SOUTHCOM.

The militarisation of Honduras is also crucial to implementing a strategy of containment of the Nicaraguan revolution, of the Salvadorean insurgent forces and, to a lesser degree, of the Guatemalan guerrillas. In Honduras, the military forces have been reinforced, particularly the Air Force (with F-5 supersonic planes), turning that country into the dominant air power of the Central American region. This is an important destabilising element since the air weapon has greater offensive capability and potentially threatens Mexico (because its most important energy resources are close to its southern border) as well as Guatemala, Belize and El Salvador. However, the build-up of the Honduran Air Force is mainly related to the US containment-dissuasion strategy towards Nicaragua.

The Venezuelan Army, in the southern part of the Basin, has a tradition similar to that of Mexico's, but which only goes back to the 1960s. Venezuela considers the Caribbean – mainly the island nations of the Eastern Caribbean and, to a lesser extent, Central America – its natural zone of influence.[14] Nevertheless, Venezuela has a dispute with Guyana over the territory of Essequibo as well as the above-mentioned conflict with Colombia. It has played a major role in supporting the Torrijo's effort towards new canal treaties, backed the *Sandinistas* in their struggle against Somoza during 1978–9 and supported Costa Rica when the *somocista* army threatened that country. It has also exercised a political influence through the links of cooperation with the Social Democratic and Christian Democratic political parties.

The geopolitics of the insular Caribbean evolved in favour of the US during the 1980s. I could mention the electoral victory of Edward Seaga in 1980, the invasion of Grenada and the support provided by the Eastern Caribbean countries in October 1983, the freezing of relations between Surinam and Cuba after the Grenada intervention, and the installation of Joaquin Balaguer in the Dominican Republic in 1986.[15] To this must be added the implementation of the Caribbean Basin Initiative[16] and the increase in US military assistance and training programmes to the security forces of the region (see previous chapter). These developments reaffirm the US presence and serve to counteract the previous tendency towards hegemonic erosion. In military and police terms, the US has standardised the armament of the security forces of the Eastern Caribbean, collective defence pacts have been established,[17] and the presence of US government agencies, such as the Drug Enforcement Agency (DEA), has been strengthened.

These changes in US strategy are designed to prevent a repetition of the Nicaraguan phenomenom in Central America and of the Grenada revolution in the Caribbean. They imply: 1) an internal militarisation in most of the countries, 2) a regionalisation of military forces and 3) the tendency towards balkanisation of the existing political forces. These three elements have appeared with greater emphasis in the English-speaking Caribbean countries with the support of conservative political forces. A similar phenomenon can be observed in Central America, though there the strength of the popular movements has held such tendencies in check.

In geopolitical terms, the military arsenals of the different countries respond, in the first place, to internal needs. In those countries which face a developed leftist insurgency, militarisation is promoted to contain it (Colombia, Guatemala and El Salvador). On the other hand, in those countries where external aggression is quite noticeable, the militarisation process responds to defensive and disuasive needs (Nicaragua and Cuba respectively). Finally, those countries with severe drug-trafficking problems have modified the structure of their armed forces in a radical way to face it (Mexico, Colombia and Jamaica), and the police forces and intelligence activities are subordinated to the war against drugs (as in most of the island nations of the insular Caribbean).

In every case, the US presence is one of the variables of the processes of militarisation. Economic and military support is given to Mexico, Venezuela and Colombia's armed forces for combatting drug-trafficking. The US is the key factor for Nicaragua and Cuba, since its threatening stance promotes the militarisation of their states and societies. In the other Central American countries implementation of the strategy of containment – low intensity war – has meant the restructuring, supply and professionalisation of the armed forces, often reaching situations of great dependency (El Salvador and Honduras). In the Lesser Antilles, in order to prevent a repetition of the Grenada experience and to combat drug-trafficking, the US has significantly enhanced its military influence. The conservative government of Balaguer in the Dominican Republic receives a high degree of support. Panama, however, is in a permanent state of political and military tension with the US. The Reagan administration was reluctant to accept the Torrijos–Carter treaties, and tried to press the government and army in every possible way to revise them so that they would allow them to stay there after the year 2000.

Table 8.2 Military forces of the USSR, UK, France and Holland in the
Caribbean basin

USSR	*2,300 (1)*
UK	*1,800 (2)*
France	—— *(3)*
Holland	—— *(4)*

Notes: (1) Corresponds to the combat brigade the US alleges is based in the eastern part of Cuba.
(2) Troops stationed in Belize.
(3) The exact figure of French troops in the Guiana space centre and Martinique and Guadaloupe is not known.
(4) Holland has a small naval air and communications base in the Dutch Antilles.
Sources: See Table 8.1.

I will make a brief balance of the existing military and political correlation that existed at the end of 1988 in the Caribbean Basin. This is to support the thesis that the existence of armies with great defensive capacity, but with limited offensive capacity (like the Cuban case), even if they do not assume a pro-US attitude, would not be able to threaten the US or its allies militarily.

Armies and governments in the Basin that are allies of the US and could be expected to collaborate militarily are: in the Greater Antilles, Dominican Republic, Haiti and Jamaica; in the Lesser Antilles, Antigua and Barbuda, Barbados, Dominica, Grenada, Saint Vincent and the Grenadines, St Lucia, St Kitts, Trinidad and Tobago, Anguilla, Aruba, Bermuda, Cayman Island, Monserrat and Turcos and Caicos;[18] in Central America, Honduras, El Salvador, and Guatemala, and in the Continental Caribbean, Colombia. The military forces of these countries plus the deployed American Forces in the Basin and the irregular forces subordinated to the US (like the Nicaraguan *contras*) amount to 245,045 army men in service.[19] Governments and armies that will most probably adopt a neutral attitude are: Belize, Costa Rica, Panama, Mexico, Venezuela, Guyana, Surinam and French, English and Dutch military men in service. These countries' armed and security forces add up to 237,515.

Finally, governments and armies that may potentially confront the US are: Cuba, Nicaragua, the *FMLN* of the El Salvador, Guatemala's *URGN*, Colombia's various revolutionary groups and Soviet military forces. All of these forces represent approximately 202,100 army men in service.

Table 8.3   US military forces in the Caribbean basin

Bermudas	1,600
Cuba	2,500
Honduras	3,000 (1)
Puerto Rico	3,600
Panama	10,000 (2)
El Salvador	150 (3)

Notes: (1) This is an estimate using 1983 as the base year.
(2) This is the upper limit established by the Torrijos–Carter Treaties.
(3) See A. J. Bacevich, J. Hallums, R. White, *et al.*, 'American Military Policy in Small Wars: The Case of El Salvador', *The John F. Kennedy School of Government*, March, 1988, p. 7.
Source: IISS, *The Military Balance, 1987–1988*, IISS, London, 1987.

This descriptive balance of politico-military forces in the Caribbean Basin obviously does not reflect what would happen if an armed conflict erupted in the region. A number of additional elements must be taken into account: 1) the breadth of the conflict with regard to the number of countries involved, 2) the forces available to be used outside their territory (as not all the forces can be used externally), 3) the fact that most of the forces are composed of infantry soldiers with a limited offensive capability, and 4) possible changes in the internal political situation in some countries which might modify their international behaviour.

The balance, however, shows the military and geopolitical advantage enjoyed by the US. Furthermore we must consider the military forces that, though not deployed in the region, could be used for regional military actions. These are the 82nd Airborne Division, based in Fort Bragg, North Carolina, where the central command of the *Rapid Deployment Force* is located, and the units under the control of the Atlantics Naval Command (LANTCOM) located in Norfolk, Virginia. LANTCOM is responsible for the military surveillance of Cuba.[20] The US has also upgraded its strategic position in the region with the new bases in Honduras that have been added to the military complexes in Panama[21] and Puerto Rico.[22] It also possesses a considerable number of military installations in other Caribbean islands.[23]

Given the military supremacy of the US, the disposition of Cuba and Nicaragua to undertake offensive actions is inhibited and their armed forces are compelled to consider only defensive war hypotheses.

However, the US government defines both countries as military threats and directs all sorts of hostile messages against them.

THE CUBAN DEFENCE DOCTRINE

Cuba faced many hostile actions during the period 1959 to 1980. Among the most notable were the Bay of Pigs invasion in 1961, isolation from the Interamerican System, particularly the Organization of American States (OAS), the rupture of diplomatic ties with most American states and the total economic blockade imposed by the US. During this period, Cuba underwent a profound process of militarisation which had the purpose of defending the revolution. This process, however, did not imply a dissociation of the interests of the state and civil society as a military linkage between the population and the government was promoted from the outset. The basis for this linkage were an intense political and social projection of the armed forces and the development of a defensive military doctrine, which reached its highest expression after 1980 in the formulation of 'Total Popular Defence' (doctrine of the 'war of all the people') and its concrete expression in the *Militia of Territorial Troops* (MTT). This explains the high percentage of GNP devoted to defence: 7.6 per cent in 1961, 8 per cent in 1962, 5.6 per cent in 1963, 5.2 per cent in 1964, between 4.5 per cent and 5.8 per cent in the period 1965–72, a low level of 3.6 per cent and 3.79 per cent in 1974 and 1975 respectively, and returning to a level between 7 and 8 per cent from 1977.[24]

The military history of the Cuban revolution can be divided into three periods roughly defined as 1960–70, 1970–80 and 1980 to the present. I mainly deal with the most recent period.

In the first period (1960–70), the revolution became consolidated along with the institutions it generated, such as the Cuban Communist Party (PCC) in 1965. In the military sphere, parallel structures – both professional and composed by the civilian population – were developed. The Ministry of the Armed Forces (MINFAR) was established on 16 October 1960 and ten days later the National Revolutionary Militia.[25] Committees for the Defence of the Revolution (CDR) were also formed in October 1960.

During the second half of the 1970s, Cuba supported different revolutionary movements in Latin America which had followed its model. This attempt failed mainly due to the defeat of Che Guevara in Bolivia in 1967. Cuba was profoundly isolated from the region until the early 1970s when it sought to normalise diplomatic relations with the Latin American countries. It intensified relations with Mexico and restablished diplomatic links with Peru, Panama and Chile. At the same time, Cuba supported the new Angolan government against military aggression by South Africa (with US support) and counter-revolutionary groups, with major military contingents. Cuban support was later extended, though with less emphasis, to other African countries such as Ethiopia, Congo, and Mozambique.

The Cuban presence in Angola undoubtedly constituted its greatest foreign policy effort and it created the opportunity for its armed forces to obtain combat experience. Towards 1987, Cuban forces in Africa totalled: 30,000 in Angola (13 infantry regiments and 8000 civilian advisors); 500 in Congo; 4000 in Ethiopia; and 600 in Mozambique.[26]

The Cuban presence in Angola began in late 1975, with the arrival of 16,000 soldiers of the Special Troops Batallion of the Ministry of the Interior (MININT) and of the regular armed forces (MINFAR). This occurred after the US had begun assisting economically and militarily, since July 1975, the counter-revolutionary groups of the FNLA through Zaire and also in response to the South African invasion of southern Angola launched on 23 October 1975.[27] According to Cuban sources, 100,000 Cubans participated in the Angolan war (on the basis of personnel rotation) in the period 1975–80.[28] The number of Cuban troops stationed in Angola averaged 20–30,000, depending on the military needs of the campaign.

In 1987, however, the military correlation of forces began to shift in favour of South Africa when its troops and UNITA were about to encircle Cuito Canavale, the concentration point of the most important Cuban-Angolan military units.[29] Cuba, however, reinforced its military forces in late 1987 and early 1988 to reverse the trend and obtained a decisive victory between February and March 1988.[30] This altered the balance of forces in Southern Africa and cleared the path for a negotiated solution with the participation of the governments of Angola, South Africa, the US and Cuba. This negotiation implied a recognition of Resolution 435 of the UN which called for the independence of Namibia. The contingent of Cuban troops in Angola reached 50,000 at the time of the victory at Cuito Canavale and their repatriation has been a central aspect of the negotiations.

Many analysts consider that Cuban participation in Angola and the rest of Africa gives that country major power status due to its military capacity and decisive influence in the course of events. It is, however, highly improbable that Cuba will seek to exercise similar influence in the Caribbean Basin. An action of this nature in the Caribbean could be considered 'suicidal' as it would move the theatre of operations to Cuba's own frontiers. According to William Leogrande, 'A Cuban attack against a US ship would be considered an act of war and probably the US would inflict important blows in retribution . . . This would mean suicide for Cuba.'[31]

This explains, in part, why Cuba did not come to the defence of Grenada when the US invaded in October 1983, in addition to the fact that the revolutionary government had collapsed due to internal struggles. The only possible scenario could be participation in the defence of Nicaragua, at the request of that government, if US-backed forces should invade, as happened in Angola.

Cuba's military structures are clearly the most complex and developed in Latin America (they are only surpassed by Brazil in quantity and quality of the armaments), given the existing relationship between the professional armed forces and those composed of the civilian population. The main elements of military organisation were developed in the 1960s, when infantry forces and individual small weapons were given priority. In the following decade, the Navy and the Air Force were modernised with the support of the USSR. In the 1980s, both elements, the professional and the irregular, were integrated with the development of the doctrine of the 'War of All the People' (announced on May Day 1980) and the creation of the MTT.[32] US sources claim that the USSR has supplied Cuba 250 thousand metric tons of armaments. It should be taken into account that a large proportion of these supplies consist of light weapons to make the new defence doctrine viable.[33]

By 1987, the Cuban irregular and professional forces amounted to the following number of effectives:

Table 8.4   Cuban military forces, 1987

Regular armed forces	
Army	145,000
Navy	12,000
Air Force	18,500
Total	175,500
Irregular Forces	
Youth Work Army	100,000
Civil Defence	50,000

Interior Ministry	17,000
Frontier Troops	3,500
MTT	1,200,000
Total	1,370,500

Source: International Institute for Strategic Studies, *The Military Balance,
1987–1988*, IISS, London, 1987, p. 189.

Cuban military equipment is clearly the most complete in the
Caribbean Basin. The infantry possesses 650 T-54 and T-55 tanks,
plus 300 T-62, and 100 T-34. It also has 1,400 anti-aircraft guns
distributed throughout the entire island as well as mobile light artillery for infantry units.[34] The Navy has two Komar-class frigates (the
most modern of the Cuban Navy, displacing 2,300 tons), 5 Osa-1,
13 Osa-2, 5 Komar, and 2 Polnocny amphibious vehicles (Cuba has
an amphibious assault batallion).[35] In addition, it has 6 submarines,
2 supplied by the USSR in 1979 and 4 in 1983.[36] The Air Force has 17
long range troop transports, 10 Il-62, 7 Tupolev Tu 154 and 2 Il-76.
It also includes 4 combat squadrons, one with 15 Mi-17 and three
with 36 Mig 23. Planes for interception are grouped in 16 squadrons,
two with 30 Mig-21-F; three with 34 Mig-21-PFM; two with 20
Mig-21- PFMA; eight with 100 Mig-21-bis; and one with 15 Mig 23
Flogger E. The helicopters are grouped in eight squadrons totalling
approximately 122: 60 Ml-4, 40 Mi-8 (20 armed), 18 Mi-24 Hind E
and 4 Mi-14.[37]

Although the Cuban military is considered to have the highest
combat capability in the Caribbean Basin and can be projected
beyond the country's borders – as was demonstrated in 1987 and 1988
with the transfer to Angola of tank and air forces – US naval forces
are clearly superior. This is recognised even by US analysts who
share the outlook of the Reagan Administration, such as Jiri and
Virginia Valenta. According to them,

Soviet modernization of the Cuban armed forces with sophisticated
elements has made them, both in size and equipments the most
awesome in the Caribbean Basin, with the exception of the US.
Although the Cubans do not have sufficient capacity to carry out
on their own air or sealift or an amphibious assault on any Central
America country or a larger island nation such as Jamaica, they
could effectively intervene in a smaller island, such as Grenada, in
support of 'fraternal' regimes.[38]

They conclude their analysis by pointing out that 'it is obvious that the essentially defensive Cuban navy cannot defy the naval power of the US in the Caribbean Basin'.[39]

In the 1980s, the most important presence of Cuba in the Basin is its support of the *Sandinista* revolution. In fact, the importance to Cuba of the consolidation of the revolution in Nicaragua is comparable to the containment of South Africa and counter-revolutionary forces in Angola. Both countries, Angola and Nicaragua, due to their broad relations with Cuba, mainly economic and military, represent priorities in Cuban foreign policy.

US analysts, such as Harold D. Sims and Theodore Schwab, share the perception that support for Nicaragua forms part of an expansionist project of 'export of the Cuban revolution'. They point out that cooperative intergovernmental relations with Cuba are concentrated in three areas: economic, military and international. They emphasise the great dependence of Nicaragua by making reference to intense cooperation in the fields of education, health and the communications infrastructure (mainly roads). With regard to the military, they assume the point of view of the Department of State regarding Cuba-Nicaragua links, support for the Salvadorean FMLN since 1979–80 and subsequent Cuban support in the war against the counter-revolutionary commandos. They also mention the broad collaboration in the international arena between the two countries and sustain their analysis with expressions of Nicaraguan politicians regarding the 'non-negotiable' character of relations with Cuba.[40]

This point of view – whose central argument is that Cuba has taken advantage of the Central American crisis precipitated by the Nicaraguan revolution to undermine the US presence – is used to justify the formulation of a new policy of containment (of Cuban-Nicaraguan 'expansionism') *vis à vis* the region. The strategic objective is to reaffirm US hegemony in changing circumstances.

By contrast, the Cuban perspective on its economic, military, political and international relationships of cooperation with countries such as Grenada and Nicaragua is based on one of the principles of the Cuban revolution: internationalism. By internationalism Cuba understands,

> . . . the subordination of Cuban positions to the international needs of the struggle for socialism and for the national liberation of peoples. Cuba, which has demonstrated its vocation for international solidarity in all possible ways – with blood, with work and

with technical collaboration –, with continue basing its international conduct on that premise.[41]

NICARAGUA

The *Sandinista* victory on 19 July 1979 produced the demise of the political and military apparatus of the Somoza regime. The widespread support of the population for Sandinista Front for National Liberation (FSLN) throughout the civil war from 1977–79 made it the main pillar of the new regime. In the second semester of 1979, the main institutions of the new system, such as the National Reconstruction Government Junta (JGRN) and the Sandinista Popular Army (EPS), were formed, complementing the socio-political effort which consisted of the creation of various popular FSLN support groups such as the Sandinista Defense Committees (CDS). Among the first decrees issued by the JGRN were the nationalisation of the financial system and foreign commerce as well as the agrarian reform and the creation of a People's Property Area (APP).

In addition to the JGRN, which was dissolved at the end of 1984 with the advent of elections, the reorganisation of the state included the formation of the Council of State. This organ, which functioned as a legislature, was launched in May 1980 and lasted until the installation in January 1985 of the National Constitutional Assembly. Representatives to the Assembly and the Supreme Court of Justice were elected in November 1984.[42] This occurred within a national context of a plurality of political parties, ranging from the extreme right to the extreme left, but with the exclusion of *somocista* representatives and the counter-revolution.

US efforts to halt the consolidation of the revolution date from 1979 under the Carter Administration when conservatives proposed the 'containment of the revolution' by cutting economic assistance (this strategy was known as 'passive containment'). With the advent of the Reagan Administration, the organisation of ex-Somoza guardsmen was promoted in Honduras and the US. Initially, this was done secretly by the CIA and through the use of third countries (like Argentina's military government). However, the enactment of the National Security Council's Directive No. 17 facilitated approval of a fund of almost $20 million at the end of 1981 'to create a 500 man army'.[43] Hence, the active containment of communism, also known as the 'Reagan Doctrine', was initiated. It became part of the 'low intensity war' strategy to promote the rollback of triumphant revolutionary processes.[44]

In the interests of defence, the Sandinistas effected a rapid quantitative increase in their armed forces, from approximately 2–3000 guerrillas grouped in the FSLN at the time of victory to 77,000 troops by 1987.[45] This was in response to the threat from the *contras* which wreaked greater destruction in quantitative terms throughout the country than did the civil war of 1977 to 1979.[46]

By 1987, the *Sandinista* army's arsenal was made up chiefly of light weaponry for individual infantry combat (it is said that they have the capacity to mobilise 250 thousand people in the event of a military invasion by the US).[47] The army is structured professionally in combat units, known as irregular combat batallions (BLI) to face the *contras*. It counts on some 150 T-54 and T-55 tanks as well as numerous anti-aircraft artillery guns (to protect the capital and infrastructural points of the economy from a probable bombing attack) and mobile artillery (to face the *contras*). The Air Force is made up of various Soviet, French, Spanish and North American combat and troop transport planes and helicopters: 3 AT-33A; 3 SF-260 Warrior; 6 Cessna 337; 4 T-28; 4 AN-26; 2 CASA C-212 A; 1 IAI-201 ARAVA; 1 C-47, 10 AN-2, 2 Aerocommander and one Twin Bonanza. Helicopters include: 4 MI-2; 34 MI-8-17; 12-MI-24 and MI-25, and 2 SA-316B Alouette III. Naval forces are almost non-existent, with approximately 20 boats for coastal duty.[48]

Both the popular and professional components of the *Sandinista* defence system have kept those countries bent on eliminating the revolution – mainly the US and Honduras – at bay. The actions of these two countries could be considered a declaration of war. In the case of the US, aggressive actions consisted of support for the *contras*, the trade embargo, political isolation, and covert actions, while Honduras restricted its actions to border clashes, which have resulted in moments of tension with its neighbour, as well as tolerance and support for the *contras*.

This strategy has suffered many ups and downs since the *contras* depend financially and militarily on the US. The US support for the *contras*, in turn, has been obstructed by Congress since the surfacing of the Iran-Contra scandal in November of 1986 and also because of Democratic control over both the House of Representatives and the Senate. Adding to the problems have also been the great military inefficiencies and internal divisions within the *contras*, which have provoked a notable decline in its defensive actions inside Nicaragua.[49]

The effects of the war with the *contras* have been very damaging for Nicaragua's economic, political and social relations. The state of emergency has been in effect since March 1982.[50] Military expenditure as a per cent of total government expenditure has jumped from 14.7 per cent in 1981 to more than 50 per cent in 1985.[51] All this has had a notable impact upon the social transformations which the *Sandinistas* have wanted to carry out. High rates of inflation, unemployment and speculation with consumer products have harmed the economy.

The impact of the war increased from 1981 to 1986 and declined thereafter. From 1980 to 1986, 18,963 deaths were registered, 9663 injuries, and 7790 civilians were either kidnapped or captured by counter-revolutionary forces.[52] Added to these losses were some 15,000 members of the *Sandinista* armed forces, among the dead and injured. More than 50,000 citizens have been directly affected by the war, a very significant number in the light of the country's total population of 3 million inhabitants. Damages to the economy, consisting of the destruction of goods, production losses, the trade embargo and blocked loans, are in the realm of 1106.2 million dollars.[53] Of the numerous sectors of the population affected by the war, northern and Atlantic coast farmers have been hit hardest, while more than 250,000 people have been uprooted from their places of origin.[54]

In 1987 and 1988, the military activity of the *contras* declined significantly because of three factors: cessation of official US aid, internal struggles, and the commitments undertaken by the Nicaraguan government at the signing of the Esquipulas II Peace Treaty in August 1987 in Guatemala. This treaty contained numerous dispositions which favored a dialogue with the *contras*,[55] thus opening up the possibility of a gradual decline in the negative effects of the war on the country. One of the most important actions of the Nicaraguan government was its fulfillment, both formal and real, of the Esquipulas II agreements between August 1987 and January 1988, compared with the track record of the other participant countries in the region with equally acute internal conflicts; e.g. El Salvador and Guatemala.[56] An effective ceasefire between warring armies was achieved afterwards with the signature of the Treaty of Sapoá in March 1988. The treaty, which represented a goal never before achieved in the region during the decade of the 1980s, was effective for 60 days.[57]

FINAL REFLECTIONS

There will probably be no significant changes in the geopolitics of the Caribbean Basin in the 1990s, although that will hinge on internal factors in each of the individual countries of the region as well as on the propensity of the great powers to meddle in regional affairs. One of the internal factors which could drastically alter the balance of power in the region is the possible advance of progressive political forces or the sharpening of internal political problems in countries like Mexico, Venezuela, Jamaica and Colombia. The situation in El Salvador will no doubt continue to be one of the most significant conflicts of the period, together with that in Panama.

The US policy towards the region will not change significantly under the Bush Administration. The document *Santa Fe II: A Strategy for Latin America in the Nineties*, places in evidence the proposed continuity of US policy towards most of the countries. It argues for the strengthening of a bilateral approach to the payment of foreign debts and rejects a multilateral solution or the possibility of a country declaring a moratorium. Problems with Cuba would again be dealt with in the context of negotiations with the USSR. The US would continue its policies of collaboration with respect to the problem of drug trafficking and would maintain the low intensity conflict doctrine when dealing with such countries as Nicaragua:

> If trends stay on their present course, the US will continue to face the export of revolution from Nicaragua into the 1990s. A containment policy will not be cheap, and in the long run it won't work. The US would have to support either a democratization of Nicaragua or pay sky-rocketing costs to combat the subversion of Nicaragua's neighbors. A policy of the democratization of Nicaragua will require a most sophisticated development of low intensity conflict doctrine.[58]

Another important document elaborated by a bipartisan group of national security experts (both Republicans and Democrats) at the beginning of 1988 shows the need to contain the emergence of new threats in the western hemisphere.

This situation might change if more pro-communist regimes come to power in the hemisphere. If the Sandinista regime consolidates its power in Nicaragua and continues to receive Soviet support, hostile communist regimes might gradually become established elsewhere in Central America – for example, in El Salvador, Honduras and Panama. Such trends could be expected to endanger the control of the Panama Canal and threaten the political stability of Mexico. These developments would force the US to divert far more foreign policy resources and defense assets to the Caribbean region leading to a reduced American role in NATO.[59]

Among the most important factors that limit the Bush administration in emulating the Reagan administration, are the fragile balance between Democrats and Republicans in the House of Representatives and the Senate, which hinder the implementation of policies which lack consensus (like aiding the *contras* in Nicaragua); also, there is a need for successful actions which will not end in failure.

Finally, it must be noted that actions which tend to strengthen military collaboration between the US and the Caribbean include the war against drug-trafficking; increased tensions in Central America, particularly the Salvadoran situation; and the possible increase in internal conflicts in the different countries of the regions such as, for instance, Panama.

Notes

1. The document which guided the neoconservative orientation of the Reagan Administration is the *Document of the Santa Fe Committee*. See Roger Fontaine, *et al.*, 'Las relaciones interamericanas: escudo de seguridad del Nuevo Mundo y espada de la proyección a nivel global de los Estados Unidos', in *Cuadernos Semestrales* (CIDE, Mexico), No. 9 (First Semester, 1981).
2. Antonio Cavalla (ed.), *Geopolítica y seguridad nacional en América Latina*, UNAM, Mexico, 1979.
3. Humberto García, 'El Caribe durante la Segunda Guerra Mundial: el Mediterraneo Americano', in Carmen Gautier (ed.), *Puerto Rico en el Caribe Hoy*, CLACSO-CEREP, Buenos Aires, 1987.
4. Humberto García, 'Defense Policy and Planning in the Caribbean: An Assessment of the Case of Jamaica on its 25th Independence Anniversary', *Caribbean Studies*, 21, 1–2, San Juan, Puerto Rico, enero–junio de 1988.
5. 'Discurso del Secretario Jorge Castañeda en la XVII Reunión de Consulta de Ministros de Relaciones Exteriores de la OEA, 21 de junio de 1979', *Unomásuno*, 22 June, 1979.

6. *Rapid Deployment Forces*, Issue Brief Number 1B-800027, Congressional Research Service, Washington, DC, 16 January 1981.
7. John Saxe-Fernéndez, 'La estrategia global estadunidense y su entorno inmediato en tiempos de guerra', *mimeo*, Political and Social Science Faculty, UNAM, 1984, p. 10. The author analyses the relationship between oil and strategic raw materials, mainly minerals, and national security in *Petróleo y estrategia, México y Estados Unidos en el contexto de la política global*, Siglo XXI, México, 1980.
8. John A. Fesmire, 'US Command Relationships in Latin America, Could they be Better?', *US Army War College*, 6 May 1982. See also Jorge Rodríguez Beruff, *Política militar y dominación, Puerto Rico en el contexto latinoamericano*, Huracán, San Juan, 1988, p. 43.
9. Drug-trafficking has been defined, particularly after 1987, as a menace to national security to be combatted even with military means. See Sam Sarkesian, 'Defensive Responses', in Uri Ra'anan, *et al.*, *Hydra of Carnage, International Linkages of Terrorism*, Lexington Books, 1986. I have dealt with this issue in 'Narcotráfico y terrorismo en las relaciones interamericanas', *Polémica* (Costa Rica), No. 5 (May–August, 1988).
10. See A. J. Bacevich, James Hallums, Richard White, *et al.*, 'American Military Policy and the Lessons Learned from El Salvador', *The John F. Kennedy School of Government*, March 1988.
11. Richard Allan White, *The Morass: US Intervention in Central America*, (New York, Harper & Row, 1984), p. 53.
12. See 'Protocolo al Tratado Relativo a la Neutralidad Permanente y al Funcionamiento del Canal de Panamá', in William J. Jorden, *Panama Odyssey*, University of Texas Press, Austin, 1984.
13. INSEH, *INSEH Informa*, Vol. 5, No. 39 (September, 1988), p. 1.
14. Rita Giacalone, 'El Caribe Oriental de habla inglesa en la política exterior de Venezuela y Cuba', *El Caribe Contemporaneo*, No. 16 (January–June 1988).
15. Roberto Cassá, 'El retorno de Balaguer en República Dominicana', *El Caribe Contemporáneo*, No. 15 (July 1985).
16. *Fact Sheet on the Caribbean Initiative*, Trade Representative, Washington, D.C., 22 February 1982; and Alfredo Guerra Borges 'Aspectos Comerciales de la Iniciativa para la Cuenca del Caribe', *El Caribe Contemporáneo*, No. 10 (July, 1985).
17. Jorge Rodríguez Beruff, op. cit., p. 141.
18. The Dominican Republic is the biggest recipient of military aid in the Antilles. In 1986 it received 10.8 million dollars in military assistance. Jamaica follows with 8.3 million dollars. The group of island-nations of the Eastern Caribbean received that same year 10.4 million dollars in military aid. See *Foreign Assistance Program: FY 1986 Budget and 1985 Supplement Request, May 1985*, US Department of State, Special Report No. 128, Washington, DC, 1985, p. 14.
19. This estimate is based in the sources cited in Table 8.1.
20. Adm. Wesley MacDonald, US C-in-C, Atlantic, 'Atlantic Security, The Cuban Factor', *Jane's Defense Weekly*, Vol. 2, No. 24 (22 December, 1984).
21. Raúl Leis, *Comando Sur, Poder Hostil*, CEASPA, Panama, 1985.

22. John Enders, *La presencia militar de Estados Unidos en Puerto Rico*, Proyecto Caribeño de Justicia y Paz, San Juan, 1985; and Jorge Rodríguez Beruff, *op. cit.*, chapter titled 'El aparato militar de Estados Unidos en Puerto Rico', pp. 145–79.
23. See Lars Shoultz, *National Security and US Policy Towards Latin America* (Princeton, Princeton University Press), 1987.
24. See Jorge Domínguez, *Cuba, Order and Revolution* (Harvard University Press, Cambridge, 1978) p. 347; and *World Armaments and Disarmament, SIPRI Yearbook 1984* (London, Taylor & Francis, 1984), pp. 126 and 129.
25. *Informe del Comité Central del PCC al Primer Congreso Presentado por el Compañero Fidel Castro Ruz*, Ed. del DOR del CC del PCC, La Habana, 1975, p. 181.
26. IISS, *The Military Balance 1987–1988*, IISS, London, 1987, p. 188.
27. See William LeoGrande, 'Cuban–Soviet Relations and Cuban Policy in Africa', in Carmelo Mesa Lago and June S. Belkin (eds), *Cuba in Africa*, Center for Latin American Studies, University of Pittsburgh, 1982.
28. *II Congreso del Partido Comunista de Cuba. Informe Central Presentado por el Compañero Fidel Castro Ruz, Primer Secretario del Comté Central del Partido Comunista de Cuba*, Editora Política, La Habana, 1980, p. 65. We calculate as 260,000 the number of Cubans who participated in Angola between 1975 and 1988.
29. René Pellicier, 'Angola, Mozambique: des guerres interminables et leurs facteurs internes', *Heterodote*, No. 46, Paris (Autumn, 1987).
30. Fidel Castro, 'Discurso pronunciado el 26 de julio en Santiago de Cuba', *Granma*, 27 July 1988.
31. William LeoGrande, 'The Author Replies', *Foreign Policy*, No. 48 (Fall 1982), pp. 181–2.
32. *II Congreso . . .*, *op. cit.*, p. 63.
33. Department of State, *Cuban Armed Forces and the Soviet Military Presence*, Special Report No. 103, Washington, DC, August, 1982.
34. IISS, *The Military Balance, 1987–1988*, p. 187.
35. *Idem.*
36. US. Department of Defense, *Annual Report to the Congress, Caspar W. Weinberger, Secretary of Defense, Fiscal Year 1983*, Washington, D.C., p. II–22, in Lars Shoultz, *National Security and US Policy Toward Latin America*, op. cit., p. 262.
37. IISS, *The Military Balance, 1987–1988*, p. 187.
38. Jiri Valenta and Virginia Valenta, 'Soviet Strategy and Policies in the Caribbean Basin', op. cit., p. 213. Translated from the Spanish version.
39. Ibid., p. 215.
40. Theodore Schwab and Harold D. Sims, 'Cuba and Nicaragua: A Key Relationship, 1979–1984', *Cuba Studies/Estudios Cubanos*, 15, 2 (Summer 1985).
41. *Informe del Comité Central del PCC al Primer Congreso, Presentado por el Compañero Fidel Castro Ruz*, op. cit., p. 230.
42. I have have discussed in greater detail in Raúl Benítez Manaut, Lucrecia Lozano, Ricardo Córdova and Antonio Cavalla, 'Fuerzas armadas, sociedad y pueblo: Cuba y Nicaragua', *Revista de Ciencias Sociales*

(Puerto Rico), 15, 3–4 (July–December 1986), pp. 649–726.

43. It was approved by President Reagan on 1 December 1981. The text appeared in *The Washington Post*, 16 March 1982.

44. Lilia Bermúdez, op. cit., pp. 161–80. See also 'Los "combatientes de la libertad" y la guerra de baja intensidad contra Nicaragua' en *Cuadernos Semestrales* (CIDE), Second Semester, 1985.

45. IISS, *The Military Balance 1987–1988*, p. 194.

46. I estimate that in the 1977 to mid-1979 period of the civil war, 35,000 people died and between 80–90,000 were injured. See CEPAL, 'Nicaragua: el impacto de la mutación política', *Estudios e informes de la CEPAL*, No. 1, Santiago de Chile, 1981, p. 18.

47. Nicaraguan Government, *El revés de la contrarrevolución, Un balance 1985–1987*, Managua, 1987, p. 6.

48. IISS, op. cit., p. 194.

49. On the Iran-Contra affair see John Tower, Edmund Muskie and Brent Scowcroft, *The Tower Commission Report* (Bantam Books-Times Books, New York, 1987); Jonathan Marshall, Peter Dale Scott and Jane Hunter, *The Iran Contra Connection, Secret Teams and Covert Operations in the Reagan Era* (South End Press, Boston, 1987).

50. The decree was revised November 1984, during the electoral struggle, to allow the exercise of certain rights.

51. For the 1981 figure see IISS, *The Military Balance, 1981–1982*, London, 1981. For 1985, *Boletín Económico Centroamericano*, ANN, Managua, 5 February 1986.

52. Nicaraguan Government, *El Revés . . .*, op. cit., p. 17.

53. *Idem.*, p. 19.

54. *Informe Anual del Presidente de la República, Comandante de la Revolución Daniel Ortega Saavedra, a la Asamblea Nacional*, Managua, 21 February 1987, p. 2.

55. 'Procedimiento para Establecer la Paz Firme y Duradera en Centroamérica' (Guatemala 7 August 1987), *Comercio Exterior*, 37, 9 (September 1987).

56. 'Conclusiones del Informe de la Comisión Internacional de Verificación y Seguimiento (CIVS) a la Reunión de Presidentes sobre los Progresos en el Cumplimiento de los Acuerdos del Procedimiento para Alcanzar la Paz Firme y Duradera en Centroamérica', Panamá, 12 January 1988 (*mimeo*, SRE, Mexico).

57. 'Acuerdo entre el Gobierno Constitucional de Nicaragua y la Resistencia Nicaraguense', Sapoá, Nicaragua, 23 March 1988.

58. 'Santa Fe II: A Strategy for Latin America in the Nineties', Committee of Santa Fe, Pre-publication copy, 13 August 1988, p. 22.

59. *Discriminate Deterrence, Report of the Commission on Integrated Long-Term Strategy*, Washington, 11 January 1988, p. 13.

Part III
Comparisons and
Implications

9 The Small State in the Caribbean: Policy Options for Survival*
Lloyd Searwar

'is it simply, as some argue (after Grenada) that there is no political or national space available to a small state in the highly polarised international arena of today which will allow it to operate independently, when it is bent on a process of radical transformation?'

Clive Thomas[1]

in spite of a certain structural dependence there is, as in the past, an area for manoeuvre which, if carefully identified and manipulated, can help to secure sovereign independence within this now interdependent world, of small entities like our own. The period of the 1960s and seventies in the Caribbean teaches us that policy flexibility and a disdain for *idees fixes* and a willingness to adjust, along with internal cohesion, are the bases from which we must play.

Vaughan Lewis[2]

In the wake of the Grenada events of 1983, the statements by two distinguished Caribbean scholars, quoted above, define the continuing dilemma which confronts the Caribbean small state. Is there a way forward out of a situation of threat which would permit such states to pursue with reasonable autonomy policy options for survival and development? The modest aim of this chapter is to look at some of the attempts made in the immediate past to diminish the situation of threats to peace in the Caribbean, attempts which have so far failed to yield significant results, and to suggest other measures which may be more effective in the future.

---

* The Caribbean for purposes of this chapter is defined as the English-speaking Caribbean or the Commonwealth Caribbean, sometimes referred to as 'the West Indies'.

PEACE

I begin as usual with a number of preliminary considerations as to what is meant by 'peace' and what is meant by 'development' and their interrelation. In the English-speaking Caribbean – the sub-region which constitutes the Caribbean Community (CARICOM)* – the threats to *peace* are of a subtle kind. Leaving aside the two mainland states of Belize and Guyana, which have been subject to territorial claims of powerful neighbors, there is no persistent threat to peace through overt hostility or the threat of the use of overt violence.

The threats are, so to speak, structural, going on day after day. They derive from the location of these small states in a region of geo-strategic significance. In the main, the threats to peace are posed as a web of constraints, a kind of latent hostility which diminishes the autonomy of these small states, many of them islands in both external and internal action.

Autonomy is defined as the capacity to maintain a close correspondence between preferences and actions.[3] So defined there is clearly no totally autonomous state. On the other hand, autonomy should at least mean that the state can translate a majority of its policy preferences into authoritative actions.

The Caribbean small state, because of its location, finds itself constrained in its choice of internal strategy for development and in its choice of a strategy of external relations designed to maintain its security and to secure resources for development.

Peace in the Caribbean of the small state is thus defined to mean the removal or, more realistically, the significant diminution of such constraints.

I note quickly in passing that those few ruling groups in the small states who have sought from time to time to reject such constraints, have been subject to destabilisation in a variety of ways including denial of aid funds from international agencies and banks, the withdrawal of investment, the withholding of technologies and spares, the encouragement of internal dissent and the mounting of hostile international propaganda campaigns.

---

* Consisting of the following states – Antigua and Barbuda, Bahamas, Barbados, Belize, Dominica, Grenada, Guyana, Jamaica, St Kitts/Nevis, Saint Lucia, St Vincent and the Grenadines, Trinidad and Tobago, together with Montserrat, not yet independent.

DEVELOPMENT

There are many ways of defining development – some in the erudite language of the economists and some reflective of ideological positions. One simple way out of such difficulties of definition is to define development as the peoples of these small states define it; i.e. in terms of the success of economic strategies which provide not only jobs but access to ever higher levels of consumer goods. Because of location, a language shared with neighbouring highly-industrialised societies, permeation by foreign mass media, especially the electronic media, good levels of education and traditional mobility, the expectations of the CARICOM peoples are steadily expanding. This is, for all practical purposes, an irreversible trend. Hence, development approaches, such as were once attempted in Guyana, which seek significant closure of the economy or the institution of measures of delinking which aim to reverse the trend towards the consumption of ever higher levels of goods, have generated unmanageable levels of dissent, leading to forms of internal repression or massive overseas migration or the dramatic reduction of production in key economic sectors.

NEED FOR A GENERAL GOAL AS A MEASURE

Given the vulnerability of the small state and the high expectations of its people, one must next try to define some general goal against which strategies for the maintenance of peace or for the promotion of development could be measured.

The question of what is the acceptable trade-off as between autonomy (relative freedom from constraint) and development must at least be asked. This point is of particular relevance to the CARICOM states, as there are cases within the region of the pursuit of extreme forms of 'dependent integration' (virtual abandonment of autonomy) into the nearby industrialised economy which appear to yield high levels of growth and of consumer living.[4] In these circumstances, how does one judge the effectiveness of strategies which promote dependent relations as against those which aim at securing, at all costs, autonomy for the small state but which put in jeopardy existing standards of living?

It could take us too far afield to enter into this complex debate. Fortunately, there is to hand a formulation by a regional expert –

William Demas – which can be considered to reflect an emerging regional consensus. In his contribution to the Distinguished Lecture series of the Institute of International Relations, University of the West Indies, St. Augustine, Trinidad and Tobago, he formulates this general goal for the small Caribbean state, as follows:

> the real issue is that of survival, combined with increasing standards of living for the people, some degree of structural transformation in the economy and avoidance of an intolerably high degree of external economic, political, diplomatic, geopolitical and even cultural dependence on some larger country or countries – most likely neighbouring but also possibly distant.[5]

LOCATION IN A SPHERE OF INFLUENCE

This chapter focuses on only one topic, namely, the situation of structural conflict which derives from the location of the small state in the sphere of influence of one super power – the US – and which it is contended is central to both peace and development.

What is the nature of US perceptions of the Caribbean or the wider region – the Caribbean Basin – which leads to the assertion of a sphere of influence?

Analysts differ as to the nature of US perceptions. Gorostiaga, drawing on his experience as a participant in the negotiations over the Panama Treaty, argues that there is a *primacy of military strategic interests over economic interests* in the formulation of US policy.[6]

Edward Gonzales, after analysing conventional approaches to the analysis of Caribbean Basin international politics which catalogue US interests in terms of strategic raw materials, economic ties and population flows, and noting that the US appears unable to find an effective formula which would decouple the process of radical change from legitimate concerns over US security interests, nevertheless identifies the major vital interest as the *geo-strategic function* which a secure and stable Caribbean Basin furnishes by facilitating the emergence and subsequent performance of the US as the leading world power with widespread global commitments.[7]

In addition to such considerations, US perceptions of Cuba as a Soviet surrogate, the withdrawal of the colonial power perceived as leaving behind a power vacuum, and the demonstrated interest of the USSR in developing relationships with responsive regimes, all these have led the US to a redefinition of the CARICOM geopolitical space as part of a strategic entity, the Caribbean Basin – which includes the CARICOM states together with the rest of the island Caribbean plus Central America – a self-confirming concept as it imports into the space thus redefined a sense of endemic crisis which is not characteristic of the English-speaking sub-region itself.

Whatever might be the roots of US concerns, the matter which is of particular relevance to our topic is the way in which these self-defined US interests are projected and safeguarded in its sphere of influence.

It is not proposed to deal herein with the question of the legitimacy of sphere of influence doctrine which in every respect disregards current international norms about the rights of the state, including in particular the right to self-determination in the choice of internal system and external relations.

It is here contended that the sphere of influence is as much a hard fact as being an island. It will not go away. Moreover, beneath the international rhetoric about the equality of states it is generally recognised that spheres of influence – for there are two – perform for this day and age an important function in ordering the international system. There is little that even a major state, let alone a small state, can do to change this situation.

SPHERE OF INFLUENCE AND THE MONROE DOCTRINE

In analytic terms the sphere of influence in this hemisphere is often confused with the Monroe Doctrine, and its roots might indeed lie in that doctrine. Petras, Erisman and Mills have defined the Monroe Doctrine as having the following essential ingredients:

It prohibited European states from further colonisation in the Western Hemisphere, it called for non-intervention, enjoining European Countries to forego involving themselves directly (i.e. generally viewed as using physical force) in the affairs of hemispheric nations and pledging the US to refrain from interfering into matters concerning the remaining European Colonies in Latin America; and it rejected the extension or imposition of European political systems into the Hemisphere, contending that European and American socio-political cultures were basically different and indeed incompatible.[8]

The existence of Cuba on the one hand and the American need to establish diplomatic relations with the new states in other regions of the world, on the other, have largely rendered the Monroe Doctrine obsolete – at least as originally formulated.

The Monroe Doctrine was a unilateral declaration. By contrast the rules for the sphere of influence – although these have never been publicly promulgated and indeed the super powers have never publicly acknowledged their existence,[9] paying in this respect lip service to international norms – are tacitly recognised not least by the diplomatic behaviour of states in both regions.

The rules of the game are basically two, namely:

1. the hegemonial power can exercise supervisory intervention within its sphere without the risk of direct military challenge by the other.[10]
2. the other super power will in the circumstances restrict itself to rhetoric or discreet poaching.[11]

What is it that triggers the exercise of supervisory intervention? Clearly it must be the perception of a threat to security. But it is the nature of the perception which is problematical, because the preservation of the self-defined security interests of the hegemonial power so often takes the form of *a concern with the choice of internal system and development strategy by the states located in its sphere of influence*.[12]

An important exercise of supervisory intervention is therefore directed to ensuring that the internal systems of neighbouring states are similar to those systems identified with the super power, any deviation being interpreted as a step towards a change of sides in the East–West conflict.

In the instant case, it has been observed by Ramesh Ramsaran that:

> the perceived connection between ideology and security leads Americans to favour systems based on free enterprise, a reduced role for the state and open policy towards foreign private capital.[13]

Ramsaran goes on to remark cryptically and without developing this point, that the Americans are often willing to recognise regimes which diverge from these ideals, but which pose no threat to US security.

FREE ENTERPRISE – THE ACCEPTABLE CHOICE

Implicit in this US position is the contention that what is called the free enterprise system is the essential concomitant of democracy.

This insistence that the so-called free enterprise system is the only acceptable choice for development strategy within the Caribbean must clearly impose severe constraints on the small Caribbean state. It is contended that in the case of the small state there are many areas of crucial importance for overall development in which, because of such factors as size, geographical hazards, and inadequate infrastructure, the private sector, whether local or foreign, is unlikely to show any interest and which in the circumstances can only be developed by the state or by other forms of economic intervention.[14]

The relationship with the US should in consequence be perceived as a source of conflict and of constraints which thwart development.

CHOICE WITHIN CARICOM

However in the Caribbean, especially at this moment, this is not so. There is a clear majority of ruling groups which affect a development strategy whose mechanisms and goals are projected as being *similar* to those of the influencing power.

In such cases, the potential situation of conflict could lie not in relations with the US but internally. Some regional experience has shown that an exclusive market-oriented approach, tending to a posture of closeness with the US, and which appears to have as its ultimate objective, forms of dependent integration into the nearby industrialised economy, 'locks' the small state into an 'approved' strategy thus denying to it urgently necessary development options involving state participation or direction, as for example in the case of Jamaica under Seaga. In these circumstances, such 'conservative' regimes are restricted from undertaking the transformation necessary to cope with structural poverty and unemployment, and the increasing marginalisation of groups within the society including, in particular, women and youths. It is for this reason that at present it appears that there is a rapid unravelling of the fabric of power available to such ruling groups.

On the other side of the political spectrum, where ruling groups responding to either domestic imperatives or ideology have projected their strategies as being part of a wider movement towards socialist transformation, they have invariably attracted the hostility of the US and have been exposed to threats and pressures from a range of sources including certain international agencies and banks. However, regional experience has also demonstrated that a near total reliance on state-controlled economic strategy is unlikely to produce, at least in the Caribbean, the new export industries so urgently needed. It is worth recalling in this connection that William Demas argued cogently more than two decades ago that the patterns of development open to the small underdeveloped country, including the small island economy, point to:

> the role of exports (as) much more that of a leading sector in the sense that the rate of growth of the GDP is tied much more closely to the rate of growth of exports than in a very large economy. It is the growth of external demand which causes the economy to move.[15]

'PURE' STRATEGY

In short, the adoption of 'pure' strategy whether on the left or on the right, whether responding to pressure or ideology, has signally failed to provide the peoples of the CARICOM region with the expected levels of development.

Before dealing with a number of initiatives which have been taken in the past to diminish the constraints, to which references have been made, so as to make the milieu more supportive of the development objectives of the small state, it is worth considering the reason why there is at present in the CARICOM sub-region so widespread an identification of the goals of the small state with those of the hegemonial power.

REASONS FOR THE TREND

This chapter suggests that there are two major reasons for this trend, namely:

1. that at the regional level institutions devised by the small states to co-ordinate action, namely, CARICOM and the Caribbean Development and Co-operation Committee (CDCC), and to advance

objectives, have in substantial measure been superceded by a new set of policy management mechanisms located for the most part outside the region, in which the CARICOM states participate but in which the decision-making power is in the hands of other major states or international agencies;
2. that at the national level there has emerged a number of penetrated systems which shape policy formulation and decision-making within these states.

POLICY MANAGEMENT MECHANISMS

In the first category one must number:

1. the Caribbean Group for Co-operation and Economic Development (CGCED) which meets under the auspices of the World Bank and includes all donor countries and agencies. Established in 1977 to consider the situation of economic difficulties in the region, the CGCED meets annually in Washington but is always preceded by a meeting of donors in Paris. While seemingly a multilateral arrangement, it in fact functions towards the region in terms of relations between donor countries and individual states. While undoubtedly it has served to mobilise some additional resources, it has in practice constrained these small states, individually and as a grouping from determining their own development strategy, objectives and priorities;
2. the annual Miami Conference, established in the context of the Caribbean Basin initiative (CBI), which attracts each year-end, as a new mecca, Caribbean Heads of Government who return to preach the gospel of free enterprise. The Conference has as its twin objectives, a review of the CBI arrangements and the bringing together of overseas investors, and officials and entrepreneurs of the Caribbean;
3. the emergence of the Caribbean Democratic Union (CDU), as at present, a powerful political body whose membership is not limited to the independent English-speaking states. The CDU apparently is in a position to determine aspects of regional political action and to sideline the CARICOM consultative and decision-making bodies, as was demonstrated by recent events in the wake of the abortive Haitian election;[16] and
4. more serious still is the penetration and practical neutralisation of

the CDCC. The CDCC, a ministerial committee established within the Economic Commission for Latin America and the Caribbean (ECLAC) on the initiative of CARICOM states, represented a major step towards bringing diplomatic coherence into the Caribbean archipelago. It included all the island states including Cuba, and opened up important possibilities for joint action and development. The difficulties encountered and which were never overcome, of holding CDCC's sixth annual meeting in Grenada during the Bishop regime and the more recent difficulties which have prevented the holding of the tenth anniversary meeting in Havana, appear to derive from the need in terms of political stance of some CARICOM ruling groups to avoid participation in a mechanism which is perceived by the super power as being of major significance for Cuban diplomacy. In consequence, there has been a steady diminution of interest in the CDCC on the side of a majority of English-speaking member states.

PENETRATION

In addition to the erosion or supercession of the mechanisms established at the regional level for the protection of sovereignty and promotion of development strategy, there is the observed phenomena of increasing penetration of systems of decision-making at high policy levels. Following Rosenau, a penetrated political system is defined as one in which:

> non-members of a national society participate directly and authoritatively, through actions taken jointly with the society's members in either the allocation of its values or the mobilisation of support on behalf of its goals.[17]

An example of such penetration is the establishment in recent times of the so-called Institutes for Democracy as arms of several of the political parties which now hold power in the CARICOM region. As political parties in CARICOM tend to play a more direct role than is usual in parliamentary government (of the Westminster type) in the making of decisions, such institutes, funded from and organised by external sources and hence susceptible to manipulation, provide opportunities for penetration of policy levels.

The phenomena of penetrated sovereignty in the CARICOM

region is a largely unresearched area but any inquiry which may be mounted would have to pay attention to such areas as the operations of trade union executives, multinational linkages and the increasing pervasiveness of certain overseas church groups implicit in whose programmes of evangelisation is support for the free enterprise system.

It is the measures outlined above which, despite the salience of the need for structural transformation and the manifest failure of an exclusive market economy approach to provide it, have led, in the Caribbean, to the pursuit of policies fundamentally supportive of the existing order.

ATTEMPTS TO BRING ABOUT CHANGE

I turn now to the attempts which have been made in the immediate past to diminish the situation of constraints, with its implicit threat to peace in the Caribbean. While some ruling groups in CARICOM had taken the initiatives leading to the establishment of the CBI and CARIBCAN (the Canadian equivalent), a number of other ruling groups in the region, sensitive to the constraints of the Caribbean milieu, have attempted to bring about change in that milieu or in the wider international system which would facilitate self-determination in the choice of internal development and external strategy. At the level of the region, a number of such proposals or arrangements have been advanced, mainly through the Co-ordination of Foreign Policy mechanism within CARICOM, as follows:

1. the proposal to declare the Region a Zone of Peace:
2. the proposal to establish a Scheme of Mutual Defence Assistance:
3. the mobilisation of Third World diplomatic solidarity:
4. the promulgation of international norms.

Each of these proposals is discussed below.

DECLARATION OF THE REGION AS A ZONE OF PEACE

The proposal to declare the Caribbean a Zone of Peace was first mooted at the Grenada Meeting of the Standing Committee of CARICOM Ministers responsible for Foreign Affairs (SCMFA) in

July 1981, the proposal being strongly supported by the then radical regimes in Grenada and Guyana. Grenada had earlier secured the adoption of a resolution at the Twelfth Session of the Organisation of American States (OAS) in La Paz on the Caribbean as a Zone of Peace which called upon all states to recognise the region as such and to devote all their efforts in appropriate regional and international fora to the advancement of the concept. The OAS resolution included the following significant paragraph:

> recognising that it is within the exclusive competence of sovereign states to *decide upon the path to be taken for the attainment of the goals of democracy, social justice and integral development for their peoples*. . . . (AG/doc. 1167/79 adopted 31 October 1979) (italics added).

In Grenada a Working Group was appointed to pursue the SCMFA proposal. But it proved difficult to convene this and, when it finally met in Belize in March 1982, a sharp conflict of views erupted with the then radical regimes of the region alone favouring the idea, while other member states indicated that their lack of enthusiasm took account of the existence of bases or installations within their territories from which the host state derived economic and other advantages. The proposal was considered a non-starter and has since been quietly dropped from the list of concerns of CARICOM Foreign Ministers.

THE SCHEME OF MUTUAL ASSISTANCE

The proposed scheme of mutual assistance suffered a somewhat similar fate. The idea that CARICOM states should seek to establish a Scheme of Mutual Defence Assistance first emerged at the Eighth Conference of Heads of Government held in Guyana in April 1973, preparatory to the establishment of the Caribbean Community. It is of significance that it was not until some *eight years* later, in July 1981, that the matter was first taken up by the CARICOM Foreign Ministers at the same Sixth Meeting in Grenada. Again, there were difficulties thereafter in pursuing the proposal. The Working Group appointed to consider the matter and to draft a scheme did not meet until some two years later, in February 1985. At this one-day Meeting of Officials, in Nassau sharp differences emerged which reflected differing perceptions of security threats, with many of the Eastern Caribbean states perceiving the matter in terms of problems of internal dissent or secession or threat of mercenary attack, while the 'radical' regimes were clearly concerned with attacks from outside the region. The meeting was deadlocked. Although there was no explicit agreement that the matter should be abandoned, that was the unspoken understanding and this proposal, like the Zone of Peace, no longer finds a place on the agenda of CARICOM Foreign Ministers.

MOBILISATION OF THIRD WORLD DIPLOMATIC SOLIDARITY

The co-ordination mechanism was clearly more successful in the mobilising of diplomatic solidarity on CARICOM territorial security issues. Such solidarity, mobilised in particular through the Non-Aligned Movement, proved effective in assisting with the maintenance of the territorial integrity of Guyana and Belize. But while such international solidarity availed as a possible deterrent in the regional conflicts with Venezuela and Guatemala, the experience of the Manley, Burnham and Bishop regimes makes it at least doubtful whether it can be significant as a countervailing influence to pressures within the sphere of influence.

THE PROMULGATION OF INTERNATIONAL NORMS – THE UN DECLARATION ON NON-INTERVENTION AND NON-INTERFERENCE

Utilising the mechanism for the Co-ordination of Foreign Policy for mobilising international support, certain regimes, especially Guyana, have sought to safeguard the capacity for self-determination through the promulgation of new international norms. Thus, the question of destabilisation was raised on Guyana's initiative at the Fifth Conference of Heads of State or Government of Non-Aligned Countries held in Colombo in August 1976. As a result that Summit, in its Political Declaration, stated:

The Conference examined, in particular, the situation of certain Non-Aligned Countries in the area (Latin America) that are the target of pressure, coercion and intimidation. The Conference especially took note of the statements by the Prime Ministers of Guyana, Jamaica and Barbados concerning attempts to 'destabilise' their governments. The so-called 'techniques of destabilisation' that are used include, among others, deliberate and well orchestrated attacks through the mass media, selective sales of arms and alleged defence service, intensification of interregional conflicts, fanning of internal problems and manipulation of servile support.[18]

Further diplomatic action was taken in 1976 by Guyana in the UN General Assembly where a Working Group of Non-Aligned States initiated the formulation of a UN Declaration on the Inadmissibility of Intervention and Interference in the Internal Affairs of States. The Declaration was finally adopted by the General Assembly some five years later, in 1981, (UNGA Resolution 36/103) and remains a remarkable example of the attempt to invoke international norms as a security shield for small states.

Of similar significance was the frequent rhetoric of Maurice Bishop on the issue of ideological pluralism. This doctrine was invoked by Bishop virtually as an international norm which might attract security by deterring intervention. In keeping with this belief, Maurice Bishop at a mass rally to mark the first anniversary of the Grenada Revolution, stated:

> Our third principle is that the principle of ideological pluralism must be respected in practice. Every single country in the world, including racist apartheid South Africa, will speak in theory of accepting the principle of ideological pluralism. But theory is not enough; we want to see in practice that the people of this region are in fact *allowed to build their own processes in their own way, free from outside interference and free from all forms of threats or attempts to force them to build a process that somebody else likes.* This principle today must be recognised and practised. It is a fundamental principle that reflects the reality of today's Caribbean.[19]

OPTIONS FOR SURVIVAL

The several proposals outlined above which have been pursued in the search for security in self-determination still inspire a familiar rhetoric in the Caribbean. However, it is considered that while such ideas may in the long term bring about significant change in international behaviour, the small states of the Caribbean, in view of the urgency of their economic situation, must now pursue options more within their grasp.

The question of decoupling the process of radical social change from the concerns of US strategic interests is of crucial importance. Up to now the ruling groups of the Caribbean, with few exceptions, have seemingly failed to identify realistic objectives which would enable them to respond to the exercise of hegemonial power in the sphere of influence in a way which would provide them with enhanced capacity:

1. for self-determination of internal strategy;
2. for the choice of external strategy which would provide both security and resources for development.

On the one hand, the posture of closeness, as already noted, has denied to its exponents imperative internal options required to meet the development problems which derive from smallness and previous colonial structures, with consequent breakdown in the development process.

On the other hand, the posture of defiance has led to an unwary reliance on doctrine and norms and ideological linkages which have attracted hostile measures including destabilisation and curtailment of assistance.

To advance the objective of self-determination, the following options are tentatively outlined below:

1. the demonstration that the choice of internal development strategy responds to the peculiar characteristics of the small open societies of the Caribbean, most of them being island states, *and not primarily to ideology*;
2. the promotion of the cohesiveness of CARICOM societies.
3. the development of an appropriate diplomacy; and
4. the reorganisation of the regional movement so that it can provide more effective mechanisms for security and for development.

Each of these inter-related options is discussed below.

APPROPRIATE DEVELOPMENT STRATEGY

The main elements of an appropriate development strategy for the so recently independent Caribbean small state should derive from a new political economy which responds to the special characteristics of these states and their location.[20] Up to now, ideology appears to have played too large a role in 'distorting' perceptions of the problems which flow from smallness and location and former colonial structures, and in devising solutions to them. In this connection La Guerre has pointed out:

> Socialism in a dependent colony was a dependent creed borrowing its visions, strategies and tools from the various metropoles. That persists even today.[21]

However, the problem exists on both sides of the political spectrum. The critique can be applied with equal force to those who advocate 'capitalist' approaches. The fact that the exponents of this latter approach have not yet, at least publicly, recognised that some aspects of the development problem posed by smallness require considerable state intervention, probably accounts for the fact that while the CBI is perceived as having failed in its objectives, criticism has so far been muted. On the other side, some revision of socialist strategy is necessary in terms of a perceived and ungrudging role for the private sector and market-oriented sectors of the economy as instruments of development.

The aim of what is described as a new political economy should be to provide a 'model' of a modernising, small and very open developing economy. It is considered that the model should include the following elements: an export sector of high-technology industries; a modernising 'traditional' export sector; import substitution in particular in food production for national and regional markets utilising foreign exchange earnings from the previous two sectors; the development of service industries which exploit the entrepot location of Caribbean states; and the diminution of economic vulnerability through diversification of markets. It is to be noted that if the states of the region are to have a 'dual' economy, there will be need to work out the right balance sector by sector between extra-regional export-oriented and national/regional import-substitution activities.

The overall objective of this exercise should be to create a 'middle ground' on which a substantial consensus on what development strategy is appropriate could be developed. Such strategy would recognise that each state must work out for itself what is right 'mix' as between state and private sectors. In short, it would be based on the recognition of the necessity for a pluriformity in techniques and entities in the development strategy for the small state in the Caribbean.

Agreement on such appropriate strategy might help to diminish the quite astonishing 'swings' or polarisation on a range of issues as between successive regimes which now characterise CARICOM politics. In the absence of a middle ground consensus as to objectives and/or strategy for their achievement, it appears that the ruling group, irrespective of its initial position on the political spectrum, is driven as a result of external influences or pressures to espouse 'extreme' positions often expressed in high rhetoric as a device for attracting external support. To put it another way, in the absence of a middle ground of political/societal agreement which the regime can consistently invoke in coping with and in limiting external pressure, or on which it can rely in the pursuit of a course more in keeping with defined national interest, the regime finds itself adopting polarised positions reflective of the ideology of the state whose assistance is being sought.

THE PROMOTION OF COHESIVENESS

It cannot seriously be disputed that a cohesive society, especially in the case of the small state, is the best safeguard against pressure or destabilisation.[22] At present our divided societies lend themselves too readily to the internalisation of external conflicts, not of their own making.

The chief instrument for the promotion of cohesiveness must continue to be the operation of parliamentary democracy after the Westminster model. However, that 'model' is defective in several respects. In the absence of the restraining conventions and customary rules which obtain in the country of its genesis, the Westminster Model can lend itself all too readily to dictatorial rule. It provides a Prime Minister with enormous residual power without the customary restraints.

Nor is it a matter of deficiencies in the electoral system alone, as has been argued by Anthony Maingot.[23] The Guyana experience can be cited against this.

Nevertheless there is a profound attachment to the Westminster 'model' among the peoples of the English-speaking Caribbean because, as Clive Thomas has pointed out, it was the primary goal in the struggle for independence.[24] Instead of attempts to discard it, thought must be given as to how it could be strengthened through such mechanisms as effective judicial review of state action in keeping with the fundamental rights' provisions now enshrined in regional constitutions.

In addition there is an apparent need to underpin the democratic process through the establishment of bodies including tripartite bodies – government, private sector and trade unions – which can provide at several levels for the 'politics of participation'.

The creation of a cohesive society will also require that special attention be given to the involvement in the development process of groups which are presently 'marginalised' including in particular women and youth. The full participation of women and youth is considered absolutely essential for at least the following reasons:

1. Without the full participation of women, these societies will neglect at their peril, at a time of difficult transition, the special skills which women in the Caribbean have historically demonstrated for devising strategies for survival; and

2. Without the full participation of youth, now the major element in the population (including women), discontent will continue to be expressed in the massive migration of young people, the accelerated growth of separatist sub-cultures such as rastafarianism or provide a catalyst for rebellion.[25]

Attention must also be given to the need for effective human rights mechanisms because the process of economic transformation will almost certainly involve infringements of human rights, unless special steps are taken to safeguard them. It has been argued from time to time, and not only on the left, that the need to cater for social and economic rights requires for the time being the curtailment of civil and political rights. This is, at least in the CARICOM region, a false dichotomy as curtailment of civil rights has led in some states to widespread demoralisation and migration, and consequent collapse of production in important sectors.[26] The recent rejection by the CARICOM Committee of Attorneys General of a proposal for a CARICOM Human Rights Commission should therefore be seen as a major setback.

DIPLOMACY FOR SURVIVAL

It is not proposed to deal here with such matters as the practical reorganisation of overseas missions to enable them to function more effectively as instruments for development.

While the CARICOM states have played eminent roles in multilateral fora, they have been altogether less successful in the area of the bilateral diplomacy which is essential for survival in view of their location. While multilateral diplomacy responds to certain general ideas of which the CARICOM states have been eloquent exponents, the pursuit of bilateral diplomacy requires the careful definition of national interest. It has been argued in this chapter that it is precisely the failure to define national interest effectively that has been one of the main weaknesses in our approach to the external environment. What is needed is a diplomacy based on principles of prudence which would include, in terms of the relationship with the US, techniques of reassurance, and which would provide the leverage which could be derived in significant part from political relations with certain major states in the Caribbean littoral and such other states as Canada and the member states of the European Economic Community (EEC).

The objective should be a diplomacy which would provide the Caricom States with a wider space in which to pursue the development strategies of their choice.

REORGANISING THE REGIONAL INTEGRATION MOVEMENT

It is not proposed to enter into a discussion here on the successes and achievements of the regional movement. However, it is indisputable that there is a clear need to make the integration movement more effective in the areas of security and economic development.[27]

Paramount consideration needs to be given to strengthening the processes of political consultation by more frequent (short and informal) meetings of Heads of Government. Such meetings should deal with issues of high politics, survival, defence and related matters. In addition, it appears necessary to institute regular consultations at high political level between CARICOM and the Organisation of Eastern Caribbean States (OECS) so as to ensure that the two groupings remain mutually supportive and pursue coherent strategies.

Perhaps an even greater challenge facing the movement is the need for it to provide assistance in the task of structural transformation. At present, the energies of the movement remain over-concentrated on revitalising intra-regional trade, although it is agreed that such trade is of high importance. However, the major crisis derives from the fact that the traditional export industries of the region (and in particular, sugar) which account for 90 per cent of total trade, have lost their growth dynamic. (Current near total dependence in some states on tourism greatly increases vulnerability.)

There is apparently an emerging regional consensus on the need for the development of a strategy of export-led growth. Such strategy is dictated on the one hand, by the nature of an international system characterised by the diffusion of technology, and on the other by the small size and the consequent structural openness of the CARICOM States.

No individual member state has the capacity by itself to monitor for technology or to pursue effective investment promotion or market strategies. Increasingly, it should be the task of CARICOM to explore as a group such industrial development opportunities in the context of the structured relations which now obtain with the EEC and under the CBI and CARIBCAN arrangements.

CONCLUSION

Given the persisting situation of threat and the failure of the policy options for survival hitherto pursued on the left or the right, whether it be proposals to declare a Zone of Peace or to promulgate new international norms or to seek deeper levels of dependence, the small state in the Caribbean must now focus its energies on measures more within its control. Such measures should include the devising of a development strategy on which a substantial political consensus might be built at national and regional levels; the promotion of cohesiveness in their societies; the pursuit of new diplomatic approaches designed to secure leverage; and the strengthening of the regional integration movement so that it can provide a countervailing force in the unequal relations in which the CARICOM states are involved, and function as a more effective instrument for structural economic transformation.

Notes

1. Clive Thomas, 'The Grenadian Crisis and the Caribbean Left', *IDS Bulletin*, 16, 2, April 1985, p. 38.
2. Vaughan Lewis, 'The World We Live In', Independence Lecture delivered at the Central Library, Castries, Saint Lucia, February 1986 (Mimeo).
3. Eric A. Nordlinger, *On the Autonomy of the Democratic State* (Cambridge: Harvard University Press, 1981), p. 8.
4. Namely, the small tourist petroleum-refining trading economies, The Bahamas, Bermuda, the US Virgin Islands and the Netherlands Antilles.
5. William Demas, 'Consolidating Our Independence: The Major Challenge for the West Indies', in *Caribbean Regionalism: Challenges and Options* (St Augustine, Trinidad and Tobago, Institute of International Relations, 1987), p. 58.
6. Zabier Gorostiaga, 'Toward Alternative Policies for the Region', in George Irvin and Zabier Gorostiaga (eds) *Towards an Alternative for Central America and the Caribbean* (London: George Allen and Unwin, 1985), p. 16.
7. Edward Gonzales, 'US Strategic Interests In the Caribbean Basin' (paper for the Conference 'International Relations of the Contemporary Caribbean' sponsored by the Caribbean Institute and Study Centre for Latin America (CISCLA), University of Puerto Rico, April 1983), p. 10.
8. James F. Petras, H. Michael Erisman and Charles Mills, 'The Monroe Doctrine and US Hegemony in Latin America', in *Spheres of Influence and the Third World* (Nottingham: Spokesman Books, 1973), p. 58.
9. President Ford reacting to allegations of complicity in the overthrow of Allende declined to pass judgement on whether it was permitted or authorised under international law. He went on to state 'It is a recognised fact that historically as well as presently such actions are taken in the best interest of the countries involved' (*Times*, 30 September 1974) as quoted in Cohen, *International Politics, The Rules of the Game* (London, Longman), p. 168.
10. Raymond Cohen, *International Politics, The Rules of the Game* (London, Longman) p. 54. See also Robert W. Tucker, writing on Central America in 'The Purposes of American Power' in *Foreign Affairs* 1980/81:
    Central America bears geographical proximity to the United States, and historically it has long been regarded as falling within our Sphere of Influence. As such, we have long exercised the role great powers have traditionally exercised over small states which fall within their respective Sphere of Influence. We have regularly played a determining role in making and unmaking governments, and we have defined what we have considered to be acceptable behaviour of governments as quoted in *Crisis in the Caribbean* (London, Heinemann, 1985) (p. 22).
11. There is an interesting example in the experience of Grenada under Bishop. It is reported that Soviet trade officials warned in 1981 that while they were trying to give Grenada 'every support possible' their assistance 'must never be provocative from the point of view of the international

situation' (Report of Grenada Mission to Moscow: 1981, GD, p. 4) as quoted in *The New Jewel Movement* (Washington, Centre for the Study of Foreign Affairs, 1985), p. 115.

12. Modesto Seara Vasquez in the *Year Book of World Affairs* (London: Stevens, 1973), pp. 301–15.
13. Ramesh Ramsaran, *US Investment in Latin America and the Caribbean* (London: Hodder and Stoughton, 1985), p. 191.
14. Substantiation of this view has been provided by the Prime Minister, Mary Eugenia Charles of Dominica who in her Independence Day Message on 3 November 1983 stated:
In countries small and poor as ours we are unable to be capitalist or communist. We have to operate so that the greatest good is obtained for the greatest number. For this reason therefore Government may have to take a larger part in the economic development of the country than can obtain in the purely capitalist state
15. William Demas, *The Economics of Development in Small Countries with Special Reference to the Caribbean* (Montreal, McGill, Queens University Press, 1965) p. 48.
16. Keith Smith, 'President or Puppet', in *Caribbean Affairs*, Second Quarter 1988 (Express, Port-of-Spain), pp. 1–12. Deals with some aspects of the disarray in CARICOM on the Haiti question.
17. James N. Rosenau, *The Scientific Study of Foreign Policy* (London, Frances Pinter, 1980) pp. 147–8.
18. *Fundamental Texts of Fifth Conference of Heads of State or Government of Non-Aligned Countries*, Colombo, August 1976, p. 34.
19. Maurice Bishop: 'Forward Ever', speech to mark the first anniversary of the Revolution in *Maurice Bishop Speaks* (New York: Pathfinder, 1984), p. 90.
20. Demas' early study already referred to remains an important step in this direction. (See note 15)
21. John Gaffer LaGuerre in his introduction to 'Ideology' and in his article 'Socialism in Trinidad and Tobago', in *Caribbean Issues*, St Augustine, Extra Mural Studies Unit, August 1978, pp. 16–29.
22. *Vulnerability, Small States in the Global Society; report of a Commonwealth Consultative Group* (London: Commonwealth Secretariat, 1985), pp. 61–3.
23. Anthony Maingot, 'Citizenship and Parliamentary Politics in the English-Speaking Caribbean', in *Forging a New Democracy* (Trinidad and Tobago, Office of Leader of the Opposition, 1985), pp. 131–153.
24. Clive Thomas, *The Grenadian Crisis*, p. 37.
25. Susan Craig, 'Background to the 1970 Confrontation in Trinidad and Tobago', in *Contemporary Caribbean; a Sociological Reader, Vol. 2* (Trinidad and Tobago) pp. 393, 394.
26. Douglas Williams, 'Human Rights and Economic Development', in *Human Rights and Development* (Barbados: The Cedar Press, 1978) pp. 26–39 remains a useful discussion of this matter.
27. See my 'The Caribbean Community in Integracion Latino-americano', Special English Issue, October 1987 (INTAL, Buenos Aires) for analysis of current problems.

10 The State, Nationalism and Security: the Case of the Anglophone Caribbean

Neville C. Duncan

As a reaction to the gradual dismemberment of formal empires in the post-World Wars era, it came to be accepted that a state's territorial boundary had become its most specific and inviolable feature (Abbott 1972). Even when the state was seen to possess questionable viability, due to small size and limited resources among other features, its right to exist as a sovereign political unit no longer came to be challenged. For a time, British imperial authorities felt that it was imperative that the states under British rule in the Caribbean move towards political and administrative integration in order to survive and function in the international system. In the post-World War period, when the constitutional decolonisation process was in full swing in the major countries of the anglophone Caribbean, the British effort was directed toward the establishment of a federation of these states. This became a reality in 1958 and a failure in 1962.

Since then efforts were made, primarily by the political class of the Eastern Caribbean states themselves, to set up a federation first of the 'Little Eight' and then the 'Little Seven'. These came to nought while several countries proceded to formal independence. In 1965 the original plan to establish the Caribbean Free Trade Area (CARIFTA) was signed between Antigua and Barbuda, Barbados and Guyana. On May Day 1968 there was a new agreement which eventually incorporated all the anglophone Caribbean states. With CARIFTA it was thought that co-operation in non-trade areas was important and, as a consequence, the seven territories of the anglophone Eastern Caribbean, in June 1968, created an Eastern Caribbean Common Market (ECCM). This presaged the creation of a Caribbean Community (CARICOM) embracing all the anglophone Caribbean. The Eastern Caribbean States transformed the ECCM into the more political institution, the Organisation of the Eastern Caribbean States (OECS), in 1981.

In none of these efforts at integration was there any overwhelming concern with collective security. It is true that a West India Regiment was established as part of the Federal experiment, but it was small, and when it was disbanded in the wake of the collapse of the Federation no comparable attempt was made, at least until recently, to revive anything similar to it.

During the 1970s there were a number of occurrences which prompted the states of the Eastern Caribbean to become more conscious of security and collective defence once again. These prompted them to take steps to protect themselves and to ensure their continuing hold of the authority structures of the state.

FORMAL ATTAINMENT OF INDEPENDENCE

The first formal factor was the attainment of independence from Britain by several of the states in the Eastern Caribbean. Between 1975 and 1984, Dominica, St Lucia, St Vincent and the Grenadines, Belize, Antigua and Barbuda, and St Kitts–Nevis obtained formal independence. Barbados had secured its independence back in 1966, and Grenada, after stormy internal protests, followed in 1974. In this regard one should note the gross inadequacy of the independence gift from Britain. Each of these countries, regardless of its size or the extent of its economic and security problems was offered the 'princely' sum of five million pounds sterling as a grant and a similar amount as a loan. Compared with the gift of the Dutch to Suriname, where between 1975–90 Holland would provide US$1400 million in aid, equivalent in 1975 to nearly half the costs of Suriname's ten-year development programme, British aid paled in significance. This inadequacy of British aid, which was never generous before nor developmentally-oriented, virtually guaranteed that these states would either become weak sub-systems in the international order, and/or more dependent on US economic penetration and dominance – a process initiated and sponsored by the British government during colonial rule. Britain's own rapid decline from being a major pre-war actor on the world scene to being a third-rate country did not offer much hope of it being an effective security umbrella for these states against external attacks, the campaign in the Malvinas Islands notwithstanding.

In the cases of Guyana and Belize, this rapid decline of Britain led to their obtaining independence with critical, unsettled border disputes with larger, richer and more powerful neighbours. Neither the Guyana/Venezuela, the Guyana/Surinam, nor the Belize/Guatemala border disputes can be deemed to have been resolved. In due course, maybe only actual war can settle the issues involved. To the extent that issues of Caribbean security were treated with any seriousness at Heads of Government conferences of anglophone Caribbean leaders, these three situations provided the cause for discussion and concern until recently. These problems hence provided the second major factor which stirred Caribbean governments out of their complacency that Britain would be a ready ally in times of trouble.

Before all this, the Cuban revolution of 1959 caused very little concern. If it had, the various indigenous colonial governments would have moved to strengthen the then existing West India Regiment quartered in Jamaica and to retain it as a regional institution, as was done for the University of the West Indies. To be sure there were reassurances which came out of implacable US hostility toward the Cuban revolution, even when US action could have provoked a nuclear war. The assumption, presumption even, in the anglophone Caribbean governing classes that their states would always remain true to the traditions of Westminster democracy, and that the US would rush to their defence against any threat, whether internal or external, prevailed. It was reinforced by the various interventions but especially in the Dominican Republic in 1965 and in Guyana during 1964.

Jamaica is closest to Cuba. On the eve of its formal independence from Britain, Jamaica's forces were made up of the British regiment and the West India Regiment (which was organised on 1 January 1959 and which was under the control of the federal government). By the passage of the Emergency Powers Bill in the federal Parliament, there was established the right by an individual territory to use the West India Regiment, after a local state of emergency was declared and after the permission of the federal government was secured. Chief Minister Norman Manley did not feel that the process was quick enough, and went further and utilised Section 58(3) of the Federal Constitution as the basis for a Jamaican law which allowed the West India Regiment to be used in Jamaica provided that there was the declared consent of the federal Governor General.

Manley's concern was sparked by the Claudius Henry Rebellion ('The Repairer of the Breach of Nations') which sought to capture power by force, and troops had to be employed in quelling the revolt. There was an apparent Cuban connection here as the security forces reported finding copies of pieces of correspondence addressed to Dr Castro and evidence of anticipated Cuban assistance. In addition, Manley noted how what started in British Guiana (Guyana) as a general strike turned out to be a general civil uprising which would not have been possible if there had been a local defence force. In arguing for Federation, Dr Eric Williams, the Trinidad and Tobago political leader, had noted that 'it is a question of who will speak for the Caribbean. Will it be Castro, or will it be the Premier of an independent West Indies Federation' (*NewsWeek*, 26 June 1961). Vivian Blake (PNP) of Jamaica probably summed up the feelings of the ruling and supportive classes in Jamaica when, in speaking in support of the federal government, he said,:

> The communists are now firmly entrenched in Cuba – just ninety miles to our north. There has been a quickening of activity, albeit on a small scale, of the same forces, in our community. The racialists, despite their pretty sounding phrases, and lip service to the principles of democracy, at this very moment threaten all that we have achieved in trying to build an integrated society

These classes were not in favour of federation but they shared the concerns expressed in this statement.

It is interesting to note that the West India Regiment was raised as part of the British army in 1795. At the end of the American War of Independence, the Black Carolina Corps was moved to and stationed in Jamaica and became the core of this Regiment. At its peak, there were at least 12 Regiments during the nineteenth century. They served in the Napoleonic, Ashanti, and the two World Wars, and were disbanded in 1926 until reformed in 1961. These, and other aspects, such as the volunteer corps in Jamaica, added up to a long tradition of military service in Jamaica and in the entire anglophone Caribbean – a fact ignored by many researchers. It meant, notwithstanding threats to security, real or imagined, that these states would find it quite comfortable to maintain the tradition.

The disbandment of the West India Regiment led to the Defence Bill in Jamaica which, on its passage, established the Jamaica Regiment and the Jamaica National Reserve (JNR) with the pre-existing Jamaica Military Band becoming a unit of the JNR. Indeed, efforts had been made to establish within the West India Regiment, located in Jamaica, a full-scale battalion to look after Jamaica's internal problems, without having to call on troops from anywhere else. This made it possible for all the foreign regiments to leave Jamaica before June 1962.

None of the anglophone Caribbean countries was fazed by the US interventions. No attempt was made to put in place institutions, structures and procedures to deal with some future possibility of this happening in their own country. Governments saw no problems then as now. There was a natural and clear identification of interests.

Part of the reason, of course, stems from the largely informal nature of the American empire and the abiding conflict between its attempt, even in intervention, 'to reconcile a capacity for control with a commitment to liberate' (Perkins, 1981, p. ix). There was a limited period of expressly formal intervention and occupancy involving as it did 'the processes of involvement, imposition, resignation, and limited disengagement' (Ibid., p. xiv). This involvement to shore up a particular *status quo* was welcomed by Caribbean leaders who had no moral difficulty in ascribing this role of policeman to the US and who did not perceive such interventions as preventing the liberation of these societies (see Barnet, 1980, pp. 319–23; and Burbach and Flynn, 1984).

THE ANGLOPHONE CARIBBEAN ON INTERVENTIONS

The anglophone Caribbean had, by 1982, evolved, conjointly, a sound position on the question of interventions. The heads of foreign ministries, meeting in Barbados had come to terms with the question of ideological pluralism in the region. Accordingly, at the major regional event for 1982, the third meeting of the Conference of Heads of Governments of CARICOM, held in Ocho Rios, Jamaica, they re-affirmed a strong commitment to maintaining and deepening the Caribbean Community, affirmed commitment to the political, civil, economic, social and cultural rights of the peoples of the region, and declared that programmes of aid channelled through regional institutions should be supportive of their own integrity. This meeting was critical in many ways because it was the first time in seven years that the conference had met (see previous chapter).

As part of the thirteen point communique, the Conference asserted that, while recognising that the emergence of ideological pluralism in the Community responds to internal processes and is an irreversible trend within the international system, it was committed to ensuring that it would not inhibit the process of integration. At the ninth meeting of the Standing Committee of Ministers responsible for foreign affairs in June 1983, it was declared that 'only through genuine respect for, and recognition of, principles of the non-use of force, non-interference and non-intervention in the internal affairs of states, could the peoples of this region hope to achieve their just goals for a better life'. Then at the 4th meeting of the CARICOM Heads of Government in July, it was stated that: The Conference deplored the increasing resort to violence as a means of resolving conflicts and disputes between States. It called on all States to abstain from all forms of aggression and to use dialogue and negotiation to settle those conflicts which now threaten the peace and security of the region.'

INTERNAL UPHEAVALS

Of major concern, amounting almost to paranoia, was the concrete evidence of widespread internal disaffection leading to direct efforts at ousting legally constituted governments from power in the Eastern Caribbean. There was a failed coup/revolution in Trinidad and Tobago in 1970 after a prolonged period of massive anti-government demonstrations. This was followed in Grenada in 1973 by broad-based public activity against the Gairy regime and its effort to take Grenada into independence the following year. The Committee of 22, which orchestrated the protests, virtually had an opportunity to bring down the legitimate government and install itself as the new authority. The more limited objectives of the protests were not achieved, but the method was successfully copied in Dominica (1979) and St Lucia (1980).

The governments of the day were toppled from power by broad-based groupings. There was an interregnum period, in which there was a pseudo-legal government, which then prepared the way for new elections to re-introduce order. Whether or not the subsequent government was a beneficiary of the 'constitutional deposition', it noted with deep concern how easy it was for a constitutionally elected government to be unceremoniously ousted. Along with both these changes were strong allegations of plots involving mercenary invasions and foreign country involvement in the process. A former

Prime Minister of Dominica, Patrick John, was sentenced to prison, after re-trial and appeals, while the head of his army was hanged, on the charge that they and others had conspired to illegally take control of Dominica and had plans to invade Barbados.

In response to a stated threat by a self-professed mercenary, Sydney Burnett-Alleyne, Barbados put its regiment and police force on alert. Burnett-Alleyne, Barbadian born, was subsequently intercepted in Martinique with a supply of weapons and jailed there. Barbados, too, had a hand in putting down a revolt in Union Island, a sister island in the state of St Vincent and the Grenadines, in 1979 by sending troops from its newly formed BDF to carry out police duties in St Vincent itself. The BDF was also involved that same year, at the request of the Government of Dominica, in standing by on patrol during the difficulties there. Later, in 1981, the Dominican Prime Minister, Eugenia Charles, requested the assistance of Barbadian troops and the French Government also sent troops from Martinique.

However bizarre some of the events were, the Eastern Caribbean leaders considered them to be deserving of the most serious response. Where local statutes did not deal with various crimes against the state and where the penalties were not stiff enough legislation was rushed through the legislatures onto the statute books. Both the British government and the US administration collaborated on offering expanded police training and the US expanded significantly its international military education training programme in the Eastern Caribbean (see part two). The US government, on its own, or in concert with French, British and Dutch forces, carried out a series of war games, some in collaboration with the local Special Support Units (SSUs) of each of the anglophone Eastern Caribbean States and with the defence forces of Jamaica and Barbados.

The Black Power challenges were effectively treated in the second half of the 1960s and the early 1970s by legislation. Highly punitive and restrictive Public Order Acts were put on the statute books. In Dominica the 'Dreads Act' was put in force and in Guyana the Security Act gave the police extensive powers. The new challenges were perceived to need the stiffer medicine of Defence Forces, Coastguard Services, and para-military training for the police forces. In addition, regional efforts at creating a standing army were seen to be vitally necessary.

C. Y. Thomas, in an article in *Caribbean Contact*, questioned whether CARICOM was in the interest of the Caribbean masses, arguing that the dismemberment of the British empire and its effects still continued to be essential for freedom and development in the region. He saw as one of the twin pillars of the institution the political principle of creating a self-reinforcing collective of the existing political leadership in the West Indies. Certainly this latter notion was one of the considerations behind the formation of the Organisation of the Eastern Caribbean States (OECS) in 1981 which was agreed in principle in 1979.

This Treaty emphasised the desirability of retaining and formalising the arrangements for joint action by its member countries. Article 3 outlined the major purposes of the OECS. Among these was to promote co-operation among the member states and at the regional and international level having due regard to the Treaty establishing CARICOM and the Charter of the UN. It proposed to promote unity and solidarity and to defend their sovereignty, territorial integrity and independence. The signatories also agreed to assist the member states in the realisation of their obligations and responsibilities to the international community and with due regard to the role of international law as a standard of conduct in their relationship. Apart from trying to promote economic integration the treaty sought to achieve the fullest possible harmonisation of foreign policy among the member states, and sought to adopt common positions on international issues and to establish and maintain arrangements for joint overseas representation and or common services. Special emphasis was given to coordinate, harmonise and pursue joint policies particularly in the fields of mutual defence and security, among others. It must also be remembered that this treaty was drafted with revolutionary Grenada very much in view and also present for the drafting deliberations.

The treaty also established a Defence and Security Committee responsible to the Authority (i.e., the Heads of Governments). This was given the power to advise the Authority on matters relating to external defence and on arrangements for collective security against external aggression, including mercenary aggression, with or without the support of internal or national elements.

There was an undoubted concern with security arrangements. When OECS states looked at the military resources at their command during the period 1979–83 it was Grenada which had a standing army, apparently well-equipped and -trained. Although Grenada had behaved with some decency, in 'returning in chains' to the Vincentian authorities the leader of the Union Island revolt when he had fled to

Grenada, there was still the highest suspicion of its Cuban and Soviet links, and also of the kinds of moral and material support and training it rendered to local radicals and dissident groups. Certainly, as poor countries, they had neither the resources nor the will to attempt matching the Grenadian forces.

In a crisis, they could turn to Barbados for support, but the BDF was relatively recent and relatively small. Further assistance might have been forthcoming from Trinidad and Tobago, and Jamaica, and perhaps even Guyana, but the absence of any sort of initial defence capability was particularly worrisome. It was not until the post-Grenada invasion period with the provision by the US of US$15 million worth of equipment and training that some of these states could begin to boast of at least some coast guard capabilities to give some meaning to the Memorandum of Understanding which they had signed with Barbados in August 1982 on Security and Military Co-operation.

Arising out of this pact the states agreed to prepare contingency plans and assist one another on request in national emergencies, prevention of smuggling, search and rescue, immigration control, maritime policing duties, protection of offshore installations, pollution control, natural and other disasters and threats to national security. Planning was to be coordinated through the operations room of the BDF.

Acceptance and use of US equipment and training has already effectively prevented the emergence of any view that the Caribbean and Central American area should become a zone of peace, where cold war concerns are pointedly avoided and where states are free to transform their societies without any interventions of any type and form from the superpowers. What has occurred instead was an attempt to secure substantial new military assistance for the establishment of a 1000-man regional defence force. It would have cost the US at least US$100 million in initial expenditure. This was in addition to the substantial assistance which each OECS state received from the US during 1984, and to a lesser extent from the UK government.

ILLEGAL DRUGS TRANSHIPMENT

The nature of the illegal drugs transhipment trade is beyond the coping capacity of any or all of the economies of the anglophone Caribbean. Yet our neighbour superpower unilaterally decides whether each country is doing enough, in terms of the US's own methodology of dealing with the problem, to stop the trade at the points of supply. When the US decides that a country is not doing enough, then it deems that country ineligible for aid, or it imposes the stiffest fines on national aircraft or ships found with illegal drugs, or it entraps leading politicians and businessmen from the state, or it uses the unerasable smear of a US Court citation to besmirch the reputation of a country's leadership. In other words, the US is using the illicit drugs trade as a major contemporary plank in achieving its foreign policy objectives in the Caribbean region. Since the tremendous earnings are also used to purchase weapons and logistical support for insurgencies, or for right-wing activity (such as death squads and armies), or to oust radical regimes, these have become surreptitious ways for the US to help its 'friends'. Going beyond these points, 'drug barons' maintain private armies in Caribbean countries which serve to drive terror into the hearts of the legitimate security forces (police and military) in most states, to the extent that the latter forces are not assuredly in control in several parts of the territories.

In all these ways, illegal drugs transhipment and earnings pose the sternest test to the viability of the Caribbean state, individually and collectively. More effective and radical solutions are urgently needed.

In almost every aspect, then, the illicit drugs trade, treated as a problem of supply, puts unnecessary and unacceptable pressures on Caribbean states. Part of the answer to this problem for the Caribbean would begin with treating the illicit drugs trade as a demand-side induced trade and thus turn the pressure back on the US. Initially, legalisation of drugs in the dominant markets of the advanced economies would become the first of major steps towards reducing the security threat for Caribbean states.

For a variety of reasons, prohibition in these small and almost defenceless states will have to stay for a while until an adequate infrastructure of related services and education can be installed. Legalisation as proposed here would mean bringing the major illegal drugs under the ambit of the law. This is a process which also involves regulated use, differing levels of regulation to deal with various drugs, and regulated sale of quality-controlled drugs and taxation. This is to be accomplished within a framework of active discouragement in the use of mind-altering drugs by providing, through public education programmes, the complete truth about alcohol, tobacco, marijuana, cocaine, heroin, and other similar drugs (Trebach, 1987).

MILITARISATION AND CIVILIAN CONTROL

There is, in the face of limited militarisation of the anglophone Caribbean, the need to examine measures, strategies, and tactics of civilian control of the military, and, by extension, of the police and the law courts of the region. Because we know the nature of being a soldier (Barnes, 1972, p. 5), civilians must take an interest in control measures.

Traditionally, civilian control seems to be facilitated as a result of international pressures, domestic political revolution, manipulation of ethnic and class factors, development of legislative institutions or through 'pay offs' accommodations to the armed forces (Welch, 1976, pp. 5–37). Generally of greatest importance, are the existence of a legitimate, widely-supported political institution, such as a parliament or a political party, along with a self-imposed and maintained sense of restraint by officers and politicians alike, in which the military is not actively solicited for resolving domestic conflicts, but is assigned to carry out relatively restricted, internationally oriented responsibilities (Welch, 1976, p. x).

It would be unwise to pretend that civilian control of the security forces is an easy objective to attain. Yet it is necessary that the issue be brought forcibly into public consciousness and be subjected to a wide-ranging debate in search of workable procedures.

GLOBAL ECONOMY CHALLENGES TO CARIBBEAN SECURITY

Another major security problem for the region lies less in economic recession in the advanced societies but more in the tremendous achievements in the materials science, biological engineering and microtechnology. These achievements are retained by the advanced societies. These developments threaten fundamentally the hope for autonomous economic survival of peripheral states which cannot begin to be able to afford the investment in research and human capital development needed to achieve market competitiveness.

There is a notion that within this impressive array of new technology Caribbean states can find niches of economic activity appropriate for their context and sufficient to maintain acceptable levels of material welfare. This may be possible but concrete suggestions are few. The Caribbean seems condemned to become a quaint outpost of economic activity in the global economy. For each of our natural products, whether in agriculture or mining, technological developments are rendering them obsolete.

The world economic system has undergone restructuring but it has not been a restructuring consistent with expectations concerning a new world economic order which offers developing countries a better chance of catching up. It is essentially one being imposed upon non-core countries and it is based on a particular form of capitalist logic. Jeffrey Henderson and Manuel Castells (1987, pp. 3–4) have outlined seven fundamental aspects of this restructuring. In brief, the anti-inflationary restructuring has yielded fiscal austerity, monetary restriction, and the near full dismemberment of the welfare state (especially through privatisation of state assets and also through the massive deterioration in state services). It has been manifested in the forcing down of wages, reducing expenditure on working conditions and social benefits. Technological innovations have led to redundancies, reductions in working time, and speed up of work. The dramatic rise in the significance of the 'informal economy' has generated a huge sector outside of state control and labour movement involvement. This informal economy includes, as Henderson and Castells points out, not merely the black market and the astronomic illegal drugs earnings but also undeclared waged work, unpaid taxes, absence of compliance with health and safety and labour regulations, and so on, as well as undocumented workers. In these and other ways, global restructuring severely affects the chances of Caribbean states developing self-sustaining economies.

As a final point in this brief discussion, there is the strong likelihood of an economic recession in the US economy in the next few years. This is the first time, in the modern world capitalist order, that the world's richest country has become the world's biggest borrower. The US's trade deficit is now qualitatively different from anything which existed in the past. So intertwined have economies become that this trade deficit has generated 4 million full-time all-year jobs in the rest of the world. A crash of the US economy or its sharp restructuring could spell disaster for all the Caribbean states which could be mitigated somewhat only if they develop more self-reliantly.

THE GENERAL ISSUES FOR THE ANGLOPHONE CARIBBEAN

Regrettably in this modern world, the international system is akin to stateless societies. There is no world government, no international court with the power to impose decisions and, although there are noble rules and guidelines subscribed to by the states comprising the system, there still exists the rule of states based on power rather than law. Within powerful states decision-making on international relations is not democratised and is virtually the exclusive property of certain specialised structures of government and the military headed by the effective head of government.

Looking back on the facts of the Grenada invasion one could extrapolate a whole series of 'what if' questions. To merely illustrate, what if Jimmy Carter had been elected President for a second term; what if the Soviet Union had not invaded Afghanistan in 1979, thus allowing President Reagan to proclaim the decade one of supreme danger to western civilisation (Graebner, 1982, p. 3); what if the US had not been repeatedly humiliated, in Iran for instance, when the American Embassy was seized? It could be asked what if the US's relative decline had not been as sharp as it was in the 1970s, from a high global position built on the wreakage of those countries which fought in the two world wars? What if Maurice Bishop had acquiesced to joint leadership of the revolution, or had not been executed? What if revolutionary Grenada had not warmly embraced Cuba and Nicaragua, and had not militarised the state to the extent that it seriously worried its CARICOM partners? Would the OECS, Barbados and Jamaica have provided the pseudo-legal reasons for invasion? What if Britain had played a more positive role in the anglophone Caribbean? There is, literally, a whole swarm of 'what ifs' which could legitimately be asked. Interesting though they may be, to pursue the quest would be interminable and almost pointless. Yet that is precisely the method adopted in most of the instant books and articles written on the Grenadian invasion.

In this situation of pervasive and unstoppable turmoil, the Caribbean and Central American states could do with a period of *détente* similar to that which made the post-war European recovery and development possible. It was not merely a Marshall economic and military plan which allowed for the transformation of Europe and Japan, but also prolonged peace, absence of internal interference and severely reduced emphasis on cold war politics.

However, the very hope of a *détente*-like arrangement or zone of peace seem unlikely in this region. It is virtually the privilege of power to define the evil it wishes to fight. Richard Barnet (1980, p. 20) noted that revolutionary or radical movements are defined as communistic if they nationalise private industry, or engage in radical land reform, or pursue autarchic trade policies, or accept Soviet or

Chinese aid, or insist upon following an anti-American or non-aligned foreign policy among others. Yet, as Roger Burbach (Burbach and Flynn, 1984, p. 20) noted,:

> there is no reformist path . . . Governments that have challenged US dominance by adopting reforms within a capitalist framework, and that have not mobilized and armed their people to resist the inevitable US intervention, have had to pay the ultimate consequence, i.e. the loss of power to US backed right-wing regimes.

To some extent, there was the possibility that countries such as Grenada, weakly-integrated into the international system, could choose some variation of the non-capitalist path approach to development and so bring about impressive levels of transformation without attracting US opprobrium and interference. Such countries could virtually make the break without experiencing sharp withdrawal symptoms such as the Manley regime had to experience in Jamaica. Alas, proximity to the US, migration, and the openness of cultural life attuned to the consumerist orientations of North Atlantic society, weigh heavily against this assumption at the non-material levels.

Max Weber would probably have argued that for revolutions to be successful they would have to develop a bureaucratic and military apparatus at the very least capable of matching, in terms of technical efficiency, those of the countries which would interfere. Barnet (1980, p. 29) argues that 'to a great extent interventionist policy is the result of the development of the technology of intervention'. Later in his book (Barnet, 1980, p. 307) he notes that the US was so deeply involved anyway in the use of coercive techniques to influence political behaviour that the overt use of force, regrettable as it is, is merely a difference in degree, not in kind.

The Eastern Caribbean states could presumably reach out and become more deeply involved in regional arrangements in Central and South America and support wider Caribbean (i.e. across linguistic boundaries) efforts at integration. But none of this has saved Latin American countries from US intervention. It is difficult to plan a strategy to ensure a country's security and sovereignty against intervention from a superpower since as James N. Rosenau (1980, p. 363) recognised, assessments of the need for and probable outcome of interventionary behaviour are more subject to the whims of individual leaders and the dynamics of bureaucratic structures than to the diplomatic, economic, military, and political policies through which nations conventionally relate themselves to the international system. Thus, while the leaders of Jamaica, Barbados and the OECS states were already decided on intervening in Grenada led by the US, they were going through the motions of a CARICOM meeting, allowing the chair of the host country, Trinidad and Tobago, who was not privy to that decision, to announce more modest CARICOM agreements on the question to the public. Additionally, the Bahamas, Guyana (which had, by far, the best military capability), and Belize (where a British military garrison was stationed) were also not privy to the invasion decision. These countries were totally embarassed by their fellow CARICOM states, especially since the decision involved a decisive role being played by a foreign power and a superpower to boot!

Ultimately, the enjoyment of collective security turns on a recognition that, in this region, the US should accept, in the words of Rosenau (1980, p. 323) 'that it is cruel and arrogant to attempt to block desperate social remedies to desperate social problems that local leaders elect to try when you have nothing better to offer'. With that recognition Barnet (1980, p. 327) would propose that the general situation would improve 'if the United States were to announce that it was no longer in the business of suppressing revolution'. In this way 'it would confront Third World governments with the choice it now helps them to avoid: learn to govern effectively and justly or face mounting insurgency'. Ultimately, however, as Barnet correctly realised, 'the successful transformation of Central America and the Caribbean is linked to a major political transition in the United States, a transition in the US ideology of empire. Other, older imperial powers finally had to adjust, however involuntarily, to anticolonial movements and to new concepts of empire'.

All oppressed and disadvantaged peoples in the metropoles and in the periphery have a stake in the outcome of these efforts. Meanwhile the states of the Eastern Caribbean owe it to themselves and to the struggle for a better life to ensure that there is a close correlation between the commendable principles of non-intervention in internal affairs of a country, the inviolability of its sovereignty, and the need for collective security and their actual deeds. There must be no more gangsterism against their sister states. The Grenada intervention, in retrospect, should teach them their lesson.

THE PRESENT SITUATION

The Question of Political Integration

The Heads of Government of the Organisation of Eastern Caribbean states met in May 1987, in the British Virgin Islands, seeking a formula to bring their 583,000 population into a single political union. They agreed to a resolution which enjoined members to start immediately a process of 'comprehensive consultation' on forming such a closer union. The major proponent was the PM of St Vincent and the Grenadines, James Mitchell, who is the strongest supporter of a unitary state. Most of the other leaders seem to be lukewarm on this aspect and PM V. C. Bird of Antigua Barbuda has spoken out strongly against a single political union. For him it represented the kind of colonialism against which he had fought with the British government. Mr Bird further stated that Montserrat and St Kitts and Nevis were interested in an association with Antigua and Barbados which would permit closer economic and trade cooperation as well as freedom of movement for each county's nationals.

So far, there has been no clear indication on what kinds of specific proposals the Heads of the OECS are going to put to their populations and with what kinds of specific rationales. Opposition and civic groups have come out in favour of a political union but so far, on all sides, there has been an insufficient sense of urgency and the consultative process has been seriously flawed.

Interest in the success of these states in forming a federation or a unitary state resides in the potential it has for providing a more sensible framework for a collective security approach, especially if widespread legitimacy can be secured for the form of union from the masses, opposition groups and general interest groups in each country. The process of attainment of union becomes as significant as the fact of it. Indeed, to achieve any form of political union would require as non-partisan-political an approach as possible since special and difficult constitutional procedures would have to be undertaken. Efforts of the ruling parties to date do not inspire confidence that they appreciate the magnitude of these tasks. Already opposition leaders are beginning to see the announced intention to form a political union as a 'smokescreen' to divert attention away from the failure of these Governments to bring about real improvements in the quality of life of the masses. Some have even seen the hand of the US government, through the Caribbean Democratic Union (CDU), as responsible for the call at this time.

The collective security system of the OECS has increasingly become dominated by the US. Through the SSUs attached to the police force of five of the states, and through the development of coastguard facilities in these islands, the US has been able to conduct a number of war games using OECS territory. Sometimes these games include other members of the NATO alliance with interests in the Caribbean and other anglophone Caribbean countries (mainly Barbados and Jamaica) but however they have been operationalised, the US forces have been the dominant actors.

OECS unity would provide a framework for reducing the need for individual capabilities in each state to deal with internal and external security threats. It would provide a better framework to guard against arbitrary and illegitimate uses of the security forces by any individual regime. Of course, it would make it more difficult for any anti-system political movement to succeed at a coup or revolution, but at the same time it should make it more difficult for dictatorial and fascist regimes to emerge and deny people a large measure of civil and political freedom.

Such a trade-off could be worthwhile. In this region we are used to the political partisanship of the Guyana Defence Force. We have seen the way in which Patrick John, a former Prime Minister of Dominica, used his fledgelling army against legitimate civilian protest action. In Jamaica, it has become commonplace to have combined police and military action in civilian matters. Antigua and Barbuda found it necessary, of all the OECS states, to establish a standing army. Its especially close and friendly co-operation and collaboration with the US armed forces was not accidental and in this light it is not at all surprising that it spurns political union for the OECS.

An OECS political union would make more possible a CARICOM wide political union, again providing a wider framework for more cost-effective security measures as well as putting more integrity into non-military aspects of security. It would do this by rationalising the number of individual units which would comprise the anglophone Caribbean federation. Of course, Barbados would have to consider joining the OECS, so too would Anguilla. Belize would pose some difficulty but its large land mass and potentialities for further absorption of migrants would solve this over time.

It is still the case, inspite of difficulties, that the Zone of Peace idea for the Caribbean and Central American area is the best for long-term security. The need to settle disputes between countries in this area through diplomacy and collectively enforced agreements without super- or middle-power interference is obvious. Certainly, this need is pressing for Guyana and Belize with their border disputes. Belize, itself, is rapidly becoming more Latin American, due to the uncontrolled in-migration problem and the humanitarian necessity to grant such persons all the rights of citizenship. Will Belize be anglophone Caribbean or Latin? And would it matter if a wider union was contemplated? The Surinamese population is now made up of significant numbers of former Guyanese citizens. Will national and ethnic problems arise which may involve Guyana, especially as there is still an unsettled border dispute between Guyana and Belize and third countries? The anglophone Caribbean has always insisted upon the territorial integrity of Belize and Guyana. Would the Anglophone Caribbean ever be in a position to come to the aid of these countries in a substantive manner, even within a political union? Elusive and difficult as it is, the anglophone Caribbean has no other recourse but to vigorously pursue the idea of a Zone of Peace.

Selected References

Abbot, George C. (1972) 'Small States: The Paradox of their Existence', Ms. (Brighton, Sussex: Institute of Development Studies).
Barnet, Richard J. (1980), *Intervention and Revolution* (New York: Macmillan).
Baynes, Lt Col. J. C. M. (1972), *The Soldier in Modern Society* (London: Eyre Methuen).
Burbach, Roger and Flynn, Patricia (1984), eds., *The Politics of Intervention: The United States in Central America* (New York: Monthly Review).
Erisman, H. Michael and Martz, John D. (1982), *Colossus Challenged: The Struggle for Caribbean Influence* (Boulder: Westview).
Graebner, Norman, 'The Decline of America: A Countering View', *Virginia Quarterly Review*, Summer, 1982, 58:3, pp. 369–91.
Henderson, Jeffrey and Castells, Manuel (eds) (1987), *Global Restructuring and Territorial Development* (London: Sage).
Perkins, Whitney T. (1981) *Constraint of Empire: The United States and Caribbean Interventions* (Oxford: Clio).
Rosenau, James N. (1980) *The Scientific Study of Foreign Policy* (New York: Nichols).
Trebach, Arnold S. (1987) *The Great Drug War* (New York: Macmillan).
Welch, Jr, Claude E. (1976) *Civilian Control of the Military* (Albany: New York State University Press).

11 Alternative Approaches to Peace and Security in Africa*

Timothy M. Shaw with E. John Inegbedion

The African perspective sees peace and development as intimately related: it sees peace not only as the resolution of conflict but as the transformation of extant social systems at both national and international levels. It is a concept which relates peace to the physical, social and existential needs of people (Hansen, 1987a, pp. 6–7).

the concept of security in the African context is necessarily broader than in the American or European situation. In the African context, state security is conceived as involving national integration, maintenance of congenial domestic ethnic and class order as well as protection of territorial integrity and defence against external intervention (Nweke, 1985, p. 11).

Security in Africa as elsewhere in the Third World is inseparable from political economy both national and global: the continuing continental crisis of the last quarter of the twentieth century has generated a series of contradictions and confrontations, which have only just begun to be recognised and analysed by students of strategic (and peace, and development) studies. As most African states and leaders have come to confront shrinking economies so security issues have expanded beyond border disputes and non-alignment to include new threats to incumbent regimes from structural adjustments and guerrilla formations: destabilisation arising from IMF conditionalities and from income declines. Thus the fine lines between 'national

* This is a considerably revised and expanded version of Timothy M. Shaw 'Security Redefined: unconventional conflict in Africa', in Stephen Wright and Jan Brownfoot (eds), *Africa in World Politics* (London: Macmillan. 1987), pp. 17–34.

interest' and regime survival and between regime survival and leadership longevity have largely disappeared as coping becomes the preoccupation. So the African debate is no longer external versus internal strategic priorities but rather security and development: security of leader, regime and state through economic renaissance or through political repression. Conversely, democratisation and development in Africa are closely correlated or, as the late Emmanuel Hansen (1987a, p. 7) asserts in his collection of indigenous perspectives on peace and development: 'For most African scholars there is no difference between the peace problematic and the development problematic.'

The thesis of this comparative chapter is, then, that peace, security and development are interrelated in Africa as elsewhere in the Third World. However, such a critical, historical and materialist perspective is not yet prevalent on the continent because so many indigenous and expatriate scholars alike are still practitioners of the established and outmoded realist paradigm. Thus the recent volumes by Nweke (1985) and by Bender, Coleman and Sklar (eds) (1985) are both cast within the traditional mold: the realist genre of great and small powers struggling over borders and resources. This mode of analysis lacks any sense of the new international divisions of labour and power: the new hierarchies of Newly Industrialising Countries (NICs) and Fourth Worlds and the new divergencies of political economies in ascendancy (e.g. Japan, Korea, Brazil and Singapore) and those in decline (e.g. US and UK, Liberia and Zambia). It therefore fails to capture or treat a new range of strategic issues related to economic contractions: weak states, alienated populations, informal exchanges, refugee exoduses, and domestic destabilisation. When these are added to already inadequate national economies and security structures then the tenuousness of many African political economies becomes apparent.

Thus, rather than territorial or political security, the primary concerns of African statespersons and scholars alike should now be economic, environmental and food securities: how Basic Human Needs (BHN) can begin to be met and nurtured again in a period of intense structural adjustment. Realists like Nweke concentrate on traditional debates over power and disarmament, including nuclear, whereas radicals like Hansen (1987a, p. 3) expand their scope beyond the orthodox to include peace and development as well as personal and social security: 'The question of peace cannot be separated from the question of the struggle for social and democratic rights and for human dignity. In other words the peace problematic is not unrelated to the issue of extant social and political conditions and the distribution of power.' Likewise, the apparent trend towards militar-isation in Africa is generating a range of unconventional strategies and struggles in response – nuclear, class and guerrilla – reflective of innovative responses to the structural adjustment syndrome of debt, devaluation, deregulation and privatisation. So the economic con-traction and political regression of the 1980s have spotlighted the substructure of Africa's strategic concerns, and produced a situation in which unconventional relations and explanations are both essential and plausible. We suggest appropriate cases of such contemporary conflicts following an overview and typology of alternate approaches and responses.

The theme of this chapter is, then, that given Africa's inheritance of dependence and under-development, 'conventional' conflict (as conceived among the industrialised states) is quite insignificant his-torically and contemporaneously; and it is likely to remain so until the end of this century. Conversely, 'unconventional' conflict has already become a major factor in Africa's security situation; given projections of ineluctable inequalities, unconventional violence – nuclear, class and guerrilla struggles – is likely to appear with in-creasing frequency, posing challenges to African statesmen and to Africanist scholars (see the essentially orthodox yet nuanced perspec-tive in Gavshon, 1981). When properly redefined, security is insepar-able from questions of the survival of states, classes, fractions and property: the 'corporatist' nexus. (Shaw, 1982).

Africa was incorporated into the world system through violence. As Walter Rodney (1982, p. 151) indicates:

> Before the 19th century, Europe was incapable of penetrating the African continent, because the balance of force at their disposal was inadequate. But the same technological changes which created the need to penetrate Africa also created the power to conquer Africa.

Yet despite the massive application of direct and latent force in the imposition, extension and perpetuation of colonialism, nationalist movements only occasionally resorted to counter-violence. The sub-sequent socialisation or incorporation of Africa's embryonic bour-geoisies is remarkable given the degree of 'structural violence' which they and their societies endured. Only when settler interests resisted change – Algeria, Angola, Kenya, South Africa and Zimbabwe – did violence become an integral part of the nationalist struggle (and, as I will suggest below, one which is of decreasing importance as the border of black Africa moves ineluctably southwards). And even in these cases the degree of radicalisation which lasted through the transitional period has been shown to be limited: Africa's cultural and psychological dependence and conservatism is ubiquitous.

Indeed, the locus of Africa's powerlessness lies in such dependence and underdevelopment: most regimes simply cannot afford – even if they wished to do so – conventional confrontation using the bulk of their national product. Moreover, those few states which are at present rich enough to develop their strategic capability – Egypt, Libya, Nigeria and South Africa – may lack the infrastructure through which to launch any sustained military attack (on the Nigerian case, see Shaw and Aluko (eds), 1983).

Despite the prospect of at least the last of these relatively richer states becoming a nuclear power (see Shaw and Dowdy, 1982), most African regimes are in general too preoccupied by national threats and global linkages to engage in sustained regional (let alone global) conflict. Their definition of non-alignment – non-partisanship in bipolar nuclear conflict – remains, yet their partisanship in sub-nuclear strategic issues and alliances has increased as the world has become more complex. Indeed, the only way in which most African regimes can sustain a battle is through 'externalisation' (that is, by accepting extra-continental intervention). Complex and changeable coalitions characterise Africa's current strategic situation, especially since the mid-1970s, although the amount of extra-continental commitment is really quite limited and constrained. As Colin Legum (1979a, p. xx) noted in his own review of Africa's future strategic position:

Looking back to the Berlin Treaty of 1884 and the carving out of separate spheres of influence by the colonial powers, Africans began to speak uneasily in 1977 about 'a new scramble' for the continent . . . the colonial memory persists, reinforcing the association of foreign power rivalries in Africa with the subjugation of the continent . . . But in the 1970s, the foreign powers had to take the interests of competing African states and groups fully into account in order to promote their own national interests. Only by offering themselves as allies to particular interest groups could they expect to expand their influence on the continent.

Elsewhere, Legum (1979b, pp. 23–4) has reflected the contemporary consensus – that African conflicts will increase – and related this to continuing extra-continental interest and intervention:

> Africa is at a most difficult and volatile stage of development. During the 1980s quarrels within one country or between hostile neighbouring countries are likely to erupt into violent conflicts . . . Such conflicts will affect not only the localities or countries directly involved, but in many cases also will provoke foreign intervention. This is not to say that Africa will be the passive victim of international power politics. On the contrary, African factions will actively seek foreign military and economic assistance to bolster fragile positions.

This fragility is a central aspect of Africa's political economies and is related to a major contradiction, one which both limits the development of Africa's own capabilities and perpetuates its dependence on external support: 'exploitation'. On the one hand, metropolitan countries and corporations extract as much surplus as possible from African economies, while on the other hand they expect strategic stability. With insufficient resources remaining at the national level, African regimes tend to be unreliable allies at the international level. So metropolitan interests may be in contradiction to each other, with economic profitability undermining strategic reliability. Alternately, such a combination of relations serves to perpetuate Africa's economic and strategic dependence, recognising the inter-relatedness between the two.

This contradiction may be expected to intensify over the next few years as protectionism among the industrialised countries further undermines the economic prospects of most African states, making them even more vulnerable to internal and external pressures. A few countries – the 'middle powers' – may benefit from the high price of oil, but most will be further impoverished. The inability of most African regimes to satisfy Basic Human Needs, let alone basic human rights, will result in increasing pressures to change internally with embattled regimes having to appeal for economic and strategic assistance externally. Africa in the 1980s, like Africa in the 1960s, may be more vulnerable to global, great-power politics as the politics of debt, food, inflation and recession erode the minimal infrastructures and industrial capacities of the majority of countries (see Gavshon, 1981).

The intensification of dependence and underdevelopment in most of the continent may, then, lead to three different outcomes, each with distinctive implications for conflict in Africa. First, the few middle powers with relatively large and still expanding economies may establish themselves as important regional powers in an impoverished and vulnerable continental system. As I. William Zartman (1976, p. 593) suggests in his revisionist work on the distribution of power in Africa:

> By the 1980s, the spread in the level of power sources is certain to increase, even dramatically. Within the decade, Algeria or Nigeria may be more developed economically than South Africa . . . several effects are likely to ensue. First, the more developed members may become more attractive to outside influence, even if greater amounts of influence will now be required in order to have an effect. Second, at this stage of development, internal gaps between socio-economic levels are likely to be magnified, as are also gaps between the states which have surged forward and those many others which have been unable to do so . . . the chances for regional leadership are increased.

Second, in some middle powers and most peripheral states, inequalities will increase between the minority in the bourgeoisie and the majority in the proletariat or peasantry. The result will be either increased antagonism or increased repression. Claude Ake (1978, p. 107) warns about the latter prospect as the global recession and contraction intensifies, with important implications for conflict control and character on the continent:

> [one] historic possibility which lies before Africa is a march to fascism. This could come about in a situation where there was protracted economic stagnation but not yet revolution . . . one thing that would surely be needed in ever-increasing quantities in this situation would be repression . . . It would appear that the choice for Africa is not between capitalism and socialism after all, but between socialism and barbarism.

Finally, third, the combination of domestic demands and external protectionism may lead some African leaders to a dramatic departure: from dependence to self-reliance – in which case, established assumptions and equations about inequalities and conflict would have to be revised. As Steven Langdon and Lynn Mytelka (1979, p. 211) argue – particularly in relation to change in Southern Africa, an issue which permeates the present chapter – disengagement may be the prerequisite of economic development and strategic stability in the 1980s:

> We expect the contradictions of periphery capitalism in Africa to become more acute in most countries on the continent in the next decade, and we expect the struggles for change in such countries to become more bitter as a result. We are confident, however, that out of such conflict can come more equitable and self-reliant development strategies that benefit the great majority of Africans.

This potential shift in development strategy has strategic as well as economic implications: post-colonial conflict may be more complex and comprehensive than the rather simple and external character of pre-colonial struggle. Indeed, notwithstanding the general poverty of Africa, a few states clearly have nuclear potential, even if not current capability.

1 NUCLEAR POWER IN AFRICA

Despite the overall pattern of short, unconventional forms of conflict on the continent, a few states may be considered potential nuclear powers. Moreover, despite schemes to declare Africa a nuclear-free zone, some statesmen and scholars insist on Africa retaining the right to achieve nuclear status if apartheid South Africa acquires nuclear weapons; some Arab African leaders may use the same argument *vis-à-vis* Israel, too. Although Egypt and one or two other Arab states may fall into the latter category, Nigeria is the leading contender in the former group. Moreover, in a continuing quest for alternative energy sources as well as for the latest technology, some African countries are interested in nuclear energy as well as in nuclear power.

Although both Nigeria and South Africa are interested in acquiring nuclear energy technology – the power station at Koeberg in Cape Province constructed with French technical expertise was due for completion and commission in 1989 – the major tension between them is nuclear weaponry. South Africa clearly needs nuclear energy more urgently than Nigeria, which has considerable, but by no means inexhaustible, petroleum and gas reserves; yet the former's acquisition of energy technology (and hence enriched uranium) is inseparable from its weapons potential.

It now seems to be widely recognised that South Africa already has the capacity to develop and detonate a nuclear bomb, probably using highly accurate 155 mm howitzer shells. After all the previous research and *exposés* (see especially Cervenka and Rogers (1978) and *Africa News* (1982)), the superpower alert of July–August 1977 about a potential nuclear test in the Kalahari and the Vela satellite recording of a probable nuclear flash in the Southern oceans in September 1979 both serve to confirm corroborative evidence. Moreover, South Africa has publicly prided itself on its ability to enrich its own uranium cheaply using an adopted gas-infusion method. Finally, while the strategic gain of nuclear capability is problematic, the pride and potential of such a status is not inconsiderable for an isolated and embattled people (Shaw and Dowdy, 1982 and Spence, 1981).

However, South Africa's nuclear power has its antithesis in Nigeria's quest for nuclear status. While Nigeria's present power base is limited, its potential military-industrial complex is considerable. Nuclear power would reinforce its claim to being *primus inter pares* in black Africa whilst also satisfying its need for both image and influence. As Robert Henderson (1981, p. 421) suggests, 'Nigeria's political leaders can point to a nuclear programme as a symbol of national power and national identity . . . it reinforces their claims to regional power status as well as their claims to speak for the independent states of black Africa.' In short, South Africa's nuclear capacity is perceived to constitute a challenge to Nigeria's security and status, one which it is determined to meet through its own nuclear programme. But unlike South Africa's nuclear research at Valindaba and Pelindaba, which makes it a relative 'nuclear independent' despite significant European and American inputs over the years, Nigeria is considerably more 'nuclear dependent' (Paneman, 1981), relying extensively on external inputs for its peaceful and strategic programmes. Moreover, South Africa is already several years ahead of Nigeria and has a scientific and technological infrastructure to support such research and development. Finally, the reaction of Africa in general and Nigeria in particular to South Africa's growing military link (nuclear as well as conventional?) with Israel – part of the 'pariah international' in terms of Robert Harkavy's analysis (1981, pp. 155–7) – constitutes one further reason for the idea of developing a continental deterrent capability.

Aside from the questions of nuclear safeguards and the considerable capital required, there is a debate over the appropriateness of such massive technological transfers and transitions: should Nigeria and/or South Africa use alternative technologies for both defence and industry? In both instances, hydro, coal, gas, sun and wind are available as alternative sources of energy; and guerrilla and conventional strategic capabilities are present. The diversion of scarce resources away from such activities and towards high-technology nuclear developments is controversial, for more appropriate forms of energy and defence might be devised, quite apart from general concerns about nuclear proliferation and pollution.

In response to such global concerns, African (and Afrikaner?) nationalists tend to be fearful of new imperialisms, respecting the Maoist argument that the multilateral nuclear Non-Proliferation Treaty and unilateral nuclear safeguards are merely attempts to divide the world into two – the nuclear 'haves' and 'have-nots'. This preemptive rejection of any new paternalism has been most clearly articulated by Ali Mazrui (1980b) and 'Tunde Adeniran (1981).

2 CLASS CONFLICT IN AFRICA

If the debate about Africa's nuclear status is 'unconventional' because it involves high technology and massive destructive potential, that about class conflict is unconventional because it involves apparently 'domestic' and 'economic' phenomena. However, given Africa's inheritance of incorporation within the world system, class struggles on the continent have 'international' connections and implications. Moreover, the treatment of class challenges by African regimes has relevance for human rights everywhere; and certainly the treatment of colour differences in South Africa has general implications for the rest of the continent. Furthermore, the growth of inequality and inflation has exacerbated tensions already, leading to a rise of crime and corruption, the former often associated with violent gang activities.

Class analysis has often been rejected as inappropriate for Africa because of the imputed embryonic character of classes on the continent. Leaving aside the pre-colonial and colonial origins of African classes, it is increasingly clear that classes remain somewhat tenuous because of other social linkages and because the bourgeoisie has been largely external or transnational. As Ian Roxborough suggests (1979, pp. 72, 73):

The class structures of the Third World differ from those of advanced nations in two principal ways: they are more complex, and the classes themselves are usually much weaker . . . Not only are the class structures of the under-developed nations complex and weak, they are frequently 'incomplete' in the sense that the dominant class, or one fraction of the dominant class, is absent. This is the case where the dominant class or fraction thereof is foreign.

Both class politics and class analysis are developing in Africa, with one result being that the more national fractions are coming to challenge the more transnational or comprador. I shall turn to this issue in the following section, dealing here only with the established transnational bourgeoisie's role in African conflict.

In a classic neo-colonial situation, the 'new class' in Africa has strong external links: the bourgeoisie is part-indigenous and part-foreign. So for the first years of independence the indigenous element came to challenge – as well as to co-operate with – the external, leading to a more balanced, if not yet equal, relationship within the transnational nexus. Strategies of indigenisation and partial national-isation produced characteristic 'state capitalist' relations in which the only changes that occurred took place within and not outside this nexus. Non-bourgeois forces were either weak or suppressed: African ruling classes shared interests and communication whereas the proletariats were divided into national institutions with minimal transnational contact. As Samir Amin (1973, p. 226) laments in his *Neo-Colonialism in West Africa*:

the deadlock . . . will . . . continue . . . until new social forces appear, open to the future rather than dominated by the past, and capable of conceiving a strategy for liberation that goes beyond the narrow horizons of minor ex-colonial civil servants.

One factor which has already broken this deadlock somewhat lies within rather than outside the bourgeoisie: the national fraction as opposed to the transnational or comprador element (Shaw, 1984b, and Shaw and Aluko (eds), 1983).

Twenty or thirty years after independence some of the results of Africanisation are beginning to show. The old Pan-African assumption about the essential equality of African states is being replaced by divergent rates of growth and accumulation. And the characteristic pattern of neo-colonialism is being superseded by new sets of tensions, particularly within the indigenous bourgeoisie between more national and more trans-national elements. Indigenisation has meant that local capitalisms of the pre-colonial era have been revived and have come to challenge the more comprador fractions.

The tension has extra- as well as intra-continental implications: the trans-national bourgeoisie could call upon neo-colonial strategic linkages for support whenever necessary. The national fraction is more autonomous, although still incorporated within the global capitalist system: any strategic support for it is contractual rather than intrinsic or automatic. Moreover, the development of national capitalism(s) may be related to the trend towards militarism on the continent as national fractions come to protect their own surplus and status. Finally, the intensification of class conflict as inflation and floating exchange rates erode the real incomes of the workers and peasants poses another challenge to embattled regimes, again calling forth an authoritarian response.

The tendency towards authoritarianism and militarism in Africa (Luckham, 1982, 1983) is not simply a function of the rise of military regimes; rather it is a function of ruling classes fearful of popular pressures. Such demands for the economic fruits of independence have increased as the post-independence period has lengthened, and as the post-war expansionist period has given way to recession and contraction. Whilst such antagonisms may still be contained in those few countries with relatively high growth rates and/or vestigial confidence in the efficacy of ethnicity, in many others they are contained only by latent or actual coercion. Moreover, populist pressures lack coherence in many countries, thus rendering them vulnerable to state retaliation.

The trend towards exclusive corporatism (Shaw, 1982) and increasing militarism in Africa constitutes an attempt by indigenous bourgeois interests to contain opposition and extend accumulation. It has serious implications for human rights in a continent in which such rights were anyway very embryonic and fragile (Shaw, 1984a); it also retards progress towards the satisfaction of Basic Human Needs (Shaw (ed), 1982). While such repression may receive international support or indifference, it will drive opposition into counter-violence – this despite Africa's awareness of the need for such violence in executing its own anti-colonialist and anti-racist struggles in Algeria, Kenya, and Southern Africa.

The rise of guerrilla conflict in independent Africa (paradoxically) coincides with the disappearance of it as a tactic against white-ruled states, although South Africa may continue to foment anti-regime forces in Angola and Mozambique through its 'destabilisation' activities. Moreover, indigenous leaders should recall the transformation of such movements from nationalist to socialist in response to regime intransigence. Hence the imperative of a more informed and sophisticated response than repression.

3 GUERRILLA STRUGGLE IN AFRICA

One result of Africa's characteristic poverty is that much of the conflict that has occurred in contemporary times has used an unconventional type of force: guerrilla struggle. Aside from its use by both Africans and Afrikaners against the expansion of the British Empire, this tactic has been employed in contemporary times as a strategy by which to overthrow colonialist and racist rule. However, with the passing of such regimes – except for South Africa – this form of resistance has been revived and re-focused to challenge repressive rule in independent Africa, whether based on class, national, professional or racial distinctions. Guerrilla activity in increasingly impoverished systems is one aspect of their decline into an anarchic state.

White rejection of black demands in Algeria, Kenya and Southern Africa led to the reluctant but ineluctable adoption of guerrilla tactics by nationalist movements. When elsewhere in Africa independence was negotiated between colonised and coloniser, in settler states a significant degree of counter-violence was necessary to create the conditions for successful negotiation. The resultant escalation of violence not only endangered established infrastructures but also produced liberation movements committed to socialism as well as to nationalism: economic independence and restructuring were demanded as well as political.

So the successor regimes in Angola and Mozambique (and possibly in Zimbabwe) are different from those in neighbouring Botswana or Zambia. The appearance of such radical rule has upset the rather benign character of the Organisation of African Unity (OAU) consensus and revived debates and coalitions reminiscent of the pre-OAU Brazzaville, Casablanca and Monrovia groupings. Hence the transition from acceptance of dependence to assertion of self-reliance as the motif of the OAU: disengagement from the world system

constitutes a form of diplomatic-cum-economic conflict, a re-defini-
tion of non-alignment.

With the successes of FRELIMO, MPLA and now ZANU, aided
by the Front Line states and the OAU Liberation Committee, the
years of guerrilla struggle in Southern Africa are beginning to come
to an end; SWAPO is achieving power and ANC's long-postponed
accession cannot be too far behind. However, at the same time as
anti-colonialist and anti-racist conflict is climaxing, the use of guerrilla tactics against African regimes is increasing: guerrilla movements in, say, Eritrea, Sudan and Uganda are merely instances of a
wider phenomenon.

Guerrilla struggles against indigenous governments do not have
the same unambiguous goal or support as those against settler states;
they often combine ethnic and economic ambitions. Moreover, they
have not always been as successful as the liberation movements in
southern Africa. Nevertheless, they have achieved control over liberated areas and have led to new political arrangements (Sudan) or
leaders (Uganda). And Polisario has secured OAU recognition for
the Saharawi Arab People's Republic even if the Eritreans cannot
shrug off Ethiopia's embrace.

Such guerrilla conflicts may be based on either historical injustices
or contemporary impoverishment. As the latter comes to be more
prevalent than the former so the continuing decline of African
economies becomes more important as a cause. Indeed, the guerrillas
and gangs may form coercive alliances at times to play 'Robin Hood'
in the countryside. And together their activities challenge and undermine the logic of the post-colonial state, accelerating its decline.

The collapse of the national economy in a few African territories –
Chad, Ghana, Uganda, Zaire (and now Tanzania?) – has accelerated
the rate of decay, with profound implications for the stability and
survival of certain African authorities. This trend towards anarchy is
likely to accelerate as most African economies experience minimal or
negative growth. It is also likely to be exacerbated as advanced
industrialised states, under the pressures of recession and protectionism, lose interest in a global reach and so decrease their investments in the African periphery (Shaw, 1984b).

One result of this economic and political decay has been the
withdrawal of the peasantry from the cash economy and its return to
subsistence agriculture: a form of effective but unplanned regional or
familial self-reliance with profound implications for the viability of the
post-colonial national economy. Such a reaction serves to exacerbate

the national crisis as commodity exports decline, foreign exchange reserves vanish and the black market-smuggling nexus takes over the remnants of the economy. This process leads not only to domestic tensions between the bourgeoisie in the city and the peasantry in the countryside but also to the demise of the neo-colonial trans-national structure: if the North is in retreat and the South in decline then the trans-national linkage withers, which enables African regimes to be more 'self-reliant' whether or not they wish to be so. So the post-neo-colonial situation is marked by more domestic than external conflict, although a revival in the world economy might yet reinvigorate certain neo-colonial relationships: trade and technology if not aid and investment. Furthermore, the semi-periphery of Algeria, Egypt, Ivory Coast, Kenya, Nigeria and Zimbabwe remains important to countries and corporations in the North. In the longer term, the outlook for the real periphery is not bright, however. Until the end of this century Africa is no more likely to be conflict-free than nuclear-free. We turn to such projections, informed by contemporary history and theory, following the next section on current cases of unconventional conflicts on the continent.

4 CONTEMPORARY UNCONVENTIONAL CONFLICTS: CONTRADICTIONS AND COALITIONS

Although Africa has not suffered as many or as intense wars since independence as have South East Asia or the Middle East (see Wurfel and Burton, 1990 and Korany and Dessouki 1984), it has experienced both short- and long-term struggles; these have served to exacerbate the tenuous condition of much of its environment as well as of its exponential population of refugees. These instances of so-called 'low intensity' conflict have also generated intra- and extra-continental coalitions of advocates and detractors and encouraged a never-ending quest for negotiaton, mediation and peacekeeping. Yet the structural conditions for sustainable peace are more elusive than ever. In this section we treat two long-standing and relatively ortho-dox conflicts – Ethiopia and Angola – along with a pair of apparently quiescent and quite unorthodox struggles – Chad and Uganda – which serve to illustrate continuities as well as changes in Africa's dialectics of war and peace, security and development.

The pair of orthodox conflicts – Ethiopia and Angola – are amongst the most violent and extended that Africa has ever experienced. The former has raged for more than a quarter-century and shows no signs of abating while the latter has evolved over the last decade from a complex nationalist-cum-civil war into a rather straight-forward and conventional stand-off between two transnational coalitions – Angola plus Cuba versus UNITA plus South Africa – with SWAPO attempting to liberate Namibia between the two. By contrast, the Ethiopian war has intensified through several stages, both exacerbating and exacerbated by the droughts and famines of the mid-1970s and -1980s. And it shows little sign of ending despite occasional attempts at mediation and occasional efforts at proliferation of the 'national' question: from Eritrea and Tigray to Oromo and Somalia. Indeed, in early 1988, the battle-tried Eritrean People's Liberation Front came closer than ever to defeating the massive and well-equipped Ethiopian military: testimony to the efficaciousness of guerilla struggle even in a barren environment after 25 years of confrontation (Selaisse, 1980). Behind the escalation in technical sophistication of the Ethiopian and Angolan militaries – Mig 23s and 21s, Russian helicopter gunships and SAM missiles – are a pair of long-suffering allies – USSR and Cuba – who, for distinctive reasons, have provided materiel and soldiers, respectively. By contrast, the allies of the Eritreans and Ovimbundu are quite different: conservative Arab states with the US and Israel on the one hand and, on the other, South Africa and the US. So the 'cold war' content is not quite complete as US support for the Eritrean and Angolan 'freedom fighters' is more conditional and covert, Stinger missiles notwithstanding. This unevenness of support has complicated prospects for and progress towards negotiation, with the more 'internal' yet internationally derived Ethiopian conflict receiving less attention than the more recent Angolan one, with its Southern African regional implications. Indeed, until the eruption of contained talks in mid-1988, the Angolan issue had tended to become a veritable 'side-show' of Namibia in particular and Southern Africa in general (Shaw and Daddieh, 1984; Shaw, 1986). The political, strategic, economic and ecological stakes in both Ethiopia and Angola are high, especially when the latter is contrasted with the bloody and anarchic conflict in Mozambique perpetruated by MNR and its South African backers.

If this pair of rather conventional wars entail high politics for primary and secondary actors alike, the other two unconventional conflicts are both less salient and less violent, even although for the citizens of the benighted territories of Chad and Uganda they were horrific. These two struggles illustrate, each in their own way, the drama of unconventional war: regional powers and guerilla tactics, respectively. The off-on stand-off in Chad became, despite well-intentioned OAU interventions, a battle between Libya on the one hand and national regime with French tactical assistance on the other. By contrast, the Uganda security nexus reflected not so much regional interests, although Tanzania played a crucial role at times and Kenya's concerns were hardly objective, as divergent domestic communities. Unlike relatively orthodox nationalist struggles as most recently in Zimbabwe, which were concluded through metropolitan peace negotiations, the Uganda wars constitute the first time that an indigenous nationalist formation has fought its way to power with minimal external material or diplomatic assistance: the Nairobi conference in 1985 merely recognised the gains of Yoweri Museveni's National Liberation Front: it did not constitute the focus of the struggle. Thus the Ugandan case is of historic significance: the first time on the continent (if not on its offshore islands – Comoros?) that an authentic, indigenous movement has seized power from an in-human national regime using popular guerrilla tactics without substantial external involvement or even interest other than, at crucial periods, from Tanzania. So if Chad represents the failure of African peacekeeping at considerable cost in financial and diplomatic terms to the OAU, Nigeria and Zaire, the Ugandan struggle indicates the potential for popular internal conflict resolution: the overthrow or undermining of, successively, authoritarian and then anarchic regimes – from Amin to Obote.

Taken together, these four examples of conflict in Africa illustrate the intractability of many tensions and the difficulty of securing satisfactory and sustainable solutions despite continental and regional, let alone global, involvements. When situated in the context of delicate economic and ecological environments they exemplify the intensity of the structural adjustment syndrome and the vulnerability of indigenous solutions. Conflict in Africa as elsewhere is inseparable from the development problematique: how to create contexts for individual and collective satisfaction of basic needs and rights. Unhappily, the character of the international division of labour emerging as the 1990s dawns is hardly propitious – advancement for some peoples and countries as the continent and triage for the rest – this despite UN and other negotiations for both development and peace (Shaw, 1990).

Hence the comparative relevance of the African case for the Caribbean: indigenous uprisings and international associations in the cyclical and problematic quest for peace and development. Although Caribbean states may in general be small, vulnerable islands in a sea of water, African political economies are in general small vulnerable territories in an ocean of problematic land. Thus we may expect similar responses in the Caribbean to the incidence of underdevelopment and structural adjustment as in Africa: local uprisings and global interventions. Although Africa may be geographically and economically more marginal than the Caribbean – in no great power's sphere of influence, neither so involved in drug, migration or capital nexuses – it has the comparative luxury of distance and diversity: no satellite TV dishes or popular tourism and travel. Yet the African (and Spanish) diasporas in the Caribbean are structurally more vulnerable than their continent of origin: marginality involves less attention and intervention.

5 FUTURE STRUGGLES IN AFRICA: TOWARDS A POLITICAL ECONOMY OF VIOLENCE

Conflict is likely to increase in Africa in the mid-term future, then, because of the continent's unsatisfactory rate of economic growth: there will be unsufficient resources to redistribute to ameliorate antagonisms. The few rich countries and classes – particularly the semi-periphery and the national bourgeoisie, respectively – will be increasingly challenged in their relative access to affluence and accumulation by the real periphery and the non-bourgeoisie. Hence the attempts by the OAU and the International Bank for Reconstruction and Development (IBRD) to propose alternative development strategies to head off an unattractive future (see Shaw, 1983a). For, as Adedeji (1977, p. 8) has warned on numerous occasions: 'Africa, more than any other third world region, is faced with a development crisis of great portent'. This crisis includes minimal or negative economic expansion, rapid population increases, declining food production, indebtedness and inflation and associated inter- and intra-national inequalities (see Shaw (ed.), 1982); all this within a world system characterised by contraction, protectionism, and competition. It is difficult, therefore, to accept the conventional wisdom based on conventional analysis as articulated by Raymond Copson (1982, p. 923): 'while large-scale armed international violence does not appear likely in most of Africa, it can occur at any of Africa's flashpoints. In the Horn and the Maghreb, conflict may not be an immediate prospect, but the underlying bases for conflict remain'.

Given Africa's increasing marginalisation it is likely to lack the financial and physical infrastructure necessary for establishing an effective and credible nuclear force. Notwithstanding all the rhetorical flourishes about Africa needing to counteract South Africa's nuclear potential and to de-colonise racist assumptions about its technological capacities (see Mazrui, 1980a) unless a Continental High Command is established by which to harness a nuclear deterrent, nuclear status will remain a chimera.

It is possible that one or two states at the semi-periphery (for example, Algeria, Egypt or Nigeria) might expand their arsenal to include nuclear weaponry (see Shaw and Fasehun, 1980) but their delivery systems would be primitive and the effect might be counter-productive; that is, lead to counter-coalitions in their immediate regions, rather than to deterrence against South Africa. The more salient aspects of Africa's depressing future as related to non-conventional forms of violence lie in intra-national rather than inter-national relations, recognising that impoverishment and inequity can be exploited by extra-continental interests.

Although class formation has been retarded and complicated in Africa it has, nevertheless, accelerated since independence, particularly since the economic shocks of the mid-1970s onwards; and projections of declining *per capita* income in most states at the periphery are likely to exacerbate such tensions. Class relations at the semi-periphery may be ameliorated somewhat by continued expansion, but such growth is likely to be uneven both between classes and over time. Moreover, the rise of a national bourgeoisie at the semi-periphery will intensify internal rather than trans-national contradictions although the several fractions in the 'triple alliance' – national, international and state capital – may collaborate as well as conflict provided the 'national cake' is growing at a sufficiently fast rate (see Shaw, 1982, 1984b). As a general strategy of containment, Africa's ruling classes are likely to move, then, towards adoption of the *Lagos Plan of Action*, expecting that national and collective self-reliance will improve rates of development and enhance political control (Shaw, 1983a).

A further global trend may exacerbate domestic tensions even as it relieves external ones: the tendency towards economic protection and isolation in the North. Recession among industrialised countries has not only reduced their demand for African products; it has also eroded the logic of neo-colonialism. In essence, only a few African states – largely those at the semi-periphery – have continuing signifi-cance for Organisation for Economic Cooperation and Development (OECD) countries and corporations. The rest are increasingly mar-ginal, and so minimal political or strategic support is available to save such regimes. Ake's formulation (1978, pp. 27–8) about the patron-client relationship of African and metropolitan classes is now rel-evant only to the semi-periphery:

> The African ruling class is the political power while the ruling class of the bourgeois countries is the economic power. The reality of economic dependence limits the political power of the African ruling class, while the reality of the political power of the African ruling class may to some extent limit the economic power of the ruling class of the bourgeois countries to manipulate and exploit Africa. The limitations frustrate both sides, and the parties in-volved strive to overcome them. So, despite the fact that the interests of the African ruling class coincide in some respects, the two classes are also in struggle.

But this struggle becomes more complex as (i) the real periphery is marginalised and (ii) the semi-periphery is fractionalised with the emergence of national as well as trans-national and state capital. One result of impoverishment in the periphery and embourgeoisement in the semi-periphery is the rise not only of class antagonism but also of guerrilla struggle.

As Namibia and then South Africa are liberated in the short- to mid-term future, so guerrilla attacks will concentrate increasingly on the African ruling class in both systems in decay (for example, Chad, Ghana and Tanzania) and in expansion (for example, Morocco and Zimbabwe). In the former case, the guerrillas may claim to be acting in the national interest whereas in the latter they are clearly acting in their class interest. There will also, of course, be secessionist and irredentist movements (for example, Eritrea, Somalia and Polisario) with implications for border conflict and continental cohersion. The map of Africa – status quo attitudes and actions notwithstanding – may continue to change as it has done over the last decade or so (for example, Senegambia and Tanzania), especially if the great powers continue their competitive meddling (Gavshon, 1981).

Guerrilla attacks on indigenous regimes may lead to extra- and intra-continental support (for example, coalitions of the socialist states to aid Angola and Ethiopia and of the capitalist states to aid

Chad and Zaire). They are also likely to lead to increasingly authoritarian responses as the ruling class seeks to protect its territory, people and profit. As Basic Human Needs are met decreasingly so human rights are likely to be decreasingly respected as indigenous regimes attempt to maintain their power, profit and accumulation (Shaw, 1984a).

Notwithstanding such unattrative scenarios, it is possible, however, that self-reliance in Africa will generate a new situation in which political struggles will be played out. Such self-reliance – albeit of distinctive forms and degrees – may be advanced in the immediate future in three ways. First, as political and economic decay continues in the real periphery, the peasantry may retreat from cash crop production to food and 'cottage' industries, so advancing local self-reliance. Second, as recession and protection are extended in the advanced industrialised states, the semi-periphery as well as the periphery may come to advocate collective and national self-reliance, albeit with differences of emphasis and expectation. And finally, third, the OAU–ECA (Economic Commission for Africa) nexus may, through the *Lagos Plan of Action* and related deliberations and declarations, provide the framework and ideology for such forms of self-reliance throughout the continent. In short, the very gloominess of projections and imminence of unconventional conflict may call forth innovative indigenous responses which may further prevent conventional violence on the continent up to the year 2000.

6   CONCLUSION: SECURITY, DEVELOPMENT AND STRUCTURAL ADJUSTMENT

The last decade of the twentieth-century is likely to be marked by a profound period of structural adjustment not just in Africa but throughout the global political economy. The impact of such a new international division of labour is likely to be particularly severe in Africa, however, and to be effected through external dictates of Bank and Fund rather than through internal pressures of regimes and constituencies. The dramatic contraction of African economies will continue to throw-up profound consequences for both security and development, especially where strategic and ecological crises coincide as in Chad, Ethiopia, Mauritania, Mozambique and Sudan. A few more resilient political economies may resist such decline (e.g. Botswana, Ivory Coast, Nigeria and Zimbabwe) but the majority are likely to suffer from the instabilities and insecurities of the structural adjustment sydrome: from debt to devaluation, deregulation, desubsidisation, etc. As Bassey Ate (1985: 65) has cautioned:

> a deepening of the present crisis of economic conditions and human rights will engender an environment which is conducive to a radical reappraisal of conceptions of security in the continent, both national and regional.

In most African states, economic and political security are endangered because structural adjustment has undermined the established post-colonial state: it is no longer neo-colonial or patrimonial as it lacks the resources to be either exploited or manipulative. As local self-reliance of African communities becomes the only means to survive – traditional, appropriate technologies, education, welfare, credit, exchange (including regional black markets in goods, currencies and labour) – so the state loses revenue, influence and status. The decay of infrastructure reinforces this trend so that most states become simultaneously weak (i.e. few resources) and strong (i.e. few opponents) until alienated and isolated communities decide that it is time to administer the *coup de grace* and finish off the moribund and irrelevant state.

However, the state never withers completely and one of its few remaining resources and recourses is control over coercion. Thus, in its declining condition, it is likely to become more directly violent as it lacks other means for control; and in return, self-reliant communities are likely to take-up arms to defend their newly-realised self-reliance. The economic and environmental 'refugees' from structural adjustment may yet organise themselves into alternative states and resist reincorporation by adoption of guerilla struggle. When they have access to foreign exchange through black markets, currency exchange and drug smuggling then their ability to arm and defend themselves improves. Such a challenge to state security is the ultimate result of structural adjustment and it may not proliferate if IMF and IBRD strictures are moderated either out of economic rationality or because of great power strategic nervousness. But the deregulation and privatisation of violence are possible results of enforced adjustments. As Hansen (1987a, p. 16) laments, 'It is not by accident that at a time of economic depression there has been an increase in inter-personal and inter-group social conflict. This has been made more likely by Africa's poor development record.'

Hansen (1987a, pp. 16–17) relates the prospects for 'peace and development' to three alternative strategies found in Africa: African capitalism, populist socialism and Marxism. Likewise, Nweke (1985) somewhat romantically relates the prospects for 'security and development' to the choices among forms of self-reliance – isolationism, regionalism and globalism – about which he is quite sceptical, except for a revival of Afro-Arab inter-regionalism. He espouses rather fanciful notions of 'African dirigisme' and nuclear options as essential to any return to development and autonomy (Nweke, pp. 73 and 91). The real costs of such grandeur are escalating, especially as devaluations multiply, so the likelihood of regional nuclear military industrial complexes outside of South Africa and Egypt are receding. However, as Ate (1985, p. 66) notes, there is

> the prospect of the emergence of local centres of power in the continent . . . (which) will serve as a rallying point in the ultimate task of constructing a truly post-colonial security order which, over time, will render redundant and, thus, delegitimise the historical role of foreign powers in the management of African security.

The African debates over peace and development cannot be separated from broader strategic and economic perspectives – materialist v. non-materialist – neither can they be divorced from issues of race and class, notably in Southern Africa. However, by contrast to Nweke's advocacy with Mazrui of the nuclear option is a proposal in Hansen (1987b, p. 229) for the demilitarisation of Africa which nicely relates security to democracy as well as development and may be seen as an antidote to the militarisation inherent in the structural adjustment syndrome:

> the military in Africa should be weakened in two fundamental ways: by attacking it directly through serious proposals to limit arms flows into African states and through legal frameworks that challenge state prerogatives to resort to violence . . . The arming of African states is an increasingly important factor in conflict. For most African states this competitive militarisation is senseless and wasteful.

References

Adedeji, Adebayo (1977) 'Africa: the crisis of development and the challenge of a new economic order. Address to the fourth meeting of the Conference of Ministers and thirteenth session of the Economic Commission for Africa, Kinshasa, February–March 1977' (Addis Ababa: ECA) July.

Adeniran, Tunde (1981) 'Nuclear Proliferation and Black Africa: the coming crisis of choice', *Third World Quarterly* 3 (4), October, pp. 673–83.

Africa News (1982) 'US/South Africa: House study probes causes of arms embargo breakdown' 18 (17), 26 April, pp. 6–10.

Ake, Claude (1978) *Revolutionary Pressures in Africa* (London: Zed).

Amin, Samir (1973) *Neo-colonialism in West Africa* (Harmondsworth: Penguin).

Ate, Bassey E. (1985) 'A Note on the Superpowers and African Security', *Nigerian Journal of International Affairs*, 11, 2, pp. 62–7.

Babu, A. M. (1982) 'Postscript' in Walter Rodney *How Europe Underdeveloped Africa* (Harare: Zimbabwe Publishing House) pp. 310–16.

Bender, Gerald J., James S. Coleman and Richard L. Sklar (eds) (1985) *African Crisis Areas and US Foreign Policy* (Berkeley: University of California Press).

Bienen, Henry S. (1982) 'Military rule and military order in Africa', *Orbis* 25 (4), Winter, pp. 949–65.

Bowman, Larry W. (1982) 'The strategic importance of South Africa to the United States', *African Affairs* 81 (323), April, pp. 159–91.

Bozeman, Adda (1976) *Conflict in Africa: concepts and realities* (Princeton: Princeton University Press).

Brayton, Abbott A. (1983) 'The politics of arms limitation in Africa', *African Studies Review* 26 (1), March, pp. 73–89.

Cervenka, Zdenek (1982) 'The conspirary of silence', *Africa* 125, January, pp. 12–15.

Cervenka, Zdenek and Barbara Rogers (1978) *The Nuclear Axis: secret collaboration between West Germany and South Africa* (New York: Times Books).

Copson, Reymond W. (1982) 'African flashpoints: prospects for armed international conflict', *Orbis* 25 (4), Winter, pp. 903–23.

Foltz, William J. and Henry S. Bienen (eds) (1985) *Arms and the Africans: military influences on Africa's international relations* (New Haven: Yale University Press).

Gavshon, Arthur (1981) *Crisis in Africa: battleground of East and West* (Harmondsworth: Pelican).

Hansen, Emmanuel (1987a) 'Introduction' to Emmanuel Hansen (eds) *Africa: perspectives on peace and development* (London: Zed for UNU) 1–23.

Hansen, Emmanuel (ed.) (1987b) *Africa: perspectives on peace and development* (London: Zed for UNU).

Harkavy, Robert E. (1981) 'Pariah states and proliferation', *International Organization* 35 (1), Winter, pp. 135–63.

Henderson, Robert D'A (1981) 'Nigeria: future nuclear power?', *Orbis* 25 (2), Summer, pp. 409–23.

Hungarian Peace Council (1987) *Development Through Disarmament: toward a comprehensive interpretation of security* (Budapest).

Korany, Bahgat and Ali E. Hillal Dessouki (eds) (1984) *The Foreign Policies of Arab States* (Boulder: Westview).

Langdon, Steven and Lynn K. Mytelka (1979) 'Africa in the changing world economy', in Colin Legum *et al.*, *Africa in the 1980s: a continent in crisis* (New York: McGraw-Hill/Council on Foreign Relations) pp. 121–211.

Legum, Colin (1979a), 'The year in perspective', in Colin Legum, *Africa Contemporary Record: annual survey and documents, Volume 10, 1977–78* (New York: Africana) pp. xx–xxiv.

Legum, Colin (1979b) 'Communal conflict and international intervention in Africa' in Colin Legum *et al.*, *Africa in the 1980s: a continent in crisis* (New York: McGraw-Hill) pp. 21–66.

Luckham, Robin (1984) 'Militarisation and the new international anarchy', *Third World Quarterly* 6 (2), April, pp. 351–73.

Luckham, Robin (1983) 'Regional security and disarmament in Africa', *Alternatives* 9 (1), Summer, pp. 203–28.

Luckham, Robin (1982) 'French militarism in Africa', *Review of African Political Economy*, 24, May–August, pp. 55–84.

Luckham, Robin (1981) 'Armaments, underdevelopment and demilitarization in Africa', *Alternatives* 6 (2), July, pp. 179–245.

MacFarlane, S. Neil (1984) 'Africa's decaying security system and the rise of intervention', *International Security* 8 (4), Spring, pp. 127–51.

M'buyinga, Elenga (1982) *Pan-Africanism or Neo-Colonialism: the bankruptcy of the OAU* (London: Zed).

McKay, Vernon (1966) 'International conflict patterns' in Vernon McKay, *African Diplomacy: studies in the determinants of foreign policy* (London: Pall Mall for SAIS) pp. 1–23.

Martin, Robert (1980) 'The use of state power to overcome underdevelopment', *Journal of Modern African Studies* 18 (2), June, pp. 315–25.

Mazrui, Ali A. (1980a) *The African Condition: a political diagnosis* (London: Heinemann).

Mazrui, Ali A. (1980b) 'Africa's nuclear future', *Survival* 22 (2), March–April, pp. 76–9.

Meynell, Charles (1984) 'How a continent at war could yet live in peace', *The Times*, 1 May.

Nweke, G. Aforka (1985) *African Security in the Nuclear Age* (Enugu: Fourth Dimension).

Nyang'oro, Julius and Timothy M. Shaw (eds) (1989) *Corporatism in Africa* (Boulder: Westview).

Paneman, Daniel (1981) 'Nuclear policies in developing countries', *International Affairs* 57 (4), Autumn 1981, pp. 568–84.

Radu, Michael (1982) 'Ideology, parties and foreign policy in sub-Saharan Africa', *Orbis* 25 (4), Winter, pp. 967–92.

Ravenhill, John (1988) 'Redrawing the Map of Africa?' in Donald Rothchild & Naomi Chazan (eds) *The Precarious Balance: state and society in Africa* (Boulder: Westview) pp. 282–306.

Rodney, Walter (1982) *How Europe Underdeveloped Africa* (Harare: Zimbabwe Publishing House).

Roxborough, Ian (1979) *Theories of Underdevelopment* (London: Macmillan).

Selassie, Bereket Habte (1980) *Conflict and Intervention in the Horn of Africa* (New York: Monthly Review Press).

Shaw, Timothy M. (1982) 'Beyond neo-colonialism: varieties of corporatism in Africa', *Journal of Modern African Studies* 20 (2), June, pp. 239–61.

Shaw, Timothy M. (ed.) (1982) *Alternative Futures for Africa* (Boulder: Westview).

Shaw, Timothy M. (1983a) 'Debates about Africa's future: the Brandt, World Bank and Lagos Plan blueprints', *Third World Quarterly* 5 (2), April, pp. 330–44.

Shaw, Timothy M. (1983b) 'The future of the great powers in Africa: towards a political economy of intervention', *University of Ife Conference on Africa and the great powers*, June.

Shaw, Timothy M. (1984a) 'The political economy of self-determination: a world systems approach to human rights in Africa', in Claude E. Welch and Ronald Meltzer (eds) *Human Rights and Development in Africa: domestic, regional and international dimensions* (Albany: SUNY Press) pp. 226–44.

Shaw, Timothy M. (1984b) *Towards a Political Economy for Africa: the dialectic of dependence* (London: Macmillan).

Shaw, Timothy M. and Olajide Aluko (eds) (1983) *Nigerian Foreign Policy: alternative perceptions and projections* (London: Macmillan).

Shaw, Timothy M. and Cyril Daddieh (1984) 'The political economy of decision-making in African foreign policy: the cases of recognition of Biafra and the MPLA', *International Political Science Review* 5 (1), January, pp. 21–46.

Shaw, Timothy M. and Lee Dowdy (1982) 'South Africa', in Edward A. Kolodziej and Robert Harkavy (eds), *Security Policies of Developing Countries* (Lexington: Heath Lexington) pp. 305–27.

Shaw, Timothy M. and Orobola Fasehun (1980) 'Nigeria in the world system: alternative approaches, explanations and projections', *Journal of Modern African Studies* 18 (4), December, pp. 551–73.

Shaw, Timothy M. (1986) 'Southern Africa in Crisis: an analysis and bibliography' (Halifax: Centre for Foreign Policy Studies).

Shaw, Timothy M. (1990) 'Dependent Development in the New International Division of Labour' in David G. Haglund and Michael K. Hawes (eds) *World Politics: power, interdependence and dependence* (Toronto: Harcourt Brace Jovanovich) pp. 333–60.

Smith, Dan (1980) *South Africa's Nuclear Capability* (London: Anti-Apartheid Movement).

Spence, J. E. (1981) 'South Africa: the nuclear option', *African Affairs* 80 (321), October, pp. 441–52.

Wurfel, David and Bruce Burton (eds) (1990) *The Political Economy of Foreign Policy in Southeast Asia* (London: Macmillan).

Zartman, I. William (1976) 'Africa', in James N. Rosenau *et al.* (eds), *World Politics: an introduction* (New York: Free Press) pp. 569–94.

Zartman, I. William (1985) *Ripe for Resolution: conflict and intervention in Africa* (New York: OUP).

Selected Bibliography

Arkin, William, 'El Tratado de Tlatelolco, las armas nucleares y Puerto Rico, Informe a la Comisión Especial para la Amenaza de Armas Nucleares del Colegio de Abogados de Puerto Rico', en *Puerto Rico ante la guerra nuclear*, Dossier No. 5, Proyecto Caribeño de Justicia y Paz, Río Piedras, 1985, pp. 6–16.

Atkins, G. Pope, *Arms and Politics in the Dominican Republic*, (Boulder, Westview Press, 1981).

Baptiste, Fitzroy, 'The British grant of air and naval bases facilities to the United States in Trinidad, St Lucia and Bermuda in 1939 (June–December)', *Caribbean Studies*, 16, July 1976, pp. 5–43.

Barnet, Richard J., *Intervention and Revolution*, (New York, Macmillan, 1980).

Bender, Lynn Darrell, 'Guantanamo: its political, military and legal status', *Caribbean Quarterly*, 19, March 1973, pp. 80–86.

Black, George, 'Mare Nostrum: US security policy in the English-speaking Caribbean', *NACLA*, 19, July–August 1985, pp. 13–48.

Bloch, Jonathan and Pat Fitzsimons, 'The Eastern Caribbean "Coast Guard"', *Covert Action Information Bulletin*, 11, December, 1980, pp. 22–3.

Brana-Shute, Gary, 'Politicians in uniform: Surinam's bedeviled revolution', *Caribbean Review*, Spring 1981, pp. 24–7, 49–50.

Bryan, Anthony, ed., *Caribbean Regionalism: Challenges and Options*, Institute for International Relations, University of the West Indies, Trinidad and Tobago, 1987.

Bryan, Anthony T., J. Edward Greene and Timothy M. Shaw, eds. *Peace, Development and Security in the Caribbean: Perspectives to the Year 2000*, Macmillan, London, 1990.

Burbach, Roger and Flynn (eds), *The Politics of Intervention: the United States in Central America*, Monthly Review Press, New York, 1984.

Burkhalter, Hollis and Alita Paine, 'Our overseas cops' *The Nation* (24 September 1985), p. 197.

Campbell, Horace, 'Crime and violence in Jamaica', *Caribbean Issues* (April 1976), pp. 22–4.

Carrión, Juan Manuel, 'Orígenes de la Guardia Nacional de Puerto Rico', *Revista de Historia*, 1, 2, (July–Dec., 1985), pp. 222–7.

CINCLANT, 'Operation Urgent Fury Report, Oct. 25– Nov. 2, 1983', Atlantic Command, Norfolk, Virginia, 6 February, 1984.

Colegio de Abogados de Puerto Rico, 'Informe de la Comisión Especial sobre Armamentos Nucleares y el Tratado para la Proscripción de las Armas Nucleares en la América Latina', Colegio de Abogados, San Juan, 17 August 1984.

Cruz, Paulina, *Puerto Rico in the Invasion of Grenada: A Threat to the Sovereignty of the Caribbean and Central American Countries*, Dossier No. 12, Proyecto Caribeño de Justicia y Paz, Río Piedras, 1984.

Danns, George K., *Domination and Power in Guyana: A Study of the Police in a Third World Context*, (New Brunswick, Transaction Books, 1982).

Davila Colón, Luis, 'The Blood Tax: The Puerto Rican Contribution to the United States War Efforts', *Revista del Colegio de Abogados de Puerto Rico*, November, 1979, pp. 603–39.

Diedrich, Bernard, 'The end of West Indian innocence: arming the police', *Caribbean Review*, Spring, 1984, pp. 10–12.

Edwards, S. Hylton, *Lengthening Shadows: Birth and Revolt of the Trinidad Army* (Imprint Caribbean Ltd., Port-of-Spain, 1982).

Enders, John, *La presencia militar norteamericana en Puerto Rico*, Serie Militarismo 1, Proyecto Caribeño de Justicia y Paz, Río Piedras, 1980.

Erisman, H. Michael (ed.), *The Caribbean Challenge, US Policy in a Volatile Region*, (Boulder, Westview Press, 1984).

Erisman, H. Michael and John D. Martz, *Colossus Challenged: The Struggle for Caribbean Influence*, (Boulder, Westview Press, 1982).

Estades, Maria Eugenia, *La presencia militar de Estados Unidos en Puerto Rico 1898–1918: Intereses estratégicos y dominación colonial*, Huracán, Río Piedras, 1988.

Fannelli, Joseph, *The Coast Guard in the Caribbean Basin: A Role for the '80's* (US Southcom, Panama, 1981).

Fauriol, Georges, 'Puerto Rico and the United States: understanding the foundations of a strategic relationship' (Final Report and Executive Summary), Center for Strategic and International Studies, Georgetown University, Washington, 8 April 1985.

Fesmire, John A., 'United States military command relationships in Latin America: could they be better?', Individual Study Project, US Army War College, 6 May 1982.

García Muñiz, Humberto, *Boots, Boots, Boots: Intervention, Regional Security and Militarization in the Caribbean*, Serie Militarismo 2, Proyecto Caribeño de Justicia y Paz, Río Piedras, 1986.

García Muñiz, Humberto, *La estratégia de Estados Unidos y la militarización del Caribe*, Instituto de Estudios del Caribe, Universidad de Puerto Rico, Río Piedras, 1988.

Gill, Henry, 'The foreign policy of the Grenada Revolution', *Bulletin of Eastern Caribbean Affairs* (Barbados), 7, 1981–1982, pp. 1–5.

Gleijeses, Piero, *La Crisis Dominicana*, FCE, Mejico, 1985.

Goldwert, Martin, *The Constabulary in the Dominican Republic and Nicaragua: Progeny and Legacy of the United States Intervention* (University of Florida Press, Gainesville, Fla., 1962).

González, Edward, *A Strategy for Dealing with Cuba in the 1980s*, Rand Corp., Santa Mónica, 1982.

González, Edward, 'The Cuban and Soviet Challenge in the Caribbean Basin', *Orbis* (Spring, 1985), pp. 73–94.

Gorman, Paul F. (General, USA), 'US Southern Command: sentinel of US interest in Latin America', *Defense*, No. 84, November–December, 1984, pp. 17–23.

Great Britain, Colonial Office, *Report of the Chaguaramas Commission*, Her Majesty's Stationery Office, London, 1958. (Colonial No. 338).

HQ, US Forces Caribbean, 'The Caribbean Regional Coast Guard', *DISAM Newsletter*, Fall 1985, pp. 53–59.

Irvin, George and Xavier Gorostiaga (eds), *Towards an Alternative for Central America and the Caribbean* (London, George Allen & Unwin, 1985).

Jaramillo, Isabel, 'La estrategia intervencionista estadounidense hacia el Medio Oriente y la Cuenca del Caribe', *Cuadernos de Nuestra América*, Vol. 1, No. 1 (January–July, 1984), pp. 78–106.

Kennedy, R., C. Wallis, G. Marcella, *et al.*, *The Role of the U.S. Military in the Caribbean Basin (Final Report)*, Strategic Studies Institute, US Army War College, Carlisle Barracks, Pa., 1981.

Lacey, Terry, *Violence and Politics in Jamaica, 1960–1970, Internal Security in a Developing Country*, (London, Frank Cass & Co.), 1977.

Leis, Raúl, 'El Comando Sur: poder hostil', *Nueva Sociedad* (enero–febrero 1986), pp. 77–88.

Lewis, Gary, 'Prospects for a Regional Security System in the Eastern Caribbean', *Millenium: Journal of International Studies*, No. 15 (1986), pp. 73–90.

Lewis, Sybil Farrell and Dale T. Mathews, comps., 'Documents on the invasion of Grenada', *Caribbean Monthly Bulletin*, Supplement No. 1, October 1983.

Louis, William Roger, *Imperialism at Bay: the United States and the Decolonization of the British Empire, 1914–1945* (New York, Oxford University Press, 1978).

Lynch, Edward, 'Moscow eyes the Caribbean', *The Heritage Foundation Backgrounder*, No. 284 (August 17, 1983), pp. 1–11.

Martin, Gary D., 'The United States Armed Services and the Puerto Rican economy: a quantitative appraisal', *Puerto Rico Business Review*, No. 9 (August 1984), pp. 3–12.

Mesa Lago, Carmelo and June Belkin, (eds), *Cuba in Africa* (University of Pittsburgh Press, Pittsburgh, 1982).

Milton, T. R. (General USAF, Ret.), 'Are we being outflanked in the Caribbean?', *Air Force Magazine* (February 1982). Reprinted in the *Jamaica Daily News*, 4 April 1982.

Morris, Curtis S. (Lt Col. USAF), *The United States-Caribbean Connection: A Perspective on Regional Military-to-Military Relationships*, The Center for Hemispheric Studies, American Enterprise Institute for Foreign Policy Research, Washington, August, 1983.

Myers, David J., *Venezuela's Pursuit of Caribbean Basin Interests: Implications for United States National Security*, Rand Corp., Santa Monica, 1985.

Post, Ken, *Strike the Iron: A Colony at War, 1939–1945*, 2 vols, Institute of Social Studies (The Hague) (Atlantic Highlands, NJ, 1981).

Preston, Richard A., 'Caribbean defence and security: a study of the implementation of Canada's "special relationship" with the Commonwealth West Indies', *South Atlantic Quarterly*, No. 70 (Summer 1971), pp. 317–331.

Regional Security System Staff, 'The Role of the Regional Security System in the Eastern Caribbean', *Bulletin of Eastern Caribbean Affairs*, No. 11 (1986), pp. 5–7.

Reiding, Alan and Reid Reiding, eds., *Confrontation in the Caribbean Basin*

(University of Pittsburgh Press, Pittsburgh, 1984).

Rodríguez Beruff, Jorge, *Política militar y dominación: Puerto Rico en el contexto latinoamericano* (Huracán, Río Piedras, 1988).

Ronfeldt, David, *Geopolitics, Security and US Strategy in the Caribbean*, Rand Corporation, Santa Monica, 1983.

Perkins, Whitney T., *Constraint of Empire: The United States and Caribbean Interventions* (Clio Press, Oxford, 1981).

Schulz, Donald E. and Douglas H. Graham, (eds), *Revolution and Counter-revolution in Central America and the Caribbean* (Boulder, Westview Press, 1984).

Serbin, Andrés, *El Caribe ¿zona de paz?, geopolitica, integración y seguridad*, Nueva Sociedad, Caracas, 1989.

Selser, Gregorio, 'Las bases de E.U. en Panamá: el destino del Comando del Sur y de la Escuela de las Américas', *Nueva Sociedad*, No. 63 (November–December, 1982), pp. 57–74.

Simmons, David, 'Militarization of the Caribbean: Concerns for National and Regional Security', *International Journal*, No. 40 (Spring, 1985), pp. 348–76.

Stodder, Joseph and Kevin McCarthy, *Profiles of the Caribbean basin in 1960–1980: Changing Political and Geostrategic Dimensions*, Rand Corp., Santa Monica, 1983.

Tiryakian, Josefina, 'The military and security dimension of US Caribbean Policy', in H. Michael Erisman (ed.), *The Caribbean Challenge: US Policy in a Volatile Region*, (Boulder, Westview Press, 1984).

Thomas, Clive, 'The Grenadian Crisis and the Caribbean Left', *IDS Bulletin*, 16, 2, April, 1985.

US Congressional Research Service, comp. *Should the United States be prohibited from military intervention in the Western Hemisphere?*, US Government Printing Office, Washington DC, 1982.

US General Accounting Office, *Assessment of factors affecting the availability of US oil supplies from the Caribbean*, GAO/NSIAD–85–127, 13 September 1985.

US House of Representatives, *US military actions in Grenada: implications for US policy in the Eastern Caribbean*. Hearing before the Sub-Committees of International Security and Scientific Affairs and on Western Hemisphere Affairs of the Committee on Foreign Affairs, House of Representatives, November 2, 3 and 16, 1983, Government Printing Office, Washington, DC, 1984.

Young, Alma H. and Dion E. Phillips, *Militarization in the Non-Hispanic Caribbean*, (Boulder, Lynn Rienner Publishers, 1986).

Index